Strange Stories,
AMAZING FACTS of
AMERICA'S
Past

Reader's
Digest

The Reader's Digest Association, Inc.
Pleasantville, NY / Montreal

PROJECT STAFF

Editor
Daryna Tobey

Designer
Rich Kershner

Copy Editor
Marcia Mangum Cronin

Indexer
Cohen Carruth Indexes

Photo Researcher
Dian Lofton, The Right Pics

Contributing Writer
Tara Gadomski

READER'S DIGEST BOOKS

Editor in Chief
Neil Wertheimer

Creative Director
Michele Laseau

Executive Managing Editor
Donna Ruvituso

**Associate Director
North America Prepress**
Douglas A. Croll

Manufacturing Manager
John L. Cassidy

Marketing Director
Dawn Nelson

**President and Publisher,
Trade Publishing**
Harold Clarke

**President, U.S. Books & Home
Entertainment**
Dawn Zier

THE READER'S DIGEST ASSOCIATION, INC.

**President and Chief
Executive Officer**
Mary Berner

Library of Congress data has been applied for.

ISBN: 978-0-7621-0773-5

Address any comments about *Strange Stories, Amazing Facts of America's Past* to:
The Reader's Digest Association, Inc.
Editor in Chief, Books
Reader's Digest Road
Pleasantville, NY 10570-7000

To order copies of *Strange Stories, Amazing Facts of America's Past,* call 1-800-846-2100.

Visit our Web site at **rd.com**

Printed in China

1 3 5 7 9 10 8 6 4 2
US 4960/G

Cover credits
Front cover: *Top*, Digital Vision/Getty Images; *center*, Alicia Buelow; *bottom*, National Geographic/Getty Images.

Back cover: *Clockwise from top left*, The Granger Collection, New York; Time Life Pictures/Getty Images; The Library of Congress; Hulton Archive/Getty Images.

Introduction

Did you hear the one about the American president who was so large that four regular-sized men could fit inside his bathtub?

Or the one about the old woman who walked into a bar, swinging a hatchet ... ?

How about the one about the millionaire who was so cheap that she wore the same tattered black dress every day, and rarely washed it, to save the cost of soap?

Stop. That's no way to start a history book, is it? Let's try this again.

The issues of the modern Republican Party are reminiscent of the term of President William Taft (1908-12), during which a philosophical split between conservatives and progressives within the Republican party led to a consistent state of conflict. Progressives within his party were frustrated at President Taft's support of the Payne-Aldrich Act, which maintained high tariff rates ....

That second example is pretty conventional as far as historical writing goes, but it's on the dry side, isn't it? For a few hours of pleasant reading, wouldn't you rather read those first stories? In that case, you've come to the right place.

Strange Stories, Amazing Facts of America's Past is the only history book we know of in which famous figures in American history actually sound like real people. They have love affairs, kill people, get sick, lose money, and do decidedly unwise things—just like the rest of us. As you read about these people, sometimes you'll laugh at them, and sometimes, your heart will bleed for them. And that's exactly our goal.

It's not until you think about American history this way—that the characters involved are human and complex and three-dimensional, just as you are—that our nation's past really comes alive. For example, Franklin Pierce is often written off as a mediocre president, but his performance becomes much more understandable when you learn that he watched his 11-year-old son die a painful death just before his inauguration. Flash forward to the extraordinary presidential election of 2000, when after weeks of legal battles, Vice President Al Gore stoically accepted a Supreme Court ruling that gave George W. Bush the presidency, even though Gore had won the popular vote. Gore, as the outgoing leader of the Senate, had to formally declare Bush the election's victor. We can only imagine the pain that caused.

The first edition of *Strange Stories* was published in 1989, and since then its unbelievable tales have made it a favorite, both among untold thousands of readers as well as those of us involved with its creation. As our staff worked on this completely updated and revised edition, we were tickled by so many of its little-known but historically important anecdotes: For example, that President Andrew Jackson's impeachment hearings were such spectacles that Congress sold tickets to them. Or that President Grover Cleveland had half his jaw surgically removed during his presidency and no one noticed. And every time I see people pouring maple syrup onto their pancakes at breakfast, I think about Boston's 1919 deadly tidal wave of maple syrup, and reach instead for some cereal.

It's precisely because *Strange Stories* leaves such lasting impressions that Reader's Digest wanted to share it with a new generation of readers. The world has changed an awful lot in the almost 20 years since this book was created, so the book had to change too. You'll find many updates in this edition, including features on recent elections, the terrorist attacks of September 11, 2001, and the space shuttle *Columbia* tragedy. Graphically, too, the book has been revitalized for both easier reading and greater visual surprise.

Enjoy reading *Strange Stories, Amazing Facts of America's Past.* We hope that it helps make our nation's history come alive for you, as it did for us.

—*Daryna Tobey, Editor*

CONTENTS

On May 10, 1869, the Central Pacific and Union Pacific railroads were joined in Promontory Summit, Utah. Opposite: Twenty-first century revelers in New York City's Times Square ring in the New Year.

CHAPTER ONE

A Diary of America

Hardly a day goes by that something remarkable doesn't happen somewhere in America, and that's the way it's always been. From lovers frozen in a block of ice to the daredevil who regularly walked a tightrope across the Niagara, this diary is a retrospective of America's oddest and most unbelievable happenings. Some of the names you'll read—like Edgar Allan Poe and George Washington—might be familiar, but our quirky anecdotes about them (why would Washington give someone a passport to *New Jersey*?) are sure to surprise you. Whether merely amusing or historically significant, all of the stories in this chapter are part of our nation's past. They are the fibers from which America is woven.

The Big Break Begins

Carpenter's Hall, Philadelphia, was the meeting place of the First and Second Continental Congresses of 1774 and 1775.

SEPTEMBER 5, 1774: THE FIRST CONTINENTAL CONGRESS MEETS

In response to December 1773's Boston Tea Party, the British Parliament imposed the Coercive Acts, which closed Boston's port and tried to crush colonial resistance. But the harsh acts had just the opposite effect; they rallied Americans to the cause of liberty.

In early September 1774, 56 delegates from every colony but Georgia (whose governor prohibited representatives from attending) met in Philadelphia. Joseph Galloway of Pennsylvania urged preserving America's place in the British Empire. Many delegates agreed, and his proposal calling for a colonial legislature—whose acts could be vetoed by the king's appointed president-general—was defeated by only one vote. By mid-October, the congress was committed to aggressive retaliation, in the form of a boycott of British goods. A revolution was about to begin.

A Passport to New Jersey

JANUARY 9, 1793: PRESIDENT WASHINGTON PERSONALLY SENDS OFF BALLOONIST

President George Washington had been intrigued by the idea of using balloons for transportation ever since the first manned flight in Paris in 1783. So, when the "greatest of the aeronauts," Frenchman Jean-Pierre Blanchard, crossed the Atlantic to give a demonstration, Washington was there.

The site chosen for the liftoff was the Walnut Street Prison courtyard in Philadelphia, the nation's capital. Arriving at 9 a.m., Washington presented Blanchard with a passport he himself had signed, not knowing how far the balloonist might travel.

When the 46-minute flight ended near Woodbury, New Jersey, 15 miles away, Blanchard was met by two astonished farmers, one carrying a gun. Blanchard, who didn't understand English, waved the paper with the presidential signature and produced a bottle of spirits. He was given a warm reception and passage back to Philadelphia.

1492
Christopher Columbus lands in the New World at the helm of a ship whose name, roughly translated, is "flirtatious Mary."
Page 240

1536
The first pleasure cruise to America leaves England; a few months into the voyage, Captain Richard Hore is compelled to give a very curious sermon.
Page 244

1541
In May, Hernando de Soto is the first white man to lay eyes on the Mississippi River. He (and his 700-plus pigs) cross it—it's just another milestone on his 4,000-mile march.
Page 243

1577
Sir Francis Drake sets sail around the world from England; during the journey, he claims California in the name of Queen Elizabeth I.
Page 243

A Royal Refuge

NOVEMBER 9, 1793: FRENCH ARISTOCRATS BUILD PENNSYLVANIA HAVEN

If the guillotine hadn't nixed the plan, the backwoods of Pennsylvania might have become home to King Louis XVI and Queen Marie Antoinette of France.

When the French Revolution exploded in 1789, thousands of aristocrats fled to America, congregating in Philadelphia, the U.S. capital. Several of these exiles hoped to create a haven for the royal family and other French refugees. Their supporters included Vicomte Louis-Marie de Noailles, a brother-in-law of General Lafayette, who used his clout to acquire the land: 2,400 acres on the Susquehanna River near present-day Towanda. Lots up to 400 acres were offered to the French for two or three dollars an acre.

The king was guillotined in January 1793, just as the project was launched, but the French exiles still hoped to save their queen. One of the first houses to be built was for her—a grand, two-storied structure with 16 fireplaces. Wishing to see the colony, Noailles arrived on November 9 and gave the town its name, Azilum (as the French pronounced the word "asylum"), to reflect its purpose.

The colony soon had some 50 houses and about 250 residents. But Queen Marie Antoinette was not among them: She had been beheaded.

Preferring a more elegant life than the rustic frontier offered, the French ached to go home. When, after a few years, they learned that they could obtain pardons, the exodus from Azilum began. By 1803, only three Frenchmen remained.

Tar and feathers often greeted tax collectors during the Whiskey Rebellion, one of the earliest challenges to the power of the young federal government.

Washington and the Moonshiners

AUGUST 7, 1794: THE PRESIDENT DEFENDS THE GOVERNMENT'S AUTHORITY

The farmers along the Monongahela River in southwestern Pennsylvania were a mere one-seventieth of the new nation's population, but they owned a quarter of its stills. They weren't drunkards, just good businessmen who had found that a jug of liquor was cheaper to transport and more profitable to sell than the grain it took to produce it. Not surprisingly, these wily frontiersmen were furious when Secretary of the Treasury Alexander Hamilton pushed Congress to adopt an excise tax on spirits in 1791. Hadn't Americans fought the Revolution to get out from under such taxes imposed by the British?

Hamilton argued that the whiskey makers wouldn't lose any money; they would just pass the tax on to buyers as higher prices. Nonetheless, in the best Sons of Liberty tradition, the Pennsylvania farmers responded to tax collectors with tar and feathers.

One moonshiner tried a different approach. When revenue men arrived, he hospitably offered them ginger cakes laced with whiskey. After a few generous helpings the officials passed out. The farmer then stepped outside, hid his still, and was a paragon of innocence when the tax collectors awoke.

> The Whiskey Rebellion was one of the greatest threats to America before the Civil War.

By the summer of 1794, however, the Whiskey Rebellion, as the frontiersmen's resistance was called, had gotten ugly. After two days of siege, the home of the district excise inspector had been overrun by a mob of 500 and burned to the ground. Terror gripped Pittsburgh shortly thereafter when 5,000 armed protesters occupied the city. There was even serious talk of secession.

On August 7, President George Washington declared that southwestern Pennsylvania was in a state of insurrection. By October 13,000 militiamen were marching to put down the rebellion. Among the commanders was Alexander Hamilton, who now was also acting secretary of war. As the army advanced, the whiskey makers' resistance collapsed. By mid-November their movement was finished. A few leaders were arrested but were ultimately pardoned. Historians have called this one of the greatest threats to the stability of the Union prior to the Civil War.

A Dim Forecast

OCTOBER 7, 1819: FIRST AMERICAN VISITS VIETNAM

A true Yankee trader, Captain John White sailed his brig out of Salem, Massachusetts, in January 1819, determined to reach a new market: Saigon. Six months later he touched the coast of present-day Vietnam near the mouth of the Donnai River, also known as the Dong Nai.

White's destination lay some 60 miles upstream. Needing a river guide and permits to proceed to the royal city, he contacted a local potentate. While putting on a show of hospitality, the chief detained him for weeks and demanded as presents just about everything on the ship. White finally bought "peace and goodwill at the expense of a pair of pistols

25 cartridges, 12 flints, one six-pound canister of powder, some shoes, much liquor, and a Dutch cheese." Impatient, White sent his own delegates to Saigon and secured permission to proceed. He and his crew reached the city on October 7.

The American was impressed by the fortifications and armaments of the walled inner city. Near one of its four great gates he noticed "two hundred and fifty pieces of cannons principally of European manufacture," evidence of Indochina's already long and stormy association with France. But in business transactions he found the capital's government officials even more rapacious than their rural counterparts. The price of the most desirable commodity, sugar, soared from "eighty to one hundred percent" after his arrival. White concluded that unless the local people shaped up, the civilized world would find nothing in that country but "a source of deep regret and commiseration."

Jumping Sam Patch

NOVEMBER 13, 1829: SHOWMAN MAKES HIS FINAL LEAP

Sam Patch's love of leaping started early. At six months, he claimed, he was leaping into a basin of bubbles from his nanny's arms. As a youngster, leapfrog was his favorite game. Soon he was leaping from boat masts into the waters below.

At the age of 20, Patch gave up his job as a cotton spinner in Paterson, New Jersey, and took to traveling from town to town, diving off bridges and other high places into bodies of water. "There's no mistake in Sam Patch," he'd tell the throng before a jump. "Some things can be done as well as others." His saying became a national catchphrase.

Friday, November 13, found Patch preparing to make his second leap of 125 feet over the Genesee Falls. After a practice dive, he had boasted to admirers: "I'll show you how it's done." From the scaffold at the brink of the falls he bragged to the crowd that Napoleon couldn't make the jump, "but I can do it, and I will." He swayed as he spoke, and onlookers realized with a shock that he was drunk. Patch jumped, but his usually graceful headfirst dive turned into a fall. He hit the water sideways and never reappeared. Some thought the stunt a hoax. But the following March a farmer discovered Patch's broken body frozen in a block of ice.

Sam Patch was so beloved that his legend grew after his death. The "doing Sam Patch" craze swept the country; clerks jumped counters, and farmers jumped fences. A touring comedian made his fame playing the part of Jumping Sam. Nathaniel Hawthorne pondered: "Was the leaper of cataracts more mad or foolish than other men who throw away life, or misspend it in pursuit of empty fame and seldom so triumphantly as he?"

1751
A great bronze bell is ordered from London to commemorate the 50th anniversary of Pennsylvania's democratic constitution; it cracks while being tested.
Page 66

1759
Ben Lay, a four-foot-seven abolitionist caveman, dies at age 82.
Page 194

1763
British soldiers use germ warfare against American Indians, and smallpox ravages tribal camps.
Page 342

1774
Mother Ann Lee and eight fellow Shakers land in New York City and subsequently found a colony near Albany, New York.
Page 199

"Too Mad a Poet"?

Edgar Allan Poe, one of the first American writers to win international acclaim, couldn't survive his first year at West Point. "Too mad a poet to like mathematics," was the judgment of a classmate.

Orphaned at the age of three, Poe had been well raised by John Allan and his wife, Frances, a friend of the child's mother. But when Poe was 15, he and his guardian quarreled. It was traumatic for both. Although Allan was wealthy, he sent Poe off to the University of Virginia with hardly a penny. When the youth finished the first term with good grades but $2,500 in debt, Allan withdrew him. In despair, Poe joined the army. After two years, Allan relented enough to help his ward get into West Point—but again, almost penniless.

Entering the military academy at the age of 21, the new cadet won high marks with little effort but again accumulated debts. Writing to a creditor, he excused his failure to get money from home with the remark, "Mr. A is not very often sober." The letter was forwarded to Allan. Outraged and hurt, he sent Poe the money to pay off the debt and then disowned him.

Frantic, Poe wrote to Allan on January 3, 1831, pouring out the bitterness that had prompted the insult. Adding that his poverty now forced him to leave West Point, he asked his guardian for written permission to do so. Contemptuous, Allan did not answer. With no alternative but to seek expulsion, Poe began skipping classes and meals. When he also refused to attend chapel, he was arrested and court-martialed. Finally, he was officially dismissed from West Point for disobedience and gross neglect of duty.

Unicorns on the Moon

The weather was steamy, and the news was even hotter. According to the *New York Sun*, Sir John Herschel, a noted British astronomer, had discovered life on the moon: blue unicorns, tailless beavers walking on two legs, and most spectacular of all, bat-like, four-foot-tall moon people covered with copper-colored fur! Males and females supposedly had animated conversations, leaving no doubt about their rationality.

1775

In May, Ethan Allen and Benedict Arnold (right) capture Fort Ticonderoga from the British without firing a shot. On June 17, the Battle of Bunker Hill is actually fought on Breed's Hill.
Page 332

1776

On July 3, John Adams predicts that the preceding day "will be the most memorable ... in the History of America.
Page 54

1780

On September 25, Peggy Arnold conveniently goes insane in the presence of General George Washington after he discovers that her husband, Benedict, has committed treason.
Page 335

More intimate moonfolk relations were said to have been observed, but good taste prohibited detailed reports, for they "would ill comport with our terrestrial notions of decorum."

Further revelations halted abruptly when reporter Richard Adams Locke confessed he had made the whole thing up. Luckily for Locke, Herschel burst out laughing when he heard that his name had been taken in vain. The *Sun* had the last laugh, though: Thanks to its inspired lunacy, daily circulation rose from 8,000 to 19,360, making it the most widely read paper in the world.

Mutiny, Murder, and Trickery

MARCH 9, 1841: SUPREME COURT FREES THE *AMISTAD* SLAVES

The case had begun on the stormy night of July 1, 1839, while the *Amistad* wallowed through rough seas off Cuba. In the hold of the Spanish vessel were 49 men and four children, all chained together by their necks, hands, and feet. They had been kidnapped from Mende, in West Africa, and sold in the Havana slave market. In a topside cabin of the *Amistad* were their owners, Cuban planters Don Josè Ruiz and Pedro Montez. Ruiz had just paid $450 a head for the men; Montez owned the children. Now they were taking their slaves to another port in Cuba.

ESCAPING FATE

Below decks, Cinquè, the tall, proud son of a chief, spoke forcefully: There was only one way to escape their fate: Mutiny. Tonight.

Quietly they pried off their chains and broke open a shipment of machetes. First Cinquè killed the cook, who had suggested the slaves would be eaten; then the captain. He was about to cleave Montez in two when the other Africans stopped him. Several of the crew had jumped overboard, and the Africans would need someone to guide the boat back to Africa. Terrified, the Cubans agreed to cooperate with them.

But Montez was determined to reach America. By day, when Cinquè could check the position of the sun, he pointed the ship eastward; but by night he sailed northwest. After zigzagging for seven weeks,

African slaves, led by Cinquè, kill Captain Ramón Ferrer during the July 1839 insurrection on board the Spanish slave ship *Amistad*.

the vessel reached the eastern tip of Long Island, where a navy patrol ship approached it. The slaves were taken to New Haven, Connecticut, and jailed to await trial for murder and piracy.

THE LANGUAGE BARRIER

Given wide publicity in the newspapers, the plight of the Africans soon became a cause célèbre in the North, but no one could get their side of the story because of the language barrier. A linguistic expert, Dr. Josiah Gibbs, went to the prison and learned to count from 1 to 10 in Mende; he then scoured the New York City waterfront, repeating the words over and over. Finally he met a black from Sierra Leone who understood—an interpreter had been found.

Meanwhile, the Spanish government claimed that the slaves belonged to Montez and Ruiz and demanded they be turned over to Spain's minister. Eager to appease the proslavery South, President Martin Van Buren was willing to comply. In January 1840, the case came before a federal judge, who was a Van Buren appointee. Unexpectedly, he declared the Africans free, under an 1817 treaty in which Spain had outlawed importing slaves to its colonies. The abolitionists rejoiced—but only briefly. At the behest of the president, the U.S. attorney appealed the case to the Supreme Court, insisting that the Africans be returned to Spanish

Cinquè's legend lived on long after the *Amistad*'s. Several books were written about the slaves' mutiny and subsequent arrest, including *Echo of Lions* by Barbara Chase-Riboud. In 1997, Steven Spielberg directed the Oscar-nominated movie *Amistad*.

jurisdiction; the defense demanded their freedom.

A SECRET LETTER

Then Congressman John Quincy Adams, former president of the United States, rose to address the court. Weeks earlier he had asked Congress for a full disclosure of all official documents touching on the case, and lo and behold a "confidential" letter had surfaced. Written by the secretary of state to the U.S. attorney in Connecticut, it contained Van Buren's instructions that the slaves be denied the right of appeal should the lower court decide against them. The 73-year-old Adams read the letter to a stunned audience and then scathingly attacked the president, asking: "Was ever such a scene of Lilliputian trickery enacted by the rulers of a great, magnanimous, and Christian nation?"

The Africans, who had spent 17 months in jail, were freed, given a year of Christian training, and then returned home. Many, including Cinquè, found that their families had been sold into slavery. Cinquè later became a slave trader.

Paper Chase

DECEMBER 30, 1842: THE ARCHIVE WAR OF TEXAS BEGINS

It was a bloodless, two-day battle over three wagon-loads of paper, in which the only shots were fired by a middle-aged woman, but they called it the Archive War.

When Austin became the capital of Texas in 1839, state documents were moved there. Sam Houston, however, wanted these archives in his namesake city; after he was elected president of Texas in 1841, he decided to get the papers. Using recent Mexican Army incursions into Texas as his excuse, he dispatched Colonel Thomas Smith with 20 men and three wagons to steal the archives from the Austin Land Office.

Arriving on the morning of December 30, the paper pilferers had the wagons almost filled when they were discovered by Angelina Eberly, a local innkeeper out for a stroll. Arousing the citizenry, she positioned herself at a howitzer (originally in place to fight American Indians) in front of the land office. Turning it toward the building, she lit its fuse.

The subsequent fusillade persuaded Smith and his men to leave the remaining archives and get out of town. The posse that followed had few weapons, but they did have the howitzer.

The chase ended the next day. The thieves, camped only 18 miles from Austin, woke up surrounded by the posse. With the cannon pointed straight at them, they prudently gave up without a fight.

A World Without End

APRIL 3, 1843: JUDGMENT DAY FOR MILLER'S MILLENARIANS

All over the Northeast, about half a million Adventist disciples of New York Baptist evangelist William Miller piously awaited the end of the world. Journalists had a field day, but their reports are so rife with tall tales that it is hard to get at the facts.

Reportedly some disciples were on mountaintops, hoping for a head start to heaven. Others were in graveyards, planning to ascend in reunion with their departed loved ones. Philadelphia society ladies clustered together outside town to avoid entering God's holy kingdom amid the common herd.

Religious leader William Miller, seated in a well-stocked safe, awaits the end of the world in 1843.

Hearing loud trumpet blasts, the faithful in Westford, Massachusetts, fell to their knees. But it was only Crazy Amos, the village idiot. "You fools!" he said. "Go dig your potatoes. Angel Gabriel won't go a-digging 'em for you."

When April 4 dawned as usual, the Millerites were disillusioned, but they took heart. Their leader had predicted a range of dates for Armageddon. They still

---

1792

In October, the White House's cornerstone is finally laid, after much debate and competition over its design.
Page 60

1793

America's first circus debuts in Philadelphia. George Washington is a big fan.
Page 201

1796

Dr. Elisha Perkins patents his medical "marvel," the Metallic Tractors, which he claimed could relieve ills using the new theory of animal electricity.
Page 294

1799

On December 14, in an effort to improve the ailing George Washington's health, his doctors draw too much blood—and hasten his death.
Page 85

had until March 21, 1844. The devout continued to make ready; but again they were disappointed. And again there was an adjustment: October 22, 1844, was now the projected Day of Doom. Amazingly, many followers were still committed. One shrewd Vermont farmer had sacred white robes made for six of his cows. "It's a very long trip, and the kids will want milk," he explained.

Again no cataclysm.

Miller never abandoned his belief that the end of the world was near, though he stopped predicting dates. His followers broke into factions, and in 1863 a union of diverse Adventist sects was organized as the Seventh-day Adventists. Today there are several million followers worldwide.

Let's Go Fly a Kite

MARCH 7, 1848: A KITE IS THE KEY TO BRIDGING THE GREAT NIAGARA

Charles Ellet had a problem: He had a contract to build an engineering marvel—a suspension bridge over the Niagara River—but no way of stretching his first cable between the shores. Any boat that tried to cross near the falls would be swept over. Then Ellet thought of kites; you could fly one to the opposite side and use its cord to pull larger cables across. He announced a kite-flying contest.

Eighteen-year-old Homan Walsh entered the contest, with an appropriately named kite, "The Union." He was successful on his second attempt: The first bridge—only 7½ feet wide—opened for business on August 1, and $5,000 in tolls

Thundering torrents and swirling mist shot through with vivid rainbows, Niagara Falls was America's foremost early tourist attraction. But building a bridge across it was a challenge that taxed both the skill and imagination of the best engineers of the time.

was collected in 10 months. Walsh, however, got no more than $50 for his invaluable service.

1801
After 36 ballots in the House of Representatives, Thomas Jefferson is elected the third U.S. president. Aaron Burr, his opponent, is elected vice president.
Page 98

1804
Vice President Aaron Burr kills former Secretary of the Treasury Alexander Hamilton in a duel on July 11.
Page 164

1806
Frederic Tudor brings to Martinique the first ice that the islanders had ever seen. On June 16, Tecumseh's prophet brother, Tenskwatawa, blots out the sun.
Pages 140 and 343

1809
Meriwether Lewis (right) dies under mysterious circumstances at an inn named Grinder's Stand, and Dr. Ephraim McDowell removes a 22½-pound ovarian tumor from Jane Crawford—without anesthesia.
Pages 249 and 294

Frozen Alive

DECEMBER 22, 1850: DEFROSTED LOVERS SURVIVE MAINE SHIPWRECK

The cold was bitter; the winds, violent. Towering waves walloped Maine's rocky coast in spray that froze into shrouds of ice more than a foot thick. When the storm hit, mate Richard Ingraham and his fiancée, Lydia Dyer, were safe and dry on a schooner anchored near Rockland. The only other person on board was seaman Roger Elliott.

Shortly before midnight, both anchor cables snapped. The boat shot out of the harbor and crashed on the ledges beyond Owls Head. As icy water cascaded into the vessel, the three passengers grabbed their blankets and struggled to the deck. The blinding blizzard made it impossible to signal for help. Then Ingraham proposed a desperate plan. Dyer wrapped herself in blankets and lay down on the deck. Her fiancé then wrapped his body and blanket around her, and Elliott did the same next to him. The seaman carried a knife so that he could chip an air hole through the protective ice that would form over them. Hours later, as the storm subsided, Elliott chiseled his way to freedom. The two lovers lay motionless. Fatigued and frostbitten, the seaman made his way across onto the point, where he was rescued by a passerby. Before he collapsed, he whispered the message, "Others on the wreck."

When a rescue party arrived, they found the two bodies entombed in a block of ice frozen to the deck. Rescuers carefully removed the ice block and carried it to a nearby house. Through delicate thawing and chipping, they peeled the ice from the lovers' bodies. Then they poured cold water over them, gradually increasing the temperature to 55 degrees, and began softly massaging the seemingly lifeless victims. After two hours, Dyer opened her eyes. An hour later, Ingraham stirred. "What is all this?" he asked. "Where are we?" Recovery was slow but complete. Six months later, in June 1851, the pair were married. Elliott, however, never fully recovered.

The Fatal Pursuit

JULY 28, 1852: STEAMBOAT RACE ENDS IN DISASTER

It was early morning when two sleek, white steamers carrying New York-bound passengers swung out from the Hudson River docks in Albany—first the *Henry Clay* and then, in its wake, the *Armenia*. Prostrated by food poisoning, the captain of the *Henry Clay*, John Tallman, lay in his cabin; Thomas Collyer, builder and part owner of the boat, was in charge.

Collyer, who had earlier built the *Armenia*, had sold it to Captain Isaac Smith with the agreement

that the two boats would never race each other and that the *Henry Clay* would make its departures well in advance. And so, when the *Henry Clay* docked at Hudson, the first scheduled stop, Collyer was outraged to see the *Armenia* race past. He rushed the *Henry Clay* back into the channel, but the *Armenia* was a good mile ahead.

As flames consumed the steamboat *Henry Clay*, Collyer and others worked to rescue victims, throwing them wooden chairs and fence boards. A train stopped abruptly, and passengers rushed to help. A Newfoundland dog joined the effort and dragged a child out of the water. Meanwhile, river pirates tried to rob the drowning of their valuables. Contrary to this rendition of the disaster, the steamboat was beached.

Determined not to be outdone, Collyer and the crew increased the pressure on boilers to 350 pounds per square inch. The blowers hummed, the boat trembled, and coal dust drifted onto the decks. Frightened, the passengers pleaded with the officers to stop the race, but the crew was too exhilarated.

After a speedy docking at Catskill, the *Henry Clay* closed the gap. Its pilot, Jim Elmendorf, nosed in beside the *Armenia*. Prow to prow, the two boats swept on. Then, as the *Henry Clay* shot a few feet ahead, Elmendorf rammed the *Armenia*, splintering its bow.

"To larboard," the passengers of the *Henry Clay* were ordered. Shrieking with fear, they ran to the far side, lifting the boat's starboard guard above the larboard of the *Armenia*. Then, crashing down, the *Henry Clay* drove the *Armenia* toward shore. To avoid being run aground, the *Armenia*'s captain quickly cut his engines, and the boat drifted clear.

Racing furiously now, with red-hot embers from the smokestacks showering its decks, the *Henry Clay* forged on. At Poughkeepsie, 20 protesting passengers debarked. At Newburgh, the *Armenia* was so far behind that new passengers, including architect Andrew Jackson Downing, gladly boarded the *Henry Clay* rather than wait.

It was 3 p.m., and the *Henry Clay*, still at top speed, had just passed Yonkers (only a few miles from its destination) when a stoker staggered up on deck. A human torch, his clothes aflame, he jumped into the river. Within seconds, the boat was ablaze.

Collyer stood dumbstruck while Elmendorf swung the boat into the east bank. It ran a full 25 feet up the embankment, with an impact that toppled a

smokestack and hurled many people, including Collyer, onto land and safety. Others were pitched into the water; some trapped on the stern by a sheet of flame had to jump into the river. Within 20 minutes the wooden boat had burned down to water level.

Throughout the hot afternoon and the moonlit night, men dredged for bodies. The next morning it was reported that of the 300 or so passengers, 80 had died—among them Maria Hawthorne, sister of novelist Nathaniel Hawthorne, and Downing.

Collyer and the officers of the *Henry Clay* were acquitted of manslaughter. The New York state legislature later outlawed steamboat racing on the Hudson River.

Rancher Races Steamer to the Bank

FEBRUARY 18, 1855: PANIC BEGINS A CALIFORNIA BANK SCARE

The next time you hurry to the bank before it closes, think of rancher Louis Remme's ordeal.

From the day a steamer arrived in San Francisco with news that a major St. Louis bank had failed, financial panic swept central California. Remme couldn't withdraw his $6,000 from Adams & Company in Sacramento, but he could see one hope. Portland, Oregon, had no telegraph. If he could beat the steamer north, he might be able to get his money from the bank's Portland branch before its managers heard of the collapse.

The anxious cattleman headed into the teeth of a northern California winter. Six days and 11 horses later, he had completed the 665-mile wilderness trek. When the steamer arrived in Portland, local banks quickly closed. But Remme already had his money.

A Trailblazer in Bloomers

·AUGUST 5, 1858: A WOMAN SCALES 14,110-FOOT PIKES PEAK

The "Pikes Peak or Bust" frenzy was a year away when Julia Archibald Holmes and her husband joined the first group of Kansas gold-seekers to head for Colorado. The 20-year-old Julia Holmes wore bloomers on the trail, for "comfort and convenience."

A pioneer in every sense, she walked beside the wagon (though women were supposed to ride in it), camped in the Garden of the Gods at the foot of Pikes Peak, and climbed the majestic mountain.

After the Holmeses scaled Pikes Peak, they marked their arrival by inscribing their names on a rock. Julia Holmes later wrote to her mother: "In all probability I am the first woman who has ever stood upon the summit of this mountain and gazed upon this wondrous scene." And indeed she was.

The Greatest Show Between U.S. and Canada

JUNE 30, 1859: BLONDIN MAKES FIRST ROPEWALK ACROSS NIAGARA

When Jean François Gravelot first saw Niagara Falls, he knew he had to cross them on a rope. That was in 1858, when the French aerialist (who called himself "The Great Blondin" to play up his fair hair) was touring America with P. T. Barnum. The next year he returned and stretched a 1,300-foot length of manila rope, two inches thick, between the steep cliffs walling the rapids below the falls. Then, as 10,000 spectators held their breath, the 35-year-old Blondin stepped onto the rope from the U.S. side. Stopping midway, he lowered a line to a waiting steamer 190 feet below, drew up a bottle of wine, drank it, and then continued to the Canadian side.

For two summers, Blondin performed above the Niagara River. He crossed it on a bicycle, on stilts, and at night. He swung by one arm, turned somersaults, and stood on his head on a chair. Once he pushed a stove in a wheelbarrow and cooked an omelet.

But his greatest feat was to carry a man across on his back. With his passenger secured by a harness with foot hooks, Blondin grasped his 35-foot balancing pole and ventured down the steep incline of the rope. Several times his brave companion dismounted to give Blondin a rest and then climbed on his back again. A gust of wind caused them to sway, and spectators quaked with terror. (According to reporters, gamblers had loosened some guylines.)

"Unless you see 'Blondin walk' you don't see Niagara," gushed a correspondent for *The Times* of London in 1860.

Blondin sprinted the last few yards and plunged with his human cargo headlong into the crowd.

In 1860, the Prince of Wales (later King Edward VII) was among the spectators. Politely refusing an invitation to be carried across, the prince persuaded Blondin to come to London's Crystal Palace. The aerialist performed in London and Europe until 1896. The next year, at the age of 71, he died in bed.

New York Part of the Confederacy?

JANUARY 7, 1861: CITY MAYOR PROPOSES SECESSION WITH THE SOUTH

Civil war and the dissolution of the Union seemed imminent when New York City Mayor Fernando Wood, a powerful pro-Southern Democrat, made a startling proposal in his annual message to the city's Common Council: If the Southern states seceded, the city should do so, too, and become "equally independent." As a "free city," he argued, it would survive with the support of the South and the sizable income provided by import duties.

Attacking the Republican state legislature's tight control and taxation of the city, Wood asked: "Why may not New York disrupt the bands which bind her to a venal and corrupt master?" Democrats in the council—and a number of businessmen—supported his idea, and secret plans were made to carry it out. But when the war's first shots were fired, New Yorkers proved to be staunchly pro-Union, and Wood was voted out of office. Later, as a leader of Northern antiwar Democrats, or Copperheads, Wood became a thorn in Abraham Lincoln's side.

The Tax Man Cometh

JULY 1, 1862: THE AGONIES OF APRIL BEGAN IN JULY

Until the Civil War there was no federal income tax; the government was supported largely by bonds, excise taxes, and "external revenue" from tariffs on imported goods. The expensive war, however, led legislators to explore new sources of "internal revenue" from citizens at home. On August 5, 1861, a 3 percent tax on annual incomes over $800 was adopted, but no one bothered to collect it, perhaps because it met such a small part of government needs. On July 1 of the following year, a new

It wasn't until after the Civil War that an income tax was adopted. The 16th Amendment made the tax legal.

tax law was signed, giving America its first operable federal income tax. This was repealed in 1872—it had just been a temporary way of funding the war debt—and no new income tax was proposed until 1894, when the government needed money to meet financial crises caused by a monetary panic. But on May 20, 1895, the Supreme Court ruled that the whole idea of an income tax was unconstitutional, since the tax would not be distributed among the states in proportion to their populations. It took the 16th Amendment (ratified on February 3, 1913) to make income tax legal.

1836
Samuel Colt patents the revolver (right) on February 25. About a week later, the Alamo falls.
Pages 124 and 346

1840
Lieutenant Charles Wilkes sights Antarctica and charts the continent for the United States.
Page 277

1841
In May, the first wagon train to California departs from Missouri.
Page 261

The doomed Mississippi riverboat *Sultana*, carrying an estimated 2,400 passengers (it was licensed to carry 376), passed Helena, Arkansas, on April 25, 1865.

Sultana Explodes

APRIL 27, 1865: POST–CIVIL WAR STEAMBOAT DISASTER THE WORST IN U.S. HISTORY

Thousands of ex-prisoners (some from the infamous Confederate prison at Andersonville) were sent north after the Civil War. When the Mississippi riverboat *Sultana*, carrying about 2,400 of them, pulled into Vicksburg, Mississippi, a repairman said that a leaky boiler should be fixed by replacing two sheets of metal. The hurried captain settled for a thin patch.

Its decks crowded with homebound veterans and other passengers, the *Sultana* pushed upstream on a flood-swollen river. Three days later, a blast tore through the midsection. Steam and hot water shot into the night sky. The boilers had exploded and the boat was on fire.

As wind-whipped flames swept toward the stern, hundreds of people clung to the bow. When the current swung the *Sultana* around, those who didn't jump were instantly incinerated.

Scalded survivors threw anything that would float into the dark water. The flooded riverbanks were a mile or more away; clinging to their bits of debris, victims were swept downstream by the current. Some grabbed onto trees jutting above the flood. Many more drowned.

The southbound *Bostonia* rescued some victims. And a flotilla of boats at Memphis, Tennessee, pulled survivors from the water. Still, about 1,500 died; the exact figure will never be known. Sadly, many veterans who had survived untold battlefield and prison horrors never made it home.

Davis's Successor

FEBRUARY 25, 1870: FIRST AFRICAN AMERICAN U.S. SENATOR TAKES HIS SEAT

After the Civil War, former Confederate states faced the onerous task of gaining readmission to the Union. In January 1870, Mississippi impressed Congress by electing a U.S. senator who had helped organize Union regiments. His name was Hiram Revels. He was a graduate of Knox College in Ohio, an ordained minister, a respected educator, and a member of the Mississippi state senate. He was also African American.

Mississippi was readmitted, but the *New York Herald* predicted that Revels would never be allowed to take his Senate seat—especially since Mississippi's most recent senator had been Jefferson Davis, who had walked out to become president of the Confederacy. In fact, political bickering did delay approval of the new senator's credentials, but he was seated. Even Davis gave him modest support: He hated to see Mississippi represented by a black man, he wrote, but if that had to be, he was glad it was Revels.

The gallery was packed and emotions ran high when Hiram Revels took his oath of office on the Senate floor.

1851
Emanuel Leutze paints Washington crossing the Delaware—by using American tourists as models and the Rhine River as his inspiration.
Page 333

1852
Harriet Beecher Stowe's *Uncle Tom's Cabin* is published.
Page 206

1853
President-elect Franklin Pierce and his family are in a train wreck; Pierce's young son, Bennie, dies.
Page 80

1854
The Know-Nothings steal the papal stone from the Washington Monument.
Page 69

Before Rosa Parks

MAY 11, 1871: TRIUMPH FOR THE FIRST FREEDOM RIDERS

On Sunday, October 30, 1870, Horace Pearce and the brothers Robert and Samuel Fox boarded a nearly empty "whites only" trolley car in Louisville, Kentucky, paid their fares, and sat down. A white passenger quickly ordered the African Americans to leave. When they quietly refused, the driver abusively forced them from the car. The next day the case came before a local judge. Pearce and the Fox brothers were fined $5 each for disorderly conduct.

Robert Fox took the case to federal court, suing the trolley company for segregation that violated his civil rights. On May 11, 1871, a U.S. district court

> African American trolley riders refused to give up their seats and incited three days of unrest in Louisville.

upheld his suit, awarding him $15. But three days of near riots followed, as city streetcar operators continued to refuse to carry African Americans in white cars. Finally the companies gave in, fearing federal enforcement and further financial loss.

Eighty-four years later, blacks in Montgomery, Alabama, still endured segregated city buses. On December 1, 1955, Rosa Parks, a middle-aged seamstress on her way home from work, refused to give up her seat and started a bus boycott that helped launch another civil rights movement. This time the victory, spearheaded by Dr. Martin Luther King Jr., would have national impact.

The Great Peshtigo Fire

OCTOBER 8, 1871: MORE PERISH IN WISCONSIN, BUT CHICAGO GETS ALL THE HEADLINES

For three days the nation's newspapers were rife with headlines about the horror of the Chicago fire. Almost unnoticed was the fierce firestorm that began in northern Wisconsin the same evening and went on to devastate Peshtigo and neighboring lumber towns in Wisconsin and upper Michigan. No soaking rain had fallen for 14 weeks, and the pine forests, piles of sawdust, stacks of raw timber, even the swamps around Peshtigo were as dry as matchsticks. Small fires, many the result of carelessness or slash-and-burn land clearing that had been done to build a railroad, gnawed at forest debris and the roots of towering pines. When the wind rose, the trees crashed to the ground, showering sparks through the underbrush. Surging autumn breezes fanned the flames into a conflagration.

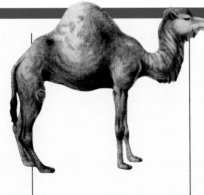

1855
In March, Congress appropriates $30,000 for a camel corps. A couple of months later, William Keil leaves Missouri for Oregon; his party is led by a preserved corpse.
Pages 347 and 262

1857
On March 6, the Supreme Court decrees that no black person can be a U.S. citizen.
Page 58

1859
Edwin Drake strikes oil in Pennsylvania.
Page 131

The widespread smaller blazes in the forest surrounding the town had created a great vacuum into which winds of hurricane force rushed. The sky became a shower of flames as fireballs burst in the treetops. Within minutes every building was ablaze. The huge woodworking factory exploded. Families who sought refuge in open fields were roasted as they lay on the ground. Those sheltered in wells were scalded. The lucky ones made it to the river, but even here they had to dunk their heads to prevent their hair from catching fire. The blaze was equivalent to the energy in a 20-kiloton bomb.

Fierce fires started in Chicago and northern Wisconsin on the same night. The Chicago fire grabbed headlines, but the fires around Peshtigo, Wisconsin, were more deadly, killing about 1,200 people.

More than a million acres (2,400 square miles) of forest were destroyed, and about 1,200 people perished. It was the worst forest fire in American history. But for days few people knew about it—the one telegraph wire into town had melted almost as soon as the fire struck. By the time word did get out, Chicago (where about 300 people died) was the fire story that had grabbed the headlines.

1860
The first Pony Express rider leaves St. Joseph, Missouri, on April 3.
Page 274

1861
In August, Allan Pinkerton arrests Rose Greenhow, leader of a Confederate spy ring.
Page 355

1856
American adventurer William Walker becomes the president of Nicaragua.
Page 348

1863
P. T. Barnum's star little people, Tom Thumb and Lavinia Warren, are married on February 10 amid great fanfare. On November 19, Abraham Lincoln, suffering from smallpox, delivers the Gettysburg Address.
Pages 211 and 118

The Case of the Costly Comma

**JUNE 6, 1872: CONGRESS PASSES
A TARIFF ACT, ERROR AND ALL**

A small punctuation mistake in legislation designed to reduce import duties nearly cost the federal government millions of dollars.

Congress intended that "fruit plants, tropical and semi-tropical for the purpose of propagation and cultivation" were to be tariff-free. But the clerk who copied the bill misplaced the comma, so the clause read: "Fruit, plants tropical and semi-tropical."

Importers took this to mean that all tropical and semitropical plants and all fruit were free of tariff. And a group of them joined forces to petition the Treasury Department for the refund that they felt was due them. At first, Secretary of the Treasury William A. Richardson agreed with the importers and on December 3, 1873, ordered hundreds of thousands of dollars worth of refunds.

But on December 10, Richardson changed his mind and suspended the refund. He reversed himself again the next day, ordering a settlement. And seven weeks after that, on January 31, 1874, the flip-flopping Cabinet member once more directed that the refunds be "revoked and cancelled." On May 9, 1874, Congress finally enacted legislation suspending, once and for all, repayments to importers. The bill corrected the errant comma, thus preventing the mistake from becoming one of the costliest typographical errors in history.

Dedicated Soldiers

**JUNE 13, 1883: WHAT A WAY
TO SALUTE CIVIL WAR HEROES**

The scene was repeated in towns and villages throughout New England. Veterans, other citizens, and perhaps a celebrity or two would gather to honor the Civil War dead and dedicate a monument to them. But when the town of Mystic, Connecticut, saw fit to pay tribute to those who fought so courageously, it became a day with a difference.

High on a pedestal, a dignified statue of a rifle-bearing Union soldier awaited unveiling. Governor Thomas Waller and a beloved senator and former general, Joseph R. Hawley, had been invited. But the festive crowd of 2,000 was gravely disappointed to find that the VIPs were delayed, and as the expectant audience shifted impatiently in their seats, the stands on which the spectators were sitting—hastily and perhaps flimsily erected for the occasion—collapsed. And that, as it turned out, was just the beginning.

One of the features of the festivities was the mustering of local troops and those from nearby Norwich. As the aging ex-soldiers marched toward town, however, shots rang out; the officer who was to give the order to fire the 38-gun salute (one for each of the 38 states of the Union) to herald the unveiling thought it might be nice to welcome the governor with it instead. The veterans, moving smartly up the street near the riflemen at that precise moment, suddenly faced the unexpected gunfire. Many were severely hurt; one officer's body was lacerated, the leg of another one was gushing blood.

Despite these injuries, no fatalities were reported.

As the sounds of gunfire and moaning faded, General Hawley delivered a stirring 40-minute speech. Then the women of Mystic served up a delicious luncheon to the deserving crowd.

It was, perhaps, altogether fitting and proper that the celebration came to an end when a drenching downpour suddenly fell upon the patriots who were assembled.

Notorious Outlaws, Model Prisoners

AUGUST 10, 1887: HEADLINER BADMEN START A PRISON NEWSPAPER

Not only was the concept of an inmate-run newspaper a novel idea in the 19th century, but having convicts put up money to get it started was even more innovative. Fifteen convicts at the Minnesota state prison in Stillwater contributed a total of $200; among the "stockholders" listed on the front page of the first edition were the Younger brothers. Notorious killers, bank robbers, and cohorts of the infamous Jesse James Gang, the trio had often grabbed headlines in national newspapers.

Convinced that the *Prison Mirror* was a worthy enterprise, Jim Younger and his brother Cole invested $20 each; their brother Bob donated $10. And on the masthead of that first edition, Cole Younger, the prison librarian, appeared as printer's devil (a minor editorial position, but listed no doubt in recognition of his exceptional notoriety as a murderer and thief).

The front page carried the maxim "God helps those who help themselves"—a motto that was later changed to "It's never too late to mend."

Published biweekly by and for inmates, the *Mirror* is today the oldest continuously published prison paper in the United States. It boasts awards as the "Best Printed Prison Newspaper," and its subscriber list eventually was extended far beyond the prison walls. But what of some of its famous founders?

Two years after the newspaper appeared, Bob Younger died at the penitentiary, a victim of tuberculosis. Cole and Jim were paroled in 1901. A year later Jim committed suicide in a St. Paul hotel because, under the terms of his parole, he could not marry the woman he loved. His surviving brother, who achieved legitimate renown with his autobiography *The Story of Cole Younger, by Himself*, died in 1916 in his hometown of Lee's Summit, Missouri, of natural causes.

1868
Impeached president Andrew Johnson is acquitted by one vote in the Senate.
Page 110

1869
John Wesley Powell's life is saved by some long underwear.
Page 265

1870
Suffragette Esther Morris becomes the first female justice of the peace.
Page 73

Split Down the Middle

NOVEMBER 23, 1889: MONTANA'S FIRST LEGISLATURE HOLDS TWIN SESSIONS

For sheer outrageousness, the first session of the Montana legislature is hard to beat. The voters had split the new state house of representatives between Democrats and Republicans, with five seats in dispute. To protect its party's claim to victory, each set of representatives met independently, in separate locations, for the entire 90-day session. Thus, Montana had two houses of representatives.

The state senate also was evenly split. Since the lieutenant governor, a Republican, held the tie-breaking vote, the Democrats refused to attend. In retaliation, the Republicans passed a resolution subjecting the absentees to arrest and stiff fines. The Democrats took it on the lam, eluding the law by fleeing the state. In the end, Montana's fractious first legislature failed to pass a single law, not even a "feed bill" to pay expenses and keep itself going—for which, no doubt, Montanans breathed a sigh of relief.

Two Robberies Mean Double Trouble

OCTOBER 5, 1892: THE DALTON GANG BITES THE DUST

Five men on horseback rode slowly into the bustling boomtown of Coffeyville, Kansas. Three of them wore false mustaches. They were the notorious Dalton brothers—Bob, Emmett, and Grat—and Coffeyville was their hometown. The other two were their henchmen, Bill Powers and Dick Broadwell. Bob Dalton, the leader, decided they would make history by robbing two banks in one raid.

The outlaws had reached the middle of town before a storekeeper recognized them and quietly spread the news. Unaware, Bob took Emmett into the First National Bank while Grat and his two

Kansas outlaws rob two banks in one raid, score $20,000, then face a shower of bullets.

chums strode into the private bank of C. M. Condon & Co.

Emerging with more than $20,000 stuffed into a grain sack, Bob and Emmett killed three townspeople and would have escaped if the other bank heist hadn't gone sour. Grat had been delayed by the Condon's bank officers long enough for gun-toting citizenry to get into position outside. When the three finally ran out, their guns blazing, rifle fire and shotgun blasts swept the street. As bullets slammed Grat backward, he killed a town marshal. Powers and Broadwell were shot dead in their saddles. Bob and Emmett rushed to help Grat.

1871
Explorer Charles Hall sets off for the North Pole on the ship, *Polaris*.
Page 276

1872
In November, Victoria Woodhull, free-love candidate for president, goes to jail. Shortly thereafter, Horace Greeley (right) goes insane then dies, three weeks after losing the presidency to Ulysses S. Grant.
Pages 95 and 94

1874
Reverend Henry Ward Beecher is sued for having an affair with a parishioner.
Page 213

Reunited for the final time, the three shot futilely at their attackers. Grat was killed, then Bob. Emmett was riddled with bullets. Only 15 minutes had passed since the Dalton Gang first entered the banks. Emmett recovered and was sent to prison. After his parole, he became a respected businessman in Los

After the shootout, the two dead Daltons (still with their false mustaches) and their companions were put on display in Coffeyville. People poured into town from miles around to view them and take their picture.

Angeles. Years later he was an adviser for the romanticized movie, *When the Daltons Rode*.

Preposterous Proposals

FEBRUARY 14, 1893: WISCONSIN REP ADDS TO THE LONG LIST OF SILLY, WANNABE CONSTITUTIONAL AMENDMENTS

Wisconsin Representative Lucas Miller proposed amending the Constitution to change our nation's name to "the United States of the Earth [because] it is possible for this republic to grow through the admission of new states until every nation on earth has become part of it."

Twenty-seven years earlier, just after the Civil War, would-be amenders wanted to call the country simply "America," "to indicate the real unity and destiny of the American people as the eventual, paramount power of the hemisphere."

1876
On July 4, America celebrates its 100th birthday.
Page 212

1877
President and "Lemonade Lucy" Hayes ban alcohol at the White House.
Page 81

1879
First group of African American "Exodusters" arrives in St. Louis aboard the steamer *Colorado*. Thomas Edison demonstrates his incandescent lightbulb at his "invention factory" in December in Menlo Park, New Jersey.
Pages 267 and 306

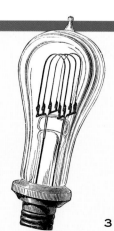

Presidential election procedures have been another favorite topic in the more than 10,000 amendments proposed since 1789. One innovator suggested that we select the president from among retiring senators—by lot. And because four of our first five presidents were from just one state (Virginia), an amendment was introduced in the early 1820s to divide the country into regions, giving each a turn at electing the chief executive.

But it was Augustus Wilson who, in 1876, went to the heart of presidential election complexities: He proposed we simply abolish the office altogether.

Leadville's Magnificent Ice Palace

NOVEMBER 25, 1895: A CORNERSTONE OF ICE IS LAID IN LEADVILLE, COLORADO, FOR THE LARGEST ICE PALACE EVER BUILT IN AMERICA

The town of Leadville, Colorado, was in the doldrums: The repeal of the Sherman Silver Purchase Act in 1893 had ended its glory days as a silver-mining center. In an effort to keep their city alive, the citizens staged a winter carnival.

On New Year's Day, 1896, the town turned out for the carnival's grand opening, and all were abuzz about its main attraction. The palace, which cost more than $40,000 and measured 450 feet long by 320 feet deep, covered more than three acres. The towers that flanked the entrance were 90 feet high. Inside was a 16,000-square-foot skating rink. Colored lights embedded in the walls and columns produced a radiant glow, and the ceiling glistened like diamonds.

A woman viewing fireworks reflecting off the palace walls finally looked away, saying it was "too unearthly a vision" to gaze upon. By the end of March, the vision was melting away.

The 1893 repeal of the Sherman Silver Purchase Act forced Leadville's citizens to think up new fundraising schemes. Though the town's winter carnival didn't raise much money, its ice palace was a sight to behold.

There was no pot of gold at the end of this rainbow; the thousands of visitors spent very little. Still, most felt it was all worthwhile. And, as Frank Vaughn, the town's poet laureate, observed: "Chances are they won't have No ice palace in hell."

A Texas-size Train Wreck

SEPTEMBER 15, 1896: THE "CRASH AT CRUSH" DRAWS THOUSANDS

Amazed that people would turn up in droves to gawk at train wrecks, William Crush, a passenger agent for the Missouri, Kansas & Texas Railroad, proposed that the line stage a crash for publicity and profit. Officials agreed, and thus was born what one reporter called "the event of the year."

Billing it as the "Monster Head-end Collision," Crush had two old steam locomotives freshly painted and arranged for each to pull six cars. A site near Waco, Texas, was chosen and named in honor of Crush, the energetic promoter. Hundreds of workmen descended and set up an instant city: a railroad depot and telegraph office appeared, as well as a restaurant in a circus tent. Statewide ballyhoo brought huge crowds; 10,000 people had arrived at Crush by 10 a.m.; by afternoon there were 40,000. As they jostled for a good view of the action, one newspaperman noted that "a wonderful recklessness marked the conduct of many." One man warned William Crush that the people were too close for safety, but he was pooh-poohed.

At 5:20 p.m. the trains thundered down the track, meeting head-on with a roaring crash. Then the boilers exploded. Debris flew through the air, killing two men; many more were injured as people ran for their lives.

Crush was fired by the railroad that night. Ever resourceful, he convinced his employers that they could turn the disaster into publicity for railroad safety and they rehired him the next day.

1888
Harold Brown tortures a dog with electrical current; a year or two later he invents the electric chair.
Page 307

1889
A Kansas City undertaker patents the automatic telephone exchange, and early birds get a jump start on the Oklahoma land rush.
Pages 302 and 269

1890
The first automated census tallies 62,622,250 Americans.
Page 308

Hopping the Train

FEBRUARY 3, 1898: FORTUNE SMILES ON PIGGYBACK LOCOMOTIVES

A blinding snowstorm had swirled across the frozen New England countryside since early evening. At around midnight, engineer Charles Eaton still struggled northward in his little Engine 684, pulling a two-car milk train on its daily run to Fitchburg, Massachusetts. Due at 5 p.m., it was seven hours late.

Simultaneously, on this same stretch of New Haven Railroad track, the giant Mogul-type Engine 823 was pushing a huge snowplow southward. Dispatcher Perry White had decided that the snow wasn't yet deep enough to stop the important milk run, so he had given 684 the right of way and diverted the plow onto a siding. These instructions had been telegraphed to a dispatcher farther up the line, who was supposed to make the appropriate track switch. But that dispatcher had gone to dinner. A sign saying "Back in 10 Minutes" hung on the door of his empty office as the telegraph receiver clicked away.

By the time he came back, it was too late. When the two engines met head-on, the little milk train was going 40 miles an hour. Its engine ran right up the plow and came to rest on top of 823, whose startled engineer furiously exclaimed: "You've got a damned nerve to be on this track!" Nerve wasn't half of it.

Fortunately, the accident was more comic than catastrophic. No one was seriously hurt. Engineer Eaton broke his nose, and his fireman, who cut the back of his head, was drenched when the tender burst and the extra water supply gushed around him. Even the cleanup was convenient. Engine 823 just carried little 684 piggyback to the depot.

"Reverence for the Mothers"

MAY 14, 1905: ANNA JARVIS'S MOTHER DIES, INSPIRES NATIONAL HOLIDAY

Anna Jarvis of Grafton, West Virginia, was devoted to her mother. Seven of her 11 siblings had died young, and the mother had clung to the survivors—especially Anna. After her mother's death, Jarvis began an impassioned crusade for a day to honor all mothers.

Eventually she devoted herself exclusively (and obsessively) to her cause. She began in her hometown with a special church service on the anniversary of her mother's death and subsequently embarked upon a sweeping letter-writing campaign. Finally, on May 9, 1914, President Woodrow Wilson proclaimed the second Sunday in May as Mother's Day, urging citizens to fly the American flag "as a public

---

1891
On October 16, Sarah Winnemucca, the first female Paiute chief, dies.
Page 257

1893
President Grover Cleveland loses part of his jaw in top-secret cancer surgery.
Page 86

1895
J. P. Morgan (right) bails the U.S. Treasury out of imminent bankruptcy.
Page 127

Mother's Day founder Anna Jarvis never had children of her own. Before she died in 1948, she had been disappointed to see how commercialized the holiday had become.

expression of our love and reverence for the mothers of our country." It is the only national observance that commemorates someone's death.

Until her death in 1948, Jarvis fought commercialization, decrying the greeting cards that replaced handwritten notes and the florists' huge profits from Mother's Day sales. Ironically, a group of grateful florists supported the impoverished crusader at the end of her life.

But not everyone credited the holiday to Anna Jarvis. Kentuckians claimed the honor for Mary Towles Sasseen, a teacher who, in 1887, celebrated her mother's birthday in her classroom and advocated the idea of schoolchildren honoring their mothers on that day with a program of song and verse. She published a pamphlet and promoted the idea for about two decades. Other schools followed suit, and after Sasseen died in childbirth in 1906, her family continued her efforts. It wasn't until a year later that Jarvis began her crusade.

Roosevelt Says, Football's a Killer

OCTOBER 9, 1905: PRESIDENT STEMS TIDE OF VIOLENCE IN COLLEGE SPORT

President Theodore Roosevelt held a tense meeting at the White House with the coaches from the three reigning football powers: Harvard, Princeton, and Yale.

The president saw merit in the game as a way to build strong bodies and character, but after seeing a horrifying photograph of Bob Maxwell, a Swarthmore College lineman who had been savagely beaten during a game, he had decided to take action. If football couldn't put an end to on-field brutality, he would abolish the game by executive decree. His concern was justified. Players wore little padding (even helmets were optional), and such popular plays as the flying wedge—in which an entire team formed a V and swept down the field like a tank—led to brawls.

During the 1905 season alone, 18 college players died and another 159 were badly injured. As a result of the meeting with Roosevelt, football representatives formed the American Football Rules Committee. The coaches issued new rules in 1906 that stressed speed rather than brute force; they banned mass formations and gang tackling and introduced the forward pass. Only six players were killed that year, including three Ivy Leaguers who died in fistfights.

1896

Harvard dropout James Connolly wins a gold medal in the first modern Olympics, and Herman W. Mudgett, owner of Chicago's "Murder Castle," is hanged.
Pages 218 and 177

1898

Frank M. Archer of New York City patents an electrical bedbug exterminator.
Page 293

1899

Frankie Baker shoots her lover, Allen (*not* Johnny) Britt, in St. Louis. She then spends decades explaining how the song, "Frankie and Johnny," got the story wrong.
Page 172

1900

On May 23, death-obsessed Frances Hiller finally gets her wish: a fancy funeral in her $20,000 funeral robe.
Page 148

Inventing the Inventor of Baseball

DECEMBER 30, 1907: ABNER DOUBLEDAY ELECTED FATHER OF AMERICA'S FAVORITE SPORT

Abner Doubleday became the father of our national pastime 68 years after the game was supposedly born. His paternity was proclaimed by a commission that A. G. Spalding had started in response to the suggestion that the sport wasn't American but had evolved from a British game called rounders. The search for American roots led to testimony by Abner Graves, who claimed to have played in the first baseball game when Doubleday marked a rough diamond in the dirt at Cooperstown, New York, in 1839. The only trouble with Graves's story was that Doubleday had been a cadet at West Point that year, and the witness himself had been only five years old. Unfortunately, Doubleday could not address the commission; he was already dead and had never mentioned the game in his letters or memoirs. Almost no one believes Graves's story today.

Albert Goodwill Spalding (left) was the premier pitcher of the 1870s. Despite the fact that he threw underhand, he was the first hurler to win 200 games. He went on to found the sporting goods firm that still bears his name.

Tale of a Comet

MAY 18, 1910: WITH ONLY SECONDS TO SPARE, A POSSE PREVENTS A SACRIFICE TO HALLEY'S COMET

Henry Heinman was the leader of a small group of fanatics in Oklahoma called the Select Followers. Heinman claimed to have received a revelation from God: On May 18, because of the poisonous gases in the tail of Halley's comet, the world would come to an end and the heavens would roll up like a scroll. Only a blood sacrifice, he declared, would avert disaster.

On that fateful day, the religious leader chose a teenager from a farm in western Oklahoma named Jane Warfield. She was tied to a stake, where she was to be knifed and allowed to bleed to death. The Select Followers were doing a ritual dance around the stake when, just in the nick of time, a sheriff's posse arrived. They rescued Warfield and arrested Heinman.

1901
In January, Spindletop sets off the Texas oil boom.
Page 132

1902
Nathan Stubblefield demonstrates his invention—the radio—in Washington, D.C., on March 20. Teddy Roosevelt's sportsmanship brings about the first plush bear, which is named after him.
Pages 303 and 108

1903
"Calamity Jane" dies, and is buried beside her friend "Wild Bill" Hickok.
Page 271

1904
Elizabeth Magie patents an amusement called "The Landlord Game," which later becomes known as "Monopoly."
Page 127

Accounts of the incident differ in several details. Was the intended victim nude or clad in virginal white? Did she have a wreath of roses atop her head? Was she really Heinman's stepdaughter? One local newspaper branded the whole thing a hoax perpetrated by the former editor of another paper. Hoax or not, newspapers from coast to coast covered the story, accurately reflecting the often hysterical mood of a comet-mad nation.

The comet named for astronomer Edmund Halley appears approximately every 76 years, most recently (and disappointingly) in 1986. In 1910, its arrival was heralded by an avalanche of advertisements and postcards and by elegant comet parties featuring exotic drinks with such names as the Comet Cocktail, Halley's Highball, and the Nucleus Brandy Cocktail (so called because the comet consisted of a nucleus and a flaming tail) that promised "a sunbeam in every sip." But gripping fear and wide-eyed terror were as common as celebrations: In addition to predictions about the end of the world, there were dire warnings to "look out for earthquakes."

"Many Moons Ago I Lived"

JULY 8, 1913: PEARL CURRAN FIRST CONTACTS PATIENCE WORTH

For almost a year Pearl Curran, a St. Louis housewife with little education and no literary ambitions, had been playing with a Ouija board. Suddenly, on a hot summer evening, some words appeared that changed her life: "Many moons ago I lived. Again I come.

Patience Worth my name. If thou shalt live, so shall I." Worth claimed to be the spirit of a 17th-century woman who had come to the New World late in life and had been murdered by Indians.

Over the next quarter-century, letters, short stories, books, poems, and plays flowed from Patience, via Pearl Curran. Hundreds of people visited the

1905
Alfred Fuller sells the first of *many* brushes.
Page 156

1906
Teddy Roosevelt tries to reform American spelling, with only moderate success.
Page 116

1907
Colorado cannibal Alferd Packer dies.
Page 176

Curran household to participate in the séances, during which Patience produced her voluminous correspondence.

Two of her books and numerous poems were published to critical acclaim. One reviewer commented that she had "a sense of humor that is rare in ghosts or secondary personalities." An expert in the field of psychic phenomena found Worth's intellect "keen, swift, subtle, and profound." And, at her insistence, the Currans adopted a child, whom the spirit considered to be "mine own bairn [baby]."

Curran continued to record communications from Patience Worth until shortly before her own death in 1937. The material filled 29 volumes.

Hello, Frisco!

JUNE 17, 1914: A TELEPHONE POLE
GOES UP IN UTAH

It was the last of 130,000 telephone poles installed across the nation to carry two circuits, each of which utilized 6,780 miles of copper wire. The linemen felt justifiable pride.

It had been decided in 1913 that transcontinental telephone service should be in operation by January 1915, when the Panama-Pacific Exposition in San Francisco was to open. The workmen had no time to waste in meeting their deadline; their job was to "nurse and coax" a tiny current of electricity across 3,400 miles.

Not only did the lines between the East and Denver have to be rehabilitated, but west of Denver there were many gaps to close. The most difficult of all was the 475-mile stretch beyond Salt Lake City, an expanse of salt basins and snow-capped mountains.

First the surveyors, camping in tents or boxcars and working despite extremes of weather, plotted a route. Having no topographical maps, they used compasses and the stars to fix their position. On their heels came the line gangs. Roads were built and chasms bridged for hauling the telephone poles, wire, and other equipment on horse-drawn wagons or sleds. Following a beeline course across shallow lakes and mud flats, the linemen propped the poles to keep them upright in the wet earth. Where the ground was rock-hard, special machinery with an auger-like drill was brought in to bore pole holes. Contending with blistering heat, record snows, and springtime floods, the crews regularly worked 11-hour days, with every third Sunday off.

January 25, 1915, found Alexander Graham Bell sitting with telephone company officials in New York while his assistant Thomas A. Watson waited in San Francisco. (Only 40 years earlier they had exchanged the first words conveyed by wire.) At 4:30 p.m. New York time, Bell lifted the receiver. "Ahoy! Ahoy! Mr. Watson! Are you there? Do you hear me?"

"Yes, Dr. Bell," came the reply from Watson. "I hear you perfectly."

1908
The Wright brothers give their first public demonstration on September 3, almost five years after having made their historic initial flight.
Page 314

1909
Alaskan miners climb Mount McKinley in record time.
Page 278

1911
Harriet Quimby (right) becomes the first American woman to get a pilot's license. And, at age 19, Cromwell Dixon becomes America's youngest licensed aviator.
Page 280

Promises, Promises

MAY 18, 1917: SELECTIVE SERVICE ACT IS PASSED, AND WOMEN START FILLING IN FOR DRAFTED RAILROADMEN

When the draft created a manpower shortage in 1917, the New York and Queens Railroad began hiring women to run its trolley cars. Within a year, 25 conductorettes were working on the Queens lines, often up to 60 hours a week. A local paper enthusiastically reported that the women "have made such a success of the work that some of them have been appointed inspectors."

The railroad was so satisfied with the conductorettes that it supplied them with khaki-colored winter overcoats (at $17 apiece), doubled their pay to $25 a week, and made a commitment to their permanent employment at the war's end. "The women conductors have come to stay on our lines just as long as they want to continue in their present jobs," an official promised. "We now have about 50 and are taking more on as fast as they apply for positions."

But alas, this pledge didn't last as long as the winter coats.

In May 1919, Governor Al Smith signed a bill to "better the conditions of women" by limiting them to only 54 working hours a week. The railroad company said it couldn't guarantee a profit with such restrictions, and in September it fired all of the women in favor of returning men.

The conductorettes "have proven remarkably steady and honest," said an official of the New York and Queens Railroad shortly after World War I ended. "They have been courteous to our patrons and we have had very few complaints." Nevertheless, the women were soon sacked.

1912
Teddy Roosevelt is denied the Republican presidential nomination although he had served as president already (and made some orthographical adjustments to American English while in office).
Page 116

1913
Joe Knowles gets nearly naked and goes back to nature.
Page 222

1914
The first true zipper, Hookless No. 2, is sold.
Page 322

1916
The Witch of Wall Street dies, leaving behind more money than J. P. Morgan.
Page 147

When Purity Distilling Corporation's steel tank full of molasses ruptured, 2.3 million gallons of molasses flooded Boston. Twenty-one people tragically died in the mess.

A Deadly, Sticky Disaster

JANUARY 15, 1919: TIDAL WAVE OF MOLASSES INUNDATES BOSTON

You may have heard your Bostonian parents or grandparents talk about the molasses flood that once engulfed the city's North End. It occurred on a day that had brought many Bostonians outdoors to bask in the unseasonable warmth. Some lunched in the shadow of the Purity Distilling Corporation's massive molasses tank. The steel-sided structure, 50 feet high and 90 feet in diameter, was filled nearly to the brim with 2.3 million gallons of molasses intended for rum. And it was about to come apart.

First, molasses sweated through the tank's looser rivets; they popped out of their holes with a sound like machine-gun fire. Then, with a muffled roar, the weakened seams split, and tons of molasses spewed out in a sudden, pitch-black flood.

The first wave, about 30 feet high, overpowered everything in its way, reducing buildings to rubble. Helpless men and animals were carried off like driftwood. A housewife died when her home collapsed around her. A boy buffeted by the surge was unable to call to his mother because his throat was clogged with molasses. A man was swept into

Boston Harbor, which was fast becoming a brown, murky mess.

The tank wreaked havoc, too, launching pieces of metal into the air like shrapnel. Flying shards sliced through a pillar of the Boston Elevated Railway, and an oncoming train braked just in time to avoid plunging into the ocean of goo.

After the flood had subsided, molasses clogged the streets, up to three feet deep in places. Victims continued to be found. A small girl still clutched firewood she had gathered. The corpse of a wagon driver was a molasses-coated statue. Survivors had to have their molasses-stiffened clothing cut off. Trapped horses had to be shot. The disaster left 21 dead (most of them drowned) and more than 50 injured.

In the ensuing weeks of cleanup, the citizens of Boston tracked molasses all over the city. People stuck to benches and sidewalks, or grappled with phone receivers glued to their ears. The molasses odor lingered for months—some say years. Even today, almost 100 years later, people claim that on a hot afternoon there is a hint of it in the air.

Mama's Yellow Rose

AUGUST 18, 1920: TENNESSEE RATIFIES 19TH AMENDMENT, ALLOWING U.S. WOMEN TO VOTE

Some called it the War of the Roses. At issue was the ratification of the 19th Amendment, guaranteeing women the right to vote. The symbol of the suffragists, or "Suffs," who supported it was a yellow rose. Their opponents, the "Antis," rallied to a red rose.

By the summer of 1920, 35 states had ratified it, one short of the three-fourths needed. The rest were very much in doubt. The Suffs pinned their hopes on Tennessee; while they tucked yellow roses into legislative lapels and pleaded their case, the Antis kept money and liquor flowing freely among the state's lawmakers.

"My mother wanted me to vote for ratification," said Harry Burn, the Tennessee legislator who swung the vote in women's favor.

When the legislature assembled on Wednesday, August 18, Suff campaign workers, counting roses from the gallery, were dismayed to see young Harry Burn, from heavily Anti McMinn County, wearing a red rose. Earlier, Burn had told them, "My vote will never hurt you."

The first ballot ended in a tie. Then, on the revote, Harry Burn changed his vote to aye. The crowd went wild—Tennessee had ratified the 19th Amendment. The next day Burn attributed his dramatic switch to a letter received from his mother. "I know that a mother's advice is always safest for her boy to follow," he said, "and my mother wanted me to vote for ratification."

1921
The first transcontinental airmail flight arrives in New York on February 21. In October, four unknown American soldiers are exhumed in France; one will lie in Arlington National Cemetery.
Pages 281 and 367

1923
Author Upton Sinclair is jailed for reading the Bill of Rights aloud in public.
Page 42

1924
Little Orphan Annie debuts, after undergoing a substantial transformation, and Ezra Meeker travels the Oregon Trail for the fourth and final time—by airplane.
Pages 226 and 261

1925
John Scopes is fined $100 for teaching evolution.
Page 229

Who Planted the Bomb?

SEPTEMBER 16, 1920: MYSTERIOUS EXPLOSION ROCKS WALL STREET

It was a boom day on Wall Street, but the results were fatal. Parked next to the new U.S. Assay Office and across the street from the handsome J. P. Morgan Building was a horse-drawn cart loaded with metal sash weights and TNT. Around noontime, when the streets were filled with lunchtime crowds, the bomb went off, hurling shrapnel into the crowd and through windows. Thirty-five died, and hundreds were wounded; many bodies were mangled

An Associated Press reporter who witnessed the blast, called it "an unexpected, death-dealing bolt, which ... turned into a shamble the busiest corner of America's financial center."

beyond recognition. The blast was widely suspected to be an anarchist attempt on the life of J. P. Morgan Jr., but the tycoon was in Europe. (His son Junius Spencer Morgan was slightly injured by flying glass.)

Finding the culprit would prove impossible. As dogged investigators sifted through the debris, they discovered a horseshoe that they finally traced to a blacksmith's shop on the Lower East Side. But the blacksmith wasn't much help, and the person who sent Wall Street skyrocketing was never found.

High Crime

MAY 15, 1923: AUTHOR JAILED FOR SPEAKING FREELY

In 1923, Upton Sinclair, the well-known muckraker and novelist, was arrested while addressing a group of striking transport workers. His crime? Reading aloud the Bill of Rights. He had just uttered part of the First Amendment—you know, the part about freedom of religion, of speech, and of the press, and the right of "the people peaceably to assemble"?—when the Los Angeles police nabbed him.

The muckraking author of *The Jungle* was reciting the Bill of Rights to a group of striking longshoremen in San Pedro, California, when he was arrested.

Charged with expressing ideas "calculated to cause hatred and contempt" of the U.S. government, he was held for 22 hours before he finally reached a courtroom.

1927
Gutzon Borglum begins sculpting Mount Rushmore.
Page 71

1929
The U.S. stock market crashes on "Black Tuesday," October 29, ushering in a decade-long economic depression.
Page 136

1931
The first Rockefeller Center Christmas tree is decorated with tin cans and paper.
Page 225

An Assassin's Bullets for FDR

FEBRUARY 15, 1933: MAYOR OF CHICAGO IS SHOT IN AN ATTEMPT ON THE PRESIDENT'S LIFE

Giuseppe Zangara always had a stomachache. He blamed it (and everything else wrong with his life) on capitalists. His discontent gave him an intense desire to kill someone in power. Once, in his native Italy, he had planned to kill the king, but he couldn't get close enough to him. After moving to the United States, he considered killing our ever-placid president, Calvin Coolidge.

Early in 1933, Zangara had targeted President Herbert Hoover but was dissuaded by the chilly Washington weather, which he feared might aggravate his stomach. Then he learned that President-elect Franklin D. Roosevelt would be speaking at Bayfront Park in Miami. The park was near Zangara's home and offered him a perfect opportunity. With an $8 revolver and 10 bullets, both newly purchased at a local pawnshop, he headed for the park.

At first he was frustrated. Stuck deep in the crowd, the five-foot assassin was too short to get off a shot when Roosevelt's open car rolled in. Five minutes later, however, at 9:35 p.m., FDR had finished delivering his brief speech from atop the backseat of the car. The crowd was beginning to disperse. Zangara lunged forward, leaped onto a vacant chair, and fired five shots. Each hit someone, but all of them missed Roosevelt entirely.

Although sullen, 32-year-old assassin Giuseppe Zangara (center) enjoyed the publicity he received after his arrest. He pleaded guilty to shooting Chicago mayor Anton Cermak and was electrocuted in a Florida prison.

Four victims survived. One bullet, however, penetrated the right lung of Chicago Mayor Anton Cermak. He died three weeks later, on March 6, two days after FDR's inauguration.

Within days of the attack, Zangara was sentenced to 80 years in prison on four counts of deadly assault. After Cermak died, a new trial resulted in a new sentence: death. The assassin never pleaded insanity; he seemed proud of his guilt.

On March 20—just 33 days after the shooting and 14 days after Cermak's death—Zangara was electrocuted. Feeling slighted to the last, he complained that no photographers were present.

1932
Bonus marchers are driven from Washington, D.C., on July 28.
Page 224

1933
"Machine Gun" Kelly coins the term "G-men." Prohibition ends on December 5, and liquor (legally) flows.
Pages 173 and 182

1934
On July 22, the FBI kills John Dillinger—or so they say.
Page 187

The First Round-the-World Phone Call

At 9:30 in the morning, AT&T president Walter S. Gifford placed a call to his vice president, T. G. Miller, from company headquarters in New York City.

The call was routed by underground and aerial wires via San Francisco to the shortwave transmitter at Dixon, California, where it was amplified and hurled 9,000 miles across the Pacific Ocean to Java. A second shortwave radio circuit took the call 7,000 miles to Amsterdam. Then land wires and underground cables sped it across the North Sea to London and on to the radio station at Rugby, England. From there, shortwave zapped the call across the Atlantic Ocean to Netcong, New Jersey, from whence a cable took it back to the AT&T Long Distance Building. A quarter of a second after Gifford placed the 23,000-mile globe-circling call, Miller's phone rang—about 50 feet away, in the next office. What a way to celebrate AT&T's 50th anniversary!

Telephone operators such as these, circa 1935, would have made the necessary connections for Gifford's call.

"Wait Till I Die"

SEPTEMBER 29, 1935: DEATH BRINGS REVELATION OF A MURDER

When Captain John Lea, a respected tobacco man, died at 92, the nation discovered he had gotten away with murder. He was the last of the perpetrators of a Ku Klux Klan execution that had taken place 65 years earlier in Caswell County, North Carolina. The victim was a state senator and justice of the peace named John Walter Stephens, who was also a white tobacco farmer and served as an agent of the Freedmen's Bureau.

1935
The frozen body of the "silver queen," Baby Doe Tabor, is found in her shack on March 7.
Page 147

1936
The Literary Digest confidently predicts on October 31 that Alf Landon will defeat Franklin Delano Roosevelt (who's related to 11 other presidents) for the presidency.
Page 103 and 84

1939
On October 13, "Shipwreck" Kelly stands on his head all day atop a 56-story building.
Page 227

1943
Norman Rockwell's Rosie the Riveter makes her debut on May 29. A few months later, James Wright's lab experiment unexpectedly yields Silly Putty.
Page 369 and 324

Lea, the scion of a slave-holding family, was a Confederate veteran of the Civil War and an organizer of the Ku Klux Klan in Caswell County. Stephens, a member of the Union League and the Republican Party, worked to politically organize the county's African American vote for the Republican Party. In his fervor, he intimidated white Democrats. He was socially ostracized from the white community and accused of many crimes, though never charged.

On Sunday morning, May 22, 1870, Stephens was found in a storeroom of the county courthouse, brutally murdered. The killing created a furor. It was widely believed that Stephens's death was a Klan execution, and numbers of white men, including Lea, were arrested and questioned. But all remained silent, and all were released.

As time passed, the various suspects died, until only Captain Lea was left. Asked repeatedly what had happened, he would cagily reply, "You all can wait till I die." In 1919, he secretly gave three state officials a statement about the murder, to be read posthumously.

Made public upon his death, the affidavit stated that Stephens had been "tried" for arson and extortion, found guilty, and sentenced to death by the Klan. Naming the Klansmen involved, Lea then described how Stephens had been lured to his execution chamber, disarmed, strangled with a rope, and stabbed "in the breast and also in the neck." Stephens "had a fair trial before a jury of twelve men," Lea commented, with no indication of remorse.

Counterfeiting on the Cheap

JANUARY 13, 1948: KIDS TIP OFF COPS TO FAKE MONEYMAKER WHO WAS ON THE LAM FOR 10 YEARS

He was no master criminal, just a former building superintendent who passed phony $1 bills. Yet the nation's most-hunted counterfeiter eluded detection for about 10 years.

A little white-haired man, 63-year-old Edward Mueller moved into a New York City tenement in 1938. Fiercely independent, he told his children he was comfortably well-off, but in fact he had little money. As his savings dwindled, he began turning out $1 bills. The results were terrible; using ordinary paper, he made no attempt to reproduce the fine details of a real bill. And his spending style was as modest as his means: Mueller would pass a bill or two each day—just enough to support himself and his dog. He never passed more than one to any given person, in time branching out from his neighborhood.

The least greedy counterfeiter on record was caught only by chance: His apartment burned, and some boys who were exploring the rubble found a cache of "stage money." One boy's father recognized the bills and turned the money in.

It wasn't easy for authorities to believe that the charming old man was their quarry. Freely admitting his crime, Mueller was sentenced to a year and a day and was ordered to pay a fine. The amount? One dollar—the genuine article, of course.

1944
Secret DD tanks sink off Omaha Beach on D-Day.
Page 373

1945
Japanese machine-gun fire kills Ernie Pyle on April 18, and Harry S. Truman plays Paderewski's Minuet for Stalin at Potsdam Conference.
Pages 370 and 78

1946
The Roosevelt dime is issued on FDR's birthday, January 30. In July, the first peacetime atom bomb test blasts the Bikini Atoll.
Pages 119 and 233

Final Flight

In 1932, Amelia Earhart became the first woman to fly solo across the Atlantic. Now she and navigator Fred Noonan were on the longest leg of a round-the-world flight.

As they neared tiny Howland Island in the Pacific, fuel was precariously low, and stormy weather made radio communication difficult. But Earhart was not broadcasting her position. Her husband, George Palmer Putnam, had sold exclusive rights to the story of her flight to the *New York Herald Tribune*, and she may have wanted to keep other newspapers from getting the scoop. Just before 8 a.m. local time, Earhart radioed Howland: "We are circling but cannot see the island. Cannot hear you." Her last message 45 minutes later was unclear. She and Noonan were never seen again. Ironically, the aviatrix had said that the round-the-world trip would be her last long-distance flight.

President Franklin D. Roosevelt ordered a search for downed flying great Amelia Earhart (above). For two weeks, seven navy ships scoured 250,000 square miles of the vast Pacific but found nothing. Even today, rumors persist that Earhart was captured by the Japanese and executed as a spy.

One Last Wave from a Dying Pilot

When radar picked up a plane coming from the direction of Japan, U.S. officials knew something was amiss. It was dusk, the sky was overcast, and the enemy never attacked in that kind of weather or at that time of day. Then two American pilots spotted a P-40 bearing markings that hadn't been used since Pearl Harbor, a year earlier. A close look revealed a bullet-riddled plane without wheels. Slumped over

---

1948
On November 2, Thomas E. Dewey fails to oust President Harry S. Truman from the White House, though Chicago newspapers report Dewey's victory.
Page 103

1951
President Truman fires General Douglas MacArthur on April 11.
Page 376

1954
Lyndon Johnson keeps America out of Vietnam, though six years earlier he wins Senate nomination by only 87 votes.
Page 78

1955
On April 12, the 10th anniversary of FDR's death, Dr. Jonas Salk announces the development of his polio vaccine. Six days later, Albert Einstein dies; his brain is preserved for research.
Pages 119 and 298

the controls was a blood-soaked pilot who turned his head and waved weakly. A few seconds later, the plane hit the ground and exploded. Little remained to identify the flier, but there was a diary.

The diary traced the mystery flight back to Mindanao, an island some 1,300 miles from the crash site. Possibly the pilot was one of 19 Americans and 7 Filipinos who refused to surrender but took to the jungle with the last P-40 on the island.

Cannibalizing parts from downed planes, they readied the fighter for one final attack on the Japanese. None of this, however, was confirmed. What is certain is that somehow a forgotten American plane made it through more than 1,000 miles of hostile airspace to once again touch friendly soil. But its pilot and his mission remain one of the mysteries of World War II. The P-40 must have used bamboo skids during takeoff—remember, it had no wheels.

"Your Island Is Moving"

NOVEMBER 29, 1944: JAPANESE SUPERSHIP SINKS ON MAIDEN VOYAGE

The submarine *Archer-Fish* (its crew, above, is shown with the sub's symbol, designed by Walt Disney) was assigned to "lifeguarding" off Tokyo Bay; its mission on November 28 had been to pick up downed U.S. airmen. But it was a quiet day, and skipper Joseph Enright ordered the radar disassembled for repair. By 8:30 p.m. the radar was in working order; immediately, it picked up a target. Since the only thing in sight was an island, Enright assumed that the radar was still broken and reprimanded its operator. Within minutes, the sailor returned. "Captain," he reported, "your island is moving."

What the radar screen had detected was a supership built in such secrecy that the mere mention of it was punishable by death. It was Japan's powerful aircraft carrier *Shinano*, on its maiden voyage. For seven hours the *Archer-Fish* pursued the zigzagging quarry, but could never position itself for an attack.

> The powerful *Shinano* was the largest Japanese aircraft carrier built before 1950. It was sunk only weeks after it was completed.

Then the *Shinano*'s captain made a fatal mistake: He headed straight at the sub.

Four torpedoes hit home, and by 11 a.m. the 72,000-ton *Shinano* had sunk, taking the captain and 1,400 crew members to their watery graves. It was the end of what the Japanese had proudly called their "unperishable castle of the sea."

1957
U.S. Air Force nearly nukes New Mexico on May 22.
Page 376

1960
Earl K. Long, the Louisina governor who once had to be declared sane, dies just months after completing his third term.
Page 92

1961
Congress declares "Uncle Sam" Wilson of Troy, N.Y., the "progenitor of America's national symbol" on September 13.
Page 69

1963
Members of the Society for Indecency to Naked Animals picket the White House, demanding that Mrs. Kennedy put clothes on her horse.
Page 236

Funeral Day

APRIL 28, 1944: SHERLOCK LAID TO REST ON IRISH CLAN'S ANNUAL BURIAL DAY

Old Mattie Sherlock, proud patriarch of the Irish horse traders who roamed the byways of the South, died on March 8, 1944, in Brownsville, Tennessee. But he wasn't laid to rest until April 28—and by then he was in Atlanta, Georgia.

No matter where or when members of Sherlock's fabled clan died, their remains were usually packed up and shipped to a funeral home on Peachtree Street in Atlanta to await Funeral Day, when horse-trader caravans from all over Dixie gathered for a family reunion. (When clan members enlisted in the army during World War I, many of them gave the funeral parlor as a permanent address.)

The eight immigrant families that formed the original horse-trader bands—they'd fled Ireland during the Potato Famine of the 1840s—had tired of city life in Washington, D.C., and taken to the open road in brightly painted wagons. Trailing behind them were the strings of horses and ponies they sold for a livelihood. When the group found a priest at Atlanta's Church of the Immaculate Conception who was willing to minister to them despite their nomadic lifestyle, they began the custom of gathering there once a year to bury their dead. But Sherlock was one of the last to be laid to rest in the old way. In 1966, after more than 100 years as vagabonds, many of the horse-trader families settled permanently in a mobile-home village in North Augusta, South Carolina.

Elvita Adams Saved by a Stiff Breeze

DECEMBER 2, 1979: EMPIRE STATE BUILDING JUMPER FAILS HER LAST MISSION

The Empire State Building's 86th-floor observation deck is surrounded by a seven-foot-high steel fence topped by curved spikes, but determined jumpers are often able to scale this obstacle. One was Elvita Adams, who managed to climb over without attracting the attention of about 50 tourists on the deck with her. Leaping off the edge, she fell about 20 feet before a 30-mph gust of wind blew her back onto a ledge two and a half feet wide. A guard, hearing her cries of pain (she'd broken her hip), rescued her.

Thus Adams joined the list of other ledge-landers like Thomas Helms, who in 1977 suffered only shock and lacerations and crawled through an open window of NBC's transmitter room, startling an engineer. But one jumper who landed on the ledge refused to accept his fate; he got right up and leaped again.

1965
Astronaut Ed White walks in space on June 3, then doesn't want to reboard the spacecraft.
Page 283

1966
Stephen Dennison is awarded $115,000 in damages after serving 34 years in prison for stealing a $5 box of candy.
Page 188

1969
On July 21, man leaves the surface of the moon for the first time, after a visit of 21 hours and 37 minutes.
Page 235

World Prays for Safe Y2K

DECEMBER 31, 1999: MILLENNIUM USHERS IN BOTH REVELRY AND FEAR

The optimists were right. As the world greeted a new millennium, key computers effortlessly flipped their dates from 1999 to 2000 at midnight without a glitch.

Pessimistic Y2K (year 2000) fears that the turnover would create havoc in our computer-dependent society were quickly laid to rest. About 72 percent of Americans stayed home that night, either out of fear or simply to share a momentous event quietly with family or friends. Twenty-four or more continuous hours of television coverage of the worldwide happening assured the stay-at-homes that all was well. Airplanes took off and landed without mishap, automatic teller machines gave out money, and electricity lit up the night.

As the new millennium rolled in, starting at the international date line and moving west, joyous celebrations from Kiribati's Millennium Island and New Zealand's Chatham Islands began an all-night party that was telecast all over the world. The global festivities continued from time zone to time zone, showing off spectacular light displays at such places as the Pyramids in Egypt and the new Millennium Dome in London, built for the occasion.

In New York City, nearly 2 million adventurous revelers saw the ball drop at midnight from the top of One Times Square. For 12 hours, giant television screens allowed the throng to watch people all over the globe greet the new millennium with cheers,

John Koskinen of the President's Council on Y2K Conversion addresses the media during a February 2000 press conference.

dances, music, grins, and almost endless pyrotechnics. Similar parties took place in big cities all across the United States.

In many suburban settings, sheepish American families who had stocked up on cash, water, and canned goods for the projected period of chaos after computer meltdown asked to join the parties of their more optimistic neighbors. Few were refused.

At the Center for Year 2000 Strategic Stability at Colorado's Peterson Air Force Base, U.S. and Russian military officers kept a joint watch over computer-controlled nuclear missiles. Applause broke out in the control room when the new year arrived in Moscow without a hitch. The Russians had spent the equivalent of $4 million on Y2K military preparations; the United States had spent almost a thousand times that amount.

Tragedy of the Twin Towers

SEPTEMBER 11, 2001: CONSPIRACY THEORISTS CAN'T TOP ODD EVENTS CENTERED AROUND WORST TERRORIST ACT ON U.S. SOIL

On September 11, 2001, members of the extremist Islamic terrorist group al-Qaeda hijacked four American airplanes and then flew them into the Twin Towers of the World Trade Center in New York and the Pentagon building in Washington, D.C. A fourth hijacked plane crashed in a field in Pennsylvania after a passenger revolt. The attacks in New York caused severe structural damage to the Twin Towers, and the two buildings collapsed within an hour and a half, trapping thousands inside. Over 2,700 people were killed in the largest ever terrorist attack on American soil.

As with most national tragedies, a number of conspiracy theories have developed to try to explain the horrific events. They include the following: the Twin Towers were brought down by a controlled explosion; it was a missile, not a plane that hit the Pentagon; United Flight 93 was shot down by the U.S. military in Pennsylvania; and the U.S. government had prior knowledge of the attacks but allowed them to take place. None of these theories was backed by mainstream media or scientific evidence.

But even stranger than some of conspiracy theories surrounding the events leading up to the day are the actual events after September 11.

New York City's World Trade Center was ablaze after two hijacked airliners crashed into the towers on Tuesday, September 11, 2001.

WELCOME TO AMERICA, TERRORISTS

Within days of the attacks, the U.S. government had identified 19 men as the suspected hijackers. Their faces and names became the focus of national outrage. Americans were shocked to find out that two of the men, Mohammed Atta and Marwan al-Shehhi, had learned to fly planes at a flight school in Florida.

Six months *after* the attacks, the U.S. Immigration and Naturalization Service (INS) sent letters to Huffman Aviation International, the Florida flight school, approving the student visa applications of Atta and al-Shehhi. The two conspirators had entered America under visitor visas and applied for the student visas once they arrived. According to the INS letters, the terrorists would be allowed to stay in the United States until October 1,

---

1983
Pioneer 10 (right) leaves the solar system on June 13. Back on Earth, grownups riot in shopping malls for Coleco's new Cabbage Patch Kids.
Pages 286 and 237

1986
On January 28, the space shuttle *Challenger* explodes over Florida, killing all seven astronauts on board.
Page 284

1991
The Gulf War cease fire goes into effect on February 28.
Page 378

50

2001. Of course the men couldn't take advantage of their new visa status—they were dead, along with thousands of people they had killed.

INS blamed a backlog of paperwork at a processing center in Kentucky for the delay in dispatching the letters. And the agency pointed out that the decision to approve the visas was made before September 11; it just took some time to send out the official written documentation.

FAKING THE DEAD

Another odd and tragic post-September 11 event illustrates the extremes to which some people will go for money. After the attacks, grieving Americans donated some $2.4 billion to charities, hoping to help the September 11 victims' families. Insurance companies also geared up for the saddening claims they would receive from spouses and parents of the dead.

But few expected the hundreds of fraudulent attempts to profit from the September 11 attacks. The American Red Cross identified about 350 cases of fraudulent claims to its charitable 9/11 funds. The New York County District Attorney's office investigated 70 cases of individual fraud related to 9/11 and arrested at least 20 people. But the fakes weren't limited to New York. As far away as Georgia and Ohio, people tried to make money from the tragedy.

Charles and Cynthia Gavett of Concord, Georgia, nearly schemed their way into a hefty life insurance payout by claiming that Mrs. Gavett had gone to an interview in the World Trade Center on September 11 and was never heard from again. The couple even got their 14-year-old daughter into the act, by having her sign an affidavit that her mother was gone. But when the insurance company began to ask questions, the couple's neighbors said the woman was alive and well. It turns out that they were hoping to pay off their mortgage. Instead, they went to jail.

In Butler County, Ohio, Ajay Chawla claimed his father went missing in the World Trade Center. He promised to send some DNA samples to the New York Police Department to help identify the remains. His father was found healthy and living in India—and probably not very happy with his son. Instead of getting a big insurance payout, Chawla got a $1,500 fine and a year in prison.

DEVASTATION REVEALED IN SMALL PIECES

Within days of the September 11 attacks, it was evident to the American public that no more survivors would be found. In New York, where the wreckage of the Twin Towers' collapse was strewn across lower Manhattan, the mission became one of recovery rather than rescue. Hundreds of workers searched for bodies at the site of the New York attacks, which soon became known as "Ground Zero."

Five years after the attacks, the families of more than 1,100 victims had still not received any remains. Construction workers building a memorial at Ground Zero were continuing to find bone fragments on nearby roofs, in abandoned manholes, and beneath asphalt haul roads. As each bone fragment was recovered, it was painstakingly registered and identified in a dignified manner. They serve as tiny, yet heart-wrenching, reminders to a city still recovering from the day.

Always a glorious sight, the Statue of Liberty is especially amazing when illuminated by fireworks. Opposite: Jean Leon Gerome Ferris's painting, *The Bell's First Note*, imagines the moment of the Liberty Bell's first peal.

CHAPTER TWO

Symbols of Our Nation

If you asked a room full of schoolchildren to draw pictures of what America means to them, what do you think they would draw? Chances are, you'd get dozens of icons and symbols that kids (and all the rest of us) associate with our free nation: The Liberty Bell. The American flag. The Statue of Liberty. Maybe you'd get something as sophisticated as an Uncle Sam. These images and ideas are ingrained in us as "American" from a young age. It's not until we're older that our forefathers' words, rather than symbols, say "America" to us. (But just because we're old and wise enough to understand the importance of the Bill of Rights doesn't mean that we don't tear up when we see the flag waving at a Fourth of July parade.)

One thing's for sure: From the Declaration of Independence and the Gettysburg Address to the White House and Mount Rushmore, they are all symbols of our nation.

America's *Real* Birthday

CONGRESS DECLARED INDEPENDENCE ON JULY 2, *NOT* JULY 4

On July 3, 1776, John Adams made the following prophesy in a letter to his wife, Abigail: "The Second Day of July 1776 will be the most memorable Epocha, in the History of America. I am apt to believe that it will be celebrated, by succeeding Generations, as the great anniversary Festival. It ought to be commemorated as the Day of Deliverance."

When the letter was later published—well into the next century—July 4 had already become the traditional day of celebration, so an editor (a nephew of Mrs. Adams's) redated the letter July 5 and changed the first line to read "The Fourth Day" rather than "The Second."

So what actually happened on July 4? Legend has it that the delegates gathered at Independence Hall in Philadelphia to sign the Declaration of Independence. In fact, they met that day to approve the final version of the Declaration, which they had scrutinized. Only two people—John Hancock, the president of Congress, and Charles Thomson, the secretary—signed anything then, and their signatures went on the draft copy. It wasn't until July 19 that the order was placed for the formal document to be printed on parchment paper. It was signed by 50 delegates on August 2. Six others signed later.

> "I am obnoxious, suspected, and unpopular. You are very much otherwise. (And) you can write 10 times better than I can."
>
> —**JOHN ADAMS**, cajoling Thomas Jefferson into writing the Declaration of Independence

THE CRUCIAL VOTE

Richard Henry Lee of Virginia first proposed the resolution "that these United Colonies are, and of right ought to be, free and independent States" on June 7. By July 1, when the Continental Congress prepared to vote on Lee's resolution, only nine of the 13 colonies were firmly in favor of it. New York was abstaining, South Carolina and Pennsylvania were opposed, and Delaware was

IMPROBABLE PIONEER

Abigail Adams: Early Liberator of Women

If Abigail Adams had gone to the Continental Congress in 1776 instead of her husband, John, the way American women were treated back then might have been quite different. In a March 31, 1776, letter to her husband, Mrs. Adams wrote: " ... in the new Code of Laws which I supposed it will be necessary for you to make I desire you would Remember the Ladies, and be more generous and favourable to them than your ancestors. Do not put such unlimited power into the hands of the Husbands.... "

To this, John Adams replied: "I cannot but laugh ... Depend upon it, We know better than to repeal our Masculine systems ... in Practice you know We are the subjects."

undecided. Two of Delaware's delegates were split in their views, and the third, Caesar Rodney, was on business 80 miles away. To break the tie, the pro-independence delegate sent for Rodney. Rodney set out before dawn on July 2 and rode furiously through driving rain; he arrived at Independence Hall just in time to cast Delaware's deciding vote.

In the meantime, Adams and others had won the support of South Carolina and Pennsylvania. Thus the tally for independence, which inspired Adams's letter to his wife, was 12 to 0. The following week New York made the Declaration unanimous.

A detail from John Trumbull's *The Declaration of Independence* shows (left to right) John Adams, Roger Sherman, Robert Livingston, Thomas Jefferson, and Benjamin Franklin presenting the document to John Hancock (seated).

Stockton Changes His Mind

Declaration signer swears allegiance to Britain

Just a few months after he had signed the Declaration of Independence, Richard Stockton of New Jersey recanted and swore allegiance to King George III. Born in 1730 into a wealthy family, Stockton became a prominent lawyer and served on the provincial council of New Jersey under its Royal governor, William Franklin (the illegitimate son of Benjamin Franklin). At first in favor of conciliation with Britain, Stockton was won over to the cause of independence, and he became a delegate to the Continental Congress in June 1776.

That fall, after signing the Declaration, Stockton was seized by New Jersey Tories, who were British loyalists. He was taken to New York, where he was imprisoned as a common criminal and subjected to cruel treatment. When his colleagues in the Continental Congress heard about it, they asked General Washington to intercede. Whether he did so is unknown, but in March 1777 Stockton was back home in Princeton.

The British command had offered to pardon all Patriots who would recant the call for independence and take a pledge of neutrality. By the time spring rolled around, 4,800 people, most of them from New Jersey, had accepted British amnesty.

Washington countered by ordering the defectors to "take the oath of allegiance to the United States of America." Those who refused were to be treated as common enemies. Stockton, ill in health and broken in spirit, finally complied. The unhappy man, shunned by his former friends, died four years later of cancer.

In this 1940 painting by Howard Chandler Christy, delegates to the 1787 Philadelphia convention sign the new Constitution.

Build Anew or Repair the Roof?

THE REAL REASONS WHY
THE CONSTITUTION WAS WRITTEN

The Constitution of the United States is actually the second governing document in the nation's history. The first, the Articles of Confederation, was in effect from 1781 to 1789. (Oddly enough, one of the document's provisions, set forth in Article 11, was that the colony of Canada could join the Union at any time, although no other colony could be admitted without the agreement of nine of the original 13 states.)

Government under the Articles failed because, as George Washington said, it was "little more than the shadow without the substance." There was no true central authority. Although Congress could declare war and enact treaties, it lacked the power to collect taxes, regulate commerce, maintain order, or even to enforce its own decisions. Interstate disputes proliferated, worthless money flooded the country, discontented people rioted, and foreign nations refused to deal with a government so powerless at home. Anarchy, rebellion, and chaos threatened the land.

The Continental Congress called for a committee to amend the Articles, but in May 1787, when the delegates met in Philadelphia, they boldly decided to ignore the directive and write a new constitution that would establish a strong federal government. "We are razing the foundations of the building, when we need only repair the roof," protested Oliver Ellsworth of Connecticut.

After a long summer of contention and compromise, their task was miraculously completed.

Ben Franklin and the Iroquois

Benjamin Franklin, that wise and witty elder statesman of Revolutionary times, helped work out the Constitution's system of representative government. Franklin was himself inspired by the Iroquois Indians, whose League of Five Nations functioned as a representative democracy for two centuries before the Constitution was written.

The five nations of the Iroquois Confederacy—Onondaga, Mohawk, Seneca, Cayuga, and Oneida—were united under the Great Law of Peace. This oral constitution, eventually written out in 117 sections, detailed the makeup of the ruling council, its methods for reaching decisions, the duties and qualifications of its members, the limitations of its power, and the rights of the people. The council, made up of 50 *sachems,* or chiefs, had no power over the inner workings of any tribe but dealt only with such mutual concerns as war and treaties. Decisions were reached through a precisely outlined procedure, with the sachems of the Mohawks and Senecas forming one deliberating body, those of the Oneidas and Cayugas another, and the Onondaga sachems wielding a kind of veto power. (A sixth nation, the Tuscarora, joined the confederacy in 1722 but did not take an active part in league councils.) All decisions had to be unanimous.

The sachems were appointed by the senior women of the communities, who themselves formed a Council of Women of the Five Nations. This women's council oversaw the deliberations of the sachems, and if it deemed that the will of the people was not being followed, it could remove any or all of the sachems from office.

In 1744, Franklin's Philadelphia press published an article about the Lancaster Treaty between the Iroquois and the British. It contained this advice from Canasatego, an Onondaga sachem: "Union and amity between the five nations have made us formidable. We are a powerful confederacy, and by your observing the same methods you will acquire fresh strength and power. Whatever befalls you, never fall out with one another."

Franklin was apparently impressed, because he then studied the system of the Iroquois Confederacy. Seven years later he himself wrote, "It would be a very strange thing if six Nations of ignorant Savages should be capable of forming a Scheme for such a Union," and yet the English colonies should find it "impracticable."

In 1754, when war with the French and their Indian allies seemed imminent, delegates of the seven northern colonies met in Albany, New York, to draw up a plan of defense. Franklin, the Pennsylvania delegate, proposed a confederacy much like that of the Iroquois. The Albany Plan failed, but it paved the way for the Articles of Confederation. The Articles, in turn, led to the formation of a new, stronger federal government under the Constitution, reflecting Iroquois concepts of liberty and democratic organization.

When the Constitution was submitted to a vote of approval, Franklin pleaded that anyone who still had objections would, with him, "doubt a little of his own infallibility" and agree to it.

Franklin was inspired by the Iroquois Indians, whose League of Five Nations functioned as a representative democracy for two centuries before the Constitution was written.

"Three-fifths of All Other Persons"

THE CONSTITUTION'S SURPRISING STANCE ON SLAVERY

Slavery: Without it there would be no America, no nation dedicated to liberty and equality. This was the paradox faced by delegates to the Constitutional Convention. The Southern states had made it clear that they would not join the Union if slavery was not accepted. And although abolitionist sentiment was strong in the North, pragmatism and politics dictated brutal compromise. As a result, it would take a civil war and 175 years to correct the injustices incorporated into the new Constitution.

The very language of the Constitution reflects the convention's spirit of compromise. Nowhere in the document is the word "slavery" found. But the continuation of the system was provided for in three separate passages.

Article I, Section 2, spelled out the formula for determining each state's popular representation in the lower house of Congress: Count all free persons, exclude Indians not taxed, then add "three fifths of all other Persons." Thus a compromise was struck between the South, which wanted slaves counted for the sake of representation, and the North, which wanted them excluded.

Article I, Section 9, stated that the importation "of such Persons as any of the States now existing shall think proper to admit" would be permitted until 1808. Thus the South conceded in return that the slave trade would end in 20 years, as it did.

Article IV, Section 2, prevented a "Person held to Service or Labour in one State" from escaping his bondage by moving to another state. Known as the "fugitive slave clause," this

> Nowhere in the Constitution is the word "slavery" found. But the continuation of the system was provided for in three separate passages.

was the Constitution's most effective protection of the institution of slavery.

In the first half of the 19th century, what rights the black slave had, if any, were at the discretion of local authority. As to the small population of free blacks, who lived mostly in the North, the situation varied from state to state. In New York, New Jersey, Pennsylvania, and most of New England some even had the right to vote before 1820, but gradually the status of free blacks deteriorated to that of noncitizen. The Supreme Court made this official with the Dred Scott decision in 1857.

Scott was a slave whose suit to gain freedom went to the nation's highest court. In delivering the majority opinion, Chief Justice Roger Taney not only rejected Scott's plea but stated that the Constitution was written only for whites and that blacks, even free blacks, could never be citizens.

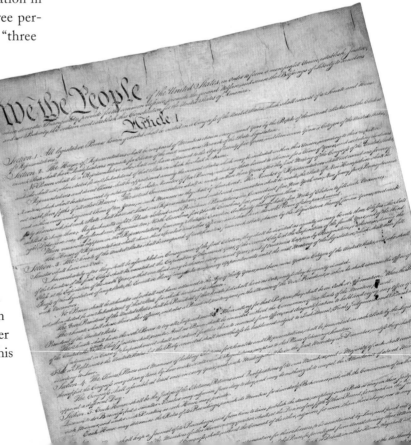

The decision was met with cries of protest from the North and cries of approval from the South. The foundation of compromise upon which the Constitution had been built began to crumble, and civil war ensued. The Emancipation Proclamation of 1863 freed slaves in the seceding states only; until the war was over, it had no practical effect. In 1865, the 13th Amendment ended slavery once and for all in the United States.

In 1868, Justice Taney's interpretation of the Constitution was nullified by the 14th Amendment, which ensured full rights of citizenship to "All persons born or naturalized in the United States." The right of citizens to vote regardless of "race, color, or previous condition of servitude" was guaranteed in 1870 by the 15th Amendment. Finally, in 1964, the 24th Amendment abolished the poll tax, making it clear that "We the People" means *all* the people.

No Rights, No Ratification

STATES INSIST ON PROTECTING INDIVIDUAL LIBERTIES

More concerned with the need for a strong central government than with the protection of people's rights, the delegates to the Constitutional Convention didn't officially discuss the idea of a bill of rights until the last week. On September 28, 1787, the Constitution was submitted to the states for ratification. It met strong opposition. In one state convention after another, the issue of a bill of rights was central to the fight for ratification. The Federalists claimed that a bill of rights was unnecessary; most state constitutions already had such provisos. The anti-Federalists, joining forces with those advocating a bill of rights, contended that the new federal government would be more powerful than any state, and that a constitution that did not specifically restrict that power was an invitation to tyranny.

The battle became intense. In Pennsylvania the opposition tried to block ratification by absenteeism, to prevent a quorum, and were literally dragged from their homes for a vote. Riots occurred, and the Pennsylvania framer of the Constitution, James Wilson, was burned in effigy.

By June 21, 1788, nine states had ratified, although Massachusetts and New Hampshire demanded a bill of rights. The Constitution was adopted, but Virginia and New York had not approved it. They were vital. Virginia was the richest and most populous state; New York was second, and without it the nation would be physically divided into north and south.

More than two-thirds of the New York delegates opposed ratification, and 31-year-old Alexander Hamilton fought alone to stem the tide. Day after day he argued the Federalist cause and prevented a final ballot, hoping to receive good news from Virginia. There the debates were heated, with Patrick Henry leading the opposition.

"The plot thickens fast," George Washington wrote to his friend the Marquis de Lafayette. "A few short weeks will determine the political fate of America." On June 25, by a vote of 89 to 79, Virginia backed the Constitution, calling for a long bill of rights. A month later New York followed, 30 to 27, with similar recommendations.

North Carolina and Rhode Island held out, and so the Union included only 11 states when Congress convened for the first time on March 4, 1789. Under James Madison's lead, a bill of rights became the main order of business, and in September Congress submitted to the states a series of amendments guaranteeing individual freedoms and property rights. A few months later, the two holdout states voted to accept the Constitution. The 10 amendments became law on December 15, 1791, upon approval by three-fourths of the states. Curiously, Massachusetts, Georgia, and Connecticut did not ratify the Bill of Rights until 1939, the 150th anniversary of the new government.

Washington's Folly

IN ITS EARLY YEARS, THE WHITE HOUSE WAS ANYTHING *BUT* A PRESIDENTIAL PALACE

President Thomas Jefferson, upon moving to the White House in 1801, asked architect Benjamin Henry Latrobe to make some structural changes, including the addition of terrace-pavilions on the sides of the main building. Above: Latrobe's plans for the renovations.

If George Washington had had his way, the president's house would have been a palace nearly five times the size of the existing mansion. At least, that was what he and the French architect Pierre Charles L'Enfant envisioned in the spring of 1791. But when the building commissioners had their first view of L'Enfant's plan, as the story goes, they were alarmed by its extravagance and grandeur.

Arrogantly assuming he needed only Washington's authority, L'Enfant commenced work at once. When Secretary of State Thomas Jefferson dismissed him in February 1792, the grounds had been staked out, the cellars dug, and some of the foundation stone delivered.

Eager to take charge, Jefferson proposed a competition for plans for the president's house and the Capitol. With Washington's consent, he drafted an announcement, offering a prize of $500. The winner was James Hoban, an Irish architect. His plan for a typical 18th-century English mansion struck Washington and the commissioners as "convenient, elegant, and within moderate expence."

In October 1792, the cornerstone was laid. But the Capitol and other government buildings took priority, and so work on the president's house was delayed.

ABIGAIL ADAMS'S EXPANSIVE (BUT EMPTY) LAUNDRY ROOM
In November 1800, John Adams and his wife, Abigail, moved into the White House. She found "a castle of a House" clearly "built for ages to come," but only half of the rooms were plastered. Shabby government furniture had been brought from Philadelphia and set about. On the lawn there were tree stumps, hacked weeds, piles of rubble, and—in full view—a presidential privy.

> "Not one room or chamber is finished of the whole," complained First Lady Abigail Adams.

"Not one room or chamber is finished of the whole," the First Lady complained. "It is habitable by fires in every part, thirteen of which we are obliged to keep daily." She needed "about thirty servants to attend," but had only six, and there were no bells with which to summon them. Worse, she wrote her daughter, "We have not the least fence, yard, or other convenience without, and the great unfinished audience-room [the East Room] I make a drying-room of, to hang up the clothes in."

Mrs. Adams had to endure her miseries only briefly. Her husband lost the presidency to Thomas Jefferson, and by March she was back home in Quincy, Massachusetts. Jefferson, challenged by a house he considered "Washington's folly," quickly set to work changing it inside and out.

The First Bathtub
A HYGIENE HOAX THAT JUST WON'T DIE

Several scholars and historians claim that Millard Fillmore installed the first bathtub in the White House in 1851. It would be an interesting bit of presidential trivia if it were true—but it isn't.

The story began in 1917, in a column written for the New York *Evening Mail* by that irrepressible author, editor, and iconoclast H. L. Mencken. Hoping to divert his readers from the gloomy news of World War I, he concocted a spoof on the history of the

continued on page 62

America's Changing Capital

For 25 years, the center of government in America moved back and forth among nine cities. In 1789, the Congress was authorized under the Constitution to choose a permanent site. Finally, after a decade of debate and a donation of land by Maryland and Virginia, the capital city of Washington, D.C., was founded.

Here are the locations where Congress met before the permanent capital was established:

Philadelphia, PA
Sept. 5, 1774, to Dec. 12, 1776

Baltimore, MD
Dec. 20, 1776, to Feb. 27, 1777

Philadelphia, PA
March 4, 1777, to Sept. 18, 1777

Lancaster, PA
Sept. 27, 1777 (only one day)

York, PA
Sept. 30, 1777, to June 27, 1778

Philadelphia, PA
July 2, 1778, to June 21, 1783

Princeton, NJ
June 30, 1783, to Nov. 4, 1783

Annapolis, MD
Nov. 26, 1783, to June 3, 1784

Trenton, NJ
Nov. 1, 1784, to Dec. 24, 1784

New York, NY
Jan 11, 1785, to Aug. 12, 1790

Philadelphia, PA
Dec. 6, 1790, to May 14, 1800

Washington, D.C.
Nov. 17, 1800, to present

A Tub for Taft

The White House staff's ability to supply creature comforts for the president was tested in 1909. There wasn't a tub big enough for William "Big Bill" Howard Taft, who carried well over 300 pounds on a six-foot frame. The solution came from the captain of the battleship *North Carolina*. Told of an approaching presidential visit, the officer had a special tub constructed. Satisfied with his soak at sea, Taft had the tub installed in the White House. Seven feet long and 41 inches wide, the bathtub could accommodate four normal-size men.

Wilson's Sheep

During World War I, in order to save manpower and set a good example for the nation, President Woodrow Wilson had sheep crop the White House lawns. The flock numbered 18 at its peak. The wool was shorn and auctioned for a total of $52,823, which was donated to the American Red Cross.

bathtub in America, and in the process he perpetrated a hoax that will not die.

The first stateside bathtub, an elegant mahogany contraption, he wrote, had been installed in the home of a Cincinnati businessman in 1842, and the odd practice of bathing soon caught on among the wealthy. When word of the fad got out, it set off a public outcry against the "epicurean and obnoxious toy from England, designed to corrupt the democratic simplicity of the republic." By bravely installing a bathtub in the White House, Mencken went on, Fillmore had helped gain public acceptance for the habit of regular bathing.

> President Franklin Pierce, not Millard Fillmore, had the first White House bathtub installed in 1853.

In 1926, alarmed that his fabrication had entered history in the guise of gospel truth, Mencken wrote a confession of his hoax. But despite his efforts to set the record straight, the story endures to this day.

So what's the actual story behind the White House's first tub? A bathing room with copper tubs and a shower was installed on the White House's first floor in 1833 or 1834; the first permanent bathtub (on the second floor) was installed by President Franklin Pierce in 1853.

Renovating "The Residence"

HOW HARRY TRUMAN NEARLY—AND *LITERALLY*—DROPPED IN ON THE DAUGHTERS OF THE AMERICAN REVOLUTION

Edgar Allan Poe himself wouldn't have blamed Harry Truman if, in 1947, Truman had compared the presidential residence to the House of Usher. Like Poe's doomed mansion, the White House was beginning to collapse.

One day while the president was bathing, he felt the tub settle. Below him, his wife, Bess, was holding a reception for the Daughters of the American Revolution. Afterward, he suggested to her the comic possibility of his unannounced appearance in his birthday suit. During a concert in the Blue Room, attended by several hundred people, the president was warned that the chains holding the two-ton chandeliers could break at any time. After

C.W. Barber, the chief structural engineer, and Lorenzo Winslow, the White House architect, inspect the East Room's sagging ceiling in 1951 during the renovations ordered by President Truman.

another event, in the East Room, the servants discovered a large pile of ceiling plaster on the floor. Finally, when a leg of daughter Margaret's piano broke through the first-floor ceiling, Truman decided that something had to be done.

An investigation showed that the second floor was on the verge of collapse and, according to one expert, the first-floor ceiling stayed in place only by "force of habit." The outer walls were solidly constructed, but the supports of the inner walls rested only on clay, thanks to hasty reconstruction after the British had burned the building in 1814. During the next 100 years, supporting walls and beams were drilled and cut through to put in running water, gas lighting, central heating, and electricity, and a fireproof floor was installed in the third story.

Congress finally approved funds to salvage the mansion. Begun in late 1948, the job cost nearly $7 million to complete. In March 1952, the first family returned to a modernized executive mansion that, architects assured them, would stand for the next 500 years.

The White House in Transition

From 1800 to the present, the president's home has been a work in progress. Here are a few of the changes our chief executives have made.

1814 James Madison orders the White House to be rebuilt after the British burn it down in the War of 1812.

1824 James Monroe has the south portico added to the house.

1829–33 Andrew Jackson adds the north portico and installs running water.

1889 Benjamin Harrison has the White House wired for electricity.

1902 Theodore Roosevelt has the entire interior remodeled and wings added; the second floor is turned into living quarters and the West Wing is extended for office space.

1941–43 Franklin Delano Roosevelt approves an East Wing extension and secretly has a bomb shelter built.

1948–52 Harry S. Truman oversees a complete reconstruction, during which a balcony is added above the south portico.

1977 Jimmy Carter installs solar heating panels on the roof of the West Wing. They were removed in the 1980s.

Betsy Ross proudly unfurls the Stars and Stripes for George Washington (center) and others in Percy Moran's circa 1917 painting, *The Birth of Old Glory*.

Mrs. Ross and Mr. Washington

WHO REALLY DESIGNED THE STARS AND STRIPES?

Legend has it that, in 1776, George Washington and two other patriots called on Philadelphia seamstress Betsy Ross and asked her to stitch the new American flag. She examined the design they produced, recommended a five-pointed star, and went to work.

But that's not how it really happened. This story originated in 1870, when Ross's grandson, William J. Canby, passed it on to the Pennsylvania Historical Society, claiming that he had heard it from Ross herself when he was a child. Years later the legend appeared in a book about the flag, the Betsy Ross Memorial Association formed, the house where Ross likely sewed flags became a historic site, and artist Ellie Wheeler portrayed Ross meeting the committee while working on the Stars and Stripes.

Thus the seamstress became enshrined. The records of her time reveal no facts to substantiate the legend, but they do show that she was paid for making flags for the Pennsylvania Navy in 1777.

> The Betsy Ross story originated in 1870 when her grandson claimed he had heard it as a child.

At the outset of the Revolution, the regiments of the 13 colonies flew their own colorful banners. The first flag to symbolize America's unity (raised by Washington on New Year's Day, 1776) was a modification of a British naval flag. The colonists imposed six white stripes upon its red field, thus creating 13 stripes representing the 13 colonies, but kept the crosses of Saint George and Saint Andrew in the top corner.

The Grand (or Great) Union flag, as it was known, became obsolete with the Declaration of Independence because the two crosses symbolized loyalty to Britain.

On June 14, 1777, the Continental Congress resolved that the national flag should have "13 stripes, alternate red and white," and that the crosses be replaced by "13 stars, white in a blue field, representing a new constellation."

It's quite possible that the Stars and Stripes was originally intended for the navy. Washington and the Board of War wanted a different standard for the army. It was not until March 1783, a month before Congress proclaimed an end to hostilities, that Washington received the first shipment of colors. What design the flags bore and what he did with them remains unknown.

FUNNY FACT

The Flag That Wasn't Flown

Legend has it that "The Spirit of '76," with its 13 red and white stripes and its circle of 13 five-pointed stars, flew proudly over American troops throughout the Revolution.

The fact is, Americans fought under many banners, but rarely the Stars and Stripes. The flag's earliest versions had various combinations of blue, red, and white stripes, with the stars usually set in rows. There is no documentation for the flag depicted in Archibald Willard's famous painting *The Spirit of '76,* above.

Coming Clean About Key

THE TRUE STORY BEHIND "THE STAR-SPANGLED BANNER"

Legend has it that Francis Scott Key wrote "The Star-Spangled Banner" while a prisoner of the British fleet. He supposedly wrote it during a 25-hour siege of Fort McHenry that ended on the morning of September 14, 1814.

In fact, Key, a Georgetown lawyer, was actually spearheading a peace mission sent to the British fleet in the Chesapeake Bay to secure the release of a physician named Dr. William Beanes. The British received Key courteously and agreed to release Dr. Beanes. But there was a snag. Inadvertently, Key had caught them preparing to launch an attack. Fearing that he would alert the Americans, the British detained Key and his party on their sloop, the *Minden*, until after the attack.

> Francis Scott Key set his lyrics to a bawdy British drinking song from 1775 called "To Anacreon in Heaven."

It was from the *Minden* that Key watched the bombardment. After the guns fell silent, Key saw in "the dawn's early light that our flag was still there." Inspired, he began the lyrics of "The Star-Spangled Banner" on the back of a letter he had in his pocket. The tune he used, popular in America for years, was that of a bawdy British drinking song called "To Anacreon in Heaven." It had been composed by John Stafford Smith around 1775 as an anthem for the Anacreontic Society, a London gentleman's club named for a Greek poet who worshiped "the Muses, Wine, and Love." Key's song was an instant hit. It grew in popularity, competing with "America the Beautiful" for first place among patriotic songs until 1931, when it was officially designated the national anthem.

The Liberty Bell

**AMERICA'S TREASURE CRACKED
LONG BEFORE INDEPENDENCE DAY**

According to the well-known story, on July 4, 1776, a boy ran to the steeple of Philadelphia's Independence Hall and told the feeble, white-haired bell ringer that independence had just been declared. Rejuvenated by the news, the old man rang the bell so vigorously that it cracked.

In fact, the bell never rang upon the news of independence. Declaration was not actually proclaimed until July 8, and the crack had occurred years before. The great bronze bell, inscribed with the words "Proclaim Liberty Throughout All The Land Unto All The Inhabitants Thereof," had been ordered from London in 1751 to commemorate the 50th anniversary of Pennsylvania's democratic constitution. On arrival, the bell was hung in the belfry of the State House, which was later known as Independence Hall. The bell first cracked at this time, while it was being tested. It was melted down, recast, and rehung. In 1835 it cracked again—perhaps, as legend has it, on the day it tolled for John Marshall's death. The clappers would have been muffled, however, which makes that legend unlikely. It pealed for the last time on George Washington's birthday, in 1846, after which it was taken down.

It was not until 1839—when it was used as a symbol by abolitionists because of its inscription—that the State House bell came to be called the Liberty Bell. In 1847, George Lippard fabricated the popular story about the bell cracking on the first Independence Day in a book called *Washington and His Generals, or Legends of the American Revolution.* This is how the Liberty Bell was launched as one of the nation's most potent and profitable symbols of patriotism and started to be depicted on every conceivable item from neckties and coffee cups to Liberty Bonds.

BRIGHT IDEA

The Liberty Bell Slot Machine

When San Francisco entrepreneur Charles Fey invented a new and improved three-reel slot machine in 1898, he chose the Liberty Bell as both its name and the symbol of the jackpot. The seaport city went wild for the Liberty Bell machine, even though the odds of getting the payoff were 10 times what they were with the single-disc slot machines that were then popular. The Liberty Bell machine should have earned Fey millions, but he stubbornly refused to have it patented. A rival slot machine mogul predictably stole Fey's design. During the fire that followed the 1906 San Francisco earthquake, Fey rescued the first Liberty Bell machine from his offices. It wound up as an exhibit in a Reno restaurant and saloon called the Liberty Belle Saloon & Restaurant, which is owned by Fey's two grandsons and managed by a great-grandson.

Hey, How 'bout a Turkey?

MOSES, PILLAR OF FIRE, AND HERCULES ALL CONTENDERS FOR THE GREAT SEAL

Over a period of six years beginning in 1776, three committees tried to come up with an acceptable design for the Great Seal of the United States, the national coat of arms that we needed to authenticate official documents.

The first committee—Thomas Jefferson, Benjamin Franklin, and John Adams—was appointed by the Continental Congress only hours after the formal adoption of the Declaration of Independence. The three turned to the Bible and classical mythology for inspiration. Jefferson proposed that the seal depict the Israelites' passage through the wilderness, led by a divine cloud and a pillar of fire. Adams suggested the mythical hero Hercules, choosing between the paths of virtue and self-indulgence. Franklin wanted to show Moses commanding the Red Sea to close over the pharaoh.

In a quandary, they called in a consultant, a Swiss-born Philadelphia artist named Pierre Eugène Du Simitière. He pointed out that the greatest thing about the United States was that it was a new nation forged out of many. To illustrate this, his design featured an escutcheon, or shield, showing the emblems of the six European homelands from which most early immigrants had come. Around the shield were 13 smaller ones representing the new states, linked by a gold chain. Supporting the shield were the goddesses of Liberty and Justice. Above was the Eye of Providence, and below was the motto *E Pluribus Unum*, Latin for "Out of Many, One."

The committee chose Du Simitière's design for the obverse, or front, and Franklin's for the reverse and submitted them to Congress. But Congress, preoccupied with the Revolutionary War, tabled the project.

A second committee, appointed in 1780, proposed a design for the obverse featuring a shield with 13 stripes, supported by a sword-bearing soldier and a woman holding the olive branch of peace.

A radiant constellation of 13 stars was the crest. The reverse featured the goddess of Liberty. The designs were rejected. A third committee, named in 1782, called upon William Barton, a Philadelphia authority on heraldry. For the obverse he introduced the European eagle, placing it in the crest, and for the reverse he conceived an unfinished 13-stepped pyramid.

Congress then turned the accumulation of designs over to Charles Thomson, secretary of Congress. Synthesizing and simplifying them, he retained the first committee's motto, *E Pluribus Unum*; the second committee's shield and olive branch; and the third's eagle and pyramid. However, he substituted a rising American bald eagle for the European heraldic eagle, making it the centerpiece, placed the shield upon the eagle's breast, and put a clutch of arrows in its talons. He handed the designs over to Barton, who arranged the stripes vertically on the shield and gave the eagle upswept wings. The results of their joint effort were instantly approved by the Continental Congress. Seven years later, the seal was adopted by the first federal Congress and put in the custody of the first secretary of state, Thomas Jefferson.

Benjamin Franklin called the bald eagle a bird of "bad moral character" and advocated the turkey as our symbol of sovereignty.

Plagued by Problems

A marble obelisk soaring more than 555 feet from its base, the Washington National Monument pierces the sky above the nation's capital, standing as a symbol of George Washington's strength and vision. But it sheathes a turbulent history.

The memorial was 105 years in the making, from its proposal by the Continental Congress in 1783 to its public opening in 1888. The first idea, much to General George Washington's pleasure, had been to erect an equestrian statue, but the plan went awry. One of the problems was money (or the lack thereof). The other was congressional disagreement about an appropriate tribute. In 1833, a group of citizens organized the Washington National Monument Society to raise funds, commission a suitable design, and oversee construction.

The marble cornerstone of the monument was laid on July 4, 1848, with a ceremony that generated enthusiastic financial response, not only from individuals but from organizations, banks, and various states. Alabama donated a commemorative plaque for the interior, and other states followed suit, as did fire companies, social clubs, Indian tribes, and even foreign countries, including the Vatican.

By 1854, the obelisk was 152 feet high. But the marble plaque given by Pope Pius IX, taken from the Temple of Concord in Rome, indirectly brought work to a halt. At dawn on March 6, 1854, some members of the superpatriotic American Party (who were known as the Know-Nothings) broke into the monument grounds, removed the papal stone, and presumably dumped it into the Potomac. It was never recovered. Then, as the result of a rigged election in 1855, the Know-Nothings took charge of the monument society. In turn, Congress, which had planned to allocate $200,000 for the project, withdrew its funding, and public support withered.

Over the next three years, the Know-Nothings (who succeeded in raising all of $285.09) added four

It took more than 105 years to finish the Washington Monument. It now showcases 190 commemorative plaques on its interior stairwell.

feet of inferior marble to the monument, which later had to be removed. Work stopped during the Civil War and little was done for more than a decade afterward. The Washington Monument remained a pitiful stub in the heart of the capital city.

On the centennial of independence in 1876, Congress funded the monument's completion. Then another problem surfaced: The U.S. Army Corps of Engineers discovered that the obelisk's foundation was inadequate to support its proposed height. Some 70 percent of the ground under the shaft had to be removed to strengthen the base with additional concrete footings. As an extra precaution, the target height of the obelisk was lowered from 600 to 555 feet 5⅛ inches. Work resumed on the shaft in 1880, and the monument rose an average of 80 feet annually until its completion on December 6, 1884.

Today 190 commemorative plaques can be viewed from the Washington Monument's interior staircase. Among them is a replacement for the stolen plaque, sent by the Vatican in 1982.

The Know-Nothings

In the 1840s a good many so-called "native Americans" felt menaced by the influx of Irish and German immigrants (most of whom were Catholic and poor). They formed a secret society, swearing to vote only for American-born Protestants and to oppose the Catholic Church. If asked about the politics of their order, members uniformly answered, "I know nothing." Hence they were called the Know-Nothings. Organized nationally as the American Party in 1854, they became quite powerful.

Alarmed by this flood of bigotry, Abraham Lincoln wrote, "As a nation, we began by declaring that 'all men are created equal.' ... When the Know-Nothings obtain control, it will read: 'All men are created equal except Negroes, and foreigners, and Catholics.'" The American Party rapidly withered away.

The Two Uncle Sams

**WHICH SAM WILSON INSPIRED
THE BELOVED AMERICAN FIGURE?**

Few people realize there was a *real* Uncle Sam—in fact, there were two of them. Both were named Samuel Wilson and both lived for many years in Troy, New York. One is buried there; the other lies in Merriam, Indiana. Although a congressional resolution honored Troy's Sam Wilson in 1961 "as the progenitor of America's national symbol of Uncle Sam," the people of Indiana stand by their Sam Wilson as the real Uncle Sam.

The New York Sam was born in Massachusetts in 1766; he later settled in Troy and opened a meatpacking plant. He was a kindly employer who became affectionately known as Uncle Sam. During the War of 1812, Wilson sold 300 barrels of beef and pork in brine to Elbert Anderson, a food wholesaler with an army contract. Each barrel was stamped "EA-US," the initials standing for Elbert Anderson and the United States. When a workman was asked what the letters stood for, he jokingly replied, "Uncle Sam Wilson," and the name stuck. This "Uncle Sam" lived to be 87.

Merriam's Sam Wilson, born in Delaware in 1778, also moved to Troy. He took a job clerking in Ebenezer Anderson's general store. During the War of 1812, the store became a war supply headquarters, and Sam oversaw the handling of government orders. Again, boxes were marked for shipment with the letters "EA-US" (the "EA" being for Ebenezer Anderson), and again someone identified the "US" as Uncle Sam. This second Sam later moved to Indiana, where he died at the age of 100.

Whichever Uncle Sam was the original, the nickname spread like wildfire, and in 1813 it began to appear in the newspapers as a synonym for the United States government.

Lady Liberty: Taller Than She Used to Be

Given by the people of France to the people of the United States as a symbol of enduring friendship and their mutual love of freedom, the Statue of Liberty reigned as the largest freestanding sculpture for eight decades. Towering 151 feet above her pedestal, MissLiberty weighs 225 tons and has a girth of more than 100 feet. Her nose is four and a half feet long, her eyes each two and a half feet wide, and her mouth three feet wide. Her upraised right arm extends 42 feet, while her hand is 16 feet 5 inches long. Her index finger is eight feet long!

In 1875, the Franco-American Union was founded to create the memorial. Incredible as it seems, the starting point for the mammoth work was a four-foot plaster model that artist Frédéric Auguste Bartholdi submitted for the Union's approval. First he translated it into a nine-foot reproduction, and then into a 36-foot quarter-size model. Next, taking thousands of measurements, he enlarged each section to its final dimensions. Full-size lathwork and plaster forms were then made, over which hundreds of plates of pure copper (hammered to a thickness of $3/32$ inch) were fitted and shaped. The project kept a large staff of craftsmen busy for five years.

To keep the enormous copper shell from toppling over, the famous engineer Gustave Eiffel designed an interior framework made of iron. In May 1884, the model was completed and assembled in Paris; the glistening lady was formally presented to "the people of the United States" on July 4. Then she was dismantled and packed. Some 200 huge wooden crates were hauled on a 70-car train to Rouen, France, and shipped to Bedloe's Island in New York harbor. Reassembled on her concrete pedestal and unveiled on October 28, 1886, Miss Liberty has been a welcoming beacon ever since.

FUNNY FACT

Sculptor Uses Mom's Face as Inspiration

The face behind the Statue of Liberty's face is that of the sculptor's mother, who lived under German domination in Alsace, his birthplace. Ironically, Madame Bartholdi was a domineering bigot, who frowned on the sculptor's marriage and contributed to her other son's eventual madness— he was afraid to tell her of his love for a Jewish woman.

Mighty Mount Rushmore

PRESIDENTIAL FACES BROUGHT TO LIFE WITH JACKHAMMERS AND DYNAMITE

"American history shall march along that skyline," announced Gutzon Borglum in 1924, gazing at the Black Hills of South Dakota. The great sculptor had been invited there by a local official familiar with his work in Georgia: a colossal bas-relief on the face of Stone Mountain, depicting Confederate heroes. Hoping to draw tourists to his state, the South Dakotan envisioned a parade of famous frontiersmen carved in rock.

But Borglum thought the memorial should represent the nation as a whole and proposed portraits of George Washington, Abraham Lincoln, Thomas Jefferson, and Theodore Roosevelt. Eleanor Roosevelt later suggested including the suffragist leader Susan B. Anthony, but she was overridden.

The site the artist chose—the nearly perpendicular face of 6,000-foot Mount Rushmore—offered a solid expanse of granite beneath its fissured surface. Facing generally southeast, it caught the sun most of the day.

Work began in the summer of 1927. Using models on a scale of one inch to a foot, Borglum plotted the presidential features, transferred his measurements to the mountainside, and instructed his crew where to cut away rock.

Most of the sculpting was done by experienced miners. Working with jackhammers and dynamite, they removed some 400,000 tons of outer rock, cutting to within three inches of the final surface. So skilled were they with the tools of their trade, even in contouring the eyes and lips, that the sculptor's traditional mallet and chisel were used very little.

As each face took shape, Borglum studied it with binoculars from several miles away and made minor adjustments. Working errors and hidden flaws in the rock repeatedly forced him to rethink the composition and alter the arrangement of figures. One mistake in cutting rock, for example, ruined Jefferson's head, which was to have been on the right side of Washington's. It was blasted away and recarved on the left. The project dragged on for 14 years, its cost escalating to $1 million. When Borglum died in 1941, his dream—the creation of the world's biggest sculpture—was near completion. His son oversaw the final work.

Eleanor Roosevelt wanted to add suffragist leader Susan B. Anthony to Mount Rushmore, but she was overruled.

The monument has evoked mixed feelings. Some see it as a desecration of nature. Others, like President Franklin Delano Roosevelt, are awed not only by its magnitude, but by "its permanent beauty and its importance."

A New Way to Vote

HOW THE ELECTORAL COLLEGE CAME TO BE

Ask Americans which constitutional right they most treasure, and the chances are that voting for president will be high on the list. In fact, the Constitution gives no such right.

Although Benjamin Franklin and a few others favored popular election of the chief executive, most of the Constitution's framers feared that less educated Americans might elect corrupt or incompetent men to the executive office. As a result, they decided that the president and vice president would be chosen by a special body of electors. The Electoral College would, they felt, exercise superior judgment. The Constitution allotted each state as many electors as it has senators and representatives and left the manner of their selection to the states.

In the early years, the electors were usually appointed by the state legislatures. By 1832, the choosing of electors by popular vote had become the rule, except in South Carolina, which retained a strong legislative system. With the steady growth of population (and hence, the number of electors), the lists of individual electors became long and unwieldy. In 1892, a trend began to group the electors by political party, requiring only a single vote.

The names of the presidential candidates did not begin to appear on ballots along with those of the electoral candidates until 1897. The voting machines that were introduced a few years later lacked space for long ballots, and so Iowa and Nebraska began to list only the names of the presidential and vice presidential candidates, dropping the names of the electors altogether. A vote for a party's candidate was taken as a vote for the electors of that party. Gradually the rest of the states followed suit and adopted the short ballot.

Despite the directive of the ballot, and despite party loyalty oaths, electors are constitutionally free

The names of the presidential candidates did not begin to appear on ballots along with those of the electoral candidates until 1897.

to vote as their judgment dictates when they meet in their state capitals in December. In the elections of 1948, 1956, and 1960, several electors ignored the voters' wishes.

Traditionally, the electors of a state vote as a bloc for the candidate receiving the most votes in that state. As a result of this strange practice, three presidents—Rutherford B. Hayes in 1876, Benjamin Harrison in 1888, and George W. Bush in 2000—won with a majority of the Electoral College while losing the popular vote to their opponents.

Stolen Suffrage

18TH-CENTURY NEW JERSEY WOMEN HAD THE RIGHT TO VOTE TAKEN AWAY FROM THEM

According to the state constitution drawn up by the Provincial Congress of New Jersey in 1776, women had the right to vote in that state. It may have been an oversight, but the document nonetheless stipulated that "all inhabitants" meeting age and residency requirements and worth at least £50 could vote. It made no reference to sex.

The women of the state had not petitioned for suffrage and, oddly enough, they seemed quite indifferent to it. There is no record of a New Jersey woman voting before 1790. But activism appeared in 1797, when John Condict of Newark ran against William Crane of Elizabeth for a seat in the state legislature. The race was tight. Condict nearly lost when, at the last minute, a group of about 75 Elizabeth women turned out to cast their ballots for their hometown candidate.

After that eye-opening election, women of all ages—including some who were underage—were hauled to the polls in carriages and wagons by candidates and party leaders who needed their votes.

In an 1807 election, the people of Newark and Elizabeth fought over the location of a new courthouse. Women were thrown into the fight by both towns in a contest that was virtually a carnival of skulduggery. Boys even dressed as women to cast ballots. Shocked by this "saturnalia of corruption and abuse," New Jersey lawmakers passed laws banning women from the polls.

You Asked For It, You Got It

WHY DID 1970s YOUNG PEOPLE NOT TAKE ADVANTAGE OF THEIR NEW RIGHT TO VOTE?

"Old enough to fight, old enough to vote"—the notion bubbled to the surface every time the United States went to war. President Dwight D. Eisenhower had endorsed it back in 1954, after the end of the Korean conflict. So, too, in the mid-1960s, did President Lyndon Johnson, who hoped to lure anti–Vietnam War student protesters from the barricades to the ballot box. And now the time had come. On June 17, 1970, Congress passed a law that lowered the voting age from 21 to 18.

Formidable barriers remained before the law took effect, however. Voting age standards had always been set by the individual states, and some state legislatures wanted to keep it that way. Several filed suits with the Supreme Court.

A constitutional amendment finally resolved the issue. In March 1971, Congress approved the 26th Amendment, and within three months it became the law of the land.

The majority of young people seemed barely to notice. Some 11 million citizens between ages 18 and 21 had suddenly won the franchise. Only half of them registered to vote in the 1972 presidential elections—and of these, only 35 percent showed up to cast their ballots.

Victorious 1948 presidential election candidate Harry Truman jubilantly hoists a copy of the *Chicago Daily Tribune*, which prematurely (and erroneously) reported his opponent's victory. Opposite: President Bill Clinton's extramarital affair with White House intern Monica Lewinsky made headlines worldwide.

CHAPTER THREE

Politics and Presidents

What is America's most popular specta-
tor sport? It's not baseball or even
football—it's politics. We watch elections and the State of
the Union addresses
with more glee than we watch the World Series. Televised debates are better than any soap opera. For over
200 years the United States has thrived on tales of
presidential peccadilloes, kooky candidates, and gubernatorial, well, goobers.

How many presidents have faced impeachment? Has
an animal ever won an American election? How many presidents died
while in office, and how many more were nearly assassinated? The
answers are inside, along with thrilling tales of election upsets, upset
presidents, unfit candidates, and so much more.

Presidential Firsts

HE	WAS THE FIRST WHO...
Jefferson	shook hands rather than bowing at White House receptions.
Jackson	rode on a train.
Van Buren	was born an American citizen.
Tyler	married while in office.
Fillmore	ate White House meals prepared on a cookstove rather than a fireplace.
Pierce	had a White House Christmas tree.
Buchanan	was a bachelor.
Lincoln	was born outside the 13 original states.
A. Johnson	received royalty (Queen Emma of Hawaii in 1866).
Hayes	had a White House telephone.
Hayes	visited the West Coast.
Cleveland	had a child born in the White House. (The Baby Ruth candy bar was named for the child.)
B. Harrison	had electricity in the White House. (He didn't trust it; so servants switched the lights on and off.)
T. Roosevelt	left the United States while in office.
T. Roosevelt	rode in an automobile.
T. Roosevelt	flew in an airplane (as ex-president; F. Roosevelt while in office).
T. Roosevelt	won the Nobel Peace Prize.
Taft	had a car at the White House.
Harding	rode in a car to his inauguration.
Wilson	crossed the Atlantic.
F. Roosevelt	appeared on TV.
Eisenhower	hit a hole-in-one.
F. Roosevelt	named a woman to the Cabinet.
L. Johnson	named an African American to the Cabinet.
Nixon	visited China.
Clinton	was a Rhodes scholar.

President *Hanson*?

MARYLAND MAN HOLDS ONE-YEAR TERM AS FIRST CHIEF EXECUTIVE—BEFORE WASHINGTON

Bells pealed, cannons boomed, and fireworks lit up the sky. It was March 1, 1781, and citizens were celebrating "the final ratification in Congress of the Articles of Confederation and perpetual union between these states." With the passage of this legislation, a man from Maryland became the first person to serve the one-year term as president. His name was John Hanson.

Born into a politically active family in 1715, Hanson served in the pre-Revolutionary Maryland assembly. He helped choose delegates for the First Continental Congress, approved funds for beleaguered Boston in 1775, and helped raise the first Southern troops to join the Continental Army under George Washington. In 1779, Hanson was elected to the Continental Congress in Philadelphia. It was a hardship to be a congressman; for one thing, the pay wasn't very good (not to mention the fact that Philly didn't recognize Maryland's money). But Hanson went, and on March 1, 1781, he and his fellow Maryland delegate, Daniel Carroll, were the last two signers of the Articles of Confederation. Thus the United States of America was born, and Hanson—perhaps in appreciation for his signature, since Maryland had been holding out—was elected "President of The United States in Congress Assembled." He served the term despite failing health and the death of his last surviving daughter.

Soon after Hanson's election, Washington delivered General Charles Cornwallis's sword to Congress, and Hanson presided over the ceremony celebrating Britain's defeat at Yorktown. On behalf of the Congress, the president congratulated the man who was to become our first president under the Constitution.

King George? Never!

WASHINGTON SHOOTS DOWN THE IDEA OF MONARCHY IN AMERICA

At best, it was a preposterous suggestion. In a long letter to George Washington in May 1782, Colonel Lewis Nicola—a respected officer who had served in the Revolutionary War as a military manual writer—complained about Congress's inadequacy. The nation's treasury lacked the funds to pay off foreign loans and support the government, let alone pay the soldiers.

"The experience of the war," Nicola argued, "must have shewn to all, but to military men in particular, the weakness of republics."

To forestall complete chaos, he suggested that America become a monarchy, with the commander in chief as king. His proposed title for Washington? George I of the United States.

From his headquarters in Newburgh, New York, Washington responded at once: "Be assured, Sir, no occurrence in the course of the War has given me more painful sensations than your information of there being such ideas existing in the Army as you have expressed and I must view [them] with abhorrence, and reprehend with severity...."

George Washington kneels in Henry Brueckner's 1866 engraving, *The Prayer at Valley Forge*. There is a long-standing historical debate as to whether he ever made such a plea at Valley Forge.

"Let me conjure you then, if you have any regard for your Country, concern for yourself or posterity, or respect for me, to banish these thoughts from your Mind, and never communicate, as from yourself, or any one else, a sentiment of the like Nature."

And thus, the great hero of the American Revolution summarily dismissed any thought of a reign of royalty. The nation had fought so hard under his leadership to win its independence.

Washington's Disappearing Chef

Hercules hits the road and leaves the president hungry

When the nation's capital was moved from New York to Philadelphia in 1790, George Washington, unimpressed with the food he was served, brought his own slave chef, Hercules, from Mount Vernon. But Hercules' arrival, and the length of his stay, posed a problem: Pennsylvania law stipulated that slaves be given their freedom after six months of residency. To get around this, Washington made up various reasons to send his household slaves, including the talented chef, back to Virginia just before the six-month deadline. Then, after several weeks, the president would bring them back to Philadelphia.

Hercules was quick to resist this sleight of hand. He had no intention of remaining a slave, and so one night he simply disappeared. After months of disappointing meals, Washington, who had vowed "never again to become the master of another slave by purchase," was faced with the prospect of buying a new slave to cook for him. His quandary was resolved, however, when he found a white housekeeper who also knew her way around in the kitchen.

And what of the fabled Hercules? Although Washington made several attempts to have him apprehended, the chef was never heard from again.

Play It Again, Mr. Chief Executive

HARRY TRUMAN CHOOSES OVAL OFFICE OVER A MUSIC-HALL GIG

Harry S. Truman took piano lessons as a child, and he was good. When he was about 12 years old, his instructor, who had studied with the European master Theodore Leschetitzky, took Truman to a Kansas City concert by the world-renowned Ignacy Jan Paderewski. It "was a wonder," Truman recalled. "I was studying [his] minuet," and afterward "we went back behind the scenes. She told him I didn't know how to make 'the turn' in his minuet, and he said, 'Sit down,' and he showed me how to do it. I played it at Potsdam for old Stalin. I think he was quite impressed." Truman considered a musical career but gave it up after his father went broke speculating on the grain market. "A good music-hall piano player is about the best I'd have ever been," Truman said. "So I went into politics and became president of the United States."

Harry S. Truman plays a tune for actress Lauren Bacall at a Press Club canteen.

On the Ballot, With Only 86 Votes to Spare

YOUNG CANDIDATE DUBBED "LANDSLIDE LYNDON"

In 1948, Lyndon Johnson was a young House representative and his opponent for the Senate seat was a seasoned former governor, Coke Stevenson. In the rough-and-tumble arena of Texas politics, the two fought hard for the Democratic Party's senatorial nomination that year.

The primary election was odd from the start. A block of votes "turned up" in Duval County after the polls had closed. Then, because of a "mix-up" in nearby Jim Wells County (which routinely boasted high voter turnout—sometimes well in excess of distributed ballots), the lead kept changing. Each side promptly accused the other of fraud. When the smoke cleared, Johnson seemed to be 87 votes ahead, finally nailing down the nomination at the state convention. But Stevenson wouldn't quit. He demanded an inquiry, and months of maneuvering led to a direct appeal to Supreme Court Justice Hugo Black. Just weeks before the election, LBJ's name was finally printed on the ballot.

As a result, the Jim Wells County investigation was halted (with voting lists "lost" or stolen), the Duval County ballots were burned by the courthouse janitor, and Johnson went on to win the Senate seat by a 2-to-1 margin and with it, a stepping-stone to the White House.

Jimmy Carter to the Rescue

BEFORE HE TOOK OFFICE, THE 39TH PRESIDENT COMPLETES 90-SECOND NUCLEAR REPAIR JOB

Having graduated from the U.S. Naval Academy, Jimmy Carter was fascinated by nuclear power, and particularly by the potential of atomic submarines. Both his expertise in nuclear theory and his practical experience in building the first nuclear propulsion components were unexpectedly put to the test in 1953, when a nuclear reactor in Chalk River, Canada, developed a leak, releasing radioactive material into the atmosphere.

Carter, who was then taking courses in reactor technology and nuclear physics at Union College in Schenectady, New York, was called in, along with two other naval officers, to help disassemble the damaged nuclear reactor core. Because of the extreme danger posed by exposure to radiation, Carter and his team had only 90 seconds to retrieve the damaged pieces of the underground reactor core.

The trio first practiced on an exact mock-up of the equipment, which had been constructed on a tennis court close by. They became familiar with the damaged pieces and the tools that would be used to remove them. When they finally descended into the core, each wearing a suit of white protective clothing, they worked frantically and accomplished the task in 89 seconds. It has been

estimated that in those few seconds each man absorbed a year's maximum dosage of radiation. Carter, later to become our 39th president, wrote in his book, *Why Not the Best?*, "There were no apparent aftereffects from this exposure—just a lot of doubtful jokes among ourselves about death versus sterility."

TRUTH OR RUMOR?

Ronald Reagan was an actor before he was president. But is it true that another president was a model before going into politics?

Yes. The nation's 38th president, Gerald Ford, was featured in a 1940 issue of *Look* magazine. The six-page article was titled, "A New York Girl and Her Yale Boy Friend Spend a Hilarious Holiday on Skis." It featured Ford as a handsome law student; at the time, he was also an assistant football coach and a partner in a New York modeling agency.

In 1952, Lieutenant Jimmy Carter (center, standing) checks equipment aboard a submarine during his seven-year tour of duty in the navy.

John Tyler's Secret Wedding

THE TWICE-MARRIED 10TH PRESIDENT FATHERED 15 CHILDREN

John Tyler became the first president to wed while in office (and the only one to do so secretly) when, at the age of 54, he married Julia Gardiner on June 26, 1844. Gardiner was a well-born, well-heeled beauty, 30 years his junior. As news of the wedding spread, eyebrows rose and tongues wagged, but Washingtonians weren't surprised—they had taken quick note of the budding romance between the lonely chief executive and the lively belle. The two had begun to see each other just months after the death of Letitia, Tyler's wife of 29 years and the mother of his first eight children (one of whom died in infancy). The wedding had been low key to assure privacy for the Gardiners, in mourning for the bride's father, who had died in an explosion in February.

Julia Tyler relished being mistress of the White House, but after only eight months she and her husband had to make way for the new president, James K. Polk. The Tylers then took up residence at Sherwood Forest, the former president's Virginia plantation, and before the year was out she was pregnant. The busybodies who had forecast frustration for the aging president's young bride were proven wrong: Julia bore her husband seven children. Tyler, in fact, was by far the most prolific of presidents, fathering eight sons and seven daughters. His first child, born in 1815, was five years older than his second wife—and 45 years older than his last child, who was born in 1860.

> Tyler was by far the most prolific of presidents, fathering eight sons and seven daughters.

In 1861, Tyler presided over a conference seeking a last-ditch formula to avert civil war. Later elected to the Confederate House of Representatives, he died in 1862, at age 71, before taking his seat. The Confederates buried him at Richmond with honors, but the federal government pointedly ignored the passing of the only president who ever subsequently became a sworn enemy of the United States.

Heartbroken and Defeated

ONE-TERM PRESIDENT FRANKLIN PIERCE PLAGUED BY POLITICAL AND PERSONAL TRAGEDY

Only one elected president, Franklin Pierce, has ever been denied renomination (in 1856) by his own party. He had tried through compromise to unite a nation that was bitterly divided over the slavery issue, and he had failed miserably.

But the tragedy of Pierce's administration was as much personal as it was political. The popular, hard-drinking extrovert had, as a young representative from New Hampshire, married a shy, puritanical woman. Jane Pierce was in poor health and hated partying, the damp Washington climate, and public life. Throughout Pierce's early political career, his wife spent much of her time at their New Hampshire home.

Two of Pierce's sons died in infancy. When a third son, Benjamin, was born in 1842, Pierce heeded his wife's pleas and retired from national politics. He virtually stopped drinking, devoted himself to his family and his successful law practice, and limited his political activities to the state level.

In June 1852, however, Pierce allowed himself to be nominated at the deadlocked Democratic convention, and on the 49th ballot he became the party's presidential candidate. When news reached the Pierces, Jane, who dreaded the day this would ever happen, fainted. Pierce argued that his being president would create a fine legacy for Bennie, then a bright 11-year-old. To everyone's surprise, he won. Shortly before the inauguration, the family was involved in a train wreck. Neither parent was hurt, but their beloved son was thrown from the car and crushed to death before their eyes. Despondent, the newly elected president went to Washington alone. He resumed drinking and contracted chronic bronchitis. (As a result, he installed a greatly improved heating system in the White House.) When Jane finally joined him in Washington, she kept to her room, writing notes to their dead son.

The youngest—and probably the handsomest—president up to that time, Franklin Pierce (left) fell short of expectations. Shortly before his inauguration, the Pierce family was in a train wreck. The president-elect and his wife, Jane Pierce (right), were not injured but their young son was killed.

Pierce was elected in the same year that Harriet Beecher Stowe's book, *Uncle Tom's Cabin*, was published. The nation was nearly aflame over slavery, but the president seemed never to have understood the intensity of the conflict. He was refused his party's renomination.

The Pierces retired to their New England home, where Jane died in 1863. Six years later, at 65, the former president passed away, a lonely and obscure man among the White Mountains of New Hampshire.

Lemonade Lucy and the Roman Punch

DURING THE HAYES ADMINISTRATION, "WATER FLOWED LIKE CHAMPAGNE AT THE WHITE HOUSE"

Rutherford B. Hayes was no teetotaler; he'd been known to lift a glass or two, though never to excess. But after taking office in 1877, he declared the White House alcohol-free, in part because his wife, Lucy, believed in temperance. Hayes, whose administration followed the whiskey-soaked years of Ulysses S. Grant, wanted to set a wholesome example for the nation.

After one official function, Secretary of State William Evarts remarked that "water flowed like Champagne at the White House." Among thirsty dignitaries, Mrs. Hayes soon became known as

Lemonade Lucy. The White House staff, however, found a way around the prohibition: The chef started serving a course called "Roman Punch" midway through dinner. In it, a hollowed-out, frozen orange filled with a sherbetlike concoction was filled with, according to one senator, "as much rum … as it could contain without being altogether liquid."

The president had the last laugh. After he died, a diary was discovered in which he confessed that his "orders were to flavor them rather strongly with the same flavor that is found in Jamaica rum. There was not a drop of spirits in them!"

Theodore Roosevelt with his second wife, Edith Carow Roosevelt, and five of his children. From left: Roosevelt, his sons Archie and Theodore Jr., daughter Alice, son Kermit, wife Edith, and daughter Ethel. Alice is his daughter by his first wife, Alice, who died after childbirth. Roosevelt and Edith had one other child, Quentin (not pictured), who died when he was 21.

"A Grief Too Deep"

FAMILY TRAGEDY DRIVES TEDDY ROOSEVELT TO SEEK A NEW LIFE IN THE WILD WEST

"There is a curse on this house," Theodore Roosevelt's brother told him. "Mother is dying and Alice is dying too." This was the news that greeted the future president on a foggy evening in 1884, as he burst into the family's New York mansion. He was there to see his infant daughter for the first time. By the next day he had lost his young wife, who had just given birth to the couple's first child, and his mother. Both of them died on Valentine's Day, which was also Teddy and Alice's fourth wedding anniversary. "The light has gone out of my life," Roosevelt later wrote in his diary.

Leaving the baby in his sister's care, the 25-year-old politician soon took his seat in the state legislature, but he was no longer the same man. "You could not talk to him about it," a fellow assemblyman noted sympathetically. "You could see at once that it was a grief too deep."

After the legislative session, Roosevelt headed west to the Dakota Badlands, where he had part interest in a cattle ranch. He bought another and ran it himself, planning to stay. The vigorous frontier life agreed with him, but in 1886, after a disastrous winter, he returned east. There he remarried and, in time, fathered five more children.

Although he mourned Alice, oddly enough she is not mentioned in his autobiography. But while out West, he did write movingly of her as "beautiful in face and form, and lovelier still in spirit; as a flower she grew, and as a fair young flower she died." And with these touching words, he laid to rest his grieving sadness and deep despair.

Trouble in the Lincoln Family

FIRST LADY BELIEVED TO BE A CLOSET CONFEDERATE

Mary Todd Lincoln's family was deeply involved in the Confederate cause, a fact not lost on gossipmongers. A half-brother was accused of brutalizing Union prisoners, her half-sisters were married to Confederate officers, and her brother thought Lincoln was "one of the greatest scoundrels unhung." It didn't help that she badgered her husband about political appointments and called Secretary of State William Seward "a dirty abolitionist sneak." Her secretary later wrote that rumors flew about Mrs. Lincoln's "constant correspondence, as a spy, with the chiefs of the Rebellion. Through her they obtained the secrets of the Cabinet and plans of generals."

A Senate committee even convened in secrecy to consider the accusations. According to one member, the meeting had just begun when the officer posted at the door opened it. The senators were "almost overwhelmed by astonishment," for there stood Lincoln, alone. Pathos was written upon his face and an "almost unhuman sadness" filled his eyes. Speaking "with infinite sorrow," he said: "I, Abraham Lincoln, President of the United States, appear of my own volition before this Committee of the Senate to say that, I, of my own knowledge, know that it is untrue that any of my family hold treasonable communication with the enemy."

Lincoln turned and left. Overcome, the committee dropped all consideration of rumors that Mrs. Lincoln was a Confederate spy.

WAS ABRAHAM LINCOLN'S SON, ROBERT, A PRESIDENTIAL JINX?

Abraham Lincoln's eldest son, Robert Todd Lincoln, was not at Ford's Theatre when his father was shot in April 1865, but he was at the president's side when he died. The event traumatized him.

Sixteen years later, the younger Lincoln was secretary of war when James A. Garfield called him in to discuss the assassination. Two days after that meeting, Garfield was

> "There is a certain fatality about presidential functions when I am present."
>
> **—ROBERT TODD LINCOLN**

shot in Washington's Baltimore & Potomac Railroad Station just as Lincoln was entering to meet him.

Twenty years after that, on September 6, 1901, Robert Todd Lincoln was invited to attend the Pan-American exposition in Buffalo. As he came into the Exposition Hall, shots rang out, and William McKinley slumped to the floor, mortally wounded.

Lincoln became a recluse. "There is a certain fatality about presidential functions when I am present," he lamented.

Even in death, presidential tragedy remains close to him. He lies in Arlington National Cemetery, scant yards from the grave of yet another assassinated president: John F. Kennedy.

Six Degrees of Franklin D. Roosevelt

Assiduously tracing the Roosevelt roots, genealogists discovered that Franklin Delano Roosevelt was related to no fewer than 11 previous presidents of the United States. Although he did not seem to attach great significance to this distinguished lineage, FDR's mother relished recalling antecedents who included "half the aristocracy of Europe and all that of the Hudson River Valley."

Franklin D. Roosevelt, 32nd President

Through his mother, Sara Delano, Roosevelt was related to seven former presidents as well as Robert E. Lee, Jefferson Davis, and Winston Churchill.

Through his father, James Roosevelt, Roosevelt was related to three former presidents.

William Taft
27th President

Benjamin Harrison
23rd President

Theodore Roosevelt
26th President

John Q. Adams
6th President

Ulysses S. Grant
18th President

Zachary Taylor
12th President

Through his father's first wife, Rebecca Howland, Roosevelt was related to one former president.

Martin Van Buren
8th President

John Adams
2nd President

William H. Harrison
9th President

James Madison
4th President

George Washington
1st President

Too Much Blood

WAS WASHINGTON BLED TO DEATH BY AMERICA'S BEST DOCTORS?

In the bleak dawn of a December day in 1799, George Washington lay ill and weak in his Mount Vernon bedroom. His throat was swollen, and he was scarcely able to breathe. Speaking with difficulty, the 67-year-old former president summoned the overseer of his estate and asked the man to draw blood from his arm.

Bleeding, a standard medical practice of the time, was based on the theory that removing diseased blood would speed the development of fresh, healthy blood. It was commonly done by opening a vein with a sharp instrument called a lancet.

"Don't be afraid," Washington told the trembling man, and the incision was made. "The orifice is not large enough," he whispered, and it was enlarged.

Martha Washington told Washington's aide, Tobias Lear, that she thought that too much blood was being taken. Lear tried to intervene, but Washington gestured for yet more blood to be drawn. Half a pint was taken.

At 9 a.m. the patient's longtime physician, James Craik, arrived. He made a preliminary diagnosis of inflammatory quinsy, an extreme form of tonsillitis, and ordered a second bleeding. There was no improvement. Washington was still unable to swallow or even to cough, and so a third bleeding was conducted.

Later that afternoon, two more physicians were summoned. After agreeing on the diagnosis, Dr. Elisha Dick favored a tracheotomy, to cut an opening in the windpipe below the obstruction. His colleagues felt that the move was too radical. Dr. Dick also argued against further bleeding. "He needs all his strength," he said. "Bleeding will diminish it." He was overruled, and Washington was bled once

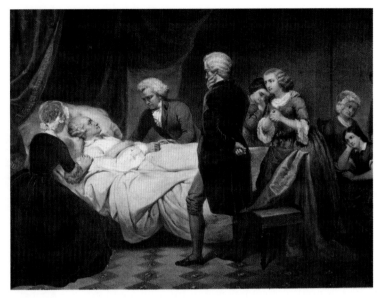

George Washington's death on December 14, 1799, may have been hastened by the four bleedings that weakened him.

more. We don't know how much blood was taken altogether, but this time alone a whole quart was removed. (The human body contains only five quarts of blood.)

Although he was in considerable pain, Washington never complained. Gradually suffocating, he expressed his thanks to the doctors for their attention and then advised them to "let me go off quietly; I cannot last long." He didn't. Hours later, he summoned Lear to his bedside and whispered: "I am just going. Have me decently buried, and do not let my body be put into the vault in less than three days after I am dead." Lear nodded and Washington asked, "Do you understand me?"

"Yes, sir," said Lear.

"'Tis well," said Washington. They were his last words.

In retrospect, as Dr. Craik wrote to one of his associates, had they "taken no more blood from him, our good friend might have been alive now. But we were governed by the best light we had."

Grover Cleveland's Classified Surgery

PRESIDENT SUFFERS BOUT WITH JAW CANCER—AND KEEPS IT A SECRET

Early in his second term as president, Grover Cleveland had a battle to win in Congress—one that he viewed as critically important to the economic health of the nation. But before he could fight and win in the public arena, he had to conquer a terrifying personal foe: cancer of the jaw.

The public battle is well documented. In 1893, the nation was on the verge of a depression, which Cleveland blamed in part on the inflationary Sherman Silver Purchase Act (passed in 1890 during Benjamin Harrison's administration). It required the Treasury to buy 4.5 million ounces of silver each month and to issue notes against it, redeemable in silver or gold. A firm believer in the gold standard, Cleveland vowed to use the full power of his office to force the repeal of the act at a special session of Congress, scheduled for August 7, 1893.

A GRIM DIAGNOSIS

Cleveland's private battle did not become public knowledge until 1917, nine years after his death. On May 27, 1893, while brushing his teeth, he discovered a small, rough patch on the roof of his mouth. Tissue tests revealed malignancy: the cigar-loving chief executive had cancer of the jaw. Cleveland needed surgery.

The 56-year-old president accepted the news stoically. To avert public panic, he took elaborate measures to ensure that word of his coming operation would not be leaked. Not even his pregnant, young wife was told about his illness or his imminent surgery.

The preparations for the operation were so secretive that they sounded like a spy mission. Cleveland's cover story was that he was vacationing at his summer home. The surgery was to take place not in a hospital, but on the *Oneida*, a friend's yacht anchored in New York's East River. He was smuggled aboard under cover of darkness; the doctors arrived separately to avoid arousing suspicion.

SECRET SURGERY

Just after noon on July 1, Cleveland settled his massive bulk into a chair that had been specially adapted to allow his head to tilt back. Five eminent medical men clustered around the chair; a dentist administered nitrous oxide—a new anesthetic later nicknamed "laughing gas"—and extracted two bicuspids to give surgeons access to the diseased area. Ether was then successfully administered, to the doctors' relief. They had worried about its effect on their corpulent patient.

To avoid telltale facial scars, all surgery was done inside Cleveland's mouth using two new medical instruments: a retractor designed to push aside his heavy jowls and a battery-operated electric knife for cauterizing the wounds. The chief surgeon was forced to cut away most of the president's upper left jaw because the cancer was more advanced than anyone had expected.

Although the president recuperated splendidly, his battle was not yet won. Because he lacked much of his upper jaw, he could barely communicate. His face was lopsided, and his speech was like that of a man with a cleft palate. But because rumors about his health had begun to spread, he could not postpone his appearance at the all-important congressional session, which was then only a month away. Cleveland was fitted with a prosthetic device made of vulcanized rubber, which gave him an artificial jaw line and made it possible for him to speak again. He labored for hours each day to improve his diction. Meanwhile, the device was refined and refitted. In the midst of these hardships, a second operation was performed to remove further malignant growth.

Cleveland kept his appointment with Congress and, speaking slowly but articulately, successfully urged the repeal of the Sherman Act. At the same time he allayed growing suspicions that he was ill. An account of the operation did appear in a newspaper (the dentist had spilled the beans), but the administration denied the report, saying that only routine dental surgery had been done. When the truth was finally revealed, it was no longer a sensational story and, in the midst of World War I, it received little public attention.

Madame President

AFTER HER HUSBAND'S STROKE, EDITH WILSON REPUTEDLY RAN THE EXECUTIVE OFFICE

The Iron Queen. The Presidentress. The Regent. These were some of the names people called Edith Wilson after her husband suffered a massive stroke while speaking in Pueblo, Colorado, in 1919. The First Lady came to dominate the White House. A senator coined the phrase that was on everyone's lips: "Petticoat Government."

Although she barred everyone, Cabinet officers and trusted aides alike, from the president, the First Lady insisted that she had no role in executive decisions: "The only decision that was mine was what was important and when to present matters to my husband." Daily bulletins assured the country that the president was recovering, but in fact, he was partially paralyzed and nearly blind. When President Woodrow Wilson was scheduled to address Congress, the message sent to Capitol Hill was instead a patchwork of reports by Cabinet members, with penciled corrections by the First Lady herself. Some lawmakers observed that Wilson knew

President Woodrow Wilson reviews documents with his second wife, Edith Bolling Galt Wilson. Edith Wilson was sometimes referred to as the "secret president" because of the role she played in Wilson's presidency during his illness.

nothing about the message. The government limped along, grimly controlled by the First Lady.

A descendant of the American Indian princess Pocahontas, Mrs. Wilson was a strange match for this president. Shrewd, with little formal education (while Wilson held a Ph.D.), she was a political innocent who, though a 20-year resident of Washington, had never visited the White House. Indeed, initially she could not even recall who she had favored in the 1912 election which Wilson, a Democrat, had won. But after their marriage, she rapidly became his confidante in all matters, enabling her to assert her influence during his illness.

> A descendant of Pocahontas, Edith Wilson was shrewd, despite little formal education.

After his death in 1924, she was as protective of his memory as she had been of him, preserving memorabilia and tirelessly attending the dedication of any public building named in his honor. And 44 years after she stood at her husband's side as he took the oath of office, Edith Wilson appeared at the inauguration of another Democratic president, John F. Kennedy. Less than a year later she died at the age of 89. In her obituary, *The New York Times* noted that "some went so far as to characterize her as the first woman President of the United States." And, indeed, many still agree.

BRIGHT IDEA

How Do You Say, "None of Your Business" in Chinese?

When Herbert Hoover and his wife, Lou, wanted to speak privately in the presence of White House guests, they spoke Chinese. They had learned the language during their post-wedding years in China (he was a mining engineer who later became a consultant to the Chinese director of the Ministry of Mines). Their time there climaxed in the nightmarish Boxer Rebellion of 1900.

JFK and Addison's Disease

AN UNANSWERED MEDICAL QUESTION HAS POLITICAL OVERTONES

"I have never had Addison's disease," said John F. Kennedy after winning the presidency in 1960. "I have been through a long campaign and my health is very good today." According to one of his many doctors, however, "Jack had been diagnosed as having Addison's disease."

It was a potentially explosive issue. Until the 1940s, the incurable adrenal disorder was always debilitating and often fatal. By the 1960 election, it was controllable with cortisone, but merely having to explain that fact would surely have cost Kennedy votes.

Perhaps it was simple curiosity that precipitated three known break-ins, or attempted break-ins, of JFK's doctors' offices. We will probably never know. The young candidate's medical files were marked with assumed names or kept in secure places, and so his privacy was protected and the issue of his "killer" disease—if, indeed, he had it—was never raised beyond the level of rumor.

This lithograph by an unknown artist depicts the attempted assassination of President Jackson on January 1, 1835, which took place after funeral services for congressman Warren R. Davis. Richard Lawrence shot at Jackson, but his pistols misfired. Lawrence was knocked to the ground and arrested. He was later tried and found innocent by reason of insanity.

The First Wannabe Assassin

MAN WHO MADE TWO TRIES ON PRESIDENT ANDREW JACKSON'S LIFE NEVER WENT TO JAIL

On a chilly January day in 1835, an aging, infirm President Andrew Jackson leaned on the arm of a Cabinet member as he emerged from the Hall of the House of Representatives, where he had attended a funeral service for Congressman Warren Davis. Waiting behind a column in the Capitol's eastern portico was his would-be killer, a handsome young man named Richard Lawrence. Concealed in the folds of Lawrence's long, dark cloak was a pair of single-shot pistols.

When Jackson was some eight feet away, Lawrence sprang out, a pistol in each hand. Raising his right hand, he drew a bead on the president's chest and confidently pulled the trigger. The explosion of the percussion cup echoed through the chamber, and chaos ensued. But Jackson did not fall. The gun had misfired.

Ever the fighter, Jackson raised his cane and charged the assassin, shouting in fury. With the old man almost upon him, Lawrence shot again. Incredibly, the second gun also misfired. The gunman was quickly wrestled to the ground and spirited away.

Two clear shots, two misfires; the odds have been calculated at 125,000 to 1. Both weapons were properly loaded and both functioned perfectly in later tests. Lawrence blamed the dampness.

A host of conspiracy theories blossomed, but it became clear at Lawrence's trial that his was an act of lunacy. He had lived a normal life until 1832, when he suddenly became delusional. At one time, he thought that he was King Richard III of England, and that Jackson had killed his father and was hiding royal funds in U.S. banks.

No precedent existed for trying a failed assassin, and so the crime was treated as a simple assault, a misdemeanor at the time. The prosecutor, Washington District Attorney Francis Scott Key (writer of "The Star-Spangled Banner"), agreed that the defendant should be treated as a madman, and Lawrence was freed on a plea of insanity.

He spent the rest of his life in asylums and died in 1861.

Bullet in the Hole

WAS IT AN ATTEMPTED ASSASSINATION OR BAD HYGIENE THAT CAUSED GARFIELD'S DEMISE?

It took James A. Garfield 11 weeks to die after he was shot in the back by assassin Charles Guiteau on July 2, 1881. The bullet nicked an artery, and the wound eventually killed the president. In spite of this injury, the earnest efforts of the country's best physicians would probably have finished him off, anyway.

Since it was believed that the bullet itself would cause infection, the physicians' first concern was to find it. They did this by poking into the president's wound, trying to follow the bullet's channel with a metal probe (or sometimes even a finger). And because most American doctors were still skeptical about Louis Pasteur's 20-year-old theory of bacterial infection, the probes were not sterilized, and the fingers rarely were washed.

District of Columbia health officer Smith Townshend was the first doctor to stick his finger into Garfield's wound. He didn't find the bullet but reported that the president complained of heaviness, numbness, and pain in his legs, and that he declared himself to be "a dead man."

Next, D. W. Bliss, a prominent Washington surgeon and Garfield's boyhood friend, got his heavy Nélaton probe (one tipped with rough porcelain) stuck in the fragments of a shattered rib. Its removal was quite painful. Undaunted, he tried again with his little finger, then with a long, thin, flexible silver probe.

Over the next few days, the list of famous doctors who poked into Garfield's wound was impressive. So was the depth to which they probed; upon withdrawing his finger, the surgeon general of the navy reported feeling a perforated liver seven inches from the bullet's entry point.

To relieve the president's discomfort in the muggy Washington heat, a Baltimore engineer improvised an air-conditioning scheme using an exhaust fan and 3,000 feet of Turkish toweling saturated with iced saltwater. It brought the temperature in the room down from 99 degrees to the mid-70s.

TRUTH OR RUMOR?

Is it true that there was a vice president who dreaded the possibility of becoming president?

Yes. Although twice elected vice president (he served in that capacity from 1913 to 1921), Thomas Riley Marshall was determined never to be president; he said it would be "a tragedy for the country." Long before Woodrow Wilson's incapacitating stroke, Marshall stopped going to Cabinet meetings and took to the lecture circuit to supplement his income. So remote did he become from affairs of state that, at first, no one at the White House thought it necessary to tell him how serious the president's illness was.

But Marshall did achieve a kind of immortality. Once, while presiding over a dull Senate debate, the vice president—who was seldom seen without a stogie clamped between his teeth—uttered the unforgettable line: "What this country needs is a good five-cent cigar."

On July 22, the wound began to form pus. To enlarge and drain it, Philadelphia doctor Hayes Agnew performed two operations—one without anesthesia. Garfield was given "nutritional enemas" of eggs, beef extract, and whiskey, which did no good at all. Inexorably, the infection spread. By August 18, the president showed signs of blood poisoning. His face was paralyzed, his mind was wandering, and he had lost 80 pounds. Again the doctors operated without anesthesia.

Resigned to death, the president begged to be taken to the New Jersey shore. On September 6, his bed was mounted on springs in a railroad car cooled with iceboxes and, by way of a specially built spur line, he was taken to his cottage door. He rallied briefly, but on September 19, when the nicked artery finally burst, he died. At his autopsy, the bullet was found safely encapsulated in scar tissue far from any of the doctors' probings, doing no harm.

Today, of course, X-rays would find the bullet, the artery would be surgically repaired, and intravenous feeding would keep up Garfield's strength. Given such modern care, he might well have lived to a ripe old age.

"Honey, I Forgot to Duck"

AFTER ATTEMPT ON HIS LIFE, REAGAN IS SHOWERED WITH JELLY BEANS AND A GOLDFISH

"Honey, I forgot to duck" was President Ronald Reagan's much-publicized comment to his wife, Nancy, after would-be assassin John Hinckley shot him on March 30, 1981. The chief executive may well have recalled the remark from a story about boxer Jack Dempsey who, after losing the heavyweight championship to Gene Tunney in 1926, used the same words to explain his battered appearance to his wife. That bit of lore could hardly have been lost on former sportscaster "Dutch" Reagan.

While the president was recovering from his gunshot wound, well-wishers showered him with cards and gifts, including 500 bouquets, a music box, a 55-pound glass pig filled with jelly beans, a 10-pound box of chocolates, and a photograph of Bob Hope and Jill St. John wearing bunny costumes. One get-well gift was outstanding, however, especially in its manner of delivery: It was a goldfish that survived a trip through the mail from Albany, New York, in a plastic bag full of water. Barney Bullard, the 10-year-old who sent it, explained in a note that

President Ronald Reagan waves to onlookers at the Washington Hilton on March 30, 1981, moments before John Hinckley Jr. tried to assassinate him.

he was enclosing "a companion, a goldfish named Ronald Reagan II. I hope you like him. Just feed him daily every morning and he will be fine." Dubbed the First Fish, Ronald Reagan II was promptly placed in a tank emblazoned with the presidential seal, where he lived happily for more than three years.

The Kingfish That Ruled Louisiana

IRREPRESSIBLE AND OFFBEAT, GOVERNOR HUEY LONG WAS ONCE CONSIDERED A REAL THREAT TO FDR'S REELECTION

When the German consul and the commander of a German cruiser paid a courtesy call on Governor Huey P. Long of Louisiana in 1930, they were hardly prepared for his sartorial splendor. For there was the Kingfish, in green silk pajamas, a red and blue robe, and blue slippers, looking, as one reporter put it, like "an explosion in a paint factory."

Seeing that the consul was flustered, the irrepressible Long returned the visit the next day dressed in pinstriped pants borrowed from a hotel manager, a waiter's boiled shirt, a swallowtail coat, and a collar "so high I had to stand on a stool to spit over it." Received cordially amid military pomp and splendor, Governor Long impressed the commander as "a very interesting, intelligent, and unusual person."

This colorful, freewheeling behavior was typical of the man who had become the state's youngest governor in 1928. Sailing into office on the campaign slogan, "Every man a king, but no man wears a crown," he made himself the virtual dictator of

Huey Long smiles while sitting behind several NBC microphones during a radio broadcast.

Louisiana. He provided free school textbooks, raised funds for a university, built a modern highway system, and expanded hospitals and other institutions

TRUTH OR RUMOR?

Is it true that there was once a governor who had to be declared *sane*?

Yes. Governor Huey P. Long's younger brother, Earl, was a three-term governor of Louisiana in the mid-1900s. In his last term, oddly enough, he had to have himself declared sane to keep his job.

When "Ol' Earl's" wild behavior caused his family to have him committed to a Texas institution, he objected violently, saying he was a "governor in exile, by force and kidnapping." Later he agreed to be treated at a New Orleans clinic. But it was a short stay; after a day he simply drove off to the capitol at Baton Rouge. Promptly recommitted, he protested that his hospitalization was unlawful imprisonment. When the state hospital board agreed to hear his case, he fired the hospital superintendent, replacing him with an old friend who declared him sane.

largely financed by the taxes imposed on utilities and oil companies. He also used every means to stifle his political enemies. When, in his habitually high-handed manner, he imposed a new, heavy tax on the oil industry, Long incurred the wrath of a hostile legislature, which promptly impeached him on 19 counts. But he wiggled off the hook by forcing 15 state senators to pledge allegiance to him, no matter what the evidence revealed.

> "Every man a king, but no man wears a crown."
>
> —**HUEY LONG**'s 1928 campaign slogan

Cleared of the charges, Long rallied his supporters and got himself elected to the U.S. Senate in 1930—yet he continued to serve as governor for two more years. Arriving in Washington in 1932, he took on bigger game: FDR and his New Deal. In short order Long was proposing a radical plan to redistribute the nation's wealth through a tax-the-rich scheme and demanding that the federal government furnish every family with an allowance, an annual income, and benefits. He called it the Share Our Wealth program.

By 1935, as a possible third-party presidential candidate, he was considered a real threat to Roosevelt's reelection. But on September 8, 1935, while preparing to curtail the New Deal program in Louisiana, the indomitable Long was shot down by an assassin in the state capitol. Although he died two days later, his spirit lives on, for the Louisiana Pied Piper left as his legacy a powerful political dynasty.

FUNNY FACT

Presidential Justice
William H. Taft, president from 1909–13, was the only chief executive who later became chief justice of the U.S. Supreme Court.

Stephen A. Douglas was reelected senator of Illinois in 1858 after a series of debates with the Republican candidate, Abraham Lincoln, who defeated him in the presidential race two years later.

A Campaign Trailblazer

STEPHEN A. DOUGLAS PEDDLED IDEAS "AS A TIN MAN PEDDLES HIS WARES"

It wasn't until 1860, when Stephen A. Douglas ran against Abraham Lincoln and two other candidates, that an American had ever declared his own candidacy, openly sought nomination, or publicly campaigned for the presidency. When Douglas hit the road on his own behalf, orating to crowds from railroad coaches and hotel balconies, many were offended by his brash behavior.

Although Douglas carried his message far and wide, his stumping was a pale version of today's barnstorming. In fact, when he set out to spread his message eastward, he announced the trip as a visit to his mother in Clifton Springs, New York. It took him almost a month of stopovers to get there. One Republican handbill taunted: "A Boy Lost! Left Washington D.C. some time in July has been seen in Philadelphia, New York City, Hartford, Conn., at a clambake in Rhode Island. He has been heard from at Boston, Portland, Augusta, and Bangor, Me. He has an idea that he is a candidate for President."

While the final vote confirmed Lincoln's popularity, Douglas nevertheless made an admirable showing. As for high-visibility presidential candidates campaigning for themselves, he started it all.

The Very Unusual Election of 1872

GRANT VERSUS GREELEY A CHOICE BETWEEN "HEMLOCK AND STRYCHNINE"

Among America's many strange presidential races, few have been stranger than that of 1872. Voters had to choose between two candidates who were almost equally unfit. It reduced both parties to squabbling shambles, and it opened the way for a bizarre parade of candidates to espouse a wide range of causes.

The incumbent was Ulysses S. Grant, whose administration had been fraught with corruption and incompetence. The prospect of his renomination split the Republican Party and brought about the Liberal Republicans. After a near-riotous convention, they nominated Horace Greeley, founder and editor of the *New York Tribune,* and champion of nearly every social reform that he could latch on to. Greeley was a brilliant journalist, but an impractical statesman; he was a gullible idealist whose public demeanor was clownish at best. "Success with such a candidate is out of the question," sighed Charles Francis Adams, the son and grandson of presidents, who lost to Greeley on the sixth ballot.

The regular Republicans renominated Grant. A month later the Democrats selected the man who once said, "All Democrats may not be rascals, but all rascals are Democrats." It was none other than Horace Greeley. (Southern Democrats, it seemed, would vote for anyone who favored amnesty for former Confederates and the withdrawal of federal troops from the South.)

Grant spent a quiet seaside summer while Republican speakers, editorialists, and cartoonists recalled his Civil War heroism and ridiculed Greeley's baby face, chin whiskers, and rumpled clothes. They jeered at the editor's support of vegetarianism, prohibition, and communal living schemes. (The *Phrenological Journal*, however, having measured Greeley's cranium, wrote glowingly of his natural qualifications for office.) Meeting ridicule everywhere, Greeley grew more frenetic and morose. He said later that he didn't know whether he was running for the presidency or the penitentiary.

Personal grief compounded his public ordeal. In September, he returned to New York to sit at the bedside of his dying wife. Grief-stricken, he slept little until her death on October 30. A week later he was massacred at the polls, capturing only six states while Grant swept 30.

A Pitiful End for Horace Greeley

Few serious candidates before Horace Greeley had ever been so thoroughly repudiated at the polls; none before or since has been so totally destroyed by defeat. Crushed by the loss of his beloved wife, he saw himself as "the worst beaten man who ever ran for high office." But further humiliation was to come. When Greeley tried to resume control of his beloved *Tribune,* he was rebuffed by acting editor Whitelaw Reid. Instead of welcoming Greeley back, Reid ran a front-page box mocking the Republican office seekers who had sought the old editor's help, then refused to print Greeley's response. Greeley's mind snapped and his health broke. He died, insane, in a physician friend's suburban retreat only three weeks after the election.

An Odd Couple in Pursuit of the Presidency

TWO COLORFUL CANDIDATES SEEK THE TOP SPOT

Among the minor-party candidates in that strange campaign of 1872, two of the most fascinating were Victoria Woodhull, whose Equal Rights Party spoke for "the unenfranchised women of the country," and George Francis Train, self-proclaimed "Champion Crank of America."

Woodhull and her sister had already invaded traditionally male territory by becoming Wall Street brokers and by publishing a political journal called *Woodhull & Claflin's Weekly*. Free-thinking reformers, they spoke out for free love, abortion, divorce, legalized prostitution, and women's voting rights. In an address to a meeting of the National Woman Suffrage Association, Woodhull delivered the clarion call that was her campaign theme: "We mean treason; we mean secession … we will [overthrow] this bogus Republic." On Election Day, she and her sister were in jail, charged with sending obscene literature through the mail. (The offensive material was an article congratulating the popular preacher, Henry Ward Beecher, for having the good sense to dally with a married lady parishioner, but chiding him for failing to openly advocate the free love he clearly practiced.) Reports about Woodhull's personal life, including her support for free love, did not help her at the polls.

Train was controversial in a different way. An eccentric and flamboyant self-made millionaire with a flair for publicity, he was obsessed with speed and drawn to struggles for freedom. Jules Verne modeled *Around the World in 80 Days* on a journey Train had made in 1870. Over the course of the trip, Train became embroiled in a revolution against the Third Republic in France and avoided the firing squad by

> Jules Verne modeled
> *Around the World in 80 Days*
> on a journey Train had
> made in 1870.

wrapping himself in both the French and American flags—it was one of 15 sojourns in foreign jails in the course of his long life. (He deducted the enforced stopover from the 80-day count.) He was later to break his own record by circling the globe in 67½ days.

During the 1872 campaign, he was a political rarity: He was a losing candidate who made a profit. Charging admission for his orations, he barnstormed the country, delivering an amazing 1,000 speeches to a total of 2 million people. Calling himself "your modest, diffident, unassuming friend, the future President of America," he held forth on his own magnificence. Finally, he became involved in the Victoria Woodhull controversy. In response to the charges against her, Train published a collection of biblical quotations that were, he said, more obscene than anything his opponent had written. He, too, was clapped in jail.

TRUTH OR RUMOR?

Is it true that President Harrison served just one year in office?

No—his term was even shorter than that. William Henry Harrison took office in 1841 but died of pneumonia just a month into his term.

Going for the Silver

PACK OF THIEVES RIDES BRYAN'S CAMPAIGN BANDWAGON

When William Jennings Bryan carried his 1896 presidential campaign across the country by train, sometimes delivering as many as 30 speeches a day, he unwittingly attracted a band of faithful followers he hadn't counted on: pickpockets.

The candidate of the Democratic, Populist, and National Silver parties, Bryan advocated the free coinage of silver, at a ratio to gold of 16 to 1. His chief purpose in stumping the country was to reach the farmers of the Midwest, who would benefit from the freer supply of money that the silver standard would bring about. A gifted orator, the energetic 36-year-old nominee addressed huge crowds at every stop, assailing Wall Street and extolling the virtues of silver. To make the point that silver was as widely accepted as gold, he would ask his listeners to raise their hands if they carried gold in their pockets and then ask the same of those who had silver.

What Bryan didn't realize was that in doing so, he was aiding some 50 pickpockets who would hop on the train at the beginning of the day, blend in with the others on board, and then pile out at each whistlestop to work the tightly packed crowd that had assembled. The thievery became such a serious problem that Bryan finally had to hire a Pinkerton detective.

A campaign button for William Jennings Bryan and his running mate, Arthur Sewall.

Congressional Violence

DIGNITY AND DECORUM HAVE NOT ALWAYS PREVAILED IN THE SENATE AND THE HOUSE

When Vice President Martin Van Buren presided over the Senate in the mid-1830s, he occasionally wore sidearms to help keep order. It is a wonder that others have not followed his example, considering how many lawmakers in both houses of Congress have resorted to fists, guns, or clubs.

One of the first was Connecticut Representative Roger Griswold. On January 30, 1798, when Matthew Lyon of Vermont slighted Griswold's state, he retaliated by insulting Lyon's war record. Lyon spit in Griswold's face. Two weeks later Griswold attacked Lyon at his desk with a stick. Lyon counterattacked with a pair of fire tongs from the fireplace behind the speaker. House members separated them.

Mississippi Senator Henry S. Foote and Missouri's Thomas Hart Benton were already enemies in 1850, when, during a rancorous speech by Foote, Benton kicked back his chair and moved menacingly forward. Foote drew a gun and aimed it at Benton. "Stand out of the way!" Benton shouted to others. "Let the assassin fire!" Foote, who was quickly disarmed, later claimed that he thought Benton, too, had a gun.

In May 1856 abolitionist Senator Charles Sumner of Massachusetts insulted Senator Andrew P. Butler of South Carolina in a tirade against slavery. Later, while Sumner was at his desk, Butler's nephew, Representative Preston Smith Brooks, entered the Senate chamber with a fellow South Carolinian and bludgeoned Sumner with a cane. Sumner's injuries kept him away from the Senate for three years.

In 1964 Strom Thurmond of South Carolina and Ralph Yarborough of Texas took off their coats in a Senate corridor and thrashed out a dispute over a civil rights appointment. Thurmond pinned Yarborough but could not get him to cry "Uncle." The two later reconciled at a picture-taking session.

Campaigning from Prison

SOCIALIST EUGENE V. DEBS GETS ALMOST A MILLION VOTES FOR PRESIDENT

Labor leader Eugene V. Debs ran for president five times as the standard-bearer of the Socialist Party, but his best showing was in 1920, when he campaigned

from a cell in the Atlanta Federal Penitentiary. He was serving time for speaking out in 1918 against the Espionage Act—by its own terms, to criticize the law was to break it. In the final weeks of the campaign, Debs was allowed to issue one press bulletin a week. On Election Eve, he wrote: "The result will be as it should be. The people will vote for what they think they want, to the extent that they think at all, and they, too, will not be disappointed."

The election, in which he received 919,799 votes (about 5.7 percent of Warren Harding's showing), marked the end of socialism as a third-party movement. It was, according to one Socialist leader, "the last flicker of the dying candle."

Presidential Trivia

HE	WAS THE ONLY PRESIDENT WHO...
Washington	was unanimously elected.
Ford	was both vice president and president without being elected to either office.
Coolidge	(right) was born on July 4.
Tyler	joined the Confederate government.
Nixon	resigned.
Lincoln	received a patent.
Garfield	could simultaneously write Greek with one hand and Latin with the other.
Wilson	earned a Ph.D.
Kennedy	received the Pulitzer Prize.
W. Harrison	was the grandfather of another.
Eisenhower	was a licensed pilot.
L. Johnson	was sworn in by a woman.
Carter	commanded a submarine.

Town Votes for Republican Mule

BOSTON CURTIS WAS AS CLOSE AS YOU COULD GET TO A *DARK HORSE* CANDIDATE

In 1936, Kenneth Simmons, who was the Democratic mayor of Milton, Washington, placed a candidate named Boston Curtis on the ballot for Republican precinct committeeman. Curtis, who ran as a dark horse, delivered no speeches and made no promises. Astonishingly, his unusual political campaign proved successful at the polls; he won by a unanimous vote of 52 to 0. But Curtis was different from other candidates for public office: He was a mule, and he became

quite famous. As "the people's choice," he was featured in national magazines, and a major film studio tried to place him under contract. His election even momentarily upstaged FDR's victory over Republican Alfred M. Landon in the presidential race that year.

Simmons claimed that he sponsored the mule's candidacy to demonstrate the carelessness of the town's voters. Perhaps he was also demonstrating a wry sense of humor, for he had shown that the offspring of a donkey—symbol of the Democrats—could win as a Republican.

A Tie? Oh, My!

JEFFERSON AND BURR DEADLOCKED FOR PRESIDENCY IN 1800 ELECTION

"The Person having the greatest Number of Votes shall be the President," says Article II, Section 1, of the Constitution, referring to the votes cast by each state's electors. It goes on to say that the candidate with the second-highest vote tally would become the vice president. Thus the framers of this historic document left a loophole that allowed Thomas Jefferson and Aaron Burr, candidates on the Republican ticket for president and vice president, respectively, to wind up with the same number of electoral votes.

The deadlock threw the election of 1800 into the House of Representatives, where many ballots and much political maneuvering were needed to resolve it. With President John Adams's term due to expire in a few months, some politicians and journalists foresaw the astonishing possibility of anarchy.

By the time the votes were cast in December, there were 73 Republican and 65 Federalist electors. As it turned out, although there appeared to be a rift in the Federalist ranks, every Republican elector had voted for both Jefferson and Burr. (Burr, while declaring that he was not in competition with Jefferson, never actually renounced the presidency.)

Balloting began in the House on February 11, 1801. Each of the 16 states had one vote; a simple majority, or nine votes, was needed to win. On the first ballot, Jefferson got eight and Burr six. Two states were undecided. The count had not changed by midnight, when the 19th ballot was cast. For six more intriguing, scheming, rumor-filled days,

Most Federalist representatives regarded Jefferson as a dangerous radical, but they lacked the votes to elect Burr.

voting continued. Alexander Hamilton, though a Federalist, urged fellow Federalists to support Jefferson, on the grounds that although Jefferson was "a contemptible hypocrite"—he did have some "pretensions to character," whereas Burr's "public principles have no other spring or aim than his own aggrandizement. His elevation can only promote the purposes of the desperate and profligate."

Most Federalist representatives regarded Jefferson as a dangerous radical, so they ignored Hamilton. They did not have enough votes to elect Burr, but as March 4—the end of Adams's term—loomed, they thought their support might swing a number of the Republican votes.

As the lobbying grew more intense, there was talk of civil war. Some accused the Federalists of planning to usurp the presidency. The Virginia militia was even reportedly prepared to march on Washington, D.C., if it became necessary.

Finally Delaware's representative decided that Burr could never be elected. The only reason to go on supporting him was "to exclude Jefferson at the expense of the Constitution," and this he would not do. Thus, after an astounding 36 ballots, the acrimonious deadlock was broken, and Jefferson was finally declared the third president of the United States, with Burr as his vice president.

By the time the next presidential election rolled around, the 12th Amendment, specifying that the electors vote separately for president and vice president, had been ratified.

A Heaven-Sent President?

When John Quincy Adams won the presidency in 1824, he did it without a majority of electoral votes. In fact, Andrew Jackson beat him in both the popular vote and the Electoral College. But because Jackson did not have an outright majority, the issue was decided in the House of Representatives, and the outcome finally hung on a single vote, cast by an aging patroon from upstate New York.

The election was an odd one from the start. The two-party system had collapsed, and all the principal candidates claimed to be Republicans. Various state legislatures nominated their own favorites, and in all some 17 candidates were in the running. By Election Day, the field had narrowed to four: Tennessee Senator Andrew Jackson, hero of the Battle of New Orleans, was the people's choice. His opponents regarded him as a semiliterate hothead, good in a fight but ill-prepared for national leadership.

John Quincy Adams of Massachusetts, secretary of state and son of a president, came in second. Though highly qualified by education and experience, he was viewed as a cold fish that lacked human warmth.

Third was William H. Crawford of Georgia. He owed much of his support to a bulging pocketful of political debts that he had collected during his term as secretary of the treasury. (So flagrant was his abuse of patronage that, in the course of a discussion on the subject, outgoing president James Monroe threatened him with a pair of fire tongs.)

Kentuckian Henry Clay, speaker of the House, was fourth. Since the 12th Amendment specified that the choice be made among the top three vote-getters, he was eliminated from the race. After a private meeting with Adams, during which Clay reportedly was offered the post of secretary of state, he threw his substantial support to the New Englander.

On February 9, voting day in the House, Adams knew that he had to win on the first ballot or be overwhelmed by Jackson's popular support. Each state had one vote, to be decided by the majority of its representatives. Adams was sure of 12 states—one short of the majority he needed, and the New York delegation was tied.

Clay felt that one of the New York representatives, the immensely rich and pious old landholder Stephen Van Rensselaer III, could be swayed, although his vote was supposedly committed to Crawford. As the delegation arrived, Clay ushered Van Rensselaer into the speaker's room, where he and Daniel Webster exercised their considerable powers of persuasion on Adams's behalf.

They failed. But the encounter flustered the old aristocrat. Before casting his vote, Van Rensselaer bowed his head in prayer, and the first thing he saw when he opened his eyes was a slip of paper marked with Adams's name—possibly a discarded ballot. Taking it as a sign of God's will, he put the slip in the ballot box and made John Quincy Adams the sixth president of the United States.

Though highly qualified, Adams was viewed as a cold fish that lacked human warmth.

The Swing Vote

**EDMUND ROSS'S POLITICAL CAREER ENDED
BECAUSE HE VOTED TO ACQUIT JOHNSON**

On May 11, 1868, Senate Republicans caucused to see how the vote would go in President Andrew Johnson's impeachment trial. Thirty-five votes were firm for conviction. Six seemed assured for acquittal. One man remained silent: Edmund Gibson Ross, the 42-year-old freshman senator from Kansas.

A newspaper publisher and editor, Ross had been appointed in 1866 to finish the term of Senator James H. Lane, who had shot himself because he had been criticized for supporting President Johnson. Later that year, Ross won an election on his own.

A staunch Republican since the party's formation in 1856, Ross had voted consistently against Johnson, but after the House impeachment he told a colleague that "so far as I am concerned he shall have as fair a trial as an accused man ever had on this earth."

Word went out that Ross was "shaky." Letters and telegrams poured in from Kansas, demanding that he vote to convict. "I have taken an oath to do impartial justice … " he wrote in one telegram to constituents on the day of the vote. "I shall have the courage and the honesty to vote according to the dictates of my judgement and for the highest good of the country."

On May 16, the day of the Senate vote, all six "renegade" Republicans were sure to vote with the Democrats for acquittal. All eyes turned to Ross. "I almost literally looked into my open grave," he later wrote. "Friends, position, fortune, everything that makes life desirable to an ambitious man, were about to be swept away by the breath of my mouth, perhaps forever."

The breath of his mouth was at first so thin that his vote could not be heard. The second time, they heard him in the gallery: "Not guilty."

A justice of the Kansas Supreme Court sent a telegram: "Unfortunately, the rope with which Judas hung himself is mislaid, but the pistol with which Jim Lane killed himself is at your service."

None of the seven who voted with the Democrats ever served in the Senate again. Ross finished his term as an Independent and returned to Kansas, where he resumed his newspaper career and became a Democrat. Badly beaten in a later race for governor, he moved to New Mexico. President Grover Cleveland appointed him governor of the territory.

Just before Ross died at the age of 80, the state of Kansas sent him a message of appreciation for his courageous conduct during Johnson's impeachment trial nearly 40 years before.

"Selling the Presidency Like Cereal"

HOW THE "TELEVISION ELECTION" OF 1952 CHANGED POLITICS FOREVER

A nation that had been hooked on radio for a generation was switching to television in 1952, buying seven million sets that year. Thus, for the first time, voters could see Republican Dwight D. Eisenhower and Democrat Adlai E. Stevenson vie for the nation's highest office—and major networks could vie for viewers' time. (During the conventions, stations paired familiar long-time radio commentators with newcomers on the screen. A happy result was the broadcaster selected to appear with Edward R. Murrow; the newcomer—who was a natural—was Walter Cronkite.)

Eisenhower's strategists, recognizing the potential of projecting his famous grin into millions of living rooms, used the small screen throughout the campaign. And as it drew to a close, they blitzed the airwaves with 60-second spots. The most effective one showed Eisenhower giving this response to a question about inflation: "My wife, Mamie, worries about the same thing."

Adlai Stevenson, on the other hand, didn't even own a TV set. What he liked was delivering a witty, carefully crafted speech to a live audience, and he was a master of the art. But he was stiff and unnatural on

A 1948 portrait of General Dwight D. Eisenhower, who, in 1952, defeated Adlai Stevenson in the presidential election.

television and did not make use of electronic campaigning. It was "selling the presidency like cereal," he complained. "How can you talk seriously about issues with one-minute spots?" Ironically, Stevenson's most effective television appearance was his speech conceding defeat. Comforting his crestfallen supporters, he confessed that he felt like a little boy who had stubbed his toe in the dark—it hurt too much to laugh, and he was too old to cry.

"You Won't Have Nixon to Kick Around Anymore"

THE POLITICIAN'S FAMOUS NEWS CONFERENCE WAS HARDLY PROPHETIC

It seemed to be the end of the political road for Richard Nixon, who had just lost the 1962 election for governor of California to the incumbent, Pat Brown. Appearing unexpectedly at a press conference, Nixon rambled on, then focused on the media.

"As I leave you I want you to know how much you're going to be missing," he said, his voice edged with bitterness. "You won't have Nixon to kick around anymore."

In fact, it was neither the last press conference for Nixon nor the end of his political career. He licked his wounds, campaigned hard for Republican candidates in 1964, and by 1968 was back in charge of the party. Snaring the presidential nomination, he was elected by more than 500,000 votes. It was quite a comeback for a man whose career had been marked by controversy. Nixon's 1950 senatorial race against Helen Gahagan Douglas was called the "dirtiest campaign on record." Later, as Dwight D. Eisenhower's 1952 running mate, he made his emotional "Checkers" speech, defending himself against charges of accepting improper campaign contributions. But he and "Ike" won the election easily (at 40, Nixon became the nation's second-youngest vice president) and were reelected in 1956. Then, in 1960, Nixon ran for president, losing to John F. Kennedy by only about 100,000 votes—out of the nearly 69 million cast.

It was just two years later that the gubernatorial defeat seemed to end Nixon's career. But he bounced

Nixon's 1950 senatorial race was called the "dirtiest campaign on record."

back as a two-term president, in the process giving rise to the Watergate scandal—and once again there was ample opportunity "to kick Nixon around."

Three Governors, but Only One Office

IN 1946, GEORGIA HAD MORE LEADERS THAN IT COULD HANDLE

When Eugene Talmadge died in 1946, before he could be sworn in as governor of Georgia, the state legislature appointed his 33-year-old son, Herman, to the job. But two other men also claimed the governorship, and the ensuing political chaos resembled what one magazine called "something conceived at night by three unemployed radio writers."

Ellis Arnall, still the incumbent governor, asserted that since Herman Talmadge had not been an announced gubernatorial candidate, he could not assume the office. Undaunted, Talmadge moved into Arnall's outer office anyway, saying, "I do not object to Ellis Arnall hanging around as long as he wants to." Arnall countered that the "pretender" was welcome to visit.

Chaos prevailed when Talmadge's men changed the office locks, forcing Arnall to camp out in the capitol lobby. Lawsuits were initiated; countersuits were filed. At one point a whiff of tear gas and a firecracker, mistaken for a gunshot, enlivened the scene.

The standoff became triangular when M. E. Thompson, the newly elected lieutenant governor, was sworn in to that office. He immediately declared himself acting governor and started appointing his own officials. The enraged Talmadge wouldn't

Herman Talmadge, candidate for the governorship of Georgia, shakes hands with constituents after an August 1948 campaign speech.

budge, on the grounds that since his father had died before taking office, Thompson had absolutely no claim to succeed him. Thus, until Arnall resigned in Thompson's favor, Georgia could boast that it indeed had three governors.

The stalemate was finally broken after two months, when the Georgia Supreme Court ruled that Thompson was the lawful governor. Talmadge did not appeal the decision. Instead, he vowed that he'd "take this to the court of last resort—the people." And when the 1948 election rolled around, he won the governorship easily in his own right.

The Loser Who Won

INCUMBENT WINS, THOUGH "TO ERR IS TRUMAN"

When the Democrats nominated Harry S. Truman for the presidency in 1948, a flock of white pigeons was released over the Philadelphia convention hall to symbolize peace. But more symbolic to observers was that one bird crashed into the ceiling and fell to the floor. Experts said that Truman had about as much chance of winning as that bird. Indeed, he had been a compromise vice presidential candidate in 1944, and when Franklin Roosevelt died the next year, Truman wasn't alone in feeling that "the moon, the stars, and all the planets had fallen on me." Many agreed that the job might overwhelm him. "To err is Truman" became a popular saying.

Meanwhile, the Republicans nominated Governor Thomas E. Dewey of New York, who had made a surprisingly strong showing against Roosevelt in 1944. Although he didn't exactly set crowds on fire, he was an efficient administrator with a rich speaking voice perfect for radio. And the icing on Dewey's presidential cake came when two wings of the Democratic Party bolted from the Truman ticket. With FDR's coalition in tatters, it seemed impossible for Truman to win (an opinion reflected in the polls). Dewey reacted by avoiding issues whenever possible. He even took time out during the campaign to plan his inauguration. But the president forged ahead. From June on, he made 556 speeches as his campaign train whistle-stopped

some 31,700 miles across the nation. "I'm going to fight hard," he declared, "and I'm going to give 'em hell."

On election night pollsters, political pundits, and professional Republicans along with a fair amount of the populace were stunned, for Dewey's cautious campaign had managed to snatch defeat "out of the jaws of victory." And Truman, the feisty man from Missouri, had handily won both the popular and electoral votes to pull off what has been called the greatest upset in American political history.

Many Happy Returns?

The *Chicago Tribune's* "Dewey Defeats Truman" wasn't the only postelection newspaper snafu in U.S. history. The *New York Sun* headlined the 1916 election of Charles Evans Hughes as the nation's 29th president; the victory, of course, went to Woodrow Wilson. Twenty years later, *The Literary Digest* poll, which had an excellent track record for presidential predictions, asked 10 million Americans "to settle November's election in October." The results showed Alf Landon defeating Franklin Roosevelt by a comfortable margin. But on Election Day the only poll that counted told a different story: Roosevelt trounced Landon, sweeping all but two states.

One Vote Decided ...

• **Texas.** The 28th state squeaked into the Union in 1845 by one vote in the Senate. Because of Texas's size, the lawmakers stipulated that four more states could be carved out of its territory.

• **Alaska.** The vote of just one senator also approved "Seward's Folly," the 1867 deal by which Secretary of State William Seward purchased the vast territory of Alaska from Russia for over $7 million.

• **President Smith.** In a caucus, Kentucky Congressman Green Clay Smith was reportedly one vote shy of becoming Abraham Lincoln's running mate. Andrew Johnson got the nod and became president after Lincoln's death.

Republican presidential candidate George W. Bush addresses supporters during an August 2000 campaign rally.

2000: President-Elect Loses Popular Vote

A woman drops her vote into an early voting ballot box in 2004 in St. Petersburg, Florida. Most people who voted on that day said they waited in line about 90 minutes to vote.

THE STRANGE AND AMAZING DETAILS OF HOW GEORGE W. BUSH BECAME PRESIDENT

It wasn't the first time that the presidential candidate with the most popular votes lost the race. But the 2000 election may well go down in history as the most confusing and litigious presidential election ever.

It was a hard-fought campaign period between the Democrat Al Gore, then vice president, and the governor of Texas, Republican candidate George W. Bush. Early in the race, voters in several states made their intentions clear. As Election Day drew nearer, the candidates realized that their fate would be decided by a handful of "swing states" with undecided voters and many electoral votes up for grabs.

ELECTION NIGHT FIASCO

As in previous modern elections, Americans gathered around their TV sets to watch the election results come in. In their quest to have the best election-night ratings, the television networks were under pressure to keep the news coming fast—perhaps too fast. The networks' insistence on predicting winners well before the votes were counted resulted in embarrassing gaffes, with news anchors forced to retract their forecasts several times.

On November 7, 2000, at about 8 p.m. Eastern Standard Time, the major TV networks all predicted that Gore had won the vote in Florida, a key "swing state" with enough electoral votes to secure the election.

> TV networks proclaimed Gore the winner in Florida, but that's when things really got strange.

But these predictions were based on exit polls, not on actual votes. It quickly became clear the Florida vote was still "too close to call." Gore's predicted win was withdrawn by the news teams. That's when things got really strange.

At about 2:15 on the morning of November 8, John Ellis, a Fox News Network consultant in charge of predicting the election winners, made the decision to declare George W. Bush the winner in Florida—and indeed, the country. Ellis was none other than Bush's cousin. Minutes later, the other major networks followed suit, prompting Gore to telephone Bush and concede. At this point, all the votes in Florida had still not been counted—the country was tossing and turning on predictions.

While Bush privately celebrated and waited for Gore to publicly admit defeat, history took another turn. At 3 a.m., as Gore was in a car on the way to face the TV cameras, a member of his staff realized that Florida was *still* "too close to call." Gore turned his car around, called Bush back, and retracted his concession—it was perhaps one of the most unusual conversations ever had between two presidential candidates. This is how it was reported:

Bush: "Let me make sure I understand. You're calling me back to retract your concession?"

Gore: "You don't have to get snippy about this."

Bush then explained that his brother, Jeb Bush, then governor of Florida, had assured him of his Florida victory.

continued on page 106

Down to the Wire

The following election results prove that it doesn't take a landslide to win the presidency: each of these political nail-biters represents a victory won with less than a 5 percent difference in the popular vote.

	% POP. VOTE	ELEC. VOTE
1880		
James Garfield, R	50.0*	214
Winfield Hancock, D	50.0	115
1884		
Grover Cleveland, D	50.2	219
James Blaine, R,	49.9	182
1888		
Benjamin Harrison, R	51.7	233
Grover Cleveland, D	48.3	168
1892		
Grover Cleveland, D	51.7	277
Benjamin Harrison, R	48.3	145
1896		
William McKinley, R	52.2	271
William J. Bryan, D	47.8	176
1916		
Woodrow Wilson, D	51.6	277
Charles Hughes, R	48.4	254
1948		
Harry Truman, D	52.3	303
Thomas Dewey, R	47.7	189
1960		
John F. Kennedy, D	50.1	303
Richard M. Nixon, R	49.9	219
1968		
Richard M. Nixon, R	50.4	301
Hubert Humphrey, D	49.6	191
1976		
Jimmy Carter, D	51.1	297
Gerald Ford, R	48.9	240
2000		
George W. Bush, R	49.7	271
Albert A. Gore Jr., D	50.3	266
2004		
George W. Bush, R	51.2	286
John Kerry, D	48.8	252

*figures have been rounded to the nearest tenth of a percent.

Who's Chad?

Before 2000, most Americans just knew Chad as a country in Africa. But after the election, the word "chad" came to stand for much more.

Several counties in Florida used a manual voting system, in which voters used a small metal stylus to punch a rectangular hole on the ballot next to the name of their preferred candidate. The tiny bits of paper that fell from the ballot after they were punched were called "chads."

This type of voting had been used, without debate, in Florida for years. But some of the styluses were worn and unable to fully punch a hole in the ballot. Sometimes they just dented the ballot. The resulting bump was a "pregnant" or "dimpled" chad. On other ballots, the little piece of paper failed to disconnect. This was called a "hanging chad." These ballots were not tallied in the machine count. Lawyers in Florida debated whether these ballots could be counted as a vote in a manual recount. Different counties had different decisions on how to count the chads.

Gore: "Let me explain something. Your younger brother is not the ultimate authority on this."

By 4:15 a.m., all the TV networks had to, once again, take back their predictions. No one realized that it would take a full 35 days for America to know the election's true outcome.

On November 9, an exhaustive five-week period of recounts and lawsuits began. The Gore and Bush teams both sent cadres of lawyers to Florida to fight over the legality of the vote. More than a dozen legal actions were taken over the vote in Florida: the role of absentee ballots, incomplete ballots, ballot layouts, voter registration cards, and most unusually, the chads (left), all became supremely important.

THE FINAL RESULT

On December 12, 2000, the legal wrangling over the Florida vote came to an end when the United States Supreme Court halted a hand recount of the "undervotes" in Florida. ("Undervotes" were ballots that did not definitely show a vote for president and included some of the "dimpled chads.") Once this recount was halted, it effectively made George W. Bush the winner in Florida—by only 537 votes. The Florida vote was certified, and Bush was declared the winner of the state's 25 electoral votes.

In total, Gore had garnered 50,996,116 votes nationwide. Bush had fewer: 50,456,169. But Bush had a 271–267 edge over Gore in the Electoral College, where 270 votes are needed to claim the presidency.

Gore publicly conceded on December 13, 2000. First, he called Bush to congratulate him and lightheartedly promised "not to call him back this time."

In a televised speech, Gore declared he "strongly disagreed" with the Supreme Court's decision, but that he would accept "the finality of this outcome." In his public address, Bush said, "I am thankful for America and thankful that we are able to resolve our electoral differences in a peaceful way."

But the saga wasn't over yet.

THE CONGRESSIONAL CONFIRMATION

Following every presidential election, a joint congressional session is held to formalize the vote. Though it is official Congressional business, this formalization tends to be just that: a formality. But it wasn't that easy on January 6, 2001.

Gore presided over the joint session in his capacities as the current vice president and head of the Senate. Several members of the U.S. House of Representatives took to the podium to object to the election results, citing irregularities in Florida's voting procedures. But these protests were largely symbolic, as congressional rules required the objections to be signed by both a representative and a senator. No senator would join in. So in an ironic scene, Gore was required to one-by-one reject the representatives' objections and formally declare George W. Bush the winner of the 2000 election.

2004: Déjà Vu All Over Again
SWING STATES TAKE CENTER STAGE ONCE MORE

The 2000 election taught America many lessons. Among them, we invested millions of dollars in upgrading the country's voting machines. Though TV newsrooms still fight for ratings on election nights, they are less quick to predict winners. In the 2004 election, the phrase "too close to call" was heard over and over on the airwaves. But voters still worried that election could end as it had in 2000: with indecision.

The 2004 presidential race between George W. Bush and Senator John Kerry was just as close, and as bitterly fought, as the 2000 race. Once again "swing states"—Ohio, Pennsylvania, Michigan, and (yes, that one again) Florida—were seen as keys to winning the election. But this time, it was Ohio and its 20 electoral votes that turned out to be the race's battleground.

Late in the night on November 2, 2004, polling results were showing Bush with a marginal lead over Kerry in Ohio. But the Democrats wanted to wait to be sure. Voters across American held their breath as Kerry declared that he wanted all absentee ballots in Ohio counted before conceding defeat. But on November 3, 2004, it became clear that a win for Kerry in Ohio was impossible, so Kerry conceded.

George W. Bush was elected to his second term, leading a deeply divided country.

> Voters across America held their breath as Kerry declared that he wanted all absentee ballots in Ohio counted before conceding defeat.

Cleric Makes a Mint Off Cherry Tree Myth

**MASON LOCKE WEEMS'S TALE ABOUT
YOUNG WASHINGTON SELLS LIKE HOTCAKES**

"I cannot tell a lie," said little Georgie Washington. "I chopped down the cherry tree with my hatchet." Everyone knows the heartwarming tale, and most people know that it never happened. The story first appeared in 1806 in a book called *The Life and Memorable Actions of George Washington.*

The author, Mason Locke Weems, was an Episcopalian minister whose fiddle-playing, bawdy sense of humor, and opposition to slavery had cost him his church. He went on the road, becoming a popular guest preacher, book peddler, and writer. After a rousing sermon, he'd step from the pulpit to sell Bibles—he sold thousands along with his own moral tracts and inspirational biographies.

In 1800, Weems wrote his publisher that he had nearly finished a new book about Washington, "enlivened with anecdotes apropos, interesting and entertaining." The first editions sold like hotcakes. In 1806, the bestselling author added several "new and valuable anecdotes," among them the famous story of the cherry tree; he also doubled the price, to 50 cents a copy. The 82nd (and last) edition appeared in 1927.

A Most Unusual Independence Day

**TWO PRESIDENTS DIE WITHIN HOURS
OF EACH OTHER ON THE FOURTH OF JULY**

About 6 p.m. on July 4, 1826, John Adams, second president of the United States, died at the age of 90 at his home in Quincy, Massachusetts. His final words were, "Thomas Jefferson still survives."

Unknown to Adams (left), the 83-year-old Jefferson, the nation's third president, had died several hours earlier at Monticello. This was an astonishing coincidence because these two friends-turned-enemies-turned-friends again were the only signers of the Declaration of Independence to become presidents of the republic they had helped to forge, and both died on the 50th anniversary of America's independence.

That Jefferson should be on Adams's mind during his last moments was not surprising. Their lives had been intertwined ever since the days when they worked together to produce the historic document—Adams had suggested that Jefferson write the Declaration and then had defended it. Both men

BRIGHT IDEA

The Teddy Bear

While hunting on the Mississippi Delta in 1902, Teddy Roosevelt refused to shoot a bear that had been run down by hounds, knocked unconscious, and tied to a tree. In depicting the scene, cartoonist Clifford Berryman inadvertently spawned a sensation: the Teddy Bear. There are two versions of how the stuffed bears came to be sold. In one, Brooklyn storeowners Rose and Morris Michtom asked Roosevelt for permission to use his nickname, and he agreed. In the other, a German woman, Margarete Steiff, made a cute bear that was an instant international hit. In any case, the results were impressive: Between 1903 and 1911 millions were sold, and what began as a fad survives as a classic.

emerged from that experience with profound respect for each other. "Laboring always at the same oar we rode through the storm with heart and hand, and made a happy port," Jefferson (left) wrote to Adams.

But after independence was won, the two followed different political paths. For a while both served in the diplomatic corps, Adams as minister to England and Jefferson as envoy to France. When they returned, each was accused by the other's supporters of harboring unhealthy ties to the nation in which he had served. Jefferson was called a sympathizer of the French Revolutionists (he was in Paris when the Bastille was stormed), while Adams was accused of trying to impose a British-style monarchy on the United States. By the end of Washington's second term as president, Adams and Jefferson were the leaders of the two factions that would become the nation's first political parties.

The Jeffersonian Republicans, suspicious of big cities and banks, believed that America should look to its vast land resources for growth. Adams's Federalists, representing the emerging capitalist urban class, favored a strong central government.

In the election of 1796, these two candidates and philosophies clashed in what is still considered one of the most venomous campaigns in U.S. history. A blizzard of pamphlets castigated each man. The Federalists denounced Jefferson as a rabble-rousing atheist, a coward, and a tool of France, while the Republicans lambasted Adams as a monarchist and an enemy of liberty. When the dust finally settled, Adams had won by three electoral votes. Four years later, Jefferson ousted Adams by eight votes.

Dr. Benjamin Rush, a mutual friend and fellow signer of the Declaration of Independence, finally brought the two rivals together in 1811. Then began a voluminous correspondence, a rich exchange of letters that would continue the rest of their lives. "Refusing to be gladiators," one historian commented, "they conversed as sages."

TRUTH OR RUMOR?

Is it true that Sidney Poitier was the first African American invited to dine at the White House?

The African American who holds that honor is not Poitier (above). It's Booker T. Washington (below), who joined Theodore Roosevelt for

dinner in 1901. Washington knew that the move might be politically dangerous, but it was the first time that a black man had been asked to dine at the White House; the head of the Tuskegee Institute felt obliged to accept. Washington, often attacked for accommodating segregation, became a hero among blacks for his "courage" in accepting the invitation.

Although almost 200 years have passed since the historic day when Thomas Jefferson and John Adams went to their graves, the spirits of the two great men survive.

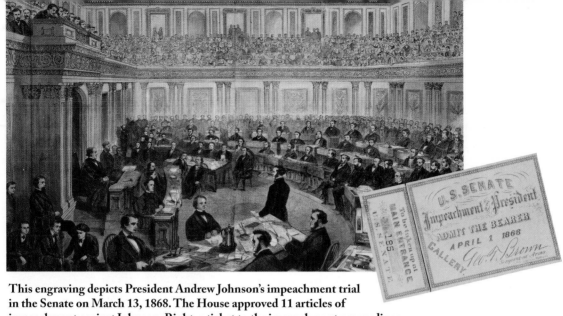

This engraving depicts President Andrew Johnson's impeachment trial in the Senate on March 13, 1868. The House approved 11 articles of impeachment against Johnson. Right, a ticket to the impeachment proceedings.

The Almost-Impeached President

ANDREW JOHNSON'S TURBULENT TENURE CLIMAXES IN TWO-MONTH TRIAL TO KICK HIM OUT

In 1824, 15-year-old Andrew Johnson and his brother ran away from the North Carolina tailor to whom they had been indentured in childhood as slavelike apprentices. The tailor posted a $10 reward for their return, warning "all persons against harboring or employing said apprentices." Johnson eventually fled to Tennessee and three years later opened his own tailor shop.

He soon married his 16-year-old sweetheart, Eliza McCardle. Unlike her husband, who could read only a few simple words, she had some education. Sitting by his side as he sewed, she shared it with him. He learned to read well, to write, and to figure. An exciting world was opened to him; he began to read voraciously and to involve himself in the issues of the day.

THE PROUD MECHANIC

The Age of the Common Man was rushing in, impelled by Andrew Jackson of Tennessee, and the young tailor rode its crest. Proudly labeling himself a "mechanic," or craftsman, he battled what he was later to call "an illegitimate, swaggering, bastard, scrub aristocracy," and rose from local to state office. In 1843 he went to Congress, where his speeches, according to *The New York Times*, "cut and slashed right and left, tore big wounds and left something behind to fester and remember."

Elected governor of Tennessee in 1853, he was soon the focal point of a number of issues that would lead to civil war. Once, after a placard was posted urging that "Andie Johnson" be shot on sight, some friends wanted to act as his bodyguards. Saying that he wanted "no man to be in the way of the bullet" meant for him, Johnson walked alone to the Capitol.

He carried a gun while running for reelection. At one point, in defiance of death threats, he put it on the rostrum at a meeting and said, "If any man has come here tonight for the purpose [of assassination] let him shoot." No one did.

TRAITOR TO THE SOUTH

"If Johnson were a snake," one Southern leader said, "he would hide himself in the grass and bite the heels of the children of rich people." He was a senator by then, fighting against the fast-growing secessionist movement. After Lincoln's inauguration in 1861,

Johnson hurriedly left for home, hoping to keep Tennessee in the Union.

In Liberty, Virginia, his train was boarded by an armed mob. "Are you Andy Johnson?" a man demanded. Johnson said he was. "Then I'm going to pull your nose!" the man said, reaching for that large, often caricatured feature. Drawing his pistol, Johnson protected his nose and cleared the car.

In Lynchburg, Virginia, he was dragged from the train, kicked, spit upon, and almost hanged. The angry mob finally let him go on the grounds that his fellow Tennesseans should not be denied the privilege of killing him.

Wearing his pistol, he stumped his home state. He was hanged and shot in effigy in Nashville, Knoxville, and Memphis, but the cool courage with which he argued his cause kept would-be attackers at bay. When Tennessee joined the Confederacy in June 1861, Johnson kept his Senate seat—and he was the only Southern senator to do so.

Appointed military governor of Tennessee by Lincoln in 1862, he persuaded the legislature to renounce secession and end slavery in the state. In 1864, because of Johnson's unique value as a loyal Southern Democrat, Lincoln chose him as his running mate on the National Union Ticket.

> In Lynchburg, Virginia, Johnson was dragged from the train, kicked, spit upon, and almost hanged.

ANDY THE SOT

Ill and exhausted on Inauguration Day in 1865, Johnson braced himself with brandy. Tipsy, he slurred his speech, and from then on the newspapers called him Andy the Sot.

Only 41 days later, on April 15, 1865, Lincoln was dead and Andy the Sot was president. Proposing to

The Affair that Sobered Washington

Clinton becomes only the second president to face impeachment

Just after noon on February 22, 1999, 100 United States senators stood poised to vote on whether to remove President Bill Clinton from office. The question was posed by Chief Justice William H. Rehnquist, who had presided over the 37-day trial in the Senate.

Clinton, the 42nd president and a Democrat, faced two impeachment counts resulting from his efforts to hide his affair with a young White House intern, Monica Lewinsky. The first count, perjury, was rejected by a vote of 55 to 45. (Ten Republicans broke ranks to join a solid block of Democrats who supported Clinton.) The second count, obstruction of justice, split the Senate 50 to 50 (only five Republicans broke ranks) and left Clinton in office. The Constitution requires a two-thirds majority of the Senate (67 votes) to remove the chief executive.

The Clinton trial tainted the president's considerable accomplishments and left the public exhausted. The sordid, 18-month-long story of the president's extramarital sex life had paralyzed Washington,

stymied the work of Congress, and made American voters more cynical than ever about politicians.

follow Lincoln's lenient Reconstruction policy, he supported amnesty for Southerners who would swear allegiance to the federal government and did not insist that the former rebel states give blacks the vote. Opposing Johnson in Congress were the Radical Republicans, who wanted to impose military rule on the South, enforce the black vote, and disenfranchise ex-rebels and confiscate their land. Johnson repeatedly vetoed such legislation. Calling him an "insolent, drunken brute," the radical press accused him of having plotted Lincoln's assassination.

THE IMPEACHMENT

Sweeping the congressional elections in 1866, the radicals gained the strength not only to override Johnson's vetoes, but to pass laws that limited his power. One of these, the Tenure of Office Act, forbade him to dismiss any official without prior Senate approval. Ignoring it, he proceeded to fire Secretary of War Edwin M. Stanton, replacing him with Ulysses S. Grant. But at the Senate's insistence, the office was restored to Stanton. When Johnson fired him a second time, the House voted 126 to 47 to impeach.

"Let them impeach and be damned," Johnson said. He did not attend the Senate trial, a sold-out, two-and-a-half-month show, presided over by Chief Justice Salmon P. Chase. The charges were flimsy (the Tenure of Office Act was later declared unconstitutional), and the conduct of the trial was scandalous. No Cabinet member was allowed to testify for Johnson, and the Senate overruled 17 of Chase's decisions to admit evidence on his behalf. The final vote was 35 to 19 for conviction, one short of the two-thirds needed, and Andy the Sot remained president of the United States.

Cloak-and-Dagger Government?

ROOSEVELT SPIES ON MEMBERS OF CONGRESS

In a controversy spawned by Capitol Hill rumors and political maneuvers, Washington in 1908 was alive with speculation that President Theodore Roosevelt had used the Secret Service to compile dossiers on the private lives of congressmen, and that he meant to use them. Congress was looking for a way to strike back.

The Secret Service, the Treasury Department's investigative branch, was at the core of the dispute. During his administration, Roosevelt had made liberal use of it in his anticorruption crusades. The Secret Service's defenders argued that, as the federal government's only corps of trained investigators, its survival was vital. Its detractors compared the service to Napoleon's secret police—perhaps inspired by the fact that Attorney General Charles Bonaparte was a great-nephew of Napoleon I. In a carefully worded bill, Congress moved to restrict the Secret Service's power. Roosevelt fought back with his major weapon: eloquence.

A WAR OF WORDS

In verbal and written attacks, legislators claimed that the president sought despotic powers and a secret police force. Roosevelt declared that he only wanted the tools to fight corruption, even if his inquiries brought him right up to the halls of Congress. Charges and countercharges in the press and on the Hill flew thick and fast. Finally, on January 8, 1909,

Congress officially defended its integrity. By an over-whelming vote of 212 to 36, the House tabled (that is, formally ignored) the section of Roosevelt's annual message that criticized the restriction of the Secret Service. Not since Andrew Jackson's administration in the 1830s had a chief executive suffered this insulting form of congressional rebuke.

In a way, both sides won. As a result of Roosevelt's maneuvering, a bureau of investigation (later called the FBI) was formed in the Justice Department. And Congress, sensitive to the slightest hint of domestic governmental spying, had sent a clear signal that such tactics would not be tolerated.

Goat Gland Brinkley's Run for Governor

A POLITICAL PATH PAVED WITH GONADS

The desperate times of the Great Depression gave rise to a new breed of populist politician, but none was stranger than John Romulus Brinkley, the so-called Goat Gland Doctor of Kansas. Brinkley—whose questionable medical certification came from several diploma mills, including the Eclectic Medical University in Kansas City, Missouri—had gained a considerable following in the 1920s, with his claims of sexual rejuvenation for aging or "tired" men. Brinkley's cure: A transplant of young buck goat sex glands into the gonads of human beings.

Brinkley owned a radio station, KFKB "Kansas First, Kansas Best," and used it to advertise his services. Men flocked to the Brinkley Gland Clinic in Milford, Kansas, where they paid a minimum of $750 for the surgery. By 1928, Goat Gland Brinkley was performing from 20 to 40 operations a week. He was reputed to be a millionaire, having implanted perhaps 5,000 pairs of goat glands.

Brinkley's activities also attracted the attention of the American Medical Association, which quickly branded him a "blatant quack of unsavory professional antecedents." In 1930, the Kansas medical board finally stripped him of his license. (A year later, the Federal Communications Commission shut down his radio station.)

Brinkley gained considerable following in the 1920s by transplanting goats' sex glands into humans' gonads.

To "avenge his reputation and save his business," Goat Gland Brinkley announced himself as a write-in candidate for governor in Kansas's 1930 election. His slogan: "Clean out, clean up and keep Kansas clean." The political joke proved to be a serious threat. He received one of the largest write-in votes in American history, finishing a close third in the race. Two years later he tried again, using his powerful, newly purchased radio station just over the Mexican border to blow his political horn. But the voters were unimpressed, and he lost to incumbent Alfred M. Landon, who would soon be a presidential candidate. On his third try, in 1934, Brinkley was trounced.

Brinkley turned again to the business of sexual rejuvenation, but this time without the use of goat glands. Establishing a practice in Del Rio, Texas, and another in Little Rock, Arkansas, he promised sexual restoration through prostate surgery and a cure-all made of a little hydrochloric acid and some blue dye. Over the years, his political views drifted far right to a growing fascist movement. By the late 1930s, lawsuits had stripped him of much of his wealth, and he died poor in 1942. Though only a minor political player, his nefarious medical career led to significant reforming legislation to protect patients.

President Warren Harding shakes hands with New York Yankees star Babe Ruth. Below: a photo of Harding as a dashing, 30-year-old senator.

Cronyism and Sex

REVELATIONS PRIVATE AND PRESIDENTIAL MARK HARDING ADMINISTRATION

Nominated by "men in a smoke-filled room," the handsome and popular Warren G. Harding was elected in 1920. By the time he died in 1923 amid rumors of suicide and murder, his administration had been "responsible in its short two years and five months for more concentrated robbery and rascality than any other in the whole history of the Federal Government," wrote a historian in 1931. His notorious love life also became grist for scandal mills.

POLITICAL CHICANERY

Easygoing and malleable, Harding hadn't wanted the presidency. Put up to running by his domineering wife and a political boss, he won by a wide margin.

Shortly after the inauguration, Secretary of the Interior Albert Fall leased naval oil reserves, including some in Teapot Dome, Wyoming, to business cronies, becoming some $300,000 richer in the process. When the deal was made public, Fall's leases were declared fraudulent, and he eventually went to jail. Others of the president's "Ohio gang" (he was from Marion, Ohio) also got rich through his freewheeling patronage.

In July 1923, on a trip west, Harding was diagnosed as having food poisoning, and then suffered a heart attack. He died on August 2. There was no autopsy, and many insiders came to believe the rumor that Mrs. Harding had poisoned her husband to save him from disgrace.

PERSONAL PECCADILLOS

A sensational book called *The President's Daughter* was published in 1927. In it, a woman named Nan Britton (right) told the story of her long love affair with Harding, and claimed that she had borne his only child. According to her tale, she fell in love with Harding at the age of 14 when he, then 45, was running for governor of Ohio. By 1917, Nan was in New York. Between their ensuing meetings in hotel rooms around the country, he wrote her love letters, all of which Britton claimed to have destroyed by agreement with Harding. She said he had destroyed her letters, too, but after his death Mrs. Harding burned most of his personal correspondence, and so the truth may never be known.

Harding's letters to Britton could yet turn up. Another cache of love letters turned up in the house of an elderly Ohio recluse named Carrie Phillips, the wife of one of Harding's best friends. They show that Carrie "was the love of Harding's life." Their torrid 10-year affair apparently began when the two couples toured Europe together in 1909. Between meetings, Harding wrote Mrs. Phillips sexually explicit, 40-page love letters and even verse, posthumously revealing an unexpectedly lyrical side of his personality.

Harding had many other affairs. He even maintained a room next to the Oval Office for quick liaisons and seemed to be insatiable. He was perhaps a victim of satyriasis, an excessive, unmanageable need for sex. The long, graphic love letters he wrote may have been another symptom of the disease.

At his death, Harding was still popular and respected. In the years that followed, however, his reputation was badly tarnished by scandals that continued to surface long after he was in his grave.

Imprudent Presidents

Love affairs ensnare chief executives in scandal

In 1884, during Grover Cleveland's first run for the presidency, it was revealed that he had fathered the child of a young widow who lived in Buffalo, New York. Determined to face the scandal head-on, Cleveland, then a bachelor, admitted paternity and went on to win the election. His honesty did much to extinguish the flame of scandal, despite a popular campaign chant that his detractors enjoyed: "Ma, Ma, where's my Pa? Gone to the White House, Ha, Ha, Ha!"

Years after his assassination, women came forward who claimed to have known John F. Kennedy intimately. The most sensational tale was that of actress Judith Campbell Exner, who readily detailed her two-year relationship with the chief executive. Records show that the FBI was onto their liaison, and that she was reputed to be the mistress of a Chicago crime boss as well. To many, it seemed inconceivable that one woman could have had simultaneous affairs with the president of the United States and a Mafia leader.

Actor William Campbell and his first wife, Judith Exner, at the premiere of the film, *To Hell and Back*.

The Filibuster Champ

**NEITHER PISTOLS NOR POISON
COULD STOP BOB LA FOLLETTE**

Filibustering—the parliamentary delaying tactic of refusing to give up the floor—has long been a favored weapon of stalwart congressional orators. One of the best was Robert La Follette Sr., who was a Wisconsin senator from 1905 to 1925. His feats of endurance provoked threats of violence and even attempted murder.

In a biography of her husband, Belle La Follette told how, during a record-breaking 1908 filibuster, he refreshed himself with occasional glasses of an eggnoglike concoction. One of these drinks was so bitter that he took one sip and then had it taken away. Analysis later showed that the beverage contained enough ptomaine bacteria to kill him.

He became ill but kept on talking and set a one-man filibuster record of 18 hours, 23 minutes. (His record held until 1953, when Senator Wayne Morse spoke for more than 22 hours. Then, in 1957, Senator Strom Thurmond set a new record of 24 hours, 18 minutes.)

Another filibuster, in 1917, brought La Follette dangerously close to a shootout with Kentucky

An early 1900s photo of Wisconsin Senator Robert La Follette Sr. in a rare quiet moment.

Senator Ollie James. An argument escalated to a confrontation between the two, both of whom were known to carry guns. La Follette's friend, Oregon Senator Harry Lane, armed himself with a sharp file, vowing to stab James if he moved toward his weapon. No gun was drawn. It was just as well, for La Follette's pistol, which he thought was in his traveling bag, had been surreptitiously removed by his son, the future Senator Robert La Follette Jr.

BRIGHT IDEA

"Mr. Rucevelt's" New Word List

Teddy Roosevelt was "surprized" at the ruckus "razed" in response to his 1906 order to the public printer. In it he listed 300 words that henceforth would be spelled according to the Simplified Spelling Board guidelines.

Funded by millionaire industrialist and philanthropist Andrew Carnegie, the organization crusaded for deleting the "u" in "honour" and "parlour," changes that eventually came into general usage. (More radical ideas, like "kist" for "kissed" and "tho" for "though" have not endured.)

Questioning the president's power to change American orthography, Congress instructed the printing office that all the material sent to its chambers contain standard spellings. Roosevelt regretfully withdrew his order in response to the general outcry.

America's Renaissance Man

THOMAS JEFFERSON: POLITICIAN, INVENTOR, ARCHITECT, AND MORE

At a White House dinner for Nobel Prize winners, John F. Kennedy called his guests "the most extraordinary collection of talents that has ever been gathered at the White House, with the possible exception of when Thomas Jefferson dined alone."

Among America's great statesmen, Jefferson stands out as a Renaissance man with an incredible range of interests, knowledge, and abilities. In the thick of politics for 40 years, he still found time for other pursuits, including farming, architecture, law, geography, botany, natural history, playing the violin, and enjoying fine food and wine. With an inquiring mind and an incisive intellect, he wrote prodigiously and insightfully about anything that interested him. His writings on agriculture alone fill a 704-page book. An avid reader, he amassed a personal library of 6,487 volumes that became the nucleus of the Library of Congress in 1815.

More than an armchair genius, Jefferson found practical application for his talents. A dedicated farmer, he was the first person in North America to raise tomatoes for food (they were considered poisonous), and his experiments with rice made the nation a leading producer of that crop. He also invented a new moldboard for the plow. Among his other inventions were a swivel chair, a pedometer to measure his walks, a chair that folded into a walking stick, a dumbwaiter, a revolving music stand, and a calendar clock. (So that others could have free use of his inventions, he patented nothing.) A talented architect, he adapted Roman classicism to native materials, developing a distinctive American style for the University of Virginia in Charlottesville. Not only did he design its buildings, he was also its general contractor, bookkeeper, overseer during construction, and landscape architect.

Perhaps Jefferson is best summed up in his own words: "Determine never to be idle. It is wonderful how much may be done if we are always doing."

Thomas Jefferson designed every detail of Monticello, his home in Virginia. An accomplished inventor, he improved the polygraph, a device with two simultaneously operated pens, so that he could make copies of his letters while he wrote them.

The Gettysburg Address

HAUNTING, MEMORABLE WORDS FROM AN AILING PRESIDENT IMPRESSED FEW ON THE DAY THEY WERE DELIVERED

"A few appropriate remarks" were requested of President Abraham Lincoln for the dedication of the cemetery on the Civil War battlefield in Pennsylvania, set for November 19, 1863. In fact, Lincoln was not the featured speaker. That honor went to the eminent orator Edward Everett, a Massachusetts clergyman, journalist, academician, and, later, a congressman and statesman. While Everett had been given two months to prepare his speech, Lincoln was not even invited to speak until two weeks before the event.

At intervals during a photographic session on November 15, he began making notes. On the 17th, the day before his departure for Gettysburg, he wrote his first draft on a sheet of White House stationery. During the train trip, the president gave his speech more thought, and on the eve of the ceremony he completed its final draft, adding another nine lines in pencil on a piece of lined foolscap.

True to form, the eloquent Everett delivered a dramatic two-hour oration. Lincoln, suffering from what was later diagnosed as smallpox, rose with his mismatched sheets in hand and in less than three minutes delivered a 10-sentence speech of some 270 words. A smattering of applause followed from an audience unsure that he was finished.

The press reaction was mixed. One paper wrote that "the cheeks of every American must tingle with shame as he reads the silly, flat and dishwatery utterances." But another accurately prophesied that "the dedicatory remarks of President Lincoln will live among the annals of man."

The FDR Dime

Today, polio is just one of several ailments against which American children must be immunized. But in 1921, when Franklin D. Roosevelt contracted polio, it inspired more fear than any other childhood disease.

Although 75 percent of polio victims were youngsters (hence the name "infantile paralysis"), FDR was 39 when polio struck him. At first, doctors thought he had a bad cold, then a spinal blood clot; finally, Roosevelt's high fever and paralyzed legs convinced his physicians that he had polio. Beyond the diagnosis, the medical men could do little—there was no cure.

Determined not to let his infirmity end his career, FDR exercised his upper body strenuously. His burly torso created such an air of well-being, in fact, that many people were unaware of the extent of his disabilities.

But if something happened to the braces and crutches that supported him when he stood, he was helpless. In 1936, when he was in Philadelphia accepting the nomination for a second presidential term, one of his braces snapped in front of the 100,000 people gathered at Franklin Field. Roosevelt fell forward, unable to move until a bodyguard righted him and refastened the support. "It was the most frightful five minutes of my life," he later admitted.

The only freedom the chief executive had from braces, canes, and crutches came when he swam; he was especially invigorated by the mineral waters at Warm Springs, Georgia. In 1926, wanting other polio victims to have the same opportunity, he donated a substantial portion of his personal wealth to establish a foundation at Warm Springs.

Despite his generosity, however, Warm Springs operated in the red. Various fundraising campaigns failed. In 1937, entertainer Eddie Cantor suggested a more effective approach: Why not ask everybody in

President Franklin Roosevelt (center left, with cane) and British Prime Minister Winston Churchill (center right) attend a Christmas service at Washington's Foundry Methodist Church on January 13, 1942. Eleanor Roosevelt is second from the left. Left: an FDR dime.

the country to send a dime for polio research to the president at the White House? Cantor even suggested a catchy name: the March of Dimes.

The response was overwhelming; sometimes as many as 150,000 dime-laden letters a day arrived at the White House. Beginning with that first campaign, contributions were used not only to pay for treatment of polio victims, but for the research necessary to triumph over the disease.

FDR didn't live to see the first polio vaccine. But he and the March of Dimes had become so closely identified that, after his death in 1945, Congress voted to honor his memory by depicting him on the coin. The first Roosevelt dimes were released on January 30, 1946, FDR's birthday and the annual kickoff of the March of Dimes appeal.

Millions of the Roosevelt coins had been contributed to the March of Dimes by April 12, 1955. On that day—exactly 10 years after Roosevelt died of a stroke at his cottage, the "Little White House," in his beloved Warm Springs—Dr. Jonas Salk's discovery of the first polio vaccine was announced.

Diamond Jim Brady at the racetrack in a 1915 photo. Opposite: Internet entrepreneur Marc Andreessen delivers a 2001 keynote address at the Oracle OpenWorld conference.

CHAPTER FOUR

From Rags to Riches

What's the American dream? To seek—and find—your own fortune. These pages chronicle bold, unbelievable tales of Americans who made millions by thinking and doing the unimaginable: Taking oil from deep in earth. Laying tracks from one end of the country to the other, for others to travel. Straightening curly hair. Developing portals that enable anyone sitting in front of a computer to find anything, anytime.

What do the eccentric rich do with their money? From banana-nut ice cream and diamond-encrusted bicycles to ornate funerals, you won't believe what they covet. Nor will you believe how easy it is for swindlers to separate fools from their money, and how quickly and easily some millionaires fall from great fortune to abject poverty.

The Business of Jamestown

AN AMERICAN PRINCESS GOES TO KING JAMES'S COURT TO RAISE MONEY

Jamestown, the first permanent English settlement in America, became a crown colony in 1624, but it didn't start out that way. The settlement was founded in 1607 as a business venture by the Virginia Company of London. The company's many investors—who were people from both upper and lower classes—pooled their shares in a common stock to finance the enterprise, hoping to reap profits from the abundant gold and silver the New World was expected to yield.

But the shareholders were soon disappointed. The gold and silver failed to materialize, and the small colony barely survived starvation, malaria, and Indian attacks. By 1616, the Virginia Company was in serious trouble, with no saleable products except cedar board for wainscoting and a small tobacco crop, which John Rolfe had begun cultivating just three years earlier. Stockholders abandoned the company in droves, leaving it on the verge of bankruptcy.

Casting about for a way to raise money, Jamestown's governor, Thomas Dale, hit upon a brilliant idea: The company would send Pocahontas across the Atlantic and have her presented at court. The 21-year-old Indian princess was already a celebrity in England, thanks to Captain John Smith, who had written of her admiringly. From the first, Pocahontas had seemed spellbound by the English colonists—she emulated them, learned their language, adopted their dress, converted to Christianity (taking the name Rebecca), married Rolfe, and bore him a

King James was impressed by the Indian girl; in his eyes, she was surrounded by a "divine aura," which was a sign of royal blood.

son, Thomas. She was the perfect model to show what the English could achieve in the New World.

In late June 1616, Pocahontas debarked at London, accompanied by her husband, her small son, and a retinue of 10 or 12 American Indians including her half-sister Matachanna (who served as the infant's nursemaid) and Matachanna's husband, Tomocomo, an agent for Powhatan.

John Smith, who was in England, wrote to Queen Anne, extolling the American princess and hinting that if she were not well received it would bode ill for the English overseas. Meanwhile, Pocahontas was fashionably outfitted and instructed in court deportment.

Finally, the poised princess was escorted to the palace and presented to Queen Anne and King James I. (Pocahontas's husband was excluded as a commoner—in fact, he was nearly imprisoned for his audacity in marrying royalty.)

King James was impressed by the Indian girl; in his eyes, she was surrounded by a "divine aura," which was a sign of royal blood. He asked his Privy Council to check whether her son might inherit America.

Pocahontas became the darling of the upper classes. When not being honored at some gala affair, she received such distinguished visitors as Sir Walter Raleigh and the poet and dramatist Ben Jonson. So successful was she in winning publicity for the Virginia Company that its management gave her a salary of £4 a week, although the sum strained its reserves.

Tomocomo, however, detested the English and their ways and made no bones about it. He wore his native dress—an ornamented breechcloth, a fur mantle, and face and body paint—and scorned the white men's food. Serving as eyes and ears for Powhatan, who had told him to count Englishmen in order to judge the threat they posed, he began by cutting notches in his staff, but quickly gave that up. Through an interpreter he argued religion with the bishop of London and other church officials, vigorously defending his own god. Before assemblies of scholars he discoursed about his homeland and social traditions and even demonstrated ritual songs and dances.

The fast pace and the damp London climate took their tolls on the Indians. Several died, and Pocahontas fell ill. On a foggy March day in 1617, she boarded a ship at Gravesend, at the mouth of the Thames, for the long voyage home. As it prepared to sail she quietly died, probably of pneumonia. She was buried in an unmarked spot beneath a church floor; her remains have never been found.

Pocahontas had done her job well. So many people wanted to go to the New World that the firm reorganized as a land company, giving each shareholder a 50-acre plot. In 1622, when the tobacco industry was flourishing and the Virginia Company was on the brink of prosperity, 347 colonists were

FUNNY FACT

Vandalia: The Colony that Never Was

In the late 1760s, Philadelphia merchant Samuel Wharton and a group of colonial businessmen sought reparations for their losses in the form of land grants from the Crown. Their consortium grew to become the Grand Ohio Company.

Officially, the company sought to create a 14th colony: Vandalia, in present-day West Virginia and Kentucky. In fact, the company was engaged in a spectacular land grab, in which its shareholders would own 20 million acres of prime frontier land.

Their scheme almost worked. The Crown approved the colony in the spring of 1775, but withheld the grant while quelling a seemingly minor disturbance caused by a few rebellious farmers at Lexington and Concord. No one involved in the deal realized that the American Revolution had begun.

killed in a massacre led by Pocahontas's uncle. Future plans were abandoned, and the king annulled the company charter.

Making Money in Maine

IN THE END, TABER BILLS WERE NO MORE VALUABLE THAN MONOPOLY BUCKS

Who hasn't dreamed of printing his or her own money? In 1804, the dream became a reality—then a nightmare—for merchant John Taber.

Taber lived in Portland, Maine, and ran a successful import-export business. Maine, which was then part of Massachusetts, was suffering a severe currency shortage because a state law forbade banks from issuing paper currency in denominations lower than $5. To help alleviate the shortage, John Taber & Son decided to use the equity of the firm to back its own notes in denominations of $1, $2, $3, and $4. The firm's reputation was so solid that the Taber

bills became popular currency in Portland. But when Congress declared a trade embargo in 1807 during the struggle between England and France, it caused many shipping businesses to fail. Among them was John Taber & Son. Taber's son, Daniel, added to the problem: Whenever he wanted extra money, he had signed a new lot of bills (without his father's knowledge and without gold reserves to back it up). Unable to redeem the bills, the company was ruined.

Later, John Taber went to collect a debt from a former associate. When the man paid him in Taber bills, Taber protested that it was now worthless. His ex-partner replied, "That is not my fault. Thee ought to have made it better."

Brown Gold

MOUNTAIN MEN RISK THEIR LIVES IN FUR TRADE

Jim Bridger (right) was only 18 in 1822, when he was recruited by Ashley Expeditions to search the wilds for furs. Jedediah Smith was only 23. But they both were to become the most celebrated of that dauntless and hardy breed called "mountain men." Along with Hugh Glass, John Colter, Joe Walker, and others, they opened the West, blazing trails through wilderness, finding passes over mountain ranges, and seeing fresh the wonders of the continent.

But they were no mere adventurers. They were in business—the fur business—and they endured hardship and risked their lives for their trade. They dealt in "brown gold," or beaver pelts, to satisfy the vogue for beaver top hats back east and in Europe. In 1826, when William H. Ashley, founder of the Rocky Mountain Fur Company, retired with his gains of $80,000, Smith and two other mountain men, David Jackson and William Sublette, bought him out.

Seasoned and savvy, the trio led the search for new trapping lands. Smith and a party of two blazed a trail across the Sierra Nevada and became the first Americans to reach California, then part of Mexico, by an overland route. They gave the British-owned Hudson's Bay Company and the American Fur Company, which was owned by the ruthless John Jacob Astor, some stiff competition. After four years, they were satisfied with their earnings, and Smith and his partners sold their company to Jim Bridger and four others in 1830. Smith retired to St. Louis; the following year, he was killed by Comanches on the Santa Fe Trail.

Astor's American Fur Company waged an all-out war to destroy the enterprise with bribes, threats, and shipments of liquor to ply the Indians. The mountain men finally sold out to Astor; in 1836, the Rocky Mountain Fur Company was dissolved. During its 14 years in business, the company had sent its home base in St. Louis about 1,000 packs of beaver pelts, netting $500,000 at a cost of 100 lives. Bridger, who was only 37 when he sold the business, went on to become a legendary guide and an army scout. Forced into retirement in 1867 by arthritis and failing eyesight, he died in Missouri in 1881.

FUNNY FACT

Samuel Colt Didn't Even Own One of His Own Revolvers

Though Samuel Colt's six-shooter saw initial success after he patented the weapon in 1836 at the age of 22, sales soon languished and the factory closed. When, 10 years later, the secretary of war ordered 1,000 revolvers for America's war with Mexico, Colt couldn't find one of his own guns to use as a prototype! The weapon maker asked a New York gunsmith, Orison Blunt, to make him another prototype; this version of the weapon incorporated suggestions made by Texas Ranger Sam Walker.

National Debt? $0.

FOR THE FIRST (AND ONLY) TIME IN U.S. HISTORY, AMERICA'S BUDGET WAS IN THE BLACK

Enriched by the sale of public lands and revenue from the Tariff of 1833, which taxed imported goods, the federal government managed to pay off its debt completely—making the United States the only major nation in modern history to accomplish this extraordinary feat. In January 1835, the national debt was a big, round zero.

During the boom years from 1835 to 1837, the government found itself in the embarrassing position of running a substantial surplus. Unable to spend it fast enough, Congress, in 1836, decided to turn over the riches—some $28 million—to the states. Most of the money went to railroad, highway, and canal construction, stimulating an economy already overheated by cheap money, easy credit, and a speculative exuberance. In the meantime, Congress did little to interfere. Indeed, many members were only too happy to join the speculators who were buying up thousands of acres of western land.

Alas, the wheel of prosperity turned all too quickly. As President Andrew Jackson watched the nation's acreage being converted to bank notes, he became increasingly concerned. Jackson had always distrusted paper currency. Toward the end of his presidency he issued a directive that only gold and silver coinage, or notes backed by gold or silver, could be used to buy federal lands.

Jackson's aim was to cool the engines of speculation; instead, he brought the economy to a crashing halt as investors raced to withdraw their funds from banks. In the ensuing financial panic, hundreds of banks and businesses went broke, and the United States suffered its worst depression to date. By 1838 America had rejoined the ranks of debtor nations.

Building Boys Up

19TH-CENTURY AUTHOR AND CHILD ABUSER TRIES TO REPENT THROUGH PHILANTHROPY

The bulk of Horatio Alger's 100-plus mass-market novels, including *Ragged Dick*, tell of poverty-stricken young boys rising up to achieve great wealth by working hard and being virtuous. But earlier in his life, the author sexually molested several Cape Cod boys. He spent the rest of his life trying to atone for his sins.

A Harvard Divinity School graduate, Alger seemed to embody all that was good. In 1864, at the age of 30, he became minister of a small parish in Brewster, Massachusetts.

But the town's gossips soon started asking questions: Why wasn't the bachelor clergyman interested in the congregation's single women? Why did he devote so much time and energy to young boys?

When a boy in the parish reported that he had been sexually molested by the minister, Alger did not deny the charges. He immediately resigned and left town.

Consumed by shame, he devoted his life to the betterment of impoverished boys. Settling in New York City in 1866, he became associated with Charles Loring Brace and the Newsboys' Lodging House, a shelter for street kids. He was also involved in the Fresh Air Fund, which took underprivileged children to the country for two weeks, and continues to do so to this day. And he gave most of the royalties of his works to disadvantaged young men.

President Franklin Roosevelt (center) visits with Chinese statesman Chiang Kai-Shek (left) and British Prime Minister Winston Churchill (right) in 1943.

"I Have a China History"

MUCH OF FDR'S INHERITANCE CAME FROM SMUGGLED DRUGS

"I do not pretend to justify the prosecution of the opium trade in a moral and philanthropic point of view," wrote Warren Delano, Franklin Delano Roosevelt's grandfather, in a letter home from China, "but as a merchant I insist that it has been a fair, honorable and legitimate trade; and to say the worst of it, liable to no further or weightier objections than is the importation of wines, Brandies & spirits into the U. States, England, &c."

THE CHINA TRADE

Only 24 years old when he arrived in China in 1833, Delano soon became the head of Russell & Company, the biggest American trading firm there. He was directly involved in what was euphemistically called the China trade. Bringing Chinese tea, silk, and porcelain to the West was an important part of that trade, but the most lucrative part was smuggling opium into China from India and Turkey.

Between 1821 and 1839, the opium trade rose from 5,000 chests per year (each weighing 133.5 pounds) to 30,000 chests, paid for by 100 million ounces of Chinese silver. Called "foreign mud" by Chinese officials, who were powerless to stop its spread, the drug had created more than two million Chinese addicts by 1835.

DELANO'S FIRST MILLION

In 1839, the emperor named a new and incorruptible high commissioner of Canton, who tried to end the opium trade. The first of a series of Opium Wars broke out between China and British traders. Delano's boat, flying a flag of truce, was ambushed from shore, and Delano was briefly held prisoner.

Undeterred, he and other Yankee traders enthusiastically resumed the opium trade at the end of the war in 1842. Delano did so well that he sailed home that autumn, married, and returned with his bride to China, where he stayed for three more years. Then he retired to New York and invested in western railroads. Delano's daughter, Sara, who was the future mother of President Roosevelt, was born in 1854.

Warren Delano was a millionaire by 1857, but his fortune was wiped out overnight in that year's financial panic. Not one to be defeated easily, he returned to the Orient and reentered the China trade; within five years he made a second fortune, again from the opium trade.

THE HERITAGE

How much FDR knew about his grandfather's career as an opium smuggler is a mystery. But the president did acquire from him a feeling of kinship for China. "You know, I have a China history," Roosevelt once told General Joe Stilwell, who was in command of U.S. forces in China during World War II. "My grandfather went out there … he made a million dollars; and when he came back he put it into western railroads. And in 8 years he lost every dollar. Then … he went out again and … made another million."

BRIGHT IDEA

Monopoly

Monopoly is probably the best known, most popular board game of all time—but there's a great deal of dispute over how the game actually came about. The "official" story is that unemployed salesman Charles Darrow sketched the original version on a piece of oilcloth and sold the game's rights to Parker Brothers in 1935.

Another version of Monopoly's history says Elizabeth J. Magie patented, in 1904, a game called The Landlord Game, to portray the evils of real estate monopolies. Then, in 1929, a teacher in the Atlantic City Friends School introduced the game (which by then went by the name "Monopoly") to her colleagues and students. They gave the spaces familiar Atlantic City place names, assigned property values, and painted the playing board as it is known today.

A visitor took the game back to Philadelphia and introduced it to a Quaker hotel manager named Charles Todd, who in turn introduced the game to Darrow. "He asked me to write up the rules and make him some copies and copy the game board for him," says Todd. Todd pointed out that, in copying the game for Darrow, he had misspelled "Marven Gardens" as "Marvin Gardens." The spelling error still persists.

J. P. Morgan Bails America Out of Bankruptcy

FINANCIER SAVES THE DAY WHEN USA ALMOST GOES BROKE

In January 1895, a crisis at the U.S. Treasury threatened to make American currency worthless.

A severe depression stifled the economy. Large financial institutions, fearing that paper money would be devalued, were nervously cashing in their greenback dollars for Treasury gold. Gold reserves were draining out at the rate of $3 million a day. Experts, especially those who supported the gold standard, feared that public confidence in paper money would collapse, and greenbacks would become worthless. Desperately, the government needed to replenish the gold supply—but how?

For political reasons, President Grover Cleveland wanted Congress to take the initiative with a bill authorizing a public sale of bonds, the money to be used to buy gold. Financier John Pierpont Morgan was certain the scheme would lead to disaster. Not only was there too little time, but the announcement of the sale acknowledging the Treasury's weakness would in itself cause a rush to cash in greenbacks.

On the morning of February 5, Morgan met with the president, who was still committed to the idea of a congressionally mandated public bond sale. Around noon, they received a report that the New York subtreasury had only $9 million in gold left. Morgan personally knew a man who might present more than $10 million in drafts that very afternoon. Collapse could be only hours away.

Morgan presented a workable solution. A forgotten Civil War law existed that allowed the Treasury to buy gold coins directly with bonds. This law gave Cleveland the authorized bonds he wanted, while at the same time allowing him to sell them privately and quickly to Morgan's syndicate without a public announcement.

There remained one problem: Morgan must guarantee that large financial institutions would stop cashing in greenbacks for the very gold that the scheme would provide. It was an astounding request: The president was asking Morgan to control the entire international financial community and to ensure its support of American paper money. Fully realizing the difficult manipulations that this would require, Morgan gave the president a promise that no one else could have made, and he kept it. The gold was delivered to the Treasury, and the gold drain was stopped. For all his efforts, Morgan's company made less than 1 percent profit on the deal.

"You've Got to Look Like Money"

DIAMONDS WERE ALWAYS JIM BRADY'S BEST FRIEND

Jim Brady bought his first diamond—a one-carat sparkler for his little finger—in 1879, when he was 23. It cost $90, nearly half of his savings; he blew the rest on clothes. He'd just landed a job selling railroad supplies, and he knew that impressions were important. "If you're going to make money, you've got to look like money" was his credo.

Diamond jewelry was common among traveling salesmen; it impressed clients and hotel clerks. But Brady made the gems his trademark. He won them in card games, bought them in pawnshops, and traded for them. Soon he was called "Diamond Jim." He even gave away sparklers to special customers; skeptics were silenced when he scratched his name on the nearest window.

Real wealth began when Brady became the exclusive agent for a steel undercarriage for railroad cars, then built mostly of wood. Eventually he introduced steel cars and formed his own company.

By the time he turned 32, Brady was a celebrity. He reveled in the role. He was a regular at Harry Hill's, a night spot frequented by

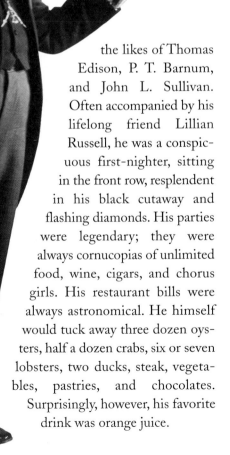

Brady owned a set of diamonds for each day of the month, complete with stickpin, shirt studs, cuff links, vest buttons, and belt buckle.

the likes of Thomas Edison, P. T. Barnum, and John L. Sullivan. Often accompanied by his lifelong friend Lillian Russell, he was a conspicuous first-nighter, sitting in the front row, resplendent in his black cutaway and flashing diamonds. His parties were legendary; they were always cornucopias of unlimited food, wine, cigars, and chorus girls. His restaurant bills were always astronomical. He himself would tuck away three dozen oysters, half a dozen crabs, six or seven lobsters, two ducks, steak, vegetables, pastries, and chocolates. Surprisingly, however, his favorite drink was orange juice.

Brady was the first to be seen in a horseless carriage in New York, streaking down Madison Avenue at 11 miles an hour. When bicycles became fashionable, he ordered several gold-plated editions with silver-plated spokes.

For Lillian Russell he had a special cycle made, complete with diamond chips, gemstones, and mother-of-pearl handlebars. When they went cycling, traffic halted and throngs gathered; the police had to clear their way.

In 1912, Brady underwent a risky operation for kidney stones. Doctors found that his stomach was six times the normal size. During his recovery, the ever-generous "Diamond Jim" presented the nurses (all 50 of them) with two-carat diamond rings. When he died in 1917, crowds gathered at his house on East 86th Street to pay their last respects. He lay in his coffin, decked out in diamonds. And they fought to get into the chapel for his funeral. Most attendees, from the famous folk on down to newsboys, wept openly.

"The Goose That Lays the Golden Eggs"

ANDREW CARNEGIE BUILDS HIS OWN FORTUNE BY INVESTING OTHERS' MONEY

Andrew Carnegie was regarded as a brilliant and aggressive steel magnate and was one of the nation's great success stories. But long before he earned millions in metals, he made his first fortune through investments—and he never used a penny of his own.

The poverty-stricken Carnegie family came to America from Scotland in 1848, and 12-year-old Carnegie took a factory job for $1.20 a week. Four years later, when he was earning $4 a week as a telegrapher, Tom Scott of the Pennsylvania Railroad hired him as his personal secretary. Carnegie idolized Scott, and the ambitious youngster became Scott's apprentice in the rapidly growing business. Scott taught Carnegie more than railroads; he introduced him to the wonders of investment.

The first lesson came in 1856. "Fortunatus knocked at our door," Carnegie later wrote. "Mr. Scott … asked me if I had $500 to make an investment for me. Five hundred cents was much nearer my capital." Scott advised him to buy 10 shares in the Adams Express Company, about which the older man had inside information. (At that time, trading on the basis of inside information was a common—and still legal—practice.)

Curiously, Carnegie later wrote that his mother had borrowed the $500 from his uncle, but his own papers contain an IOU to Scott, who clearly lent the

Scottish industralist Andrew Carnegie emigrated to Pittsburgh in 1848 and went on to become one of the richest men in America. Over the course of his life, the tycoon donated over $350 million to charities and libraries.

young man the funds himself. Nearly six months later, when the note came due, Carnegie had saved $200 and borrowed the rest from another man, offering his Adams shares as security. Thus began Carnegie's method of using dividends from stock to make payments against loans; when the loans were paid off, the dividends were his. This was a system he would use repeatedly to build his assets and income without having to invest his own capital.

The cunning Carnegie went on to amass a staggering fortune in the steel business. (J. P. Morgan once called him "the richest man in the world.") But for the rest of his life, Carnegie would recall vividly the envelope that contained his first monthly dividend of $10. "It gave me the first penny of revenue from capital—something that I had not worked for with the sweat of my brow. 'Eureka!' I cried. 'Here's the goose that lays the golden eggs.'"

Carnegie's "Daughter"

A sweet-talking swindler bilks banks of millions

Elizabeth "Cassie" Bigley was born beautiful but not rich. To remedy this oversight, she took up the art of the con, first passing herself off as an heiress in Toronto, then as Mme. Lydia De Vere, Clairvoyant, in Toledo. In that guise, she persuaded one gentleman to obtain $10,000 in cash for her forged notes and wound up in jail for her trouble. In 1893, she was pardoned by Governor William McKinley.

Settling in Cleveland, she met Dr. Leroy Chadwick in a bordello. They married and soon became one of the city's most celebrated couples. Their large, ornate home bespoke Cassie Chadwick's fondness for spending lots of money and so did their lavish entertaining and extravagant gifts. To support this lifestyle, she pulled her biggest con yet: She persuaded bankers that she was Andrew Carnegie's illegitimate daughter.

Clever and convincing, she once took some Ohio lawyers to Carnegie's New York mansion.

Asking them to wait in the carriage, she entered the mansion, talked to the maid, then left, waving a friendly farewell. Once outside, she showed the lawyers notes for almost $1 million signed "Andrew Carnegie." The signatures were impressive, but bogus. In another scam, Chadwick claimed that Carnegie had given her $7 million in securities and got a bank receipt for the tidy sum; the securities, of course, were more of her artful forgeries.

Using the credit inspired by her receipt and the Carnegie name, Chadwick continued to litter banks with forged paper, managing to spend about $1 million a year. Finally one lender sued, and when Carnegie disavowed any knowledge of this supposed daughter, the banks immediately panicked. One

Cassie Chadwick loved to spend money, and the hoax that allowed her to indulge her luxurious ways—she claimed to be Andrew Carnegie's illegitimate daughter—lasted seven years. When the steel magnate publicly stated that he did "not know Mrs. Chadwick," her glittering world crumbled.

banker, having lent Chadwick four times his institution's entire capitalization and quite a bit of his own money, begged her for repayment. When she refused, he fainted.

Chadwick was later arrested and tried. Despite her powers of persuasion, she couldn't con her way out of prison, where she died, penniless, at age 48 in 1907.

Black Gold, Pennsylvania Tea

**DRAKE WAS THE FIRST TO STRIKE OIL
COMMERCIALLY, BUT HE DIDN'T STRIKE IT RICH**

"I bot by Townsend's advice without investigating," Edwin Laurentine Drake reminisced, "and a few months afterwards when I did try to investigate I made up my mind my friend had pulled me in, in trying to get out himself."

Drake, who had retired as a railroad conductor in 1858 because of his bad back, lived with his wife and child at the Tontine Hotel in New Haven, Connecticut. Money was scarce, so he couldn't help but be interested when a fellow boarder named James Townsend talked about the potential commercial value of Seneca oil. Native Americans had long used the stuff found in creeks and salt wells to soothe aching joints. Townsend thought it might sell as a substitute for whale oil in lamps, or even as a lubricant. The problem was that no one had yet found a way to extract large quantities of it from the ground.

It so happened that Townsend, a bank president, was one of three New Englanders—the others were Dr. Francis Brewer and lawyer George Bissell— who had formed the Seneca Oil Company and bought a tract of 100 acres on the aptly named Oil Creek, near Titusville in western Pennsylvania. They needed a "general agent" for their wild venture. Who better than Drake, an innocent who resembled a deacon with his black clothes, dark beard, and sorrowful eyes?

Drake was made president of the company, awarded a huge block of stock (which he was quickly relieved of), and promised a year's salary of $1,000 for operating expenses. He was also gulled into sinking his entire savings—all $200—into the project. Drake and his family took the train to Titusville.

Having no idea how to get oil out of the ground, he employed men for a dollar a day to dig with picks and shovels. They failed, and so he turned to drilling. Keeping precise records of his expenses, he bought

When Edwin L. Drake arrived in Titusville in 1858 to raise oil from the ground, local people felt sorry for him. They wondered how such a nice fellow could have been so badly gulled by the "fancy stock company." Several years later the unlikely hero of the oil industry revisited the well that changed their lives. In the background is the derrick he built.

lumber to build a derrick, and a $500 nautical engine for power. Searching for a dependable helper, he met and hired "Uncle Billy" Smith, a blacksmith with salt-boring experience.

By the spring of 1859, the directors had lost interest in the project. But Drake doggedly persisted. Thwarted by sand and clay clogging the drill hole, he had a brainstorm: He would drive pipe down to bedrock to form a shaft for the drill. Drake's brilliant innovation made oil wells possible, but it never occurred to him to patent it. On August 28, 1859, he saw something glistening in the hole, almost 70 feet down.

"What's that?" Drake asked. "That is your fortune," replied Uncle Billy. Soon gushing oil filled all the barrels they could find. Drake had drilled the world's first commercial oil well.

Overnight, Titusville became a boomtown; Brewer, Bissell, and Townsend scrambled to buy up all the shares of Seneca Oil. All the men, except Drake, were on their way to becoming millionaires. Inept in money matters, Drake hung around for four years as an agent and justice of the peace. He saved a measly $16,000. Then he lost it all speculating on Wall Street.

Years later, when Drake and his family were found living in destitution, the state of Pennsylvania granted him an annual $1,500 pension. After his death in 1880, the citizens of Titusville erected a monument to honor him as the man who launched the oil industry.

IMPROBABLE PIONEER

"Tol" Barret: The First Texas Oilman

Most people in Melrose, Texas, thought the land around Oil Springs was worthless. But not storekeeper Lyne Taliaferro "Tol" Barret; in 1859, he leased 279 acres there.

Had he been able to get the right machinery then, Barret would have drilled the first producing oil well in America. But the Civil War intervened, and it was 1866 before he got started. Just as he struck oil 106 feet underground, the price of crude dropped sharply because of conditions during Reconstruction.

His savings gone, Barret abandoned his oil field and returned to the store. Before he died in 1913, there had been so much drilling at Oil Springs that he could no longer locate the site of his original well.

The Day Spindletop Roared

NO ONE COULD STOP A MILLION BARRELS OF OIL FROM SPEWING FROM THE EARTH

Back in 1900, the modest lumber and rice marketing town of Beaumont, Texas, wasn't a very exciting place. The youngsters were thrilled when their Sunday school teacher, Pattillo Higgins, took them out to Spindletop, a knoll south of town named for a cone-shaped tree. They delighted in the eerie way the natural gas burned when Higgins poked a small hole in the ground and lit a match.

Higgins, a brickmaker and real estate promoter, had a passion for geology. He was sure that where there was gas, there was oil. The adults of Beaumont scoffed, especially after four shallow wells were drilled on Spindletop without success.

Anthony F. Lucas, an Austrian-born mining engineer, shared Higgins's view. Answering the promoter's ad in a trade journal, Lucas leased land for exploration and got the backing of banker Andrew Mellon and two Pittsburgh oilmen. The investors hired brothers Al, Jim, and Curt Hamill, all of whom had drilled at Corsicana, the first major oil field in Texas. The Hamill brothers started drilling in October, but it was slow going for them. First they hit quicksand, then rock. But they worked around the clock, stopping only for a Christmas break.

They'd gone down 1,020 feet on January 10, 1901, when the drill stuck. They pulled it out, replaced the bit, and began to lower it. Suddenly mud started boiling up from the hole, pushing the drill pipe with it. Then, with an explosive roar, mud and debris shot into the air, followed by a geyser of oil more than twice the height of the derrick. The men, backing off in alarm, were drenched.

People could hear the explosion for miles. Awestruck farmers rushed to the scene. No one in America had ever seen such a gusher before. Oil spewed out at a record 80,000 barrels a day. Fire was a deadly threat, but no one knew how to stop the flow. The well roared and gushed for nine days, hurling

Visiting Spindletop in 1901, a Standard Oil official shrugged: "Too big, too big; more oil here than will supply the world for the next century—not for us!" But the age of liquid fuel soon ensued.

nearly a million barrels of crude into the air, before the Hamills devised a way to cap it. Fashioning a T-shaped pipe fitted with valves, they risked their lives against the tremendous power that steadily burst from the earth and screwed the device to the drill pipe.

Spindletop was transformed. A forest of oil derricks sprouted near the first well, so dense that their supports overlapped. An acre of land sold for $1 million. Shantytowns sprang up, including Gladys City, named for one of Higgins's young pupils. Wildcatters lured by the boom lived in tents or rented pool tables or barber chairs for the night. Saloons, gambling parlors, and brothels prospered—but so did crime. Con men sold so much worthless stock that the hill became known as Swindletop.

Overproduction quickly drove oil prices down to three cents a barrel, while a scarcer commodity, water, cost $6 a barrel. Spindletop's boom was over by 1903, but it sure knighted the first of many Texas millionaires.

Famous Achievement, Infamous Scandal

THE "UNMITIGATED FRAUDS" THAT BUILT THE CROSS-COUNTRY RAILROAD

One of America's greatest achievements—building a railroad system that stretches from coast to coast—was also one of our greatest scandals.

The owners of the Central Pacific and the Union Pacific railroads had devised a clever scheme to reap enormous profits. They created their own construction companies and charged the railroads exorbitant rates to lay tracks. Thus they made money two ways: by pocketing the extra fees and by inflating the price of the railroads' stock with padded holdings.

The Central Pacific's owners, including the well-known Charles Crocker and Collis P. Huntington, set up a construction arm called the Contract and Finance Company. Similarly, the Union Pacific, headed by Thomas C. Durant and Oakes Ames, created the Crédit Mobilier of America construction

Laborers lay rails for Union Pacific Railroad in 1866. On average, workers could lay about two miles of track per day.

company. The Central Pacific, building eastward from Sacramento, California, completed 742 miles at an expense of about $120 million (actual cost: some $58 million). The Union Pacific, building westward from Omaha, Nebraska, paid $94 million for 1,038 miles of track (actual cost: only about $50 million).

To ensure the success of the scheme, the plotters bribed congressmen and government officials, including future President James Garfield and Speaker of the House Schuyler Colfax. Almost $500,000 went for that purpose, including 343 shares of railroad stock.

Scandal erupted after a series of articles in the *New York Sun*, beginning in September 1872, revealed that the owners of Crédit Mobilier held more than 367,000 shares of Union Pacific stock that had not

cost them a cent. Congress created the Poland Committee to investigate, but many of the central figures could not be identified. Moreover, so convoluted and secretive were their dealings that the investigators were unable to sort what had really happened.

A few ringleaders, principally U.S. Representative Oakes Ames, were censured. Congress enacted legislation in 1873 directing the attorney general to sue Union Pacific stockholders for illegal profits from contracts the owners had made with themselves.

The Supreme Court ruled on the suit in 1878, saying that "more unmitigated frauds were never perpetrated on a helpless corporation by its managing directors." But, it further stated, since "the government has received all the advantages for which it has bargained," it could collect nothing.

A Reluctant Rider on the Money Train

VANDERBILT *HATED* RAILROADS—THAT IS, UNTIL HE MADE A MINT OFF OF THEM

When Cornelius Vanderbilt died on January 4, 1877, at the age of 83, he was probably the richest man in the world. He left an estate of some $104 million— $2 million more than the entire U.S. Treasury. About

90 percent of his fortune came from railroads, though he hated railroads and refused to have anything to do with them until the last 15 years of his life.

His antipathy dated from November 1833, when he was a passenger, along with former President John Quincy Adams, on the Camden and Amboy

Railroad. The train, bound for Perth Amboy, New Jersey, broke an axle and jumped the track, killing two people. It was the first fatal train wreck in U.S. history, and it critically injured Vanderbilt.

Not until the railroad boom of the 1860s did the lure of high profits help Vanderbilt surmount his deep aversion to trains. He was worth about $11 million by then, most of it earned from his large fleet of steamships. He reasoned that if he could control the railroads, he would be able to extend his freight-carrying capacity from the coastal docks into the heart of the country.

First, he secretly bought the New York & Harlem Railroad, which ran 52 miles from 42nd Street in Manhattan to Brewster, New York. The stock cost him $9 per share; it soon reached $50, earning millions. His acquisition of a Broadway streetcar franchise, extending his rail service all the way down to the Battery seaport, made the Harlem stock even more valuable.

Vanderbilt's injury in an 1833 train wreck caused him to despise railroads for much of his life.

Vanderbilt's rivals tried to have the streetcar franchise annulled while they sold Harlem stock short, but the shrewd commodore bought up all the available Harlem stock until it was cornered.

EXPANDING THE TRANSPORT EMPIRE

Now fully launched, Vanderbilt began to expand his empire. He acquired the Hudson River Railroad, which ran parallel to his own Harlem line but continued on to Albany. He then set his sights on the New York Central, which ran from Albany to Buffalo, and in less than a year he had amassed a controlling interest of $2.5 million in shares.

Vanderbilt was dissatisfied, however, with the comparatively small amount of freight that was being transferred from the Central to his southbound Hudson River line, which turned over most of its westbound freight to the Central. That winter—he waited until midwinter, when boats could not ply the frozen Hudson River—Vanderbilt informed the Central's management that the Hudson would no longer accept its freight. In addition, he directed his trains to stop some two miles short of a bridge near Albany, forcing the Central's passengers to make the connection on foot. The railroad's stock plummeted, and Vanderbilt snatched up the shares—about $6 million worth.

Vanderbilt merged the Central and Hudson lines, thinking that the move would make both more valuable. Yet, much to his disgust, freight rates were on the decline. He tried to get the Pennsylvania and the Erie lines to agree on higher rates; but the Erie blocked his every move to establish connections to the Midwest. Vanderbilt attempted an age-old solution: buy out your rival.

The Erie was not easily bought. It was run by a trio of unscrupulous rascals: Daniel Drew, Jim Fisk, and Jay Gould. As fast as Vanderbilt could buy Erie stock, they kept selling. They converted Erie bonds into stock, sometimes illegally; and when an old printing press was found, they churned out some 100,000 counterfeit shares to sell him. The four-year war of the Erie reached its turning point in 1868.

The enraged Vanderbilt called on one of his "tame" New York State judges to order the arrest of Drew, Fisk, and Gould. But they had been warned. Hurriedly gathering all incriminating evidence and $6 million in illegal profits, the trio fled to New Jersey.

This defeat was one of the darkest occasions in Vanderbilt's life. His opponents had cheated him—worse, they had outwitted him! Their dispute almost plunged the railroad industry into financial disaster. Vanderbilt relented, however, and agreed to settle.

Vanderbilt emerged triumphant in 1875. After conquering the Lake Shore & Michigan Southern, the Canada Southern, and the Michigan Central railroads, he was finally able to link them with the New York Central line, thus creating one of the world's greatest systems of rail transport, stretching all the way from the eastern seaboard to the industrial heart of the country.

Frederick Burr Opper's lithograph shows Cornelius Vanderbilt, Jay Gould, Russell Sage, and Cyrus W. Field carving the United States into a railroad monopoly.

Thank Jay Gould, It's Black Friday

Stock-exchange traders keep a close eye on the ticker tape following the October 1929 Wall Street crash.

A 19TH-CENTURY MONEY SCHEME OF RUINOUS PROPORTIONS

Modern stockbrokers and speculators still shudder at the thought of Black Tuesday: October 29, 1929, when the market's spectacular nose-dive set off the Great Depression. That's how their great-grandfathers felt about Black Friday—September 24, 1869, when a scheme to corner the nation's gold market brought about a near-ruinous collapse.

The mastermind of the 1869 plan was the brilliant and cagey Jay Gould, recently victorious against Commodore Cornelius Vanderbilt in the fight for control of the Erie Railroad. Gould's gold-market plan hinged on the fact that gold was always in demand; businessmen needed it to conduct foreign trade. If Gould could corner the market, the needs of international merchants would drive the price of gold upward. And since there was only some $15 million to $20 million in gold in New York, a corner seemed easy if the U.S. Treasury's holdings of $80 million could be kept off the market.

Inside connections were vital to the plan, so Gould contacted Abel Corbin, brother-in-law of President Ulysses S. Grant; Corbin often bragged of his influence with the president. Gould had Corbin arrange for Daniel Butterfield to be appointed assistant U.S. treasurer in New York. He even met with the president, to convince him that a higher gold price would avert a national currency crisis. But Grant, a "sound money man," was noncommittal.

> In the ensuing pandemonium some brokers fainted, others were taken to hospitals, and one, Solomon Mahler, committed suicide.

The scheme went into full swing that September, with Gould buying gold contracts secretly, through various brokers. And to secure the alliances of his henchmen, he also bought millions in gold contracts for them without demanding payment.

But rumors about Gould's gold corner soon leaked out, and a counterattack to force the price down stalled the market. Gould enlisted the help of Jim Fisk, an old cohort who had previously backed out of the scheme. Fisk was to openly purchase gold, building confidence and driving up the price. He complied, loudly predicting that gold would soon hit $200 per ounce. His ruse worked, and the price of gold climbed steadily.

But Gould had stacked the deck: While Fisk bought furiously at ever-inflated prices, Gould secretly sold through dozens of brokers. Gold finally reached $162 per ounce, and that's when the secretary of the treasury put $4 million in government gold on the market. Gold quickly fell to $133. Black Friday had come.

In the ensuing pandemonium some brokers fainted, others were taken to hospitals, and one, Solomon Mahler, committed suicide. Fisk saved himself from financial ruin by repudiating his contracts. Gould had "tame" judges issue injunctions halting the payoffs of various financing agreements.

Estimates of Gould's profits ranged from $11 million to $40 million—some claimed that he later shared the bonanza with Fisk.

continued on page 138

A Chronology of America's Biggest Financial Panics

1819 A sudden drop in cotton prices bursts a speculative bubble. As a result, banks fold, Western real estate depreciates, and credit tightens.

1857 Financial panic is set off by several factors, including a drop in food prices, the failure of the Ohio Life Insurance and Trust Company, and the loss of $2 million in gold when the uninsured ship *Central America* sinks on its way from California.

1873 A financial crisis in Europe results in the withdrawal of investments in the United States, the failure of a prominent banking house, and the closing of some 100 banks.

1893 U.S. gold reserves fall below a safe minimum. The securities on the New York Stock Exchange fall to their lowest point ever. Some 600 banks close.

1907 A run on New York's Knickerbocker Trust Company forces the bank to close its doors. Other banks follow suit. J. P. Morgan intercedes.

1929 Following an alarming decline in stock prices beginning on October 21, the market collapses on October 29. It triggers a 10-year depression, the worst in the country's history.

1987 On October 19, an apparently healthy market plummets. By the end of the day, the stock market has lost $500 billion in value.

The Tax Bite: Feeling the Pain

Paying taxes was an American tradition long before 1914, when the grueling spring ritual of federal income tax filings began. Here are the words of some noteworthy Americans on the topic.

"Nothing in this world is certain but death and taxes."
—*Benjamin Franklin*

"Taxes are what we pay for a civilized society."
—*Oliver Wendell Holmes*

"What is the difference between a taxidermist and a tax collector? The taxidermist takes only your skin."
—*Mark Twain*

"Anybody has the right to evade taxes if he can get away with it. No citizen has a moral obligation to assist in maintaining the government. If Congress insists on making stupid mistakes and passing foolish tax laws, millionaires should not be condemned if they take advantage of them."
—*J. P. Morgan*

"The income tax has made more liars out of the American people than golf has."
—*Will Rogers*

"The hardest thing in the world to understand is the income tax."
—*Albert Einstein*

Black Tuesday

THE GREATEST STOCK MARKET CRASH IN HISTORY USHERS IN THE GREAT DEPRESSION

More than 16 million shares of stock were sold, and about $15 billion was lost in the greatest crash in New York Stock Exchange history, on Black Tuesday, October 29, 1929.

The crash capped a two-month decline in stock prices and came only days after a steep slide on October 24. At the market's low point in mid-November, the value of stocks listed on the Exchange had fallen by some $30 billion.

Black Tuesday by itself did not cause the Great Depression that followed, but because the economy was already shaky, the crash opened the door to a national catastrophe. Contributing factors were years of overproduction in industry and agriculture, plus easy credit that allowed many consumers, investors, and businesses to pile up excessive debt.

At first, business, finance, and government leaders generally downplayed the event, as did most newspapers. Industrialist Andrew

In February 1936, a group of transient men is directed onto a train leaving Los Angeles. The men had arrived in California by hiding in the freight cars.

Mellon saw "nothing in the present situation that is either menacing or warrants pessimism." President Herbert Hoover loudly proclaimed that "the fundamental business of the country is sound." A headline in *The Wall Street Journal* of October 30, 1929, sounded equally reassuring: "Stocks Steady After Decline: Spokesman Expresses View Hysteria Is Passing."

The show-business periodical *Variety* put it differently: "Wall St. Lays an Egg." Within months of the crash, thousands of businesses were crippled or bankrupt, banks had failed, and unemployment had spread like wildfire.

Black Monday

IN 1987, STOCKS FALL 508 POINTS *IN ONE DAY*

Monday, October 19, 1987, was not a good day on the New York Stock Exchange. When the closing bell rang at 4 p.m., a record 604 million shares had been traded, nearly all at a loss. The panic had been aggravated by something called program trading—huge blocks of stocks bought and sold by computers as the market fell. After months of scoring one new high after another, the Dow Jones Industrial Average was hit by a loss of 508 points, the largest one-day decline in its history.

Not since the crash of 1929, which kicked off the Great Depression, had the future seemed so bleak. In just seven hours, on what would become known as Black Monday, stock prices had plunged a sickening 22.6 percent. Stock Exchange chairman John Phelan called it "the nearest thing to a financial meltdown I ever want to see."

Tuesday started out even worse. So many sell orders flooded the exchange that trading in some securities came to a halt. Nobody wanted to buy. Banks refused to extend short-term credit, thus drying up potential funds. Relief came from the Federal Reserve Board in Washington, D.C., which acted to flood the market with sorely needed dollars. Corporations began to buy back their own stocks. By the end of that "Terrible Tuesday," the Dow index had risen more than 100 points. Wednesday's rally was even more robust—a record gain of 187 points.

The market did recover, but the panic sent a clear message that ballooning federal and trade deficits had put the nation's economy on shaky ground. By week's end, Wall Street had returned to business as usual.

> In just seven hours, on what became known as Black Monday, stock prices had plunged a sickening 22.6 percent.

The Ice King Cometh

**FREDERIC TUDOR MAKES A COOL
FORTUNE REFRESHING HOT CLIMES**

Ice was unknown in the Caribbean until 1806, the year in which a 22-year-old Bostonian named Frederic Tudor took a boatload of it to Martinique. Insulated with hay, it didn't melt on the way, as laughing skeptics had predicted. Tudor persuaded the owner of the Tivoli Garden to let him make ice cream. The man had never heard of the stuff, but after selling $300 worth in one night, he clamored for more, but there was no more. The young entrepreneur had failed to provide insulated storage, and his exotic cargo dissolved at the docks.

Nine years passed before Tudor brought ice to the tropics again; personal debts and the War of 1812 had prevented him. Tudor's next trip was to Havana—and this time he brought enough lumber to build an icehouse. He earned a tidy sum. "Drink, Spaniards, and be cool," he wrote in his Ice House Diary, "that I, who have suffered so much in the cause, may be able to go home and keep myself warm." He returned by way of Martinique, where he obtained a 10-year monopoly on ice.

By the 1820s, Tudor also had icehouses in Charleston and New Orleans. He invented the refrigerating jar, a precursor of the Thermos, and his agents gave them to bartenders—they even gave away free ice until the public was hooked on it. One happy result was the frosted mint julep: Without plenty of Yankee ice, the quintessential southern drink could never have been born.

As Tudor developed better ways to store ice, his business became an international one. In 1833, his ship docked in Calcutta, India, after a four-month voyage. Almost two-thirds of its 180-ton cargo of ice was intact.

The Ice King lived to be 80. The business he founded flourished for another quarter of a century, managed by one of his sons, until manufactured ice made it obsolete.

The Paperback Shopping Mall

**HOW THE MONTGOMERY WARD CATALOG
TURNED MIDDLE AMERICA UPSIDE DOWN**

As a salesman traveling through the South in 1870, Aaron Montgomery Ward saw how local merchants exploited rural people by selling their wares at heavily marked-up prices. If he could pay cash for goods in large quantities, he could sell them for much less.

Ward's first one-page mailing listed 163 items, but his business boomed so rapidly that he was, before long, sending out bound catalogs. In 1875, Chicago-based Montgomery Ward was the first company to offer its customers a money-back guarantee—a revolutionary move at a time when the warning, "Let the buyer beware," was customary. Because of federal weight restrictions on packages, the company had to be resourceful: Heavy coats, for example, were shipped in two halves, with a needle and thread included, so that they could be sewn back together.

Ward's customers often requested products that the catalog just didn't sell: Hundreds of letters came from men seeking wives; some wanted this or that model featured in the catalog's pages. Others asked for summer boarders, good lawyers, and babies to adopt. Other correspondents wanted marital advice.

Occasionally the company tried retail areas beyond its capabilities. It marketed a stylish automobile called the Modoc, but the venture failed because no one had foreseen the need to have Modoc dealers and service garages.

When Rural Free Delivery was initiated, brick-and-mortar merchants—who were angry because customers would no longer need to come to town to pick up their mail—staged catalog-burnings in the town squares, to no avail. Over the years Montgomery Ward & Co. grew from its small mail-order origins into a chain of hundreds of retail stores. The story of Rudolph the Red-nosed Reindeer originated as a Ward's sales promotion. The company discontinued the catalog in 1985.

Paging Dr. Kellogg

THE IDEA FOR HIS WHEAT FLAKE CEREAL CAME TO HIM IN A DREAM

When young John Harvey Kellogg attended the Bellevue Hospital Medical College in New York, he sustained himself on breakfasts of seven Graham crackers, supplemented by an occasional coconut, potato, or bowl of oatmeal. He'd been sent to medical school by the Western Health Reform Institute of Battle Creek, Michigan, a retreat whose founder, Ellen G. White, followed literally the advice of Genesis: "Behold, I have given you every herb-bearing seed … to you it shall be for meat."

Offering only the blandest of foods—largely whole-grain cereals without flavoring—and no entertainment, the institute had difficulty competing with more posh spas. It needed, at the very least, a staff physician.

EARLY EFFORTS

Medical degree in hand, Kellogg returned in 1876 to take his place as the institute's medical superintendent. Renaming it the Medical and Surgical Sanitarium, he introduced such amenities as wheelchair socials and string orchestra concerts.

The spa expanded and thrived. Remembering his difficulty in maintaining "dietary correctness" in New York, Kellogg set to work developing a precooked, ready-to-eat health food, which he called "Granula." In 1881, after finding that the name had already been used by James C. Jackson of Dansville, New York (who sued Kellogg), the doctor renamed his product "Granola."

By then he had married Ella Eaton, a fellow dietary activist, and had hired his younger brother, William K. Kellogg, as an assistant. Together, they ran the Sanitas Food Company and the Sanitas Nut Food Company. These tiny concerns produced not only health foods, but also such exercise equipment as muscle beaters and flesh brushes.

BROKEN TEETH AND INSPIRATION

Kellogg's biggest breakthrough came as a result of an old lady's false teeth: She broke them on some zwieback he had prescribed, and she sued, collecting $10 from him. He began to think about softer, ready-cooked food. Then he was awakened one night in the midst of what he would later call "a most important dream … a way to make flaked foods. The next morning I boiled some wheat, and, while it was soft, I ran it through a machine Mrs. Kellogg had for rolling dough out thin. This made the wheat into thin films, and I scraped it off with a case knife and baked it in the oven."

These first wheat flakes were christened Granose. Distribution was limited, for Kellogg was adamantly noncommercial, and he guarded his secrets. But potential profits were great, and dozens of imitators flocked to Battle Creek to produce their own nutritious brands. One of Kellogg's patients, C. W. Post, created thicker flakes with crispy bubbles, which he called Elijah's Manna. The biblical name created a storm of protest among religious groups, so he renamed the cereal Post Toasties. He was a millionaire within seven years.

When, after decades of working on the sidelines, William Kellogg bought his brother's cornflake company, he leaped on the commercial bandwagon. "The Genuine Bears This Signature—W. K. Kellogg," read the legend on each box of cereal he sold.

TRUTH OR RUMOR?

Is it true that the inventor of Hershey's chocolate made the product by accident?

No. Milton Hershey began his fortune by producing caramels—he only made chocolate novelties on the side. But it wasn't long before he decided to concentrate on chocolate. Why? It would retain the impression of his name in hot weather, which caramel would not.

In 1893, inspired by Swiss milk chocolate bars, he hit on the idea of mass-producing a five-cent bar from his own recipe, using fresh milk. The Hershey Bar was an instant success, as was his 1907 creation, the Hershey Kiss.

Obsessing Over Every Stride, Pattern, and Gesture

FREDERICK TAYLOR'S SYSTEMS STILL RULE THE LIVES OF TODAY'S WORKERS

As giant factories revolutionized American industry during the late 1800s, work patterns also drastically changed. Much of this was due to the obsessive, controlling personality of Frederick W. Taylor, nicknamed the Father of Scientific Management.

Taylor was born in Philadelphia in 1856. As a boy, he tested various strides when walking, to see which one yielded the greatest distance with the least effort. Other children disliked playing with him, because his games were more efficient than fun. Before a party, he made lists of pretty and plain girls so that he could spend equal time with those in each category. As an adult, he continued to live by a rigidly precise pattern of counted steps and measured gestures. Neither a smoker nor a drinker, he worked compulsively and slept little.

He became a pattern maker and machinist at the Midvale Steel Company, but soon rose in station by imposing his precision on others. Studying time and motion, he defined strict work standards.

Taylor's rules were ruthlessly enforced. There were fines for broken parts (which in one case amounted to more than two months' pay), carelessness, tardiness, and unexplained absences. Some workers resisted by staging slowdowns, sabotaging equipment, and even threatening physical violence.

By the time Taylor published *The Principles of Scientific Management* in 1911, his methods had been instituted in several major factories. Even the Bolshevik leader V. I. Lenin was a strong advocate of the system. Perhaps only Taylor could have thrived for long under his own regimen.

The Tale of the 20-Mule Team

DEATH VALLEY TREKS BROUGHT SUCCESS OVER THE LONG HAUL FOR "BORAX" SMITH

F. M. Smith quit seeking gold in 1872, when he found huge deposits of white crystalline "cottonballs" in the Nevada desert. The stuff was valuable and he knew it. Soon he monopolized the borax mineral bonanza, earning the nickname "Borax" Smith.

Eight years later, a chance encounter abruptly changed the scenario. Aaron Winters had spent most of his 60 years prospecting for gold. But his efforts never panned out, and by 1880 he was resigned to spending his twilight years with his wife in a shack just east of California's Death Valley. Then an itinerant prospector told Winters how folks in Nevada were making a fortune from borax, and described how you test it to tell it apart from salt. Winters suppressed his excitement. So that was the white stuff littering acres of Death Valley!

Winters and his wife set out to test the powder—it *was* borax. But reality set in. Death Valley was one hell of a place to make your fortune—it was 130°F in the shade some days, and there was no water. Winters

> To monopolize the bonanza, Smith bought out rivals and held others off at gunpoint.

knew he'd never be able to haul the borax across 165 miles of desert to the nearest railroad junction. When San Francisco entrepreneur William Coleman offered him $20,000 for discovery rights, he took it.

Coleman had carried cargo with multiple mule teams before, so one of his superintendents suggested they hitch a pair of teams to two wagons at a time. The wagons Coleman designed, with rear wheels seven feet in diameter, could haul 36.5 tons not only of borax but enough water, food, and fodder to supply the crew and 20 animals for the duration of a 10-day trek.

So successful were these spectacular desert freight trains that the product became known as 20-mule-team borax. But because of the great new supply, prices plummeted. Coleman went broke in 1890. Who bought him out? None other than "Borax" Smith, the fellow who had first found the stuff 20 years earlier. Adopting the 20-mule-team name as a trademark, Smith promoted borax into a household panacea for aiding digestion, softening water, keeping milk sweet, and curing epilepsy and bunions.

Make a Million, Bet a Million

FOR JOHN GATES, A DOLLAR EARNED WAS A DOLLAR THAT MUST BE GAMBLED

John W. "Bet-a-Million" Gates loved to gamble on everything. He earned his nickname by plunking down $1 million on a horse at the Saratoga racetrack. They wouldn't take the bet.

It was the love of taking chances that earned him millions. An Illinois country boy with a high-school education, he had saved enough money at 19 to buy a half-share in a small hardware store. In 1874, that same year, he gambled on a new invention called barbed wire. Maneuvering a partnership with a manufacturer, Gates took to the road selling the product. To convince skeptical Texans, he built a barbed-wire corral in a San Antonio plaza and penned up 30 snorting longhorns for an afternoon. Before long, Gates owned the American Steel and Wire Company, the nation's largest such business. Described by his secretary as "a great boy with an extraordinary money sense annexed," Gates outraged Wall Street financiers with his ability to best them. When J. P. Morgan sought the Louisville & Nashville Railroad, Gates grabbed control of the line and made Morgan pay through the nose. But the day came when Gates's luck ran out, and he went begging to Morgan. Morgan told him to get out.

His finances still somewhat shaky, Gates went to Texas in 1901, right after Spindletop, one of the great gushers in petroleum history, had been struck. Gambling again, he formed an oil company on the spot. In a few years, he had at least $50 million. In 1911, "Bet-a-Million" sent Morgan a copy of his firm's financial statement, just to rub it in. He died later that year.

TRUTH OR RUMOR?

Is it true that someone once bilked P. T. Barnum, the showman who said, "There's a sucker born every minute," of millions?

Sort of. In 1855, in what became known as the Jerome Clock Company episode, one of the nation's largest clock businesses asked Barnum to lend them $110,000. In return, the company would relocate to East Bridgeport, Connecticut—a community that Barnum and investor William H. Noble had founded four years earlier. In so doing, Barnum would help save the jobs of the company's 700 employees.

Over several months, Barnum endorsed a series of $3,000, $5,000, and $10,000 notes. The repayment periods were to range from 5 to 60 days, but he left the dates blank to ease transactions.

When the banks began to refuse his notes, Barnum discovered that the clock company had dated them as long as two years into the future, while taking new paper from Barnum. They had taken the showman for about half a million dollars. Barnum liquidated assets to pay off most of his debts and began rebuilding his fortune.

A Banker with a Heart

BANK OF AMERICA FOUNDER CHANGES THE COUNTRY'S TRUST IN, AND USE OF, COMMERCIAL BANKS

Amadeo Peter Giannini was a banker who disliked banks. To him, the world's most precious commodity was not money but people. Though he cared little for riches, he created one of America's most powerful financial institutions. Today it is known as the Bank of America.

Giannini's impeccable business sense was recognized very early by his stepfather, for whom he worked in a produce market in San Francisco. He became a full partner in the business at age 19. The tireless young Giannini invested in real estate, and at the age of 31 he announced his retirement. He explained that the $250 a month he earned on his investments was enough for him and his family to live on. "I don't want to be rich," he stated. "No man actually owns a fortune; it owns him."

His "retirement" ended a year later, in 1902, when he was made a director of a small bank in San Francisco's Italian North Beach neighborhood. Banking interested him, but he disliked its practices; they ignored the needs of the common man. In 1904, Giannini organized his own bank called the Bank of Italy. Made up of small shareholders, it would change banking practices in America.

Giannini did what was then unheard of for a banker: He solicited business. Through advertisements and personal persuasion, he convinced people that their money was safer in his bank than hidden under mattresses. He then recycled this newfound capital back into the community by giving small loans to individuals with only their wages as collateral. Recognizing that local banks could distribute capital more efficiently, he pioneered the idea of branch banking.

When the great earthquake of 1906 struck San Francisco, Giannini quickly removed all of the bank's cash (about $2 million) and hid it. The day after the disaster, his was the only institution open for business, dispensing loans over a wooden plank. Giannini foresaw the crash of 1907, when unbridled financial speculation ruined many banks, and hoarded gold. He stacked the gold in his tellers' windows in plain sight; it was a display of confidence that convinced customers that their money was safe with him.

By the time he retired in 1934, Giannini had built the world's largest commercial bank, with more than $5 billion in assets. Yet he remained true to his principles about personal wealth: Upon his death in 1949, his estate was no larger than it had been in 1904. By the end of the 20th century, Bank of America was the country's number-two bank (behind Citigroup), with assets of $572 billion.

The Spruce Goose, an eight-engine plywood flying boat designed by Hughes, cost $18 million to build. With Hughes at the controls, it flew for just one mile, skimming the water, in 1947.

The Inmate Who Owned the Asylum

BILLIONAIRE HOWARD HUGHES LIVES HIS LAST DAYS ALWAYS NAKED, EATING BASKIN-ROBBINS

In the 1930s and 1940s, Howard Robard Hughes cut a dashing figure as a white-scarfed aviator, a tuxedoed film producer escorting a screen goddess, and an aggressive industrialist. But in his private life, Howard Hughes was a man sick with phobias, living in his own personal hell.

Born in Texas in 1905, Hughes was the son of a rich industrialist and an obsessive mother. His mother dosed him with mineral oil and kept him from playing with other children, lest he be exposed to germs. She died when he was 16; his father died two years later.

In 1924, the young man became head of the Hughes Tool Company. He proved to be a very able businessman—some said a genius. But Hughes grew restless and went to Hollywood to produce movies. Among his best efforts were *Scarface*, with Paul Muni, and *Hell's Angels*, which was Jean Harlow's big break. In 1941, Hughes produced *The Outlaw*, starring the buxom Jane Russell, for whom he designed a clever push-up bra.

In the meantime, Hughes, who loved flying, formed the Hughes Aircraft Company and test-piloted his own planes. By 1938 he was a national hero, having set three world speed records. He also crashed several times; his injuries resulted in lifelong pain and a dependence on codeine.

After a series of mental breakdowns in the 1950s, the public idol insulated himself from the world and conducted all his business through intermediaries. Most of his staff were Mormons, whom Hughes considered pure of body and spirit. Visitors had to perform bizarre cleansing procedures and wear white cotton gloves. He himself dispensed with clothes for sanitary reasons.

In his later years, the recluse became an inmate in his own asylum (a Las Vegas hotel that he bought so he wouldn't have to move), his every whim catered to. Lying naked in a darkened penthouse, Hughes watched old movies around the clock. When he complained that a local TV station didn't show late-night movies, his aides arranged to buy it. When he developed a passion for Baskin-Robbins banana-nut ice cream, a flavor that was about to be discontinued, they special-ordered 350 gallons of it. Undernourished, the six-foot four-inch Texan weighed scarcely 90 pounds when he died at the age of 70. Fittingly, death came to him aboard an airplane.

The Witch of Wall Street

THOUGH SHE HAD RICHES APLENTY, HETTY GREEN WAS STILL A RAG-WEARING CHEAPSKATE

Hetty Green could read the newspaper's financial pages by the age of six. In 1864, at the age of 30, she inherited her father's million-dollar fortune and began trading on Wall Street with a bold audacity that became legendary. She bought Civil War bonds when others spurned them, and they paid off. Green made ailing businesses profitable by driving stocks up and down. But it was her personal style as much as her skill against such fierce competitors as Jay Gould that earned her the title "the Witch of Wall Street."

While her peers lived in opulence, Green lived like a pauper. She worked alone on the floor of a bank where she had coerced free space, and for lunch she'd pull a ham sandwich from her grubby pocket.

She married so that her inheritance would go to her children rather than to other relatives. But the children, Ned and Sylvia, were subjected to her brutal thrift. They ate and traveled as cheaply as possible, shuttling to and from dingy hotels to avoid paying property taxes. When Ned was injured in a sledding accident, Green took him to a charity ward, but she was recognized and charged. Refusing to pay, she treated the wound herself. It festered, and Ned's leg later had to be amputated.

Hetty Green died in 1916 of a stroke suffered while arguing with a maid over the price of milk. She left her children about $50 million each.

Hetty Green was a well-known figure on Wall Street. She always wore the same black dress and, to save the cost of soap, she seldom washed it. Her petticoat's pockets bulged with stocks, bonds, and wads of cash.

Nobody's Baby

THE TALE OF A SILVER QUEEN WHO ENDED HER DAYS IN SQUALOR

Among America's most poignant and scandalous love stories is that of Horace Tabor and Elizabeth Bonduel McCourt Doe (known as Baby Doe), who met in Leadville, Colorado, in 1880.

Tabor, who was 50 years old at the time, was a prominent silver king and the state's lieutenant governor. While he enjoyed his newfound wealth and position, Augusta, his wife of some 20 years, remained haunted by past poverty and nagged him constantly about money.

LOVE STRIKES

Then Baby Doe, a young divorcée, came to town. Five feet two inches tall with eyes of blue, a head full of golden curls, and a curvaceous figure, she was an eyeful and a charmer. Tabor fell wildly in love; he secretly divorced Augusta in Durango, a remote Colorado town. In September 1882, Tabor and Baby Doe were clandestinely married in St. Louis.

On March 1, 1883, they were remarried by a priest in Washington, D.C., where Tabor was serving as an interim U.S. senator. A week before the ceremony, Tabor wrote to his "Darling Babe": "I love you to death and we will be so happy. Nothing shall mar our happiness for you are all my very own and I am yours from hair to toes and back again. I love you I love you Kiss Kiss for ever and ever."

SNOBBERY AND SCANDAL

Government wives shunned the wedding, described as "picturesquely vulgar," but many notables attended, among them

President Chester A. Arthur. The national attention that the event received stirred up plenty of gossip, and before long, news of the Tabors' St. Louis marriage surfaced. The priest was outraged by the deception. The public relished one delicious revelation after another, including the juicy news of the illegal Durango divorce.

The Tabors returned to Denver. Snubbed by society, they lived in ostentatious style until 1893, the year Tabor's financial empire collapsed, and the one-time gentleman went back to pushing a slag-heap wheelbarrow. Political friends had him appointed postmaster of Denver—he worked in a building located on land that he had once given to the city. To everyone's surprise, Baby Doe stuck with him.

Tabor died in 1899, leaving his wife an unintentionally cruel legacy. "Hold on to the Matchless," he had advised her, referring to a once-great Leadville mine that he still owned. Baby Doe obediently took her two daughters to Leadville. When they finally left her—one to renounce the family forever and the other to die in a Chicago slum—she became a recluse, living in a shack near the defunct Matchless Mine, which she claimed was "her mission and her life." For 35 years she struggled in poverty, working the mine by day and tormented at night by visions of her beloved Tabor, her daughters, the devil, and Jesus Christ.

On March 7, 1935, after a three-day blizzard, her frozen body was found on the floor of the shack, her arms outstretched in the form of a cross. Baby Doe Tabor's mission had finally ended.

Living Only to Die

FRANCES HILLER DREAMED OF THE PERFECT FUNERAL—HER OWN

During the 1890s, Mrs. Frances Hiller displayed her own $30,000 coffin in her front parlor in Wilmington, Massachusetts. She frequently climbed into it to show visitors how she would look when she was finally laid out. Later, she added a life-size wax dummy of herself, dressed in a $20,000 funeral robe. Her fascination with funerals may have derived from the fact that all 23 of her children (including seven sets of twins) died in infancy. At any rate, her husband, Dr. Henry Hiller, had hired a renowned wood carver to fashion ornate caskets for the couple.

Dr. Hiller, whose fortune came from a patent medicine he had invented, had always indulged his wife's eccentric tastes. She owned hundreds of hats and wore costly jewelry while gardening. When he died in 1888, the first custom-carved coffin—the one that Mrs. Hiller had intended for herself—was only half-finished. Her husband's body was kept in a vault until

> Frances Hiller kept her own $30,000 coffin in her front parlor—complete with a wax dummy of herself dressed in a funeral robe.

the funerary masterpiece was ready. It sported hand-carved ivy vines, angels, cupids, dragons, bats, and a lizard crawling out of a skull's eye socket. It was borne to a resplendent tomb in a procession that included a military band and 2,000 people carrying lighted torches.

Five years later, Frances married her chauffeur, on the provision that he change his name to Henry Hiller. When she died, in 1900, she was placed in her casket, a duplicate of the first Mr. Hiller's; her casket was so heavy that 10 men had to carry it. The funeral car, drawn by four coal-black horses covered with black netting, sagged and almost capsized under the weight. A journalist described the ceremonies as matching the excitement of the local cattle fair.

In 1935 the ostentatious Hiller mausoleum was declared an eyesore and was destroyed. The magnificent coffins were buried. Only a pair of urns and simple bronze plaques now mark their location.

Mme. C. J. Walker's Dream Came True

Wilma Soss: Stockholders' Advocate

Wilma Soss owned a few shares of this and a couple of that, but she always made sure her voice was heard. For nearly 40 years, this unlikely crusader attended annual meetings, attired for the occasion and armed with sharp questions and quips. When quiz-show scandals rocked television, Soss personified the need for a cleanup by carrying a mop and broom to a CBS meeting. Once, U.S. Steel held an annual meeting on the day before Thanksgiving. When the chairman suggested she go home and start basting her turkey, she retorted, "I'm here to talk turkey, not to baste turkey."

When she died in 1986 at age 86, *New York Times* Chairman Arthur Ochs Sulzberger noted that Soss "represented the small shareholders with dignity, pride, and courtesy." Ahead of her time, she demanded sensitivity to stockholders' interests, condemned excessive stock options for executives, and campaigned for more female board members.

A SHARECROPPER'S DAUGHTER MAKES BEAUTY PRODUCTS AND BECOMES A MILLIONAIRE

She was born to poverty in 1867, but she had a dream—literally. One night Sarah Breedlove dreamed of producing and selling a formula to straighten and improve the appearance of African American women's hair. Few success stories compare with that of Breedlove, better known as Mme. C. J. Walker.

Orphaned at age seven, married at 14, and widowed at 20, Breedlove took her two-year-old daughter to St. Louis, where for 18 years she struggled to make ends meet as a washerwoman. In 1905, she decided to go into business for herself. With just a $2 investment, she mixed up shampoos and ointments and used heated iron combs to develop a treatment that later became famous as the Walker Method (or Walker System). Her treatment made hair smooth and lustrous.

The business caught on, and she moved to Denver, where she married Charles J. Walker and soon established her reputation as the hard-working Mme. C. J. Walker, traveling widely to demonstrate and sell her products. She extolled "cleanliness and loveliness," hoping it would not only prove good business, but also encourage self-respect and advancement among black women.

At its peak, her company employed thousands of Walker Agents; they touted more than a dozen beauty products. All packages were adorned with Mme. Walker's picture, making her one of the nation's best-known women, and, eventually, its wealthiest black woman. When she died in 1919, an editorial noted that Mme. Walker had "revolutionized the personal habits and appearance of millions." And in the process she *made* millions as well.

Ding Dong, Avon Calling!

COSMETICS COMPANY GIVES WOMEN A NEW CAREER OPTION

Peddling books door-to-door in the late 1870s, David McConnell found a surefire way to make himself more welcome as he traveled throughout the East. On each stop, the young pitchman gave his customers—mostly women—a small vial of perfume he had concocted in exchange for their time. Much to his surprise, on return trips he discovered that his perfume was more in demand than his books.

In 1886, McConnell gave up the book trade, created the Little Dot Perfume Set—five home-brewed floral fragrances in little bottles—and launched a business of his own. Operating out of "a room scarcely larger than an ordinary kitchen pantry" in New York City with his wife as sole assistant, he was "bookkeeper, cashier, correspondent, shipping clerk, office boy, and manufacturing chemist" for the new enterprise, which he called the California Perfume Company.

> Women responded enthusiastically to the flexible, respectable employment that Avon offered.

Soon, however, McConnell hired Mrs. P. F. E. Albee, a former colleague in the book business, to sell his product door to door. When the New Hampshire widow took to the road, she sold not only the five fragrances, but also a new career option for women. Inspired by McConnell and encouraged by Albee, women responded enthusiastically to the opportunity for flexible, respectable employment.

Like the oak tree that became its symbol, McConnell's company grew from a small beginning into a mighty thing. In 1928, impressed by how the countrysides of Suffern, New York (where McConnell's lab was located) and those of Shakespeare's hometown, Stratford-upon-Avon, were so similar, McConnell dubbed a new product line

"Avon." In 1950, the California Perfume Company officially changed its name to Avon Products, Inc. By the time the beauty products giant reached its centennial, some 40 million women across the nation and around the world had worked as "Avon ladies."

Charge!

IN 1950, AN EMBARRASSED BUSINESSMAN REVOLUTIONIZES THE CREDIT CARD INDUSTRY

After enjoying an excellent dinner at a fine New York restaurant, Frank McNamara (right) discovered that he had no cash on hand to pay the bill. His embarrassment that evening inspired McNamara to launch a credit-card business. Thus began America's love affair with buy-now, pay-later financing.

Soon after the dinner, McNamara, the manager of a credit company, borrowed $10,000 from attorney Ralph Schneider. McNamara founded Diners' Club on February 28, 1950; by the end of that year, McNamara had persuaded about 200 people to pay a $5 annual fee for a pressed-paper card that was accepted at 27 New York restaurants. There would soon be other merchants. Although the merchants had to pay Diners' Club a commission of up to 10 percent of their credit-card sales, more and more businesses signed on. They had learned that credit-card users often spent considerably more than those carrying only cash.

At first it was difficult to persuade a skeptical public that membership came with no strings attached. It seemed too good to be true: Joining the club required nothing more than filling out an application and paying dues. For a time the company had to resort to costly promotions, such as all-expenses-paid vacations, to gain new members.

In fact, Diners' Club was not the first credit card issued in the United States. Fancy New York hotels like the Waldorf–Astoria and the Ritz had offered their best customers such cards in the early 1900s. In the 1920s, Filene's department store in Boston and California's General Petroleum Company had started their own credit-card programs. It's unlikely that McNamara (who sold his share of Diners' Club for $200,000 in 1952), envisioned the growth spurt that lay ahead—an estimated $1 trillion in credit-card purchases by the year 2000.

Divine Intervention at the ATM

BANK MACHINE SHOWS BROKE MAN A BLESSED BALANCE OF OVER $5 MILLION

In Santa Cruz, California, an arthritic 40-year-old artist named Stanton Lee Powers eked out an existence on Social Security disability payments and the odd pen-and-ink drawing that he could sell. But, God willing, his life would change dramatically over the course of a few days in 1982.

THE MIRACLE

One fall evening, Powers went to a branch of the County Bank, where he had a grand total of $1.17 in his account. He paused in front of the automatic teller machine and began to pray. And lo, as he later told it, a miracle occurred. His balance had grown to $1,600. He returned to the machine two days later and once again bowed his head in supplication. Again his prayers were answered—the balance shown was in excess of $5 million.

Powers, who promptly made a withdrawal, did what many devout but desperate Americans might do when confronted by such a test of faith. He got himself a lawyer. After reviewing the facts of the case, the attorney felt that some research was in order.

First he had the artist sign a document giving him one-third of the book, movie, and TV rights to the Miracle of the Automated Teller; then he and his client went to a County Bank cash machine. There they again witnessed the Miracle: the $5 million-plus sum appeared in response to a balance inquiry. The lawyer had Powers withdraw some money, then took him to another machine. Within a few days, a bit more than $2,000 was taken.

THE LETDOWN

But good fortune did not continue to shine upon Powers. The bank froze his account, and the next time he tried to withdraw some money, the machine took his card. In the eyes of Powers's legal counsel, the bank's action was akin to blasphemy. He demanded empirical proof that the fortune wasn't God's handiwork. If the Almighty could turn water into wine and bread into fish, he argued, he should be able to put $5 million into a bank account.

Bank officials didn't take Powers's account of his account on faith. "It's the first time I've heard of God being active in this type of thing," said one banker. Another noted that the Divine Deposit was invalid if it wasn't accompanied by a check from God.

And so it came to pass that Stanton Lee Powers was charged with grand theft and brought to trial. And lo, when it was time for him to take the witness stand, he changed his story.

THE "HAVINGNESS MACHINE"

Powers told of being given a reading by a psychic—appropriately named Fortune—who, he said, "told me things about my past I've never told anyone." Fortune offered to rid his life of obstacles. "I visualized the color green flowing into my aura. 'That's the color of self-love,' she said." Now that Powers was fully in touch with his personal aura, Fortune told

> If the Almighty could turn water into wine and bread into fish, Powers argued, he should be able to put $5 million into a bank account.

him to "turn up your shock roots to experience a havingness machine."

This state of transcendence was abetted, no doubt, by some 16 Ritalin pills, several codeine tablets, and the 10 or 12 wine coolers Powers had recently consumed. He then went to the cash machine, his "havingness machine" turned up to 100 percent. He stopped and meditated. And then it happened.

Powers recalled discussing his enriching meditation with a couple of people. And one of them had offered a recommendation: "The public won't understand it if you say meditation. Tell everybody God did it." So Powers did just that.

THE UNBELIEVERS

Powers's trial lawyer (not the same one who had led him from machine to machine) thought that once the jury heard the defendant's testimony, it couldn't hold him responsible for anything, much less masterminding a $5-million scam. But the prosecutor argued otherwise by showing that Powers had punched in large deposits on the automatic teller keyboard without putting in a great deal of money.

Because of a bank holiday, the institution did not immediately reconcile the very impressive keyed-in sums with Powers's very small deposit. And because of a programming tic, the bank's computer credited and deposited over $5 million at once, so withdrawing a mere $2,000 or so was certainly no problem.

Powers was found guilty. But in view of his precarious mental state, his sentence was lenient: Pay back the money and perform 750 hours of community service. (He gave art classes in a senior citizens' home.) Of the episode, Powers complained: "I lost everything I had—my money, my friends. And I was rear-ended four times by hit-and-run drivers."

Yes, the Lord does work in strange ways.

Geeks Rule

HOW A BUNCH OF YOUNG WHIPPERSNAPPERS WITH COMPUTERS SHOOK WALL STREET TO ITS CORE

For decades in America, there existed a certain model of a high-powered business executive: MBA, expensive suit, experience, in a corner office. But all that changed in February 1996 when Netscape founder Marc Andreessen smiled out from the cover of *Time* magazine next to the headline, "The Golden Geeks."

The 24-year-old Andreessen was dressed in blue jeans and a polo shirt, with bare feet. He looked like a nerdy kid—the complete opposite of what America knew to be a successful businessman. He was worth $58 million.

Just six months earlier, Andreessen's Internet browser company, Netscape, held its initial public offering on the stock market. The shares were expected to debut at $28. They opened at $71. Overnight, Andreessen and several of his colleagues went from working-class, young computer geeks to darlings of the business world, at a time when many Americans still didn't even know what a "browser" was.

The successful Netscape IPO marked the start of the "dot-com" boom, a five-year period of rapid stock market growth due mostly to new Internet-based companies and technology stocks. Many of these startups were based in the Silicon Valley area of California and traded on the NASDAQ—a younger alternative to the New York Stock Exchange. Venture capitalists flocked to this new property called "the Internet." It was like the gold rush and a land grab all rolled into one.

But Andreessen, and the rest of the young "golden geeks," did more than just make lots of money. They revolutionized the American workplace. Some dot-com companies gave outrageous perks to employees: on-site massages, pet-sitting services, and in-office air-hockey tables. Beanbags replaced executive chairs. Many of them were just out of college. Some had never even graduated.

The dot-com boom peaked at the beginning of 2000, but it couldn't last forever. The boom was based heavily on speculation and the raising of market value rather than actual company assets. Several high-profile failures, like Pets.com (kitty litter didn't sell very well online) marred the popularity of Internet companies. Some investors began to question the business model of these upstarts, and profit warnings began to flood the market as fast as IPOs once had. The total value of the NASDAQ was cut in half. By the end of 2000, an e-mail parodying the famous Don McLean song, "American Pie," was making the rounds. The joke e-mail read, "I can't remember if I cried, the day the NASDAQ died." But it's certain that there were tears on Wall Street. The bubble had burst and only the strongest, like Amazon, Yahoo, and yes, Andreessen's Netscape (already bought by another internet firm, AOL), would survive.

Despite the dramatic demise of the dot-com era, the golden geeks left their mark on the American corporate world. These days, it's almost inconceivable for a company to operate without a Web site. American consumers now feel comfortable shopping online. The open-plan office is seen as a friendlier alternative to closed-door offices, and even workplace clothing is more relaxed, as "Casual Fridays" have become commonplace. But unlike in Andreessen's 1996 photo shoot, shoes are required.

From the Ground Up

HOW SMALL BUSINESSES BLOSSOMED INTO AMERICAN ICONS

SEARS, ROEBUCK AND CO.

Managing a railroad and express office in North Redwood, Minnesota, a town with three houses in 1886, left Richard Warren Sears plenty of time to freelance. In those days wholesalers would often ship goods on consignment; if the shipment was unclaimed, the freight agent could have it at a reduced price so he could resell the wares at a profit.

When Sears acquired a box of $25 gold-filled watches this way, he offered them at bargain rates to other agents. In six months, he made $5,000. Quitting his job, he set up a watch company and advertised for a watchmaker. Alvah Curtis Roebuck responded. Before long the pair branched out; in 1893 they formed Sears, Roebuck and Co. and began issuing their catalog soon known as the Wish Book and the Farmer's Bible. But customers had to be wary: One Sears ad offered a "sewing machine" for $1. The "machine" consisted of a needle and thread.

JELL-O

"America's Most Famous Dessert" did not take shape quickly. Peter Cooper, a New York industrialist and philanthropist, received the first patent for this gelatin dessert in 1845 but did little with the patent. It wasn't until 1897, when a successful building contractor named Pearl B. Wait entered the blossoming packaged-food business, that the dessert went into large-scale production.

Wait's wife, May, was the one who coined the name "Jell-O." The company was a bust, so Wait sold it to his neighbor Orator F. Woodward for $450. At first Woodward fared no better than Wait had. One day, in despair, he offered to sell the whole kit and caboodle to his plant superintendent for $35. The superintendent refused and probably rued the day he did. By 1906, sales of Jell-O had reached almost $1 million.

BIRDSEYE FROZEN FOOD

When Clarence Birdseye went fishing in Labrador, Canada, it was so cold that the fish froze as they came through the ice. Thawed in water, they began to swim. This led Birdseye to try quick-freezing food to retain its fresh flavor. His experiments worked. In 1924, Birdseye launched a seafood company in Gloucester, Massachusetts. Five years later, he sold it for $22 million.

TOBACCO

From its beginning in Jamestown, the tobacco business flourished despite fierce opposition. King James I called smoking "a custome lothsome to the eye, hatefull to the Nose, harmefull to the braine, [and] dangerous to the Lungs" and did all he could to stop it. But men smoked on, and Virginia grew wealthy on their addiction. Tobacco was even legal tender in the colony; until the 1750s the salaries of clergymen were paid in it. (Later the tobacco industry featured its Virginia origin: The 1860s tobacco label shows the rescue of John Smith by Pocahontas.) In 1760, a Huguenot named Pierre Lorillard began selling highly flavored pipe and chewing tobacco and snuff concocted in his

continued on page 156

Household Words

Here's how the names of some of America's most famous companies and brands came to be:

• Phillips 66

When Frank and L. E. Phillips, founders of a new oil company, needed a catchy sign for their first gas station in 1917, the combination of a number and a name was quite fashionable.

For them the answer seemed ordained: The company's scientists suggested it because the high quality of gas was due to its specific high gravity, and theirs was near 66. On top of that, their first oil refinery was on Texas State Route 66.

Still, they weren't sure. Then a Phillips official, road-testing the new gas on Route 66, remarked, "This car goes like 60."

"Sixty, nothing," his driver replied. "We're doing 66!" The combination of coincidences was too much to resist, and the Phillips 66 logo was born.

• Shell Oil

Back in the 1830s, Marcus Samuel ran a curio shop in

London's East End. During a seaside vacation, his children began decorating their lunch boxes with shells, and Samuel, aware of the Victorian craze for decorative knickknacks, immediately recognized a potential bestseller. He began making and selling shell boxes. People loved them, and his place became widely known as The Shell Shop.

Years later his son, Marcus Jr., built up an oil business. By 1897, it had become so big that he formed a new company and named it after his father's shop. A few years after that, he adopted the Shell symbol. The rest, as they say, is history.

• Heinz 57

As businessman Henry J. Heinz rode the elevated train through New York City in the early 1890s, his imagination was sparked by an advertisement touting "21 Styles" of shoes. He felt 57 had a catchy cadence and greater "psychological influence"; so even though his company was marketing over 60 products at the time, Heinz 57 became its symbol.

• Dr Pepper

Dr. Pepper lived in Rural Retreat, Virginia. When Wade B. Morrison wooed his

New York City plant. His success brought tobacco new popularity and new condemnation. For a century P. Lorillard and Sons dominated the market with imaginative sales devices, such as the wooden cigar store Indian. On its 100th anniversary, the company stuffed $100 bills into random packages of Century cigarette tobacco.

Ready-made cigarettes were hand-rolled and costly until 1881, when James Duke introduced machines that could roll 200 a minute. At five cents a pack, sales skyrocketed. In 1890 Duke merged America's five largest cigarette companies into the American Tobacco Company.

FULLER BRUSH MAN

"I washed babies with a back brush," related the original Fuller brush man, "swept stairs, cleaned radiators and milk bottles, dusted floors, anything that would prove the worth of what I had to sell."

Born in January 1885 on a farm in Nova Scotia, Canada,, Alfred G. Fuller left home at 18 to find work in the Boston area. The shy youth eventually began selling brushes. On the eve of his 21st birthday, in response to his customers' complaints and suggestions, he invested $65 in equipment and began modifying stock items. He also made a few brushes of his own design. Within a few years, Fuller had salesmen all over the country, trained in the high art of opening doors. When he died in 1973, saleswomen called Fullerettes outnumbered the men.

MGM'S LEO THE LION

Bitten by the showbiz bug, Sam Goldfish knew the importance of a name. So when he formed his own film production company, he combined his name with that of his partner, Edgar Selwyn.

Eager for an image to enhance the name, Sam Goldwyn hired a promoter who found inspiration at a football game: As Columbia University fans sang "Roar, Lion, Roar," their team's mascot ran onto the field. Success! The king of beasts was a natural trademark. And when a merger created Metro-Goldwyn-Mayer, Leo won out over Metro's parrot.

MGM acquired a real, 350-pound lion in 1927. Charles Lindbergh's transatlantic flight dominated the headlines at the time, so MGM cashed in on the excitement by arranging for Leo to embark on a well-publicized, cross-country jaunt. When his plane went down near the Grand Canyon, a bring-him-back-alive lion hunt resulted, generating enough headlines to warm the heart of the stoniest press agent. Leo survived to roar on as the enduring symbol of MGM.

FANNIE FARMER

Born in Boston in 1857, Fannie Merritt Farmer suffered a childhood illness that left her with a limp. Doctors forbade her from attending college, so in 1887 she entered the Boston Cooking School. By 1891, she was running it.

In those days, cooking was hit-or-miss: a pinch of this, a dab of that. But Farmer believed in scientific cookery. In 1896, for the first edition of *The Boston Cooking-School Cook Book*—predecessor of the bestselling *Fannie Farmer Cookbook*—she standardized measurements (we owe the "level teaspoon" to her). She also offered the reassurance of firm authority. "It is the duty of every housekeeper to learn the art of soupmaking," she wrote. Then she taught it.

daughter, Pepper discouraged the match. Morrison later opened Morrison's Old Corner Drug Store in Waco, Texas. In 1885 his pharmacist, Charles Alderton, came up with a soda-fountain flavor that became a local favorite. People asked what it was called, and the father of Morrison's fondly remembered lost love became immortalized.

• Betty Crocker

"How do you make a one-crust pie?" "What's a good recipe for apple dumplings?"

In 1921, when the Washburn Crosby Company, makers of Gold Medal Flour, needed a name to sign replies to the questions contained in an avalanche of customer mail, they invented Betty Crocker.

The surname belonged to William Crocker, a director of the company, and Betty was a popular nickname at the time. Today, as the General Mills trademark, Betty Crocker still stands for the positive attitude in homemaking. Indeed, she became "the eternal and supreme housewife, all-wise, generous of time, advice, sympathy."

John Dillinger (right) sits handcuffed to Deputy Chief Carroll Holby while on trial in Crown Point, Indiana. Opposite: Keeping Enron's corporate logo spic and span in 2002, though its reputation was severely tarnished.

CHAPTER FIVE

Laws and Outlaws

merica is a nation ruled by laws. As in any society, there are citizens whose duty it is to make sure that these rules are followed, and those who think that they operate above the law (or outside it altogether).

This chapter spins the yarns of America's most outrageous criminals, including gruesome murderers, cannibals, counterfeiters, and present-day corporate thieves. However shocking their misdeeds, one thing is almost always true: In the end, outlaws got the justice that was coming to them.

Herein are also tales of America's unsung heroes: the law officers who protect us. We chronicle the foundations of the nation's first private investigation company and police force, as well as old-time sheriffs and governors who brought order to an unstable, young country. Some of these "heroes," believe it or not, were no more law-abiding than the crooks they arrested.

Harboring the King Killers

ASSASSINS ACCUSED OF REGICIDE FIND REFUGE IN NEW ENGLAND

A long, futile manhunt in 17th-century New England involved three men who were no ordinary criminals. John Dixwell, William Goffe, and Edward Whalley were wanted by British authorities. As officers in the army of Whalley's cousin, Oliver Cromwell, they were among the 59 signers of the death warrant for King Charles I, who was executed in 1649.

When the Stuart monarchy was restored in 1660, Charles II declared amnesty for all except those who had helped behead his father. Before the new king was crowned, Goffe and Whalley sailed for Boston. Dixwell took off for Prussia.

A NEW WORLD WELCOME

Warmly received in New England, Goffe and Whalley remained proud and unrepentant for the rest of their lives. The king posted a handsome reward for their capture. By the time an arrest warrant was issued, however, the men had left Massachusetts.

Fleeing to New Haven, Connecticut, they were again welcomed and given shelter. But the refuge was temporary, for they were being sought by two royalist zealots. The hunters had difficulty convincing the deputy governor of their need for secrecy. The delay gave the killers time to escape to a nearby cave, where a sympathetic farmer left food for them.

ROYAL TROOPS SEARCH BOSTON

Strangers all along the way took grave risks for Goffe and Whalley. By 1664, the enraged Charles II sent troops to Boston to snare the elusive men, who promptly fled to Hadley, Massachusetts. There they lived in freedom, secretly communicating with their families back home. They even enjoyed a visit from Dixwell. Disguised as a retired merchant, he lived in Connecticut until his death in 1688.

THE BEARDED SAVIOR

The hunt for Whalley failed; he died peacefully in Hadley in 1674. But Goffe made one more appearance—one that helped save the community. Legend has it that while the townsfolk, including some of the king's men, were at church, Indians attacked. Seemingly out of nowhere an elderly, bearded man appeared. He rallied the town's defenses and then, just as suddenly, disappeared. Later, he was spotted in Hartford and reported to local officials, who refused to arrest him. Goffe died of natural causes in 1679.

FUNNY FACT

New Jersey Had a Cross-Dressing Governor

In 1702, Queen Anne appointed her cousin Edward Hyde, Viscount Cornbury, as governor-general of New York and New Jersey. At his welcoming banquet, he paid tribute to his wife's ears, inviting the men present to feel them. One evening not long afterward, a woman rushed up to a watchman and pulled his ears. "She" turned out to be the royal governor. Thereafter Cornbury would often parade around in his wife's dresses and, shrieking with laughter, pounce on other men's ears. He even wore a dress to his wife's funeral. All the time, Cornbury claimed that he was simply trying to represent the queen by resembling her "as faithfully as I can."

The Scheme to Kill Washington

HOW A PLATE OF POISONED PEAS MIGHT HAVE CHANGED AMERICAN HISTORY

If George Washington had not led the Continental Army in the Revolution, there might never have been a United States. It could have happened that way if it hadn't been for Phoebe Fraunces, daughter of New York City tavern keeper Samuel Fraunces.

Phoebe Fraunces was a housekeeper for Washington when Thomas Hickey, a member of his guard, enlisted her help in killing the general. Fraunces's role was to serve Washington a plate of poisoned peas, and she agreed to play it. But as she was serving Washington, she warned him, and he flipped the peas out the window.

The failed plot came to light on June 17, 1776. By then Hickey, in jail for passing counterfeit money, was hatching another plot. He was trying to enroll prisoners in a secret Tory corps within the rebel army; some 700 soldiers, Hickey boasted, were on the payroll of New York's Tory governor, William Tryon, and New York City's mayor, David Matthews. The men planned to support a British invasion by turning their guns on their comrades. New York City would be set ablaze while a drummer in Washington's guard would stab the general.

Warned his peas were poisoned, Washington tossed them out a window. Chickens ate them and fell dead.

An investigation was launched. Mayor Matthews surrendered and was jailed; he later escaped to England. Hickey was hanged in New York City on June 28, 1776, before a crowd of 20,000.

In reporting to Congress, Washington wrote: "I am hopeful this example will produce many salutary consequences and deter others from entering into like traitorous practices."

TRUTH OR RUMOR?

Did Benjamin Franklin's son really side with the British during the Revolutionary War?

Yes. Sometime around 1730, in what he later described as the "hard-to-be-govern'd passions of youth," Ben Franklin sired an illegitimate son, William. William Franklin was never slighted in his upbringing; the elder Franklin even managed to have him appointed colonial governor of New Jersey.

During the Revolution, the father championed American independence; the son remained loyal to the Crown. When the Revolutionary War began, William refused to give up his office and was imprisoned. When he was released two years later, William organized a band of Loyalist guerrillas. But the group so embarrassed the British with its wanton pillage, arson, rape, torture, and murder that it was disbanded in 1782. His cause lost, William fled to England.

Captain William Kidd, the Scottish privateer, welcomes ladies onto his ship in Jean Leone Gerome Ferris's painting, *Captain William Kidd in New York Harbour, 1696*. This Turkish rug was the first to be seen in the New World.

A Relatively Well-Behaved Kidd

"EVIL" CAPTAIN'S REPUTATION LARGELY UNFOUNDED

Perhaps he did commit an act or two of piracy, but Captain William Kidd was never the bloodthirsty buccaneer created by legend. In the late 1680s he was a British privateer, licensed by the government to prey on enemy merchant ships. (A pirate, on the other hand, was licensed only by his cannon and cutlass.)

By 1691, Kidd had moved to New York, where he settled in to married life, became a reputable trader, and even helped to build Trinity Church. Privateering lured him back, however, and 1695 found him hunting pirates for William III. But since there were no encounters with treasure-laden enemy vessels, his crew, who shared the plunder, advocated piracy. Kidd concurred, so they took a couple of small ships as prizes. As he sailed from port to port, Kidd's drunken speeches rang more of pirating than pirate hunting. Finally, when he took the one great prize of the voyage, Kidd thought his luck had changed. And

it had, but for the worse. Though the captured ship was a legitimate privateer's prize, its influential owners protested to the king. In addition, Kidd's backers worried about their involvement with the privateer-turned-pirate—no matter how briefly—and denounced the captain.

> Kidd was hanged in London in 1701. His body was left to rot near the Thames as a warning.

Meanwhile, Kidd, after a brief stop at Gardiners Island to bury a treasure (possibly still interred on that dot of land in Long Island Sound), returned to New York. There the governor trapped him into turning himself in. He was sent to England to stand trial, and it went badly: Evidence was withheld that might have proven him innocent, and members of his crew testified against him. And so Kidd went to the gallows, "a man neither very good nor very bad, the fool of fortune and the tool of politicians."

Ahoy, Ladies!

FIERCE FEMALES PLUNDER UNSUSPECTING SHIPS

Anne Bonny, the daughter of a prominent attorney in Charleston, South Carolina, was married and living in the Bahamas when she met up with John "Calico Jack" Rackham. Smitten, she left her husband, helped Rackham steal a merchant sloop, and set sea with him as his devoted mistress and eager comrade in arms.

One day, Calico Jack flew into a jealous rage when he saw his Bonny whispering with a young sailor. In time to avert murder, she revealed that the sailor was no rival, but another woman, Mary Read.

Reared as a boy in England, Read was serving as a seaman on a Dutch ship when the ship was seized by Rackham's pirates. Forced to join Rackham's crew, Read proved willing and courageous. Only Bonny and Rackham knew her true sex—that is, until the day she "accidentally" showed her breasts to a handsome sailor who had also been pressed into piracy from a plundered ship. The pair became secret lovers; on one occasion Read picked a fight with—and killed—one of Rackham's

From New Providence in the Bahamas, two pirates—both of them women—set out to plunder ship after ship. Praising their boldness, one witness noted that nobody "was more resolute, or ready to board or undertake any Thing that was hazardous, than she [Mary Read] or Anne Bonny." In 1720 they were caught, tried, and convicted, but they avoided execution by "pleading their bellies." Both of the women were pregnant.

veteran pirates to keep him from dispatching the youth in a duel.

When Rackham's ship was captured by the law in 1720, all of the male pirates lay drunk below deck. But Bonny and Read fought furiously to the end, to no avail. Bonny, allowed to see Calico Jack before his execution, taunted him: "Had you fought like a man, you need not have been hanged like a dog."

Uptight Citizens Brigade

It was a crime in Puritan New England …

- for ministers to perform wedding ceremonies (marriages, considered to be secular, were conducted by magistrates until the law was changed in 1692).
- to dance in a tavern or at a wedding.
- to smite your parents if you were over 16—or simply to be a rebellious son above the same age.
- for theatrical performances or sports events to occur.
- to celebrate Christmas.
- to practice blasphemy, idolatry, or witchcraft.
- for religious music to be performed.
- for the poor to adopt "excessive dress" such as lace, frills, or shoe buckles.
- to question the word of God.

A Duel to the Death

AARON BURR IS THE ONLY VICE PRESIDENT EVER INDICTED FOR MURDER

Sunrise on July 11, 1804, found Vice President Aaron Burr and former Secretary of the Treasury Alexander Hamilton standing 10 paces apart, each holding a loaded, cocked pistol. They were on a bluff in Weehawken, New Jersey, overlooking the Hudson River. The spot was a popular dueling ground beyond the reach of New York law. Their seconds had measured off the distance. Raising his gun, Hamilton turned it this way and that, and then, apologizing for the delay, he put on his spectacles. This suggested that Hamilton intended to shoot to kill.

On the signal to fire, two shots rang out. Hamilton's bullet embedded itself in an overhead branch, but Burr's slammed into Hamilton's side, sliced through his liver, and lodged in his spine. He died the next day, and the nation he had helped to found reeled in shock.

FORMER FRIENDS

In the early days of the Republic, there was no law that made dueling illegal; it was a common way for gentlemen to settle differences. Those who refused a challenge were branded cowards, a disgrace to avoid even at the cost of life.

Oddly enough, Hamilton and Burr had once been friends: Both had served in the Continental Army and, after the Revolution, had established successful law practices in New York, occasionally working on cases together. They both also became involved in politics, Hamilton a Federalist to the core, and Burr favoring a looser coalition of states. Clashing head-on, they became implacable foes, with incident upon incident fueling the fire.

Burr unseated Hamilton's father-in-law, General Schuyler, as the U.S. senator from New York. Six years later, as the result of a public scandal that undermined his political career, Hamilton challenged James Monroe to a duel. The duel never took place, but the fact that Monroe had named Burr as his second, or assistant, increased the enmity between the two. When Senator Burr was up for reelection, Hamilton engineered his defeat. Still another incident led to a duel between Burr and Hamilton's brother-in-law, John B. Church, in which neither was harmed. Hamilton's involvement in Burr's losing the 1800 presidential election further widened the rift. The last straw occurred in 1804, when Burr made a bid for the governorship of New York and Hamilton blocked him.

In April of that year, the *Albany Register* published letters claiming that Hamilton had called Burr "a dangerous man," regarded him as unfit to govern, and had privately expressed "a still more despicable opinion" of him. Burr called Hamilton to account, but the reply was evasive. On June 27, after futile exchanges of letters, Burr forwarded his challenge.

DID HAMILTON HOLD HIS FIRE?
Although Hamilton deplored dueling, he feared that a refusal to meet the challenge would discredit him. Both men put their affairs in order, with Hamilton writing an explanation of his actions, admitting he

Hamilton's Sordid Affair

Rumors of blackmail, extortion, and criminal mischief surround secretary of the treasury

Despite his diminutive stature, Alexander Hamilton, with his red hair and deep blue eyes, had a well-deserved reputation as a ladies' man. Of his many liaisons, none was as embarrassing to him as his affair with Maria Reynolds.

The relationship began in 1791, when Reynolds appeared at Hamilton's doorstep in Philadelphia begging for a loan. Though she did not know Hamilton, then secretary of the treasury, the comely Reynolds explained that she and her child had been abandoned by her husband and needed money to return to New York. Instead of giving her cash on the spot, however, Hamilton visited her boardinghouse with $30 that evening. Ushered into her bedroom, he quickly took advantage of the opportunity.

The amorous meetings with Reynolds continued, often taking place at Hamilton's own home while his wife and children were away. But then *Mister* Reynolds appeared and demanded cash for his wife's favors.

Hamilton paid the man $1,000 in blackmail money, yet he did not stop the meetings. Her husband, his wounded pride apparently forgotten, begged Hamilton not to curtail his visits because, he claimed: "I find when ever you have been with her she is Chearful and kind, but when you have not in some time she is Quite to Reverse."

Wearying of James Reynolds's requests (which by now included demands for a government job), Hamilton sought to bring the affair to a close. The whole affair came to a head after James Reynolds was arrested for a swindle involving fake veterans' claims. Attempting to trade for his freedom, he broadly hinted that the secretary of the treasury had participated in the fraudulent scheme.

As rumors began to circulate, three congressmen confronted Hamilton and demanded an explanation. In his defense, he produced the blackmail letters— 20 in all—that he said he had received from James and Maria Reynolds and denied any wrongdoing beyond a foolish dalliance. Hamilton was so convincing that the matter was dropped.

The sordid affair resurfaced several years later when James Callender, a notorious drunk with a venomous pen and a distaste for Hamilton, told it in a widely circulated pamphlet. In response, the outraged Hamilton published the embarrassing letters. "My real crime," he said, "is an amorous connection with his wife."

Publication of the letters raised a question that scholars debate to this day. Did Hamilton forge the blackmail demands to clear himself of the more serious charge of fiscal misconduct? Reynolds was poorly educated, but the letters contained elevated language; although simple words were misspelled, the complex vocabulary was without error.

It is impossible to resolve the situation now: All of the letters were allegedly burned by Hamilton's wife, Elizabeth, after his death.

might have wronged Burr. Hamilton wrote that he planned to hold his fire, a statement friends would cite to brand Burr a cold-blooded killer.

Speculation on the outcome abounded: Had Hamilton secretly set his pistol's hair trigger—capable of providing a split-second advantage—and then accidentally fired before he had Burr in his sights? Did Hamilton suicidally withhold his fire, pulling the trigger inadvertently from the impact of Burr's bullet? There were many questions and few answers.

On July 14, a great public funeral was held for the 47-year-old Hamilton; thousands of angry citizens mourned. Burr was bewildered by their reaction—the duel had been conducted honorably. He remained in seclusion. Despite murder indictments in New York and New Jersey, he was able to slip away, heading south to Philadelphia and beyond. Eventually he returned to Washington, taking up his duties as vice president. The next year he completed his term and, after an eloquent farewell speech, left for dubious adventures in the Mississippi Valley. Hamilton's death had knelled his own political demise.

Empire, Power, and Glory

Aaron Burr's ambitious dreams and grand schemes

After his farewell speech to the Senate in March 1805, Vice President Aaron Burr found himself unemployed. The duel with Hamilton had made him a political pariah. His former colleagues waited to see how a man of such intellect, energy, and ego would repair his fortunes.

No one could have imagined the bizarre path on which Burr's ambition would put him: He proposed carving a personal domain from the American West, which was greatly enlarged by the recent Louisiana Purchase. Burr found a willing ally in James Wilkinson, the commanding general of the U.S. Army. Wilkinson had visions as grandiose as those of Burr himself. Burr dreamed of conquering Mexico, uniting it with the frontier states, and apparently ruling his own empire.

Traveling the Ohio and Mississippi rivers to New Orleans, buying supplies and recruiting followers, Burr talked of the area's future in glowing terms. Chief among his converts was Harman Blennerhassett, who lived in splendor on a private island in the Ohio River in what is now West Virginia. He fell under Burr's spell and bankrolled the plan, offering his island as its home base. Burr's force—fewer than 100 strong—stored food and ammunition there, waiting for a call to action. Finally Burr sent Wilkinson the long-awaited message that on August 1, 1806, he would embark on his western expedition "never to return. The gods invite us to glory and fortune."

But Wilkinson saw that the plans had no chance of success and, turning informer, wrote Thomas Jefferson a full account of the proceedings. The president, who called Burr's scheme "the most extraordinary quest since the days of Don Quixote," decided he had to act. When Burr was apprehended in February 1807, he was brought to Richmond to be tried for treason. The prosecution could not produce witnesses to support the charges, and Burr was acquitted.

Even so, Burr thought it prudent to leave the country—though not before he had the audacity to ask the ruined Blennerhassett for introductions to Britons who might be interested in his plans. In France he wrote to Napoleon Bonaparte, proposing to reconquer Louisiana and Canada if the French emperor provided the money. Both England and France turned him down flat.

In 1812 he returned to New York; Burr died in 1836 at the age of 80, and contemporary accounts confirm that his ego remained intact to the end. Told of his deteriorating condition, he cried, "I can't die!" But his doctor replied, "Mr. Burr, you are already dying."

The Not-Dead-Yet President

FEISTY OLD HICKORY WAS FULL OF BULLETS BUT KEPT ON KICKING

By the time Andrew Jackson won the presidency, in 1828, the 60-year-old general had been involved in 103 duels and altercations, 14 times as a principal. As a legacy from two of these jousts, bullets lodged near his heart and in his left arm gave him decades of agony. For one of his antagonists, however, the legacy was death.

THE DICKINSON DUEL

In 1806, Jackson engaged in a duel with 27-year-old lawyer Charles Dickinson; the two had quarreled over a bet on a forfeited horse race. The day before the duel, Jackson and his second, General Thomas Overton, discussed strategy as they rode toward the dueling field at Harrison's Mills, Kentucky. Not only was Dickinson 12 years younger than Jackson, but he was known to be a superior marksman. A snapshooter, he was called, for his speed and accuracy in leveling and firing his weapon without taking deliberate aim. The two generals agreed to risk letting Dickinson fire first, so that Jackson (if he was lucky) could take time to aim carefully.

Traveling with friends via a different route, Dickinson showed a cheery confidence. At a tavern along the way, he stopped to practice his marksmanship and severed a string at a dueling distance of 24 feet. "If General Jackson comes along this road, show him that," he called to the proprietor.

A FATAL SHOT

The next morning the two parties met, Dickinson properly clad in a close-fitting waistcoat and snug trousers, Jackson sporting a loose frock coat that concealed his thin frame. At the signal, Dickinson whipped up his pistol and fired.

Unflinching, Jackson pressed his left arm against his chest and raised his gun. Reeling back in

A portrait of the indefatigable Andrew Jackson in the 1814–1815 Battle of New Orleans.

disbelief, Dickinson cried out, "Great God! Have I missed him?"

Returning to his mark, he waited, eyes averted. Jackson coolly squeezed the trigger, but the gun stuck at half-cock. Recocking, he carefully aimed again and fired. The bullet tore into Dickinson's abdomen, fatally wounding him.

Overton, startled to see blood filling one of Jackson's shoes, asked if he had been hit. "Oh, I believe he has pinked me a little," he replied, determined that Dickinson not have the satisfaction of knowing. In fact, Dickinson's bullet had broken some ribs and lodged within an inch of his heart—too close for removal. Because of the loose coat, Dickinson had slightly misjudged. Back at the inn, Jackson ordered that a bottle of wine be sent to his dying antagonist.

THE BENTON BRAWL

A very different chain of circumstances led to an 1813 shootout between Jackson and his close friend and personal attorney, Thomas Hart Benton. It began because, in a duel fought by Benton's younger brother,

Jesse, Jackson had acted as his opponent's second. This disloyalty outraged Benton.

The confrontation between Jackson and the Benton brothers was more of a free-for-all than a duel. It took place at Nashville's City Hotel. Jackson, backing Tom Benton onto a rear porch, shouted, "Defend yourself!" As Benton edged away, his brother sneaked up on Old Hickory and shot him, shattering his left shoulder and leaving a ball embedded in his left arm. Falling, Jackson fired twice at Tom Benton, singeing the cloth of his sleeve. (At least one bullet went through the wall into a nearby room, narrowly missing a young couple and their baby. The infant was John Charles Frémont, future presidential candidate and husband of Jessie Benton, Tom Benton's daughter.)

While Jackson was being ministered to, two of his friends carried on the battle with the Bentons. Jesse Benton just missed being killed, and Tom Benton took a nasty fall down the porch stairs. Jackson, carried into the hotel, bled profusely, and the doctors advised amputation. "I'll keep my arm," he snapped.

The Original Private Eye

PINKERTON, MASTER OF DISGUISE, ONCE SAVED LINCOLN FROM MURDER

Allan Pinkerton was born in 1819, in a tough section of Glasgow, Scotland. He grew up amid poverty and crime. His father died when he was eight; after his father's death, he had to drop out of school. He eventually became apprenticed to a pattern maker. By the time he was 20, he was a militant member of the Chartists, a radical reform movement whose mission was to make the government more democratic.

As the Chartists became more aggressive, warrants were issued for their arrests. In the winter of 1842, Pinkerton found himself "an outlaw with a price on my head," dependent on friends to hide him from the police. He wasn't able to escape until April, when he was smuggled out at night aboard a ship bound for America, taking with him his new bride. The ship wrecked in ice off the Nova Scotia coast, and the party had to escape on lifeboats. Eventually they made their way to Dundee, a settlement of Scottish immigrants 50 miles northeast of Chicago. Pinkerton thrived there as a cooper, and it was only by chance that he found himself in a new career.

One day in 1847, Pinkerton was out on a deserted island, cutting wood for barrels when he found evidence that someone had been camping

Left to right: Private eye Allan Pinkerton with President Abraham Lincoln and Major General John A. McClernand in 1862, at the Battle of Antietam.

there. Suspicious, he informed the local sheriff. After a long stakeout, the pair captured a counterfeiting gang that had used the spot as a rendezvous. As a result, Pinkerton was made a deputy. He then moved to Chicago and joined the sheriff's department. By 1849, he had become the city's first detective. He performed so well that hoodlums even attempted to assassinate him.

Chicago in 1850 was a burgeoning frontier metropolis bursting with opportunity, and Pinkerton fit right in. He soon started his own company of professional private detectives, who became famous for their use of disguise. Their office has been compared to a theater's backstage area, with a large costume closet and agents who carefully rehearsed for their undercover roles. Much of Pinkerton's business involved protecting railroads. While working for the Illinois Central, he met with the line's attorney and on a later occasion, actually saved his life. That attorney was Abraham Lincoln.

In the early months of 1861, Pinkerton, a staunch abolitionist, uncovered a plot to assassinate Lincoln as he changed trains in Baltimore en route to his inauguration. Infiltrating rebel groups, Pinkerton and his agents were able to thwart the assassins and sneak the president-elect through the city at night. The next morning, Pinkerton sent a message

announcing Lincoln's safe arrival in Washington: "Plums arrived with Nuts this morning." The silly code, in which "Nuts" referred to Lincoln, led to Pinkerton's ridicule, and even today many people doubt that the plot really existed. However, one of Pinkerton's loudest detractors was a man who had himself offered Lincoln a gun and bowie knife for the trip. Lincoln smiled and declined.

Drugstore Justice

THE PRESCRIPTION FOR IMPUDENCE?
TWO WEEKS ON THE CHAIN GANG

Dr. Charles Meyer, a German druggist and an educated man, was often called upon to settle disputes in the lawless town of Tucson, Arizona, in the mid-1800s. He owned two books—perhaps the only two in town. Both were in German. One was about setting broken bones; the other was a *materia medica*, dealing with medicinal drugs.

Meyer became the town's justice of the peace and set up court in his drugstore. When confronted with a difficult case, he would open his materia medica and study it solemnly. Then he would declare something like, "I find here a case quite similar to the one we face. It says that the plaintiff

> For people who challenged Meyer's decisions, the fines would be doubled.

is correct, and the defendant is guilty and owes him $10. Case dismissed."

People seldom challenged Meyer's decisions. If they did, he doubled the fine. A lawyer once demanded a trial by jury. "What is a jury?" Meyer asked. When told, he sentenced the client to two weeks on a chain gang, cleaning the streets and removing sewage. The lawyer got one week. The druggist-justice asked, "Now, how do you like that trial by jury?"

Another time, after Meyer and a friend had been stopped by the town marshal for exceeding the five-mile-an-hour speed limit behind a team of spirited horses, he fined his friend $15, then doffed his robe, stood before the bench, and fined himself $25.

Sandra Day O'Connor is sworn in before the Senate Judiciary committee during her 1981 confirmation hearings.

First Woman on the Big Bench

**FRESH OUT OF LAW SCHOOL, SANDRA
DAY O'CONNOR HAD TROUBLE GETTING A JOB**

In 1981, Sandra Day O'Connor became the nation's first female Supreme Court justice—a great accomplishment for anyone. Who would ever believe that, right after graduating law school, almost no one wanted to hire her?

It didn't matter that 22-year-old Sandra Day O'Connor had graduated third in her class from the prestigious Stanford Law School. (A young man named William Rehnquist, who would go on to become chief justice of the Supreme Court, graduated first.) Back in 1952, none of the firms to which she applied was interested in hiring a female lawyer. Only one law office offered her a position—as a legal secretary. She turned it down.

Undeterred, O'Connor found a job as a deputy county attorney in San Mateo, California, and later went into private practice with a partner near Phoenix, Arizona. She devoted much of the next five years to raising her three sons. She then returned to the public sector as an assistant attorney general and later ran successfully for the state senate. In 1975, O'Connor won her first judicial position as a superior court judge in Maricopa County; four years later, she was appointed to the Arizona Court of Appeals.

Known as a judicial conservative in most matters (save women's rights), O'Connor soon caught the attention of Washington's Republican leadership. In 1981, President Reagan, fulfilling a campaign pledge to appoint a woman to the bench, nominated her to be the 102nd justice of the Supreme Court. The Senate confirmed O'Connor's nomination by a vote of 99 to 0. On September 25, 1981, the nation's first female Supreme Court justice was sworn in, ending 191 years of an all-male high court.

FUNNY FACT

How the World's Worst Musical Act Set a Supreme Court Precedent

The Cherry Sisters burst upon an unsuspecting public in 1893, performing an act so awful that it became a hit—people flocked to see them so that they could heckle them and throw things at the stage. When the *Des Moines Leader* carried a review calling one sister a "capering monstrosity" and described their sound as "like the wailings of damned souls," the "capering monstrosity" sister sued. After the sisters performed their act in court, the *Leader* won the suit. The Iowa Supreme Court decided that "Freedom of discussion is guaranteed by our fundamental law." Today the standard textbooks on First Amendment law cite the Cherry Sisters' case.

Where's the Beef?

**"CATTLE KATE" WATSON TRADED
STOLEN STEER FOR SEX**

Born in 1866 with far too restless a spirit for the Kansas plains, Ella Watson ran away from home to become a dance-hall girl. She later changed her name to Kate. According to her father, she was "a fine girl of handsome form" with a "robust physique" who weighed "between 160 and 180 pounds."

In 1888, Watson received a business proposition from Jim Averill to come to Sweetwater Valley, Wyoming. There she set up a homestead about a mile from Averill's saloon and went into the business of "entertaining" his customers. Now, Averill was no ordinary saloonkeeper. An articulate man, he was the leader of the area's small ranchers and homesteaders and had written to the local newspapers denouncing the cattle barons' greed.

A savage winter had intensified the bitter range war that raged around Sweetwater Valley. As small ranchers struggled to survive, they openly rustled cattle from the barons' vast herds to feed their families. Kate Watson made it known that she would accept livestock in return for her favors, thus earning the nickname "Cattle Kate." More than a few of her growing herd bore a baron's brand.

When an angry cattleman confronted Kate, claiming that 20 of his stolen steers were in her pen, she insisted she had bought them. He demanded proof. She produced a rifle, and the mere sight of it concluded the argument. Then a spy was sent to watch Watson's ranch; he reported that she had at least 50 stolen steer.

On July 20, 1889, a vigilante party of 20 men abducted Watson and Averill, took them to a nearby canyon, and hanged them from a cottonwood tree. Although four prominent barons were charged with the murders, they never stood trial. "We didn't mean to hang 'em," said one, "only scare 'em a little."

Dames Duel over "Solid Man"

**WORKING GIRLS END UP SHOOTING
THE LOVER THEY FOUGHT OVER—BUT
WHICH ONE OF THEM DID IT?**

During the silver boom years of the 1870s, Mattie Silks ran such a successful brothel that she became known as the Queen of the Denver Tenderloin. And she looked the part in her elaborate French-styled gowns, complete with cloaks and trains. Her skirts, though, had two hidden pockets: In one she carried gold coins; in the other, a pearl-handled pistol.

Silks was madly in love with her "solid man," a drinking, gambling, two-timing dude named Cort Thompson. Trouble erupted when another working girl, Katie Fulton, tried to win him away from Silks. Fulton's fiery temper clashed with Silks's indomitable pride, and the two rivals agreed that pistols would be the only way to decide who got Thompson.

Much of Denver, including Thompson himself, turned out to witness the duel. At the count, the two women whirled and fired. Both were still standing when the smoke cleared, but Thompson was on the ground, blood spurting from his neck.

Silks rushed to his side and tried to stop the bleeding with her lace kerchief. She took her man home and thereafter spent a fortune supporting his vices, until he died in 1900. To this day, no one is sure who shot Cort Thompson, or whether it was done accidentally or on purpose.

Frankie and Johnny

The ballad tells a poignant tale of two-timing love. And nothing made Frances Baker—the "Frankie" of the familiar lyrics—angrier than hearing "Frankie and Johnny." Especially since her St. Louis neighbors identified her as the female immortalized in it.

Baker never denied that, as an emotional 22-year-old in 1899, she shot her 17-year-old boyfriend (who was named Allen and was called Albert, *not* Johnny). What really got her feathers ruffled was the song's description of her as a woman of, shall we say, easy virtue.

Even after she was acquitted of murder on the grounds of self-defense, there seemed no escaping the song, with its lyric calling her a "queen sport" who killed her boyfriend when she found him with another woman. "I just did not care for that humiliation having me in front of the public all the time," she'd complain.

Two years after the incident, Baker thought she could end the unwelcome serenading by moving first  to Omaha and then to Portland, where she ran a shoeshine stand. But the song followed her. "I was pointed out as the worst woman in the world," she lamented. "You'd think it happened yesterday."

Nor did matters end there: a play and then a movie, released in 1936, dramatized the song's love triangle. In 1942, Baker decided she had suffered enough and sued Republic Pictures for $200,000, for defamation of character. At last, 42 years after the shooting, "Frankie" had a chance to tell her side of the story.

Baker wasn't anything like the girl celebrated in the ballad, she testified. "If I was a 'queen sport,' they did not call me that to my face," she said. Nor did she wear big diamonds or fancy clothes. Her dresses were "just plain ordinary cotton ones." A neighbor pointed out that Baker's income was not derived from loose morals at all but from "washing and ironing and scrubbing steps."

She even claimed she hadn't been upset when she learned that her boyfriend was also seeing Alice Pryor. "I never fussed with her about it," she told the court. Moreover, she was at home in bed when Al came by. In fact, it seems it was Al who had designs on Frankie's life.

Al threatened Baker, first with a lamp and then with a knife. "He ran a hand into his pocket, opened his knife, and started to cut me," she said. But she was well prepared—with a silver-plated pistol at her bedside. "Just run my hand under the pillow and shot him, and he says, 'Oh, you have me,'" she recounted. And, unlike the song, Baker never shot

TRUTH OR RUMOR?

Did a person with the nickname "Typhoid Mary" really exist?

Yes. Her name was Mary Mallon; she was a cook but not a criminal. After a wealthy New York family hired her in 1906, six people in the household came down with typhoid fever. George A. Soper, a Department of Health sanitary engineer, traced her work history and discovered that she had fled typhoid outbreaks in at least five other homes. Mallon was tracked down and determined to be a breeder and carrier of the deadly *Salmonella typhosa* bacteria. She was isolated in a hospital for two years and released on the condition that she find another occupation.

Against orders, Mallon went back to cooking and was recaptured after five years on the lam. She was confined to a hospital for the rest of her life; she died of a stroke in 1938, at age 70. Though "Typhoid Mary" was herself immune from the deadly disease she carried, she infected at least 57 people and caused three deaths … that we know of.

her lover three times. "Didn't shoot him but one time," she testified, "standing by the bed."

The more convincing Baker's story became, the less convinced the court was that the song was about her at all. Although one witness claimed that a St. Louis songwriter, Jim Dooley, had penned the ballad after hearing about the shooting, others pointed out that versions of it, with heroines whose names ranged from Annie to Lilly, had been in existence in at least 11 other states long before Baker shot her boyfriend. In the end, Baker lost the suit. She returned to Portland and, in 1950, was committed to a mental institution. She died there two years later, at the age of 75.

Mrs. "Machine Gun" Kelly

THE TALE OF THE WOMAN BEHIND THE MAN BEHIND THE GUN

Kathryn Shannon Thorne might have been a good wife for a corporation executive. She knew how to help her man's career along. In 1929, soon after she married George Kelly—a big, broad-shouldered bruiser who had often bragged, "No copper will ever take me alive"—she bought him a machine gun at a pawnshop. Though he hated guns, she told him to learn how to use it.

After much practice, George Kelly got the hang of the thing. At his wife's urging, he organized a gang and started robbing and killing. Mrs. Kelly phoned newspapers regularly to brag about "Machine Gun" Kelly's exploits, and the band was soon known as "the most dangerous ever encountered." But bank takes were low during the Depression, so Kathryn pressed for a more profitable venture: kidnapping.

The Kelly Gang snatched an Oklahoma businessman, netting a $200,000 ransom. But even though the victim had been blindfolded, he was able to lead the police to Kathryn Kelly's parents' farm, where most of the gang was arrested—all except the Kellys, who were on a spending spree with their share of the loot.

When the FBI finally cornered the couple in a Memphis hideout, Kelly reportedly hollered out, "Don't shoot, G-men," thus coining a lasting nickname for J. Edgar Hoover's gang-busting brigade.

In 1933, George and Kathryn Kelly were among the first to be sentenced to life imprisonment under the new Lindbergh kidnapping law. Ironically, the amiable George died in prison in 1954, while his glamorous wife (above), the instigator of the crimes, was released in 1958.

As they were dragged into custody, Kathryn Kelly shouted at her husband, "You rat! You've brought disgrace to my family."

Don't Mess With Texas (or Kansas, or Illinois …)

Most towns and states have had (or still have) some off-the-wall laws. For example, it's a crime:

- to go to church in Georgia without a loaded rifle.
- to enter Urbana, Illinois, if you are a monster.
- to carry bees in your hat in Lawrence, Kansas.
- to let a cat run loose in Sterling, Colorado, without a taillight.
- to give your sweetheart in Idaho a box of candy weighing less than 50 pounds.
- to sing the song "It Ain't Goin' to Rain No Mo'" in Oneida, Texas.
- to wear cowboy boots in Blythe, California, unless you own two cows.

- to divorce your wife in Tennessee without giving her 10 pounds of dried beans, 5 pounds of dried apples, a side of meat, and enough yarn to knit her own stockings for a year.
- to kiss in Riverside, California, without wiping your lips with carbolized rose water.
- to eat a snake on Sunday anywhere in Kansas.
- to ride in a baby carriage in Roderfield, West Virginia, unless you are a baby.
- to carry an uncaged bear down a highway in Missouri.
- to drive buffalo through the streets of Newton, Kansas.

- to whistle or sing "After the Ball" between 6 a.m. and 10 p.m. in Mankato, Kansas.
- to eat in a place that is on fire in Chicago.
- to drive a mule through Lang, Kansas, in August unless it is wearing a straw hat.
- to throw an onion in Princeton, Texas.
- to carry an ice cream cone in your pocket in Lexington, Kentucky.
- to mistreat rats in Denver.
- to go to bed with your boots on in North Dakota.
- to practice knife-throwing at a man wearing a striped suit in Natoma, Kansas.

Love 'em and Leave 'em … in Nevada

HOW RENO BECAME THE DIVORCE CAPITAL OF AMERICA

Mrs. William Corey's highly publicized divorce from her wealthy industrialist husband established Reno, Nevada, as a mecca for divorce seekers.

Nevada's legislators decided to establish a state residency requirement of six months to accommodate the needs of their transient population of miners and entrepreneurs. This brief waiting period for residency and the state's liberal grounds for divorce inadvertently transformed Reno into a prime destination for couples who wanted to end their marriages.

One would-be divorcée who traveled to Reno to take advantage of the six-month rule was Pittsburgh, Pennsylvania, resident Laura Corey. After her husband, U.S. Steel Corporation President William

Corey, left her for a dancer, Laura filed for divorce. The two-timing industrialist fought his wife's lawsuit in vain. On July 30, 1906, a judge awarded Laura a staggering $2 million divorce settlement, which made headlines nationwide.

Of the other unhappily married spouses who followed Laura's lead, the most famous one in the early part of the century was silent-screen star Mary Pickford, who divorced her first husband in Nevada in 1920 and promptly married Douglas Fairbanks. Seeing the prosperity that the divorce trade was bringing to Nevada (flourishing enterprises included dude ranches for the soon-to-be-single), neighboring states began to change their own residency rules. Not to be outdone, Nevada reduced its residency requirement to three months in 1927 and to six weeks in 1931.

The Delaware Murderess

PATTY CANNON'S HEINOUS CRIMES SHOOK THE LAND

On an April day in 1829, the town crier of Seaford, Delaware, called out: "Three o'clock and Patty Cannon taken."

The arrest of the woman, then in her sixties, followed a discovery made by a tenant on her farm at Johnson's Cross Roads (renamed Reliance in 1882 to escape its infamous past). He had been plowing "when his horse sunk in a grave, and on digging, he found a blue-painted chest" containing the bones of a man who had been missing for about 12 years. The victim, a slave trader from Georgia, had been carrying $15,000 on his person, too much money for Cannon and her son-in-law, Joe Johnson, to resist. They murdered him at the supper table in her house.

It was no accident that the Georgian was there. Cannon, a widow accused by some of having poisoned her husband, was in the business of kidnapping free blacks in her region and selling them into slavery for as much as $1,100 each. It was rumored that she and Johnson kept them chained in the attic until they could be shipped south.

Digging around the farm, authorities found the remains of other victims, including children. A servant claimed that Cannon had murdered at least one black child she thought unsalable and had bludgeoned to death another, about seven years old, with a thick stick of wood.

Patty Cannon was never brought to trial; she killed herself in jail. Her body was exhumed in the early 1900s, and before it was reburied, her skull fell into the hands of a Delaware resident, whose nephew lent it to the Dover public library. For years it was put on display every Halloween. Now the skull and a few teeth are kept in a hatbox in the staff area, available for viewing upon request.

TRUTH OR RUMOR?

Is the tale of the Donner Party cannibals true?

We still don't know for sure. America's best-known case of cannibalism involved the Donner Party, a California-bound wagon train of 82 souls that was snowbound in the High Sierras during the 1846–47 winter. Less well known is the fact that they were led to their tragic fate by a lie told by Jim Bridger, the famed mountain man.

This 19th-century engraving depicts members of the Donner Party, trapped by snow in a Sierra Nevada pass.

Bridger owned a supply post along a new route known as the Hastings Cutoff, and he wanted the route used. He told the Donners it was "a fine, level road." They set out on July 31. By October—after struggling across boulder-strewn terrain and trackless desert—they were snowed in. It was six months before help reached them. Thirty-three party members perished; many of the rest survived by eating the dead. Jacob Donner was eaten by his children. James Reed, the only leader who survived, later wrote that, at Bridger's post, letters had been withheld advising, "by no means to go the Hastings Cutoff."

As certain as the tragedy seems to have occurred, modern-day anthropologists aren't so convinced that the cannibalism ever happened. Using modern forensic methods to examine bone remains, some scientists now conclude that there's no evidence to support cannibalism at the supposed campsite. The debate will likely rage on for some time to come.

Above: The remains of the men murdered and cannibalized by Alferd Packer (below).

Colorado Cannibal

ALFERD (*NOT* ALFRED) PACKER ATE FIVE MEN

The snow was deep and the weather bitter when 21 hopeful miners arrived in Colorado in January 1874. Despite the advice of a local American Indian that they delay their quest for silver, Alferd Packer convinced five of the men to follow him into the San Juan Mountains. Foolhardy from the start, the expedition party got lost. The ordeal ended in a crime so bizarre that it boggles the mind: Packer was convicted of murdering his companions and living off their remains.

Some 65 days after starting out, Packer strolled into an Indian agency alone, with an extraordinary tale about being abandoned by the others. When he later displayed a large wad of cash and a gun belonging to one of the miners, suspicions arose. Finally, he admitted that the members of his party had killed and eaten each other, one by one, until only two remained: Packer and Wilson Bell. One night after a tense standoff, Packer claimed, Bell attacked him

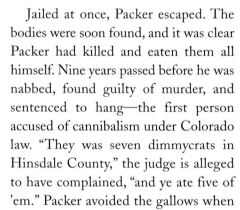

with a rifle butt, but Packer prevailed and Bell became his meal.

Jailed at once, Packer escaped. The bodies were soon found, and it was clear Packer had killed and eaten them all himself. Nine years passed before he was nabbed, found guilty of murder, and sentenced to hang—the first person accused of cannibalism under Colorado law. "They was seven dimmycrats in Hinsdale County," the judge is alleged to have complained, "and ye ate five of 'em." Packer avoided the gallows when the law under which he was sentenced was declared unconstitutional.

Three years later, in 1886, Packer was retried and sentenced to 40 years in prison. He left behind a few memorials to his dubious claim to fame: His victims' remains are buried on Cannibal Plateau, just above Dead Man's Gulch, and a snack shop at the University of Colorado is called the Alferd A. Packer Memorial Grill. Its most popular item? The Packerburger.

Murder Castle

CHICAGO PHARMACIST KILLS AND DISMEMBERS DOZENS IN HIS HOUSE OF HORRORS

Herman W. Mudgett was a handsome, charming, intelligent man. He was also one of the most monstrous criminals America has ever produced. A doctor by trade, he moved to Chicago in the mid-1880s and changed his name to Henry H. Holmes to avoid creditors and a wife he had abandoned. Holmes established himself as a pharmacist and entrepreneur on the city's South Side, near the site of the World's Columbian Exposition. By 1893, he had finished a large building—he said he planned to rent rooms to fairgoers—that the press would later call "Murder Castle."

The imposing three-story structure, ostensibly containing apartments and shops, concealed a labyrinth of windowless rooms, secret passageways, and torture chambers. An enormous safe on the second floor could be filled with gas from a set of valves in Holmes's bedroom closet. One room had sheet-iron walls lined with asbestos; human bones were found in the stove in the third-floor office.

It was in the basement that the most ghastly evidence was found: Vaults of quicklime, a barrel of acid, a huge wood-burning stove, and a zinc-lined cedar vat connected to a tangle of oil pipes all provided for the discreet, efficient disposal of bodies. A system of trap doors connected the upper floors to the cellar via a secret stairway, and a chute ran from the third floor to a dissecting room in the basement. The "Elasticity Determinator," a rack with pulleys at both ends, was used for experiments in stretching the human body.

Holmes was arrested in 1894 for insurance fraud and the murder of a business partner in Philadelphia. Police work and a few lucky breaks led the trail back to Chicago and the grisly revelations of Murder Castle. Authorities compiled a list of at least 50 missing persons (including many young secretaries to whom

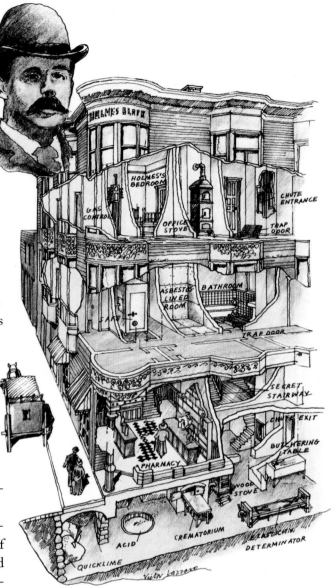

Herman W. Mudgett achieved infamy as the fiendish killer Henry H. Holmes. He is presumed to have killed at least 50 people over the course of about two years, all the while running his Chicago pharmacy. The bodies of his victims were efficiently disposed of in the elaborately diabolical house that he built.

Holmes had promised marriage) who had last been seen when they took up residence in the building. We'll probably never know how many people he actually killed or why. Convicted of the single Philadelphia murder, Holmes was hanged in 1896 and buried (at his own expense) in a reinforced coffin beneath two feet of concrete.

The Lincoln Assassination Conspiracy

**Above: an early 1860s portrait
of John Wilkes Booth.
Top: President Lincoln's
assassination at Ford's Theatre.**

DID MARY SURRATT HANG FOR HER SON'S GUILT?

A military court convicted eight people as John Wilkes Booth's accessories to President Abraham Lincoln's murder on April 14, 1865. Four were put to death. One, Mary Surratt, was the first woman ever hanged by the U.S. government. The evidence against the 45-year-old widow was inconclusive at best, and her guilt has been debated ever since.

Surratt's son, John, who had been a spy for the Confederacy, was in on Booth's plot; as a result, Mary Surratt's D.C. boardinghouse had been a meeting place for the plotters. It was even rumored that they were the agents of a more powerful conspiracy, headed by Secretary of War Edwin M. Stanton. No evidence of a larger plot, however, has ever been produced.

Mary Surratt may have suspected what the group was up to. Their plotting was open enough to arouse the suspicions of another boarder, Louis Weichmann, who became a chief witness against her. Yet no other testimony suggested that Mary Surratt knew details of the scheme.

As it turned out, Weichmann may have testified to save himself, for it was he who drove Mary Surratt into town on the day Lincoln was shot. Booth had asked her to deliver a package. It contained binoculars that he used in his escape; Surratt later denied all knowledge of its contents.

By the time the trial began, less than a month after the assassination, Booth was dead. John Surratt, considered by prosecutors to be the second most important figure in the case, had fled to Canada. By default, Mary Surratt became the trial's focal point. The prosecutors  may well have hoped that, by bringing her to trial, they would shame her son into turning himself in. But not even the urgent threat of his mother's execution impelled John Surratt to return to the States.

No one was surprised when three of the conspirators—Lewis Paine, George Atzerodt, and David Herold—were condemned to die. But the country was shocked by Mary Surratt's death sentence. Five of the nine military judges signed a petition asking President Andrew Johnson for clemency.

Mary Surratt was hanged on July 7, 1865.

Her execution was delayed in hopes of a reprieve, but a reprieve never came. (Johnson later denied receiving the request.)

Two years after Surratt's execution, it was discovered that the prosecutors had suppressed key evidence: a diary that had been found on Booth's body at the time of his death. It revealed that the original plan had been to kidnap Lincoln, not to kill him, and that Booth had not decided to assassinate the president until the very day he committed the act. It was unlikely that Mary Surratt could have known about it.

TRUTH OR RUMOR?

Is it true that President Lincoln's remains were once stolen?

Almost. On the night of November 7, 1876, three counterfeiters broke into the National Lincoln Monument in Oak Ridge Cemetery, Springfield, Illinois, and pried open the sarcophagus containing Lincoln's coffin. The men planned to ransom the body for $200,000 and the release of a fellow counterfeiter from prison. But one of the men was an undercover Secret Service agent. He alerted the police, and Lincoln's remains were let be. Following the incident, the coffin was moved about a dozen times before it was finally sealed, in 1901, inside a steel and concrete vault beneath the burial chamber in Springfield.

Who Shot John Wilkes Booth?

"Providence directed me to shoot John Wilkes Booth," claimed Thomas "Boston" Corbett (below), a sergeant in the 16th New York Cavalry. The unit had tracked the fugitive to a tobacco barn near Fort Royal, Virginia, and Corbett fired, despite orders that Booth was to be taken alive.

Corbett avowed that he  took orders only from God. When the Almighty had ordered him to avoid sexual temptation in 1858, he had castrated himself with a pair of scissors.

Did Corbett actually inflict Booth's mortal wound? He later testified that he fired a carbine. An autopsy showed that Booth was killed by a pistol bullet that the commanding officer of the 16th New York Cavalry claimed was self-inflicted.

Corbett continued to claim the credit for the assassin's death and became a national hero. Appointed doorkeeper for the Kansas state legislature, he threatened the lawmakers with a gun in 1887 and was committed to an insane asylum. He escaped and was never heard from again.

Just Die, Won't You?

"WILD BILL" LONGLEY HAD TO BE HANGED THREE TIMES

A 27-year-old gunman cheerfully mounted the scaffold at Giddings, Texas, in October 1878. He was smoking a cigar and joking with the crowd. A few days earlier he had written, "Hanging's my favorite way of dying." After all, William Preston "Wild Bill" Longley had been hanged once already.

A few years before, a group of vigilantes had mistaken Longley for a horse thief, strung him up from a limb, and fired a departing volley at him. A bullet split the rope above his head, and he dropped to the ground, unscathed.

A ruthless murderer with a short fuse, the tall, handsome Longley killed men at the slightest hint of an insult. He especially enjoyed gunning down freed slaves during the post-Civil War years.

> Before he put his head in the noose, Longley kissed the sheriff and a priest.

Altogether, between 1867 and his execution in 1878, Longley killed 32 people—more than most other gunfighters—but he never achieved the notoriety of such fabled outlaws as Billy the Kid.

This time Longley was convicted in Giddings, near his father's hometown of Evergreen, for the murder of a man he believed had killed his cousin. Before he put his head in the noose, he addressed the crowd of more than 4,000 spectators on the virtues of a Christian life. Then he kissed the sheriff and a priest and waved farewell. The trap was sprung, and Wild Bill dropped through it all the way to the ground, falling on his knees. He may have thought he was safe again, but the hangman had other ideas. The rope was adjusted, and Longley was properly hanged. The authorities let him swing for more than 11 minutes, and three doctors pronounced him dead.

The Legend of Joe Hill

MAN FRAMED FOR MURDER GIVES HIS OWN ORDER FOR EXECUTION

In the early morning of November 19, 1915, Joe Hill, known as the Hobo Poet, was led to the execution yard of the Salt Lake City prison. He had been convicted of killing a grocer and his son, perhaps in an attempted holdup. The conviction held, even though the bullets were not from Hill's revolver, and no one had identified him as the murderer. The only evidence against him was that he himself had been shot in the chest at about the same time, under circumstances he refused to explain—it had to do with a woman, he said.

Hill, born Joel Hägglund in Sweden in 1879, had immigrated to America in 1902 and Americanized his name. He toiled in the mines, on ranches, and on the docks. Although a loner, he became well known for his songs about the down-and-out. One, "The Preacher and the Slave," sung to the tune of "In the Sweet Bye and Bye," satirized religious leaders who urged pious resignation: "Work and pray, live on hay; You'll get pie in the sky when you die."

Following Hill's death sentence, the governor of Utah turned down thousands of demands for clemency and a request from President Woodrow Wilson for a stay of execution. Hill, who had chosen to be shot rather than hanged, reportedly refused a blindfold. After declaring his innocence, he shouted to the squad of five men poised with their guns, "Fire—go on and fire!" And they did.

Beyond the Call of Duty

THE LAWYER WHO GAVE HIS LIFE TO DEFEND A CLIENT

As a congressman, Clement L. Vallandigham led the Copperheads (Northerners who were vociferously opposed to the Civil War) and was banished to the Confederacy as a traitor. But by 1871, back in his native Ohio, he had built an outstanding reputation as a defense lawyer.

One of Vallandigham's clients, the raffish Thomas McGehan, was accused of murder, though he swore he'd never fired his pistol. Vallandigham thought of a way he could clear him: by showing, in court, how the victim could have shot himself while drawing his own gun. In his hotel room the day before the trial, the attorney demonstrated his dramatic ploy for colleagues. Taking one of two pistols from atop his dresser and pressing it to his chest, he pulled the trigger. Unfortunately, he'd picked up the wrong one—the loaded one.

"My God, I've shot myself!" Vallandigham shouted, staggering backward. Twelve hours later, he was dead. No one knows how the gambit might have influenced a jury, but McGehan was acquitted at a subsequent trial.

I Go to Pieces

HOW A DEAD OUTLAW NAMED BIG NOSE GEORGE PARROTT COULD BE FOUND ALL OVER TOWN

The outlaw George Parrott, also known as George Francis Warden and Big Nose George, was a "tiny, squeaky man," with a rather prominent proboscis. In 1878, he led a Wyoming gang in an attempt to hold up a Union Pacific train by prying the spikes off the rail bed. Foiled, they took off. Pursued by two deputy sheriffs who had tried to join the gang as undercover agents, the bandits waited to ambush them. They killed their men and got away. Two years later, Parrott bragged about the killings in a Montana saloon and was arrested.

Awaiting trial in Rawlins, Wyoming, Parrott nearly escaped by attacking the jailer, but the jailer's wife grabbed a rifle and said, "George, get back into your cell or I'll kill you." She was later awarded a watch.

That very night, on March 22, 1881, a masked lynch mob, angered by the escape attempt, dragged Parrott out and stood him on a barrel under a telegraph pole to hang him. Something went wrong, so they tried again, propping a ladder against the pole. In the meantime, Parrott worked his hands free. When someone kicked the ladder away, Big Nose George grabbed the pole and screamed: "For God's sake, someone shoot me. Don't let me choke to death." He finally slipped and, weighted by leg irons, slowly strangled.

The undertaker had a problem with Parrott, whose nose "was so large it interfered with the lid of the coffin and much pressure had to be exerted in nailing it down." A local doctor, John E. Osborne, had the casket opened and the body removed for research. He cut off the skullcap to see whether the brain of a criminal like Parrott differed from a normal brain. Osborne's behavior went a bit beyond the bounds of medical ethics of the time when he also removed the skin from the dead man's chest and thighs and had it tanned and made into a medicine bag and a pair of two-toned shoes, which he wore around town. He gave the skullcap to his young assistant, Lillian Heath, who filled it with rocks and used it as a doorstop.

Osborne, who later served as governor of Wyoming, a congressman, and an assistant secretary of state, donated the skin shoes and Parrott's death mask to the Rawlins National Bank.

King of the Bootleggers

GEORGE REMUS BUYS DISTILLERIES—AND THEN HAS THEM ROBBED

Top: George Remus behind bars, in 1925. Above, New York City Deputy Police Commissioner John A. Leach, right, watches agents pour liquor into the sewer following a raid during Prohibition, circa 1920.

During his reign as King of the Bootleggers, George Remus lived very well. At his 1920 Cincinnati housewarming, the party favors were jewelry for the men and a new Pontiac for each woman (the vehicles' titles were tastefully left under the women's dinner plates). He swam in a marble pool and collected rare books and fine art.

A German immigrant and former pharmacist, Remus was a respected lawyer who quickly saw how he could make money off of Prohibition. Selling his law practice and some property to raise $100,000 for his scheme, he purchased Death Valley Farm near Cincinnati, the hub of the American liquor industry. Then he bought up a number of distilleries that the government allowed to remain in operation for the production of medicinal alcohol.

Remus hired some 3,000 men to drive around in trucks and steal alcohol from the distilleries he now owned. At Death Valley Farm, the stuff was converted into booze, sold, and shipped. Remus had an inventory of 3 million gallons of liquor hidden in barns and chicken coops; his gross profits were between $60 million and $75 million.

Bragging that he had cornered the market, Remus bribed public officials to the tune of $20 million. But the law caught up, and he was sentenced to two years in the federal penitentiary in Atlanta. After a huge send-off party, which was called Ohio's social event of 1924, he traveled to Atlanta in a luxurious railroad car he had rented, accompanied by a number of friends—and federal marshals. In jail Remus got the cushy job of prison librarian, arranged for maid service and fresh flowers in his cell, and secured permission to dine with the chaplain.

By the time Remus was released from jail, gangsters had muscled in on the bootlegging business and dethroned him. But Remus made headlines once more: In 1927, he shot and killed his wife, claiming she had been having an affair with the federal agent whose evidence had convicted him. The jury found him insane, and he was sent to an asylum. But he soon convinced the Ohio Court of Appeals that he was sane after all, and he was released. He retired to an obscure life in Covington, Kentucky, where he died in 1952, at the age of 78.

Officer Capone?

LEGENDARY GANGSTER'S BROTHER, JIM, WAS A COP

Almost no one knows that the gangster Al Capone, who made a fortune from bootleg whiskey in the 1920s, had a brother, Jim, who was a law-enforcement officer specializing in Prohibition violations.

As a boy, Jim Capone ran away to join a circus. After traveling extensively, he arrived in Homer, Nebraska, on a train and decided to stay. At some point he changed his name to Richard Joseph Hart.

Known as "Two-Gun Hart" in Homer because he carried a pistol on each hip, he was a crack shot who could hit a bottle cap from 100 feet away—shooting with either hand. He became town marshal and then sheriff, busting stills statewide. As a Prohibition investigator for the Indian Service, Hart earned a reputation among American Indians for brutality. In Sioux City, Iowa, he killed an Indian in a barroom brawl but was acquitted when the victim turned out to be a bootlegger.

Reappointed Homer's town marshal, Hart was suspected of petty thievery while on night patrol and was relieved of his duties. Broke, he appealed to his family for help in 1940. Only then did Richard Hart tell his wife that he was "Scarface" Al Capone's brother. Two-Gun Hart died in 1952.

It's Miller Time . . .

Except in these locales. Here are some laws, past and present, that made it a crime . . .

- to buy a beer in the state of Maine unless you are standing up at the time.
- to drink a beer in Cartersville, Georgia, unless you're sitting down in your house.
- to drink beer in your underwear in Cushing, Oklahoma.
- to own or sell anything that tastes like, smells like, or looks like beer anywhere in the state of Alabama.
- to buy whiskey in Greenville, South Carolina, if the sun isn't shining.
- to sell liquor to a married man in Cold Springs, Pennsylvania, unless you have his wife's written consent.
- to own a copy of the *Encyclopaedia Britannica* in Texas (it contains a liquor recipe).
- to tap your foot, nod your head, or otherwise keep time to music anywhere that liquor is sold in New Hampshire.
- to do a fan dance in a bar in Montana while wearing a costume that weighs less than 3 pounds, 2 ounces.
- to wiggle while dancing in a bar in Stockton, California.
- to operate a still in Kentucky unless you blow a whistle.
- to play baseball or climb a tree while intoxicated in Council Bluffs, Iowa.
- to get a fish drunk anywhere in the state of Oklahoma.

Forger Forges through Southwest

JAMES ADDISON REAVIS ALMOST SWINDLES HIS WAY INTO A FABULOUS EMPIRE

For about a decade—between the years 1871 and 1883—a man named James Addison Reavis laid personal claim to some 17,000 square miles of what is now Arizona and New Mexico. It was a bold and clever swindle; but for a sharp-eyed newspaperman, Reavis might have gotten away with it.

While in the Confederate Army, Reavis had developed a talent for forging officers' signatures onto military passes. After his discharge, he refined his skill by forging deeds in a St. Louis real estate office. Thus he was well prepared when, in 1871, another swindler, Dr. George M. Willing Jr., asked Reavis to go in on a grandiose scheme with him. Willing died three years later (he was probably poisoned), and Reavis went on with the plan alone.

First, he got a job in the federal land records office in Santa Fe, New Mexico, and spent years studying treaties between the United States and Mexico. He was especially interested in the Gadsden Purchase, which pledged to honor Spanish land grants. He also made a study of the Spanish idiom, the penmanship, and the special parchments used in 18th-century documents. Traveling to Mexico (and possibly to Spain), he forged new names on very old documents, sometimes inserting whole pages of text, and obtained notarized copies from Mexican officials.

In 1883, he finally filed a land claim, based on the following carefully fabricated story: In 1748, in return for services rendered to the king of Spain, Don Miguel de Peralta de la Cordoba was made baron of the Colorados and received 300 leagues (about 1.3 million acres) of territory. The childless second baron deeded the land to George M. Willing, whose widow sold it to Reavis.

The claim brought panic to the territory and an outpouring of riches to the new baron Peralta-Reavis. The Southern Pacific paid Reavis $50,000 for its right-of-way. And with promises of more to follow, the Silver King Mine paid $25,000 for the right to stay open. Thousands of ranchers and businesses paid dearly for quitclaim deeds to their property. When Reavis married an "heiress" (an innocent girl he had groomed for the job), more than doubling his claim, the money burgeoned.

Then disaster struck. A newspaper publisher noticed that the type on one of the documents was of recent origin and that the watermark on the paper belonged to a fairly new Wisconsin paper mill. State Department agents were dispatched to Mexico and Spain. With chemical and microscopic tests, they found that the final pages of the Peralta grants were written in the wrong kind of ink on 10-year-old parchment.

Reavis was convicted in 1896 and sentenced to six years in jail. He died in 1908, penniless.

BRIGHT IDEA

Identifying Criminals by Their Fingerprints

The first Americans identified by their fingerprints were both named Will West. One was already in the Leavenworth penitentiary when the other arrived in 1903. Confused officials first thought their prisoner had escaped and been returned. The two denied kinship, but they looked so much alike that, according to the then-current Bertillion System of identification based on bone measurements, they were the same person.

Fingerprinting, which had just been perfected by Scotland Yard in England, resolved the dilemma, and a precedent was set.

Rhymin' and Stealin'

BLACK BART'S PILFERING AND "PO-8-RY" WERE THE STUFF OF LEGEND

Riding home from school one evening—or so the story goes—Charles E. Boles, a teacher in California's northern mine country, heard a stagecoach approaching. He knew the driver and decided to play a practical joke on him. Tying a scarf over his face and holding a pistol-size stick, he commanded the driver to halt. The driver, having no shotgun rider, threw out the strongbox and, laying whip to the horses, dashed off. Boles found himself with a fortune in gold coins and bullion. This, he decided, was a good way to make a living.

He went to San Francisco and deposited his haul in a bank, claiming to be in the mining business. From then on, Boles lived a life of leisure in San Francisco, occasionally taking a few days to roam the countryside, listening for news of a sizable shipment. Then, brandishing an empty shotgun and wearing a sack over his head, he would rob the stagecoach, leaving behind a bit of verse signed "Black Bart, Po-8."

Between 1875 and 1883, Black Bart robbed 28 stagecoaches. His "po-8-ry" entertained everyone, except the Wells Fargo detectives. Especially unamused was J. B. Hume, whose job was to follow Black Bart's trail.

After every robbery, dapper "Po-8" Black Bart (left) left a rhyme in the empty strongbox. One read: Blame me not for what I've done, / I don't deserve your curses; / and if for some cause I must be hung / Let it be for my verses."

Bart's luck ran out when he dropped a handkerchief, which bore the laundry mark FX07. Hume traced the kerchief to a San Francisco laundry and then to the name, C. E. Bolton (Black Bart's banking name).

The teacher-bandit spent four years in San Quentin. A few weeks after his release, the robberies began again, but these were deemed copycat robberies. Boles disappeared, giving rise to rumors that Wells Fargo authorities paid him a pension to stay out of the robbery business.

FUNNY FACT

A "Lady" Bandit Visits the Plummers

Like other 1870s frontier families, the Plummer family of Muscotah, Kansas, kept a candle in the window at night to guide luckless travelers in need of shelter. But such hospitality had its risks.

One evening "a tall, ungainly looking woman, queerly dressed, carrying a heavy satchel," appeared. Mrs. Plummer, alone at the time, let her come in. The woman went to bed shortly thereafter, keeping her satchel within easy reach, and left the next morning before the Plummers awoke.

Afterward they learned that their guest was none other than the killer-bandit Jesse James, on the run from the law.

The Scammer Who Wore Yellow

WEIL PERFECTS THE ART OF SEPARATING SUCKERS FROM THEIR MONEY

Born in Chicago in 1877, Joseph "Yellow Kid" Weil once said, "I never cheated an honest man, only rascals." Weil may have been the first con who really brought good old American ingenuity to the art of swindling.

In one of his favorite cons, he'd take a dog into a bar, show the bartender its well-forged pedigree, and ask him to mind the canine. Another man would enter, admire the dog, and offer to buy it for an outrageous sum. Later, when Weil returned and the greedy bartender offered him a few hundred for the dog, he'd reluctantly accept. The second

Swindler Joseph "Yellow Kid" Weil often wore yellow gloves. His nickname came from a popular 1890s comic strip.

man would never return, of course, and the bartender would be stuck with a costly mutt of dubious descent.

The drama of a Weil scam could rival that of a grand opera. Once he set up shop in a vacant bank; staffing it with tellers, guards, and customers (all fellow con artists), he relieved an "investor" of $50,000.

Sporting a trim beard and impeccably tailored suits, the dapper Weil raked in some $8 million with his scams. In later years, after he'd spent time in prison, he continued to proclaim his rob-the-rich Robin Hood views: "Our victims were mostly big industrialists and bankers," he boasted. "We never picked on poor people."

Train Robber, Trial Lawyer

AL JENNINGS PLAYS BOTH SIDES OF THE LAW

In his brief career as a train robber, Al Jennings was a dismal failure. But he sure knew how to make the best of his checkered past.

Jennings, whose father was a judge, began practicing law in Oklahoma in 1889. Eventually he joined his brothers, Ed and John, in their law firm in the sleepy town of Woodward. In October 1895, Ed Jennings was shot dead in a barroom fight by a noted lawyer named Temple Houston; their disagreement had begun in the courtroom and carried on into off hours. When Houston got off scot-free, Jennings and another brother, Frank, vowed to avenge Ed Jennings's murder. "I reverted to the primitive man that was within me," Al Jennings once said, but he never caught up with Houston.

Al and Frank Jennings then joined a gang of outlaws. In August 1897, they tried to hold up a Santa

Fe train so that they could rob the mail car, but the conductor chased them away. Two weeks later, the bandits piled ties on the tracks to stop a train, but the engineer opened his throttle and barreled right through. In October, they flagged down a Rock Island passenger train and tried to blow open its two safes. The safes wouldn't budge, but the boxcar exploded. The bandits managed to collect $300 from the passengers.

The outlaws were soon caught and sentenced to jail. All but Al Jennings got five-year sentences; Al got a life sentence for robbery with intent to kill. President William McKinley commuted his sentence and, by late 1902, he was free.

Jennings went back to the law, married, and, in 1907, got a "full citizenship" pardon from President Theodore Roosevelt. By 1912, he was making $5,000 a year as a lawyer in Oklahoma City. He ran for county attorney, promising: "When I was a train robber I was a good train robber, and if you choose me, I will be a good prosecuting attorney." He won the nomination but lost the election. When he ran for governor in 1914, newspapers editorialized against him, and he came in third.

Jennings went to California in 1915 to write, a talent he had been encouraged to develop by the writer O. Henry, a former cellmate. There he worked on a novel and ghost-wrote movies based on his life. He died in 1961 at the age of 98.

TRUTH OR RUMOR?

Is it true that the FBI killed the famous robber John Dillinger?

No one knows for sure. The FBI files say that the infamous bank robber John Dillinger died in a hail of bullets in front of Chicago's Biograph Theater in July 1934. And maybe he did. But

according to Jay Robert Nash, an authority on the history of American crime, the bureau was duped into killing the wrong man and, ashamed to admit the mistake, falsified evidence in an elaborate cover-up.

Anna Sage, a madam who was with "Dillinger" on that fateful 1934 night, had tipped off the FBI to his whereabouts; she was a Romanian citizen hoping for clemency from the immigration department. Nash claims that the man was an impostor—a minor underworld character named James Lawrence—and that Sage and her lover helped Dillinger escape. Nash came to this conclusion based on some of the details from "Dillinger's" autopsy report, which included: The dead man's eyes were brown; Dillinger's were bluish gray. The corpse had more teeth than Dillinger did and lacked the robber's birthmark. The FBI denies Nash's allegations.

Get-Rich-Quick Ponzi

THE SUPER SWINDLER WHO ENDED UP CONNING HIMSELF

Charles Ponzi saw himself as a man of substance, a mover and a shaker on the order of J. P. Morgan and John D. Rockefeller. The jaunty Italian immigrant felt confident that, if he could only amass enough capital, he could buy his way into the rarefied world of high finance, and then nothing could stop him from taking his rightful position on top of the heap.

In the summer of 1919, he discovered international reply coupons, issued to compensate for erratic rates of foreign exchange. You could buy a coupon in Spain for a penny and redeem it for a six-cent stamp in the United States. "Why can't I buy hundreds, thousands, millions of these coupons?" he wondered. So he borrowed money and invested. Then he learned that postal regulations forbade his plan.

Still, the coupons looked impressive, and the plan sounded good. Setting up shop in Boston, he printed an investment prospectus that promised a 50 percent return in 90 days. When he paid off on time, the word spread. Soon cash was pouring in, as it had to, because he was using the money from the front of the line to pay those at the end who didn't reinvest.

In eight months, Ponzi took in $15 million. He was negotiating to merge with the Bank of America when the bubble burst, and he came up $5 million short. Ponzi tried to recoup at the Saratoga gaming tables, but three days later and broke, he returned to Boston to face the music.

Jailed in Massachusetts, then deported to Italy, he ended up in Rio de Janeiro. There, in 1949, he died in a charity ward, leaving behind his unfinished autobiography. He'd named it *The Fall of Mister Ponzi*.

Stolen Sweets

A 34-YEAR PRISON SENTENCE …
FOR PILFERING A BOX OF CANDY

Stephen Dennison, a 16-year-old from a broken home near Salem, New York, stole a $5 box of candy from a roadside stand in 1925. He pleaded guilty and was given a 10-year suspended sentence. But because he failed to report monthly to a minister in his home town, Dennison was sent to the Elmira Reformatory in 1926. He remained imprisoned for the next 34 years.

In 1927, Dennison was classified as a "low-grade moron" and was transferred to the Institution for Male Defective Delinquents. Only six months before the 10-year term was up, he was sent without a court hearing or judicial review to Dannemora, a state hospital for the criminally insane, on a certificate of lunacy.

It took his half-brother, George, 24 years to win his release on a writ of habeas corpus in 1960. Stephen, who was by then 51 years old, sued the state over his illegal incarceration and was awarded $115,000. According to Judge Richard Heller, "No sum of money would be adequate to compensate the claimant."

Cooking the Books

ENRON LEFT ITS 21,000 EMPLOYEES
VIRTUALLY PENNILESS

In 2001, Wall Street was shocked by the downfall of one of America's most respected companies. But no one was more surprised than the 21,000 employees of Enron Corporation, many of whom lost their life savings because of their deceitful bosses.

From the late 1980s through the 1990s, the Houston-based corporation grew from a small gas company to become a leading energy supplier and market-maker. It made energy through its vast network of power plants and created financial instruments so that energy could be traded like stocks and bonds. Enron was regarded as an aggressive, innovative firm that attracted top executive talent; the company inspired loyalty and pride in its employees. In 1999 and 2000, *Fortune* magazine named Enron one of the "100 Best Companies to Work For in America," a distinction based largely on employee feedback.

Unbeknownst to these devoted employees, several top Enron executives were involved in devious accounting fraud. Chief Financial Officer Andrew Fastow was the architect of this creative book-cooking method. He created a network of dubious external "partnership" companies, even naming one after the Star Wars character Chewbacca. Fastow then used these partnerships to hide Enron's financial losses, keeping its official balance sheet in the black and making sure investors stayed interested. A valued stock on Wall Street, Enron soared to a high of about $90 per share in 2000. All those loyal employees were encouraged to place most of their retirement funds into Enron stock.

In the fall of 2001, the Enron downfall began. *Fortune*, which had once praised Enron, began to question how the company made money. Then, one of the executives who wasn't involved in the scheme began to internally question the firm's accounting

lost nearly all of its market value. Its share price fell below $1, The Securities and Exchange Commission launched an inquiry, and by December, Enron had declared bankruptcy.

PIRATES GET THEIR DUE

As the investigation into Enron progressed, it was revealed that several of those top executives involved in the accounting fraud—including Fastow, Chief Executive Officer Jeffrey Skilling and founder Kenneth Lay—had made millions by dumping their shares of Enron in the months before the company fell. All the while, however, they had been encouraging employees to hold on to the stock, even banning most lower-level staff from selling their Enron shares.

Not only did the employees of Enron lose their jobs when one of "the best companies to work for in America" was brought down by greedy bosses, but many of them also saw their retirement savings wiped out and continue to struggle financially today. They can at least take some comfort in knowing that the company's top conspirators, including Lay, Skilling, and Fastow, were all convicted of fraud. Fastow turned state's evidence to get a reduced sentence of six years. Skilling is serving 24 years of hard time. While awaiting sentencing, Lay died of a heart attack while on vacation in Aspen.

Today, the word "Enron" is synonymous with corporate greed and corruption. In 2002, in the wake of the Enron scandal and several other high-profile cases of U.S. corporate fraud, the government passed the Sarbanes-Oxley Act. The act places stricter controls on financial reporting and holds executives criminally responsible for fraud.

Top: Former Enron chairman Kenneth Lay in April 2006 during his fraud and conspiracy trial. Above, left to right: Former Enron Chief Financial Officer Andrew Fastow, the star witness for the prosecution in the trial of Enron's two former chief executives. Former Enron CEO Jeffrey Skilling in May 2006, at the end of his fraud and conspiracy trial.

irregularities. Sensing the inevitable, Enron bosses finally disclosed that the company had overstated its earnings since 1997 by some $586 million. In other words, the company was deeply in debt. This once-proud symbol of American corporate success crumbled as the extent of the fraud was revealed. In a matter of weeks, the company worth $77 billion

A circa-1880 American rider risks the high-wheeling bicycle. Opposite: Xavier Roberts surrounded by a pile of his Cabbage Patch Kids. The dolls that Roberts designed were wildly popular in the early 1980s.

CHAPTER SIX

Signs of the Times

I f television had existed four hundred years ago, what would the headline news have been? This chapter is a panorama of America's past, era by era: What we were thinking, what made big news, and who the movers and the shakers were.

Many of these tales—like Thanksgiving's origins, what it took to construct the Erie Canal, and how the song "The Swanee River" came to be—are *surprising but true* retellings of common stories that we just never think to challenge. Still others are hysterical short takes from America's history that you probably haven't heard—like how a man rode cross-country on a bicycle with no brakes, and how Congress closed down so that members wouldn't miss a ballet performance.

By the end, you'll surely ask of our ancestors, "What were they thinking?" The truth is, one day, the next generation will say the same thing about us.

Jean Leon Gerome Ferris imagined the Pilgrims' first feast with American Indians in his painting, *The First Thanksgiving 1621*.

The First Thanksgiving

THE PURITANS WOULD NOT BE PLEASED WITH OUR VERSION OF THEIR HOLIDAY

If there's one thing that all Americans know about or think they know about, it's the first Thanksgiving: how, in the fall of 1621, the Pilgrims, wearing their funny hats and bonnets, sat down with the friendly Indians and, as a way of giving thanks to God, shared a mighty feast.

PRAYER IN VIRGINIA

In fact, the first recorded American Thanksgiving took place in Virginia more than 11 years earlier, and it wasn't a feast. The spring of 1610 at Jamestown ended a winter that came to be called "the starving time." The original contingent of 409 colonists had been reduced to 60 survivors. They prayed for help, with no way of knowing if or when any might come.

When help did arrive, in the form of a ship filled with food and supplies from England, they held a prayer service to give thanks.

Although, in years to come, the Jamestown colonists surely thought back on that heartfelt Thanksgiving, they never commemorated it. Another Virginia group did that, also before the Pilgrims. On December 4, 1619, 38 colonists landed at a place they called Berkeley Hundred. "Wee ordaine," read an instruction in their charter, "that the day of our ships arrival … in the land of Virginia shall be yearly and perpetually kept holy as a day of Thanksgiving to Almighty God." On the first anniversary they fasted and prayed. But before the December holiday rolled around again, the entire colony had been massacred by Indians.

HARVEST HOME

The Puritans in Plymouth (who called themselves Saints, not Pilgrims—that term didn't become popular until the 1790s) also observed days of thanksgiving. But the 1621 feast we commemorate with full bellies and football wasn't one of them. A Puritan thanksgiving day was one of fasting and solemn prayer; it might be declared when a drought broke or a battle was won. Failure to observe it was a crime (as was participation in a sporting event on the Sabbath).

The famous feast was not a thanksgiving, but a three-day Harvest Home celebration, an ancient tradition; the best way to preserve food for the winter was in the form of body fat. Governor William Bradford invited the Indian chief Massasoit and his brother to join the feast, not because they'd helped grow the food, but because he still deemed it wise to stay friendly with them. To his surprise, they showed up with some 90 tribesmen.

If turkey was eaten (and there is no proof that it was), it wasn't the main course; venison was. There were no potatoes; although the Spanish had brought the tubers to Europe from South America, they were still considered poisonous. There was no grain, and so no rolls; no cattle, and so no butter. There was corn, but not on the cob; the tough kernels were boiled, mashed, kneaded, and fried into flat cakes. There were cranberries, to be sure, and other wild fruits; but no oranges or apples (hence, no apple cider). There were squash and pumpkins aplenty, but alas, lacking flour, no pumpkin pie.

Harvard's Indian College

A GRAND DREAM OF CONVERSION
THAT CAME TO NAUGHT

When the Massachusetts Bay Colony founded America's first college in 1636, its major goal was to educate Puritan ministers. Two years later, the school was named for John Harvard (right), a clergyman who had left it his library of 400 books and half his estate.

Harvard's first president, Henry Dunster, had a dream: to train Indians to preach Puritanism to their people. In 1653, the English Society for the Propagation of the Gospel in New England sponsored "one Intyre Rome att the College for the Conveniencye of six hopfull Indians youthes." Dunster put up a two-story brick building to house 20 Indians and two tutors. On the ground floor was the college press.

Four youths are known to have attended Harvard's Indian College; others were chosen, but died of "hecktick fevers" or other diseases before entering. Only one, Caleb Cheeshahteaumuck, who could speak Latin and Greek, graduated. He died of tuberculosis the following spring. Another, Joel Iacoomis, was shipwrecked on the Nantucket shoals while returning from a visit to Martha's Vineyard and was "murthered by some wicked Indians of that place." A third, Eleazer, wrote a Latin and Greek elegy before he died. The sole survivor, John Wompas, "a towardly lad and apt witt for a scholler," left Harvard after a year and bought a house on Boston Common. Jailed for debt, he escaped to become a real estate agent, of sorts—he sold an entire township he didn't own. For years, the Indian College housed only the press, on which, in 1663, was printed the first American Bible—an Algonquin translation. The building was torn down in 1698.

Buying Manhattan

DID PETER MINUIT SWINDLE THE INDIANS, OR VICE VERSA?

Manahatin ("hill island" in Algonquian) was a rich land occupied by two Indian tribes. The Weckquaesgeeks ranged over the northern three-quarters of the island, hunting beaver, deer, bear, and even bison. They fished for sturgeon in the Hudson River and harvested oysters from its huge beds. The Canarsees, from what is now Brooklyn, made forays to the southern tip of the island. Neither tribe owned Manahatin or even recognized ownership in the European sense, but the Canarsees certainly had less claim to it than the Weckquaesgeeks.

Yet when Peter Minuit, the new director-general of the Dutch colony, arrived on May 4, 1626, the Canarsees were the American Indians he met. His instructions from

The name "Manhattan" comes from the Algonquian word for "hill island."

Holland were that "in case the said Island is inhabited by some Indians these should not be driven away by force or threats, but should be persuaded by kind words or otherwise by giving them something, to let us live amongst them."

Mindful of powerful English settlements to the north and south and anxious to establish a legal claim, Minuit didn't quibble. Nor did Seyseys, the Canarsee chief. Happily accepting 60 guilders (or about $24) worth of beads, knives, axes, clothes, and (perhaps) rum in return for real estate he didn't own, he paddled back to Brooklyn.

If there had been banks in Brooklyn back then, and if the Canarsees had invested their $24 windfall at 6 percent interest, compounded annually, they would have amassed nearly $70 billion by 2000.

IMPROBABLE PIONEER

Benjamin Lay: The Conscientious Caveman

Benjamin Lay was a gnome of a man—four feet seven inches tall, with a hunched back and stick-like legs—who inhabited a cave near Philadelphia in the mid-1700s. Appalled that his fellow Quakers condoned slavery, he and his dwarf wife, Sarah, refused to live among them (although he made forays into town to disrupt meetings). Among his friends was Benjamin Franklin, who once dined in the cave. Later called by the poet John Greenleaf Whittier the community's "pertinacious gad-fly on the sore places of its conscience," Lay's way of thinking eventually won out. In 1758, a year before his death at the age of 82, the Quakers finally denounced slavery.

Lost and Found

So common was slavery throughout the American colonies that most newspapers featured classified advertisements offering slaves for sale, want ads seeking slaves with specific skills, and lost-and-found ads asking for the return of slaves. Escapes were so routine that printers kept woodcuts in stock to accompany the ads; the owner supplied a specific description of the escapee and often offered a reward.

Charles Stanley Reinhart's late 19th-century painting, *The Duckingstool*, depicts an accused witch being put through a judgment trial. She is dunked in water to prove that she's guilty of practicing witchcraft.

Salem's Psychedelic Witchcraft

In December 1691, some girls in Salem Village, Massachusetts, began to twitch, convulse, and scream that devils were pinching them. After they were fed special "witch cakes," they began accusing women of consorting with Satan. Before history's most famous witch hunt was over a year later, 19 citizens had been hanged and one pressed to death beneath heavy weights. Of the many possible theories about what happened, perhaps the most intriguing is that the girls had eaten grain contaminated with the poisonous fungus, ergot; its principal component, an alkaloid called lysergic acid amide, is closely related to lysergic acid diethylamide—or LSD.

Pueblo Popé's Rebellion

**TRIBE LEADER LED A PEACEFUL PEOPLE
TO REVOLT AGAINST SPANISH RULE**

Pueblo Indians in New Mexico had been living under the Spanish colonial government since the late 1500s. Although there had been sporadic, easily subdued uprisings from time to time, things seemed peaceful.

A docile, agricultural people, the Pueblos fought for defense, not conquest. Their villages—multistoried adobe structures—had high walls to keep out the Apaches, their enemies. But the muskets of Spanish soldiers offered better protection than their walls and weapons, just as European plowshares yielded richer harvests than the Pueblos could get with their own tools, and so there seemed little reason to resist. The Pueblos obligingly attended the Spanish Franciscan missions, sang in choirs, and served the Spaniards as best they could without giving up their own ways entirely.

But in 1675, church officials enlisted the aid of the colonial governor in a campaign to stamp out pagan practices. A *kiva*, or underground prayer room, was raided, and 47 Pueblo men were arrested for participating in a traditional ceremony. Three were hanged; the others were whipped, imprisoned, and warned against further blasphemy.

From their ranks rose the man who would unite his people, lead them in a bloody revolt, and drive their oppressors from the land. His name was Popé, and he came from the village of Ohke.

Retreating to a kiva at Taos, he and his counselor spent the next five years weaving plans for rebellion. When, in 1680, Popé finally sent Indian leaders knotted skeins, telling them in code the date of the uprising, many agreed to participate. Others, however, informed the Spanish, and so the date was moved up.

On the morning of August 10, 1680, Popé's warriors struck. Their victory was swift, sure, and brutal. They murdered men, women, and children all over the territory, taking special care to kill all priests. By August 21 the Indians had driven the Spanish into Mexico. It was the only totally successful Indian revolt in American history.

But Popé, inspirational in war, became tyrannical in victory. He decreed that every trace of the Spanish occupation be destroyed. Only the governor's mansion and carriage in Santa Fe were spared; Popé kept them for himself. Speaking Spanish was forbidden under cruel penalty. Popé died in 1688. His harsh, oppressive rule had left his people so destitute that when Diego de Vargas and a force of some 200 soldiers besieged the capital at Santa Fe in 1692, the defending Pueblos greeted their conquerors with open arms.

The Rogerenes

JOHN ROGERS AND HIS FOLLOWERS FOUGHT—IN RATHER ODD WAYS—FOR RELIGIOUS FREEDOM

John Rogers, born into a wealthy Connecticut family in 1648, was an early American who took a stand for religious freedom. Believing Christians answered to God alone, Rogers opposed salaried clergy, meetinghouses, and formal prayers. He held that states' religious laws were invalid, and advocated passive resistance to them. He and his followers, the Rogerenes, had a knack for dramatic public protest.

"The madness, immodesty, and tumultuous conduct of Rogers and those who followed him, at this day, is hardly conceivable," fumed the biased historian Benjamin Trumbull a century later, in his *A Complete History of Connecticut*. "It seemed to be their study and delight to violate the sabbath, insult magistrates and ministers, and to trample on all law and authority, human and divine. They would come, on the Lord's day, into the most public assemblies nearly or quite naked...."

Trumbull's outrage was based on exaggeration, but Rogers *was* tried and convicted of everything from entertaining two Quakers in his home to burning a New London meetinghouse. He was imprisoned seven times and once received 76 lashes for blasphemy. Many of his followers were publicly stripped and whipped, or tarred and feathered.

When his first wife divorced him, Rogers declared that neither marriage nor divorce laws had any validity. Later, since he considered himself still married in the eyes of God, he tried unsuccessfully to kidnap his wife from the bed of her new husband.

He eventually took a second wife, without the formality of a wedding. But when she was convicted of bearing Rogers's child out of wedlock and was given the choice of leaving him or receiving 40 lashes for the offense, she left him.

Rogers eventually pushed his belief in God's protection too far. In 1721, at the age of 72, he traveled to Boston during a smallpox epidemic and visited the sick, as was his habit. Returning home to New London, he died of the disease within a few days. The group he founded didn't peter out until the 19th century.

Ravaging New York

DIMWIT INDENTURED SERVANT STARTS RUMORS OF SLAVE CONSPIRACY

In 1741, Mary Burton was 17 years old and a not-too-bright indentured servant to a New York tavern keeper when she became the center of public attention. Before she was done, she had set off a wave of persecution that ravaged the city like a disease.

It began with a burglary in a tobacco shop. Burton led the authorities to a hoard of silver coins that she said two slaves had stolen on behalf of her master. While the three were being held, a series of fires broke out, rumored to have been set by slaves.

Of New York City's 12,000 inhabitants, some 2,000 were black slaves, and tensions ran high. Many New Yorkers still remembered an abortive 1712 uprising that had resulted in some 21 executions by fire, hanging, and torture; anxious rumors of new slave revolts circulated regularly. So when Burton began embellishing her story, people were ready to listen. The tavern keeper, she said, was the center of a plot in which slaves would burn the city, slaughter the whites, and divide the surviving women among them.

Two more slaves were arrested, tried without counsel—no lawyer would defend them—and burned alive. Flushed by her newfound celebrity, the young woman kept coming up with fresh, grandiose accusations. Her targets, to save their skins, accused

Mary Burton's wild accusations of a slave uprising in New York City brought about an orgy of persecution. Over the course of six months, some 20 people were hanged, 13 burned at the stake, and 70 deported. Burton collected a reward and disappeared.

others, and hysteria spread. Only when Burton pointed the finger at leading citizens did the attorney general come to doubt her word.

A Lady of Louisiana

BORN INTO SLAVERY, COINCOIN FREED HERSELF AND HER CHILDREN, THEN BUILT A GREAT ESTATE

Born a slave in 1742 at Natchitoches, Louisiana, a young girl faced a life of bondage. She was baptized Marie Thérèze, but she preferred to be called Coincoin, the African name her slave parents gave her. Through luck, hard work, determination, courage, and

extraordinary intelligence, she achieved the impossible for a black woman in that time and place.

PLANTATION LIFE

Unlike most slave children, Coincoin enjoyed a fairly solid family life. Although the "law of the plantation" was a perfectly acceptable means of marriage in the region, her parents were wed in the Catholic Church because their owners were deeply religious; like all of their slaves' children, Coincoin was baptized. Circumstances changed, however, when the owners died, and Coincoin was inherited by their daughter. By the time she was 25, the unmarried slave had borne four children.

In 1767, Coincoin caught the eye of a newly arrived French merchant, the worldly, city-bred Claude Metoyer. He soon arranged to lease the young house servant, who already had four children, and thus began a liaison that would last for nearly 20 years and produce 10 children.

This is the sitting room of Melrose Plantation House, in Natchez, Mississippi. The house is located on a 912-acre tract that slave-turned-free landowner Coincoin received through a land grant.

A SLAVE MISTRESS

Coincoin might have ended her days as a concubine had it not been for the arrival of a Spanish priest named Father Luis de Quintanilla. The priest hated that a shortage of marriageable women in Louisiana had led many young men to take up with slaves, so he set out to make an example of Metoyer and Coincoin, who were very open about their relationship.

Metoyer was forbidden by law from marrying Coincoin, but he maintained their relationship by purchasing Coincoin and her latest son and executing a deed setting them free. They lived together eight more years, before Metoyer decided to marry a friend's widow, who could bear him a legitimate heir.

A PLOT OF LAND

In 1786, their union came to an end. Metoyer deeded to the mother of his children about 70 acres of land and a modest annuity.

Though she was now in her forties and had been a house and bedroom slave all her life, Coincoin set up housekeeping in her own small cabin and began to farm her own fields. It was a meager start, but her courage, resolve, and hard work began to pay off; year by year her tobacco crop grew bigger and better.

Coincoin ran her plantation with great skill and efficiency, and she invested her growing income in the best possible way: One by one, for cash or for barter, this remarkable woman bought her own 14 children out of slavery.

SUCCESSFUL LANDOWNER

In 1793, Coincoin increased her holdings by applying for and receiving a land grant; she acquired a tract of 912 acres, which became a profitable cotton operation. (This is today Melrose Plantation, a National Historic Landmark and popular tourist attraction.) In addition to tobacco and cotton, Coincoin sold bear grease and pelts. She was so successful that at one time she owned 16 slaves.

Coincoin, who had moved from slave mistress to successful matriarchal planter, died in 1816 or 1817. To her free children and grandchildren she bequeathed not only her property, but her grit and her wisdom, which produced one of the richest plantation systems in antebellum Louisiana.

Boston's Slave Poetess Laureate

THE TRIUMPH AND TRAGEDY OF PHILLIS WHEATLEY

Kidnapped in Africa, the child who would later become known as Phillis Wheatley was shipped to Boston in 1761. She was probably about seven years old at the time. Put on the auction block naked, she stood shivering until she was bought by John Wheatley, a prosperous tailor, to be a servant for his wife.

Mrs. Wheatley named the girl Phillis. Impressed by her precocity, she decided the child should learn to read and write. The young girl soon could translate Ovid's poetry from Latin and wrote English verse in imitation of Alexander Pope. When, at about 17, she wrote an elegy on the death of a popular preacher and it was published, skeptical Bostonians came to call. They were won over by her articulate conversation and unassuming manner. She became known as Boston's poetess laureate and was invited to literary banquets—but, fully aware of the prejudice against her "sable race," she always chose to sit at a separate table.

In 1773, the poetess went to England, where she met aristocrats and writers. They, too, were captivated. She was about to meet King George III when Mrs. Wheatley fell ill. Returning home, Phillis stayed with her mistress until her death. Then she was set free.

A portrait of Phillis Wheatley appeared in a volume of her work, *Poems on Various Subjects, Religious and Moral.*

Phillis Wheatley moved out on her own. During the American Revolution, she dedicated a poem to George Washington, who expressed gratitude to "a person so favored by the muses" and invited her to visit his headquarters. Still, it was hard for her to make a living. In 1778 she married John Peters, an African American grocery-store manager—and a deadbeat. All three of her children died young. Her own health failed. She died in her early thirties, penniless, in a rooming house.

The Second Coming

MOTHER ANN LEE FOUNDED A STRICT RELIGIOUS SECT THAT FLOURISHED FOR MORE THAN A CENTURY

In 1774, Mother Ann Lee, who proclaimed herself the female incarnation of Christ, arrived in New York from England with a band of eight followers. Two years later, after much hardship, she founded a small communal settlement at Watervliet, near Albany.

Born in 1736 in the smoke-blackened industrial city of Manchester, England, Ann Lee had joined a radical Quaker sect at the age of 23. Called Shaking Quakers, or Shakers, for their practice of jumping and jerking as the spirit moved them while at worship, the sect was millenarian—in other words, they believed that the second coming of Christ was at hand. In 1770, while serving a jail term for her beliefs, Lee experienced a series of visions that persuaded her that she was the reborn Messiah.

Sexual relations, she said, were the root of humanity's problems; only strict celibacy could make up for past sins. (She herself had endured a late and unhappy marriage, and all four of her children had died in infancy.) Her doctrine not only split the sect, it increased the persecution of her remaining followers in England. In response to another vision, she brought them to America.

By 1780 Mother Ann's Shaker community was beginning to thrive, but suspicions of its English origin led to her arrest and brief imprisonment as a suspected spy. Upon her release, she spent two years on a pilgrimage throughout New England, gaining a wide reputation as a faith healer.

> Believing in the sanctity of honest, simple labor, the Shakers earned a reputation as fine craftspeople and farmers.

Her death in 1784 at the age of 48 might have ended the Shaker experiment, but new leaders emerged, and the sect survived and spread. To keep in touch with Mother Ann, spiritualism—already a Shaker practice—became increasingly important. At the height of Shaker popularity, in the 1840s, there were 19 communities from Maine to Indiana, and about 6,000 adherents.

The Shakers, believing in segregated equality of the sexes (many of the leaders were women), housed males and females in separate wings of huge dormitories. They did not procreate, of course, but increased their numbers with converts and, later, by adopting orphans. Holding to the sanctity of honest, simple labor, they earned a reputation as fine craftspeople and farmers. Their meticulous villages attracted tourists from around the world, and Shaker furniture is still prized for its quality and for its blend of function and form.

TRUTH OR RUMOR?

Is it true that George Washington once bowed to a painting, because it looked so realistic?

Yes. A 1795 portrait titled *The Staircase Group* by Charles Willson Peale shows two of his sons climbing stairs. To enhance the realism, Peale mounted the painting in a doorway, a wooden step at its base. The illusion was so spectacular that Washington actually bowed to the young men. Over the course of 59 years and three wives, Peale sired 17 children, naming many of them for classical artists. Titian and Raphaelle Peale appear above.

America's First Census

IN 1790, COUNTING ALMOST 4 MILLION HEADS WAS A *VERY* TOUGH JOB

Making his way on dirt roads and wilderness trails, the deputy marshal of the U.S. District Court combed the area assigned to him. He stopped at farms, plantations, and backwoods cabins, and quizzed those around him. The year was 1790; he was participating in the new nation's first census.

The marshal's questions were simple: How many free persons are in the family? What sex and color? How many slaves? What is the name and address of the head of family? He didn't ask about age (except to separate the men from the boys), religion, occupation, or income. He was simply counting heads. Even so, many folk were suspicious that the census had to do with their taxes. Others just didn't like being counted.

The census took 18 months to complete. The final tally: 3,929,214. Of this number, 19.3 percent were blacks, most of whom were enslaved (according to Article I, Section 2, of the Constitution, each was counted as three-fifths of a person).

America's 10 Largest Communities in 1790

1.	New York	33,131
2.	Philadelphia	28,522
3.	Boston	18,320
4.	Charleston	16,359
5.	Baltimore	13,503
6.	Northern Liberty, PA	9,913
7.	Salem, MA	7,921
8.	Watervliet, NY	7,419
9.	Ballstown, NY	7,333
10.	Stephentown, NY	6,795

The tabulation was needed primarily to determine the number of delegates each state could send to the House of Representatives. The count was also necessary for apportioning taxes among the states.

Some Americans expected the first census to show a population topping 4 million and feared that the unimpressive statistic might weaken the country's influence in Europe. But President George Washington reassured them that "our real numbers will exceed, greatly, the official returns."

James Madison had hoped that the census would obtain other useful information for study. In subsequent years it did. Among the most unwieldy questionnaires of all time was the 1890 census form, which asked for 13,000 bits of information. The world's first punch-card tabulation made it possible to process all the data gathered.

Although Virginia, with nearly a fifth of the nation's inhabitants, was the most populous state, New Yorkers could boast that 4 of the 10 largest communities were in their state.

Ladies and Gentlemen, and Children of All Ages …

AMERICA SEES ITS FIRST CIRCUS IN 1793

When John Bill Ricketts and his small troupe put on America's first complete circus performance in 1793, they dazzled the Philadelphia audience. The circus delighted George Washington, and soon the performer and the president became friends. When Washington's white steed, Jack, was put out to pasture, Ricketts offered Washington $150 for him, and Jack became a favorite circus attraction. Soon Ricketts added fireworks, a trained horse named Cornplanter, and a dwarf called the Warsaw Wonder. Then the showman took his wonders on the road.

The circus was hailed as "a place to dispel the gloom of the thoughtful … and to relax the mind of the sedentary and industrious trader." Then disaster struck: In 1799, Ricketts's amphitheaters in Philadelphia and New York burned to the ground. The staggering losses brought bankruptcy. Distraught, the enterprising Scot decided to return to Britain, but his ship (and all aboard) was lost at sea.

The President's Biblical Gems

JEFFERSON, AN ACCUSED ATHEIST, PUBLISHED A VOLUME OF RELIGIOUS VERSE

His enemies called him an atheist, and he never publicly denied the label. His religion, he felt, was his own affair. If he became president, they shrilled, America's Bibles would be burned.

In fact, according to a respected 20th-century clergyman, Thomas Jefferson's "knowledge of and admiration for the teachings of Jesus have never been equaled by any other president." So deep was his admiration that he compiled his own New Testament, consisting of extracts from the Gospels that he regarded as the actual words of Jesus. It was originally meant for the benefit of the American Indians, but later versions, titled *The Life and Morals of Jesus of Nazareth*, were published in Greek, Latin, French, and English.

Although Jefferson claimed to have spent only two or three nights on the project while he was president, he wrote in a letter to a friend that reading the volume every night before bedtime had become part of his daily routine. "A more precious morsel of ethics was never seen," he said.

Clinton's Ditch

THE ERIE CANAL JOINS HUDSON RIVER AND GREAT LAKES

Some 363 miles of deep forest and swampland separated Albany, New York, from Buffalo. The rise in elevation was 675 feet. Yet DeWitt Clinton staked his political career on the promise of digging a canal through that wilderness. When he became governor of New York in 1817 with nearly 97 percent of the vote, he took it as a mandate to get the job done.

The idea of linking the Great Lakes with the Hudson River had been around since 1784. The young nation had to find a way over or around the Appalachian Mountains or it could lose its frontier to France or England. But no project of this size and scope had ever been attempted, and the controversy was fierce.

In 1810, Clinton had served on a New York state commission to study the question. Chaired by Gouverneur Morris, an early proponent of the canal, the group deemed the job beyond the state's means and called for federal funding. Other states objected: Since New York state would benefit, let New York build the thing.

Building the thing became Clinton's crusade, and in March 1817 the state legislature passed his funding bill. But the approval of a five-man Council of Revision was still necessary. Two were in favor, two opposed. The swing man, Chief Justice James Kent of the New York Supreme Court, was preparing to vote "no" when the vice president of the United States, Daniel Tompkins, paid a surprise visit.

BRIGHT IDEA

A Fire-Breathing Boat

Because Major Stephen H. Long was worried about encountering hostile American Indians while exploring the Missouri River in 1819–20, he designed a steamboat that looked like a dragon. "The bow of this vessel exhibits the form of a huge serpent," wrote a newspaperman, "black and scaly, his mouth open, vomiting smoke, and apparently carrying the boat on his back." The *Western Engineer* completed its explorations without Indian interference to the vicinity of present-day Omaha.

The Erie Canal opened the West and changed the destiny of the nation.

Another war with England was imminent, Tompkins told the committee. New York should not waste its time and money on such foolishness. Kent, deeply offended at this saber-rattling intrusion, spoke up: "If we must have war, or have a canal, I am in favor of the canal."

No American engineers had expertise in building such a canal, and so two lawyers, Benjamin Wright and James Geddes, were chosen to head the project. "A brace of country lawyers with a compass and a spirit level," one newspaper mockingly called them.

They started in the middle in July 1817. The land west of Frankfort, in Oneida County, was soft and level—a good place to begin on-the-job training.

The canal was to be 4 feet deep and 40 feet wide at the water surface, tapering to 28 feet at the bottom. Before it could be dug, underbrush had to be cut, trees chopped down, and stumps uprooted. The work was done in sections, some only a quarter-mile long, by farmers and local contractors. Muscle—human and animal—was the only source of power, but devices were invented to help.

Cement was needed that would harden underwater. A young man named Canvass White found suitable limestone and created the new substance. Aqueducts were built over rivers, streams diverted through pipelines. When, in the marshes of western New York, malaria became a threat, men wore small, necklacelike smudge pots to keep mosquitoes at bay.

In all, 83 locks were constructed, including five blasted from solid rock at the future site of Lockport, New York. Designed by Nathan S. Roberts, they lifted the canal 76 feet over the Niagara Escarpment.

In November 1825, the a packet boat named *Seneca Chief* brought a keg of Lake Erie water to New York Harbor for a symbolic Wedding of the Waters. The canal's cost, $7 million, was repaid by tolls, averaging only pennies a mile, in 12 years. Today, most of the traffic on the canal is recreational—just small boats, with limited commercial traffic.

Mix-and-Match Mating

TWO 19TH-CENTURY UTOPIAN COMMUNITIES ADVOCATE UNUSUAL PRACTICES

The great religious revival that swept the United States in the 1830s inspired two extraordinary New Englanders, Theophilus Ransom Gates and John Humphrey Noyes, to set up their own unique utopian communities.

Gates, a descendant of Connecticut clergymen, was an itinerant schoolteacher who wended his way southward in the course of pursuing his profession.

Religion was revealed to the frail and melancholy misfit during a night of agonized prayer in the Virginia woods. A local minister was told of Gates's mystical experience, and he welcomed him as a guest preacher.

NO MORE MARRIAGE
Moving to Philadelphia, Gates kept busy preaching and publishing religious tracts. He attacked existing churches and foretold worldwide destruction,

followed by a new order in which everyone would live together in "primitive love and affection." Marriage, he prophesied, would disappear. His newsletter, the *Battle-Axe*, cited Jeremiah: "Thou art my battle-axe and weapons of war: for with thee will I break in pieces the nations."

Gates's first convert was a prostitute, who readily embraced his notion that women could be chosen by God as "brides in Christ" of unhappily married men. One father of 10 to whom she proposed such a union became so distraught that he committed suicide.

FREE LOVE VALLEY

Gates soon left town and, with about 30 followers, formed a community called Free Love Valley on the Schuylkill River. Neighbors were shocked by such practices as communal nude bathing and expressions of free love during ecstatic revival meetings. At least two babies were born out of wedlock, each hailed as Christ. (Both died young but were expected to rise again.) Gates reportedly shunned sex and was not among the four disciples tried for flouting Pennsylvania's marriage laws. After his death in 1846, the group disbanded.

Meanwhile, along came Noyes, a member of a prominent Vermont family. Younger and more practical than Gates, Noyes—a Dartmouth graduate who had studied theology at Yale—became a devotee of perfectionism. He believed that A.D. 70 had marked the second coming of Christ. Since the kingdom of heaven was literally at hand, those who lived pure, perfect lives could enjoy it on earth, and in 1834 he declared that he himself had achieved perfection. His license to preach was revoked, but he nevertheless attracted disciples. He shared some views with Gates, whom he once visited to express friendship while "correcting" the older man's excesses. Noyes, too, disavowed marriage. But when his letter on the subject was printed anonymously in Gates's *Battle-Axe*, the two evangelists became bitter enemies.

Noyes founded his own religious community in Putney, Vermont, and, despite his anti-marriage

views, wed Harriet Holton, who had begun to financially support his work. Perhaps inspired by her four painful stillbirths, he decided that "it is as foolish and cruel to expend one's seed on a wife merely for the sake of getting rid of it, as it would be to fire a gun at one's best friend merely for the sake of unloading it." Thus began his doctrine of male continence, or non-ejaculatory sex.

Later, when Noyes was attracted to a disciple and convinced her husband and Harriet Holton to agree to marriage "in quartette form," he proclaimed the doctrine of complex marriage. This he soon expanded to include the marriage of all men to all women in the community. Arrested for adultery, Noyes jumped bail and fled to Oneida, New York. His disciples followed.

> "It is ... foolish and cruel to expend one's seed on a wife merely for the sake of getting rid of it ..."
>
> —JOHN HUMPHREY NOYES, in his doctrine of male continence

An able administrator, he established the manufacture of steel traps, canned goods, silk, and silverware as the economic base of the Oneida community, which eventually numbered 300 people. Men and women were considered equals and worked side by side. A committee of elders ruled on their requests for various sexual partners. Anyone had the right to refuse (one man who resisted a woman's "no" was thrown into a snowdrift to cool off). To perpetuate the community, Noyes later introduced "selective childbearing," also known as stirpicultural breeding or scientific breeding and described in his book, *Scientific Propagation*. The idea was to control breeding in the community in an effort to improve hereditary qualities. About 100 chosen men and women took part; Noyes himself fathered 9 of the 58 resulting children.

Like Free Love Valley, Oneida aroused antagonism. Eventually Noyes fled to Canada, where he died in 1886. After he left, his disciples paired off in conventional marriages. Unlike Gates's community, Oneida survived as a joint stock corporation. In time, it became America's leading producer of stainless-steel flatware.

Matters of Great National Importance

CONGRESS ADJOURNS FOR BALLERINA

They called it Elssler Mania. During her two-year tour in the early 1840s, the Viennese ballerina Fanny Elssler (left, in *La Gypsy*), a true superstar, took America by storm. Wherever she went, the Divine Fanny drew vast hordes of admirers. They rioted outside her hotel in New York and mobbed her carriage in Baltimore. In Washington, Congress adjourned so lawmakers wouldn't miss her performance. Poems and songs were written about her. (One said the whole city of New Orleans had "got Elssler fever.") Parasols, garters, shaving soaps, and cigars bore her name—as did the boiler of a railroad engine that was dedicated to her. Philosopher Ralph Waldo Emerson found her performance transcendental, and novelist Nathaniel Hawthorne placed her portrait between his pictures of saints Ignatius Loyola and Francis Xavier.

"OK" Okay with Everyone

Theories of how our favorite Americanism came to be

The earliest known appearance of "OK" in print, in a March 23, 1839, edition of Boston's *Morning Post*, explains its meaning as "all correct," spelled "oll korrect." But as the years passed and the expression gained wide circulation, speculation grew about how OK came to be. Was it the abbreviation for Old Kinderhook, President Martin Van Buren's nickname (he was from Kinderhook, New York)? Did it refer to Old Keokuk, an Indian chief who signed treaties with his initials? Or perhaps it came from the Finnish word *oikea*, which means "correct"?

OK reached the West Indies by 1847, England a few years later, India by 1883, and the Philippines around 1908. American soldiers carried it to Japan and Korea in the mid-20th century. OK is now part of the language nearly everywhere, no matter how it is spelled: o.k., O.K., okay, okey, oke, or even okeh.

The Abolitionist Who Hated African Americans

RACIST REPUBLICAN STIRS UP CONTROVERSY IN THE CAPITAL

Politics creates strange bedfellows, and certainly Hinton Rowan Helper was among the strangest that humanitarian Republicans could have embraced, despite his antislavery views. Helper was the son of an illiterate North Carolina backwoods farmer. Orphaned early, he came to dislike African Americans; he saw them as the foundation of an economic system that enriched slave owners while impoverishing the Southern whites. In 1857 he published *The Impending Crisis of the South: How to Meet It*, a raging polemic in which he castigated slavery, not for exploiting blacks, but for causing "unparalleled illiteracy and degradation" among the white Southern masses. His solution: form a political party to bring about abolition.

The book ignited a controversy even more sensational than the one *Uncle Tom's Cabin* had caused five years earlier. Four ministers were banished from North Carolina for owning copies, and three men were lynched in Arkansas for possessing the book.

Ohio Congressman John Sherman lost the speakership of the House of Representatives because he supposedly supported Helper's views. But Republicans, embracing the book as an endorsement of their fledgling party's bid for power, distributed more than 100,000 abridged copies during the 1860 campaign. In 1861, President Lincoln appointed Helper to a diplomatic post in Argentina—perhaps to remove him from the capital's political turmoil.

After the war, Helper returned to America, continued his racist writings, and went broke in a scheme to build a railroad from Hudson Bay to the tip of South America. Insane and impoverished, he killed himself in a Washington boardinghouse in 1909.

FUNNY FACT

Why the Song Doesn't Go, "Way Down Upon the Yazoo River ..."

The lyrics to the song, "Old Folks at Home," which begins with the famous line, "Way down upon the Swanee River," were written by Stephen Foster. Foster, a man of Anglo-Irish ancestry, never set foot in the South; he wrote "Old Folks at Home" in 1851 for the minstrel shows that were popular at the time. He thought little of what became his most famous song and allowed the leader of the Christy Minstrels to publish it under his own name.

The words for "Old Folks at Home" were chosen casually. Foster asked his brother, Morrison, to think of a southern river with a two-syllable name to fit a tune he was writing. Morrison proposed the Yazoo, but Stephen rejected this suggestion. Running his finger down a U.S. map, Morrison stopped at the Suwannee in Florida. "That's it!" Stephen said. And so it was almost by chance that the song did not start, "Way down upon the Yazoo River."

The Little Woman Who Made a Big War

HARRIET BEECHER STOWE PENS *UNCLE TOM'S CABIN* AND GETS COUNTRY UP IN ARMS

After Abraham Lincoln issued the Emancipation Proclamation in September 1862, he was visited by Harriet Beecher Stowe, the author of *Uncle Tom's Cabin*. Shaking her hand, Lincoln reportedly said, "So this is the little woman who made this big war." It was not much of an overstatement. Her book had been the first American novel to take African Americans seriously; it was also the first to have a black hero. Its vivid portrait of slavery's evils had polarized the nation.

THE FIRST UNCLE TOM

Eleven years earlier, Stowe—daughter of a Congregational minister, wife of a religion professor, and mother of seven—had written a sketch for the *National Era*, an abolitionist newspaper in Washington, D.C. She had published other stories, but this one, about the death of a slave named Uncle Tom, got a lot of attention. An impassioned cause since colonial days, abolition had become a fiery crusade in the North. Two of Stowe's brothers, the preachers Edward Beecher and Henry Ward Beecher, were deeply involved in the cause. She herself taught African American children in a Cincinnati Sunday school, and she had once helped a black mother and child evade a slave hunter.

Yet Stowe saw herself as a reformer, not a radical abolitionist. Writing, to her, was holy work. But how did the book come about? Edward Beecher's wife once wrote to her: "Hattie, if I could use the pen as you can, I would write something which would make this whole nation feel what an accursed thing slavery is." Stowe replied, "I will write that thing if I live." And she did.

"GOD WROTE IT"

When she finished expanding the sketch into a novel, she said it had come to her in a vision and that "God wrote it." Although John P. Jewett thought *Uncle Tom's Cabin* was a long book on an unpopular subject, he published it, in two volumes, in 1852. Stowe feared that abolitionists would find the book mild, but it sold 10,000 copies in the first week and 300,000 in the first year.

Reaction was intense. Within three years, almost 30 anti-Uncle Tom novels were published. Stowe received mountains of threatening mail (one package included the severed ear of a slave), and her Georgian cousin asked her not to put her name on the outside of letters. Critics hooted at her inaccuracies; she had seen a plantation only once and had asked

Frederick Douglass, the prominent black abolitionist, for help in learning many details of slave life.

Yet in Boston, Stowe was idolized, receiving a standing ovation while attending a concert on the day the Emancipation Proclamation took effect. Virtually every Northern intellectual read her book; the poet Longfellow wrote, "How she is shaking the world."

CARICATURES ON STAGE

Although Stowe's own dramatization of *Uncle Tom's Cabin* was unsuccessful, nine unauthorized stage versions appeared and were performed well into the 20th century. The first, by actor George L. Aiken, opened in Troy, New York, on September 27, 1852, and ran for 100 performances. Most of these plays distorted Stowe's original heroic view of the characters. The character of Uncle Tom, a strong, Christlike figure in the novel, was debased into a shuffling, subservient old man, the source for our disparaging use of the term "Uncle Tom" today.

Ladies' Fashion Blooms

PANTALOONS FAD SUITS MIDCENTURY FEMINISTS' IDEAL

"At the outset, I had no idea of fully adopting the style; no thought of setting a fashion. I stood amazed at the furor I had unwittingly caused." Thus Amelia Jenks Bloomer, suffragist and temperance reformer, recalled the outfit that she made famous when she began writing about it in her newspaper in 1849.

As editor of *The Lily*, one of the rare newspapers owned and published by a woman, Bloomer wrote enthusiastically of

A woman sports a corseted dress and bloomers in this 19th-century illustration.

the innovative garb—an adaptation of Turkish pantaloons worn under a knee-length dress meant to replace the cumbersome skirts of the time. Feminist awareness was blossoming, and *The Lily* exerted considerable influence. The pantaloons became known as "bloomers." The comfortable, unrestricted clothing suited the feminists' ideal, and it caught on quickly. "For some six or eight years," Bloomer later reminisced, "I wore no other costume." The style even provided inspiration for a song, as well as many bitter jokes and cartoons about who was to wear the pants in the family.

The feminist struggle continued, but by 1860 the garb had faded into obscurity, given up by women who believed that the attention paid to clothes distracted from more substantial issues. And, although Bloomer vowed that she never thought her support "would create an excitement throughout the civilized world," her name will forever identify the outfit she popularized.

Showing Skin on Stage

Mazeppa's "Naked Lady" actually wore tights

In 1861, Adah Isaacs Menken transformed a tired old melodrama into one of the most successful theatrical spectacles of its day. *Mazeppa,* penned in 1830 by Henry M. Milner (based on a poem by Lord Byron), was the swashbuckling tale of a Polish prince. For 30 years, a stunt by a live horse had been the play's main appeal. But when an Albany theater owner cast buxom young Menken in the leading role and

lashed her—clad in a loose-fitting tunic and flesh-colored tights to the horse—a star was born.

Menken, whose acting career had gotten off to a slow start due to her lack of talent, found herself a celebrity. She took *Mazeppa* to New York, where she opened to rave reviews, then went on to wow 'em out west. Neophyte journalist Mark Twain was smitten. Mormon leader Brigham Young, though expressing shock, managed to sit through the whole show. And

souvenirs of the risqué performance sold like hotcakes.

Lusty Menken divorced one husband, married another, then shed him, too, before leaving for Europe. There she repeated her successes, both theatrical and amorous. She was at the height of her fame in 1868 when she collapsed onstage in Paris. Within a month the theater's "Naked Lady" was dead of tuberculosis in her early thirties.

The Bearded Bard

**WHY A GREAT AMERICAN POET
GREW HIS FLOWING WHISKERS**

Henry Wadsworth Longfellow's impressive beard was a painful reminder of the bizarre and heartrending circumstances of his second wife's death. In the summer of 1861, as Fanny Longfellow was using hot wax to  seal locks of her two youngest daughters' hair in paper packets, a wayward spark ignited her dress. Whipped by a breeze from an open window, the flames quickly enveloped Fanny, who fled in panic to her husband in his study. Seeing his wife ablaze, Longfellow smothered the flames by wrapping a rug around her.

Terribly burned, Fanny survived the night, but died the next day. Longfellow's grief was all the more painful because, in his valiant attempt to save her, he himself had suffered severe burns on his face and hands. So badly burned was the poet that he could not even attend Fanny's funeral, though it was held right in the library of their home in Cambridge, Massachusetts. To hide the disfiguring scars left on his face by the flames, Longfellow let his beard grow.

TRUTH OR RUMOR?

Was it really the Dutch who came up with the image of what Santa Claus looks like?

Well, 17th-century Dutch settlers did bring Saint Nicholas to America, but their version of the saint didn't look too jolly. It wasn't until cartoonist Thomas Nast (the same fellow who developed the elephant and donkey cartoons that came to represent Republicans and Democrats) drew Saint Nick in 1863 that he became the rotund, red-cheeked man with the white beard whom we know and love as Santa Claus.

Every Christmas, Nast, who was also famous for his Civil War illustrations, depicted buoyant scenes as a respite from the clever and often biting cartoons that made his reputation. It was with these forays into the land of make-believe that Nast did a lot to popularize Santa Claus and his beloved world of holiday merriment, North Pole workshops, and a gift-filled sleigh pulled by reindeer.

The Literary Debut of "Mike Swain"

**MARK TWAIN'S POOR PENMANSHIP DAMPENS
EXCITEMENT OVER HIS FIRST *HARPER'S* ARTICLE**

When the 30-year-old Mark Twain went to Hawaii in 1866 as the correspondent for a California newspaper, he had already won journalistic acclaim for his story "The Celebrated Jumping Frog of Calaveras County." But Twain had bigger dreams. "In my view," the writer later confessed, "a person who published things in a mere newspaper could not properly claim recognition as a Literary Person; he must rise above that; he must appear in a magazine."

The disaster that struck the clipper ship *Hornet* gave Twain the opportunity he needed. The three-masted ship left New York for San Francisco with a highly flammable cargo of kerosene and candles. But 108 days later, after a careless sailor ignited a barrel of kerosene, the ship burned like a torch. All 33 people aboard abandoned the doomed vessel in three small boats. The survivors, adrift more than 1,000 miles from land, had enough supplies for only 10 days. Two lifeboats were never heard from again. In the end, it was 43 days before Captain Josiah

Mitchell, in an act of astounding seamanship, piloted his longboat to Hawaii. Incredibly, after the 4,000-mile ordeal, all the men in the open boat were still alive.

An embarrassing affliction nearly kept Twain from getting the story of the *Hornet* survivors: He was suffering so badly from saddle sores that he had to be carried on a stretcher to their hospital and was forced to take notes lying down. Still, after working on his article all night, he got it aboard a California-bound ship at the last minute. It was a scoop—the first detailed report to reach the mainland, for which he requested, and was paid, an extraordinary $300 bonus.

On his return to California several months later, Twain found that his shipmates included Captain Mitchell and two brothers, 18-year-old Henry and 28-year-old Samuel Ferguson, who had been passengers on the *Hornet*. Twain persuaded the Fergusons to let him copy the diaries both had kept throughout their harrowing experience. He also copied entries from the captain's log.

To his delight, the more detailed narrative was accepted by *Harper's New Monthly Magazine*. It appeared in the December 1866 issue. Still, Twain's debut as a "Literary Person" was far from perfect:

American author Samuel Langhorne Clemens, who wrote under the pen name Mark Twain, is shown in a circa-1870 portrait.

Unable to decipher his handwriting, the editors listed the author of "Forty-Three Days in an Open Boat" as "Mike Swain."

Al Reach: Baseball's First Pro Player

In 1864, hard-hitting second baseman Al Reach left the Brooklyn Atlantics for the Philadelphia Athletics so that he could earn $25 a week. Fans objected to a player taking money for the privilege of batting a horsehide sphere with a wooden stick. But Reach set a precedent: He became the first salaried baseball player, thereby transforming an amateur sport into a professional one. Before Reach joined the A's, outstanding athletes had been given money under the table—shares of gate receipts, gifts, and promises of political favor. By the end of the decade, baseball players were openly earning as much as $1,400 a year.

Amber Waves of Grain

HOW THE RAILROAD CREATED AN AMERICAN BREADBASKET

In 1873 the Northern Pacific built a railroad to Bismarck, North Dakota, but it was doing absolutely no business. The railroad's major assets were tremendous land holdings on both sides of the track. Since northern Plains land was considered worthless, something had to be done to prevent bankruptcy, and railroad agent James Power did it.

Inspired by the appearance in Fargo of a farmer with 1,600 bushels of wheat that sold for an unheard-of $1.25 a bushel, Power convinced two railroad officers to put up money for a 13,400-acre farm. "Minnesota Wheat King" Oliver Dalrymple came on board to manage it, and when his first harvest netted $1 a bushel, the boom was on.

In three years, the railroad sold over a million acres. Hundreds of people bought tracts that averaged about 300 acres each, and everyone raised wheat. As manager of two spreads totaling more than 80,000 acres, Dalrymple ran the world's biggest wheat empire. The Northern Pacific carried the harvest east. (In 1880 alone, it took 1,440 railroad cars to do it.)

Ably directing his workers, and using self-binding harvesters and steam-powered threshers as well as draft animals, Dalrymple created a virtual "factory in the field." Bonanza farms of 3,000-plus acres flourished. Publicity attracted wealthy easterners, and trains routinely stopped near Fargo so that passengers could tour the farms. Even President Rutherford B. Hayes visited Dalrymple's domain, which became a showplace for the latest machinery. The owners of one vast farm started a telephone network (one of the nation's first) with equipment they bought at the Centennial Exposition.

This abandoned farmstead in Maida, North Dakota, is located not far from where the 19th-century wheat boom began.

But by the 1890s, economic crises doomed the huge spreads, and no longer could a farmer "start out in the spring and plow a straight furrow until fall. Then turn around and harvest back."

A Big Wedding for Little People

In the dark days of the Civil War, the wedding of 35-inch-tall Tom Thumb and 32-inch Lavinia Warren was a good diversion indeed. Global tours under the guidance of P. T. Barnum had made General Tom Thumb, stage name for Charles Sherwood Stratton, a millionaire at 25. When Thumb retired, Barnum found another attraction and, as it turned out, a wife for Thumb. The February 10, 1863, wedding was at New York's Grace Church, followed by a reception at the Metropolitan Hotel. The event boasted a guest list of 2,000, including "the élite, the crème de la crème." New York's streets were filled with crowds eager for a glimpse of the well-publicized tiny wedding carriage. Gifts were lavish, and the couple met with President Abraham Lincoln during their honeymoon tour. For a while, the nation forgot the horrors of war.

New York City's Madison Square is illuminated in celebration of the U.S. centennial on July 4, 1876.

The Centennial Celebration

A REUNITED NATION'S 100TH BIRTHDAY PARTY HIGHLIGHTS AMERICAN INVENTIONS

It was hailed as "an international exhibition of arts, manufactures, and products of the soil and mine"—but in the wake of a financial panic and the ensuing depression, our nation's centennial celebration almost didn't get off the ground. And while critics said that European royalty wouldn't celebrate a democracy's birth, others wondered whether Americans themselves, still recovering from a bitter civil war, would attend.

FAIREST OF FAIRS

The Old World did help the New World mark America's 100th birthday. Fifty nations sent displays to the 1876 Centennial Exposition in Philadelphia, and before it was over, 8 million people had paid 50 cents each to see the fair.

Landscaped gardens and lawns transformed West Fairmount Park into a 285-acre wonderland. The exhibit boasted 249 buildings and its own railroad.

Amid speeches, music, and hoopla, President Ulysses S. Grant opened the fair on May 10, and visitors streamed in. Foreigners were impressed, and Americans took time out to sample life as tourists. They were shocked by nudity in French paintings, delighted by a graceful Japanese teahouse, fascinated by the exotic taste of Russia's reindeer meat, and intrigued by Austrian bath shoes.

SCIENCE AND INDUSTRY

The fair was also a setting for the exchange of technical information, and visitors to these shores were awed by America's industry and inventiveness. Thomas Edison's multiple telegraph was displayed, as was Alexander Graham Bell's telephone. And the typewriter on exhibit no doubt inspired Mark Twain to buy one. (He was the first U.S. author to switch from a pen.) As an English observer reported: "The American invents as the Greek sculptured and the Italian painted: it is genius."

The Year the Horses Died

EQUINE FLU FORCES AMERICA TO FIND ALTERNATIVES TO "HORSE POWER"

It was an urban disaster. Cities that depended on horses to pull streetcars, delivery trucks, and other vehicles were swept in 1872 by an epidemic of equine influenza that brought them to a virtual standstill. The flu started in Canada, spread quickly south to Louisiana, and then west. Few horses died at first, but soon some 200 were dying daily in Philadelphia.

At the height of the Great Epizootic, 18,000 horses were too sick to work in New York City; in Rochester, New York, not a horse was to be seen in the streets. Horsecar service came to a halt. Some cities tried using oxen to pull the cars, but they were too slow and their hooves too tender. In New York, gangs of unemployed men were put to work. Construction sites shut down for lack of materials; food stores and restaurants had to be supplied by men lugging sacks and cans. Fire departments were immobilized, and so the Great Boston Fire burned out of control, destroying a 67-acre swath of the downtown area.

There were probably as many theories about the cause of the disease as there were sick horses. Some said it was what the animals had eaten; others said they were breathing poisonous gas. The epidemic ran its course in a few months, but by then streetcar officials had begun looking for alternatives to the horse.

Fallen Angel

AN 1870s SEX SCANDAL ROCKS A RELIGIOUS GIANT

In 1874, Henry Ward Beecher was not only the most famous and highly paid preacher in America, he was a national symbol of morality and virtue. When civil charges were filed alleging that the pastor of Brooklyn's Plymouth Church had seduced the wife of a friend, supporters across the country cried slander. But the facts of the case, and the sensational trial that followed, reveal the pathetic hypocrisy of the Gilded Age.

BETTER PAID THAN THE PRESIDENT

Beecher had risen to prominence through his passionate espousal of abolition. Aided by the public relations genius of publisher Henry Bowen and editor Theodore Tilton, the preacher was big business. Pew rentals and contributions from his affluent Brooklyn Heights congregation amounted to $100,000 a year. His popular writings and lecture tours extended his pastoral influence across the country and netted him a neat $15,000 annually beyond his $20,000 salary. In the early 1870s currency, his income was nearly one

Shy and quiet Elizabeth Tilton was convinced that her affair with her pastor, Henry Ward Beecher (above), "had never proceeded from low or vulgar thoughts ... but always from pure affection and a high religious love."

and a half times that of the president. So popular were his energetic sermons that the Sunday morning ferries crossing New York Harbor to Brooklyn were called Beecher Boats.

But the private Beecher could not measure up to the public image. Burdened with a severe and sexless wife, he sought release in the arms of other women. In 1868 the corpulent cleric began an affair with Elizabeth Tilton, the attractive but somewhat naive wife of his editor.

Two years later Mrs. Tilton confessed to her husband. Outraged, Tilton confronted his former friend and threatened public revelation; then, for the good of all, he decided to keep things quiet.

TILTON'S FOLLY, WOODHULL'S REVENGE

But Tilton made a mistake. He confided his frustrations to Elizabeth Cady Stanton, a prominent suffragist and something of a gossip. Stanton let the story slip to, of all people, Victoria Woodhull. Woodhull was a fiery feminist, outspoken leader of the free love movement, and coeditor of *Woodhull and Claflin's Weekly*. Woodhull's views had been attacked by Beecher's sister, Harriet Beecher Stowe (author of *Uncle Tom's Cabin*); in retaliation, Woodhull went public in 1872 with Beecher's steamy story as an example of free love among the mighty. The preacher, to the disappointment of his advocates, answered her allegations only with stony silence. But in Brooklyn the silence was broken by clumsy cover-ups and scathing whispers. Finally the cuckolded Tilton, who was excommunicated by the church, could stand it no more, and in 1874 he sued Beecher. The heavily publicized trial produced damning evidence, but the all-male jury was unable or unwilling to reach a verdict.

Exonerated by a council of Congregational churches, Beecher survived the stain on his reputation and remained at Plymouth Church until his death in 1887. Theodore Tilton died in self-imposed exile in Paris. Mrs. Tilton also remained in Brooklyn, living with her mother. She died in 1897 and was buried in the same Brooklyn cemetery as Henry Ward Beecher.

Can You Type and Take Shorthand?

THE YWCA BEGINS A REVOLUTION FOR WORKING WOMEN

If there had been a National Secretaries' Week back in 1879, the boss probably would not have brought a dozen roses to the office. In those days, secretaries were almost always men.

But the Young Women's Christian Association was about to change all that.

America's YWCA was founded in February 1870 by Georgianna Ballard and 30 other privileged young New York women. Its mission was to assist working-class young women who came to the city seeking education and jobs. In its very first year, the organization took a radical step toward fulfilling its goal by establishing a public library. This may not seem like such a big deal today, but the 500-volume collection was the first free library in New York that would lend books to women.

The YWCA's shorthand classes changed America's idea of what "women's work" was.

The group was no less daring when it came to employment. At a time when most of New York's working women held tedious, low-paying jobs as servants and factory workers, the YWCA's directors did a survey of work opportunities and discovered that "stenography is the most lucrative of all professions, the demand for stenographers being in large excess of the supply."

To fill that demand, they offered shorthand classes for women in 1879. Those who completed the classes found jobs so quickly that the YWCA added a typing course the following year. Although the typewriter was still a newfangled gadget, the far-sighted directors of the YWCA thought that it might catch on. Unorthodox as the idea must have seemed, "some businessmen preferred to have their letters done on the typewriter."

Time for Change

AMERICA GETS ON BOARD WITH STANDARD RAILWAY TIME

To regularize railroad schedules across the country, in 1883 the railroad industry established Standard Railway Time, resulting in the four time zones still used today.

Even before the golden spike linked the transcontinental railroad at Promontory Point, Utah, in 1869, the rail industry faced a daunting task: how to get the trains to run on a reliable schedule. The problem lay not in the quality of the trains but in the varieties of time observed throughout the country. Because each town set its clock by the noonday sun in the public square, a distance of a few miles could mean a difference of minutes per day from one place to the next.

When most U.S. citizens made their living from the land, the day was governed by sunrise and sunset, not minutes. With the rise of industry in the 19th century, however, minutes mattered—not just to railroads but to factories, offices, and weather-reporting stations. And so, on November 18, 1883, after years of debate, a group of railroad owners, scientists, and businessmen launched a uniform time system called Standard Railway Time. It instituted a set of four time zones across the country, replacing the countless local time belts that marked time in every small town in America.

For the next three decades, Standard Railway Time was widely accepted. But a few cities and states ignored it, and it was challenged in the state supreme courts. Finally, in 1918 the federal government ended the controversy with the passage of the Standard Time Act, legalizing Standard Railway Time. Progress had triumphed over the dictates of the noonday sun.

Mr. President—or Should We Say, Captain?

RESOLUTE DESK A SYMBOL OF BRITAIN'S FRIENDSHIP WITH AMERICA

In May 1845, British explorer John Franklin led 128 men into the Arctic to search for the Northwest Passage. None of them ever returned. Rescue parties were launched as early as 1848. Four years later, Edward Belcher set out with five ships, among them the sturdy 600-ton HMS *Resolute*.

Belcher searched for the Franklin party for two years. Then, in the spring of 1854, he ordered all his men into one ship and abandoned his other four vessels as they lay trapped in ice. The order was foolish: the ships were sound, supplies were plentiful, and the thaw was near. Returning to England, Belcher was court-martialed for his decision and only narrowly escaped condemnation. But at the time he issued the command, his men had little choice but to obey.

Sixteen months later, in September 1855, American whalers spotted the *Resolute* floating freely more than a thousand miles from where it had been abandoned. By right of salvage, the ship now belonged to the whalers, who sailed it into port at New London, Connecticut, just before Christmas. Belcher's other three ships were never found.

The U.S. government bought the *Resolute* from the whalers for $40,000, had it refitted, and returned the ship to the British as a symbol of friendship. The *Resolute* continued to serve for more than 20 years.

When the *Resolute* was finally scrapped, Queen Victoria ordered an oak desk six feet long and four feet wide made from its timbers. The desk was presented to President Rutherford B. Hayes in 1880 as a memorial to American courtesy in returning the ship.

Social Climbing

MIDDLE-CLASS AMERICA GOES "HIGH SOCIETY" WITH CALLING CARDS

For those late 19th-century visitors who wished to observe proper etiquette, a well-placed calling card was an absolute necessity. Taking their cues from the rituals of high society, middle-class Americans spent a large portion of their leisure time exchanging afternoon calls. Proper form demanded that each visit be announced—in advance—with a calling card.

The basic tool of social intercourse, calling cards were imprinted with the owner's name and often a personal design, making them, as *The Art of Correspondence* put it in 1884, "the representative of the individual." A would-be visitor left his or her card at the front door with a servant, who might place it on a silver "card receiver." The lady of the house would then decide to accept the visit, decline it, or put it off, softening the rebuff by sending her own card to the caller the next day. Conversely, a would-be hostess would distribute cards declaring herself to be "At Home" on a certain day.

Leaving a card was a way to introduce oneself to society or to one's neighbors. Even in the college dorms at Bryn Mawr, proper young ladies arranged meetings by slipping cards under each other's doors. People also sent cards to fulfill social obligations and maintain existing friendships. "The annual visits are made and returned with peaceful regularity," Mark Twain wryly noted in *The Gilded Age*. "It is not necessary that … two ladies shall actually see each other oftener than once every few years."

Men presented cards to schedule business meetings, announce address changes, offer congratulations and—when the chance arose—to meet young ladies.

After World War I the widespread use of telephones and automobiles, along with more relaxed social standards, led to a decline in formal visiting and its herald, the calling card.

Legendary Exotic Dancer Saves Fair from Ruin

BUT DID LITTLE EGYPT *REALLY* EXIST?

In 1893, there was a big fair in Chicago, celebrating the 400th anniversary of Columbus's voyage. The fair had astounding scientific exhibits, but it also had trouble paying its bills. Then Little Egypt arrived. She danced sensually, drew huge crowds, and saved the fair from financial ruin. Sound like a fairy tale?

Thousands later claimed to remember Little Egypt, but historians have been unable to find any mention of such a dancer at the World's Columbian

Exposition of 1893. To be sure, there were "belly dancers" on the midway. But these modest maidens' gyrations were fully covered by long ethnic costumes. A bored observer recalled "inordinately thick ankles and large, voluptuous feet."

SEELEY'S DINNER GUEST

In his autobiography, Sol Bloom, the man who managed the midway, denied that Little Egypt was there. He said the dancer first appeared at Coney Island, where "she acquired great renown for her actual or reputed stage appearances in the nude. A couple of years after the fair a young woman identified in the papers simply as Little Egypt became famous when she rose unclad out of an enormous pie served in the Waldorf-Astoria at the stag affair that is still so felicitously called the Awful Seeley Dinner." Following this, Little Egypts burst out all over America, and presumably this is the source of the myth of Chicago's nude dancer.

Amid all the confusion, of course, several former Exposition performers claimed to be Chicago's own Little Egypt. One was a midway belly dancer who, in 1936, sued Metro-Goldwyn-Mayer over a movie. Another was a camel, also named Little Egypt, who gave rides to midway tourists. One thing, however, is certain: The camel is not the Little Egypt who popped so memorably out of Mr. Seeley's pie.

FUNNY FACT

How the Seventh-Inning Stretch Came to Be

It happened in 1882 during a baseball game between New York's Manhattan College and the semipro Metropolitans: Brother Jasper, the college athletic director, took pity on fidgety students and, calling a time-out during the seventh inning, told them to stand up and stretch for a couple of minutes. The practice was copied by New York Giants fans during an exhibition game against the college team at the Polo Grounds and has since become a baseball tradition.

The UFOs of 1896

"ALIEN" ABOARD IS BURIED NEAR DALLAS

A former Sacramento street railway employee was among the first to see it: "Two men seated as though on bicycle frames" below a balloon. Five days later Sacramento's district attorney saw it, and so did the mayor's daughter. It was even seen as far away as San Francisco. Soon sightings were being reported from Canada to Los Angeles. Two fishermen claimed to have talked to the crew.

People skeptical of invaders from outer space stepped forward claiming to know the craft's earthly origin. Among them was a former California attorney general, who claimed acquaintance with the ship's inventor and declared that it could carry half a ton of dynamite, with which it would soon bomb Havana.

The craze faded on the Pacific Coast, only to bloom all over the Midwest. A Kansas farmer claimed a heifer had been cow-napped, and the distinguished *St. Louis Post-Dispatch* reported that "an Elderly Christian Gentleman" had come upon a 20-foot-long vessel on four legs, in front of which sat a "majestic" bearded man and a beautiful golden-haired girl "in nature's garb."

Predictably, messages from the ship began to appear; the most sensational of them was addressed to Thomas A. Edison. Signed "C. L. Harris, electrician, airship N.3," it was indecipherable. Edison declared it a hoax. Airships would be invented someday, he predicted, but "at best" they "would be only toys."

The ship supposedly crashed near Dallas, and the pilot, identified as "not an inhabitant of this world," was buried in the local cemetery. Meanwhile, in Yonkers, New York, the craft was seen heading out to sea.

Scientists suggest that people were merely seeing Venus or some other planet. Or perhaps it was just one more of the hoaxes that were popular in the period. Whatever the source, it's a story that's hard to kill: In 1973 someone made news by stealing the Texas "spaceman's" tombstone.

America's First Gold

HARVARD DROPOUT WINS TOP MEDAL AT 1896 OLYMPICS

James Brendan Connolly was the son of Irish immigrants from the tough South End of Boston. Forced to leave school at an early age, he educated himself, and was admitted to Harvard in 1895 at the age of 27. Determined to compete the following year in the Olympics (the first since the Romans abolished the Games in A.D. 394), he asked Harvard for a leave of absence. When the college refused, he went to Athens anyway, paying his own expenses.

Connolly's event was the hop, step, and jump—what we now know as the triple jump. Its final, set for the Games' opening day, was the first on the Olympic schedule. This was a real problem for Connolly and the other U.S. competitors. The Americans hadn't realized that the Greeks used the Hellenic calendar; so instead of arriving 12 days before the Games, the team arrived just hours before the opening ceremony.

Connolly, tired and 12 pounds overweight, still longed for the first Olympic prize to be awarded in more than 1,500 years. The last to jump, he cleared nearly 45 feet, outdistancing his closest competitor by more than a yard.

The gold medalist never returned to Harvard as a student and rejected its offer of an honorary degree. At his 50th class reunion, the college awarded him a Harvard "H" in track.

Them's the Brakes

GEORGE LOHER IMPROVISES ON TRANSCONTINENTAL BIKE RIDE

Butcher George Loher wanted to take a big bite out of life. In 1895, he decided to bicycle from his hometown of Oakland, California, to New York. It was a trip of more than 4,300 miles.

Fully loaded, his Stearns Yellow Fellow, weighed 53½ pounds: a saddlebag was strapped to the frame, a bedroll to the handlebars, and a suit of clothes was stuffed under the seat. Nonetheless, Loher lacked some things that most of us would consider necessities: maps and brakes. When he wanted to slow the bike on a downhill run, he "displayed a wheelman's ingenuity by tying a quantity of brush together and trailing it through the dust."

Certainly Loher saw the country: He almost ran into a train in Oregon, and broke a wheel in Montana. At the Sing Sing penitentiary outside New York City, he was invited by the warden to sit in the electric chair. "I found it a comfortable piece of furniture (that is, when the dynamo is not running)," he wrote. Loher completed his odyssey in 80 days. His wanderlust satisfied, he returned to his butcher shop—by train.

Bonkers for Bikes

The leap onto a high-wheeler bicycle was too much for most Americans. But when the first American-made "safety" bike was introduced in 1886, even the unathletic got rolling. Actress Lillian Russell had a special seat made from a clay mold of her delicate posterior, and the wealthy Goulds and Vanderbilts cycled at exclusive clubs to the music of live bands. There were 100,000 cyclists in America in 1890; by 1896, the height of the craze, there were 4 million. Not bad, considering that brakes weren't introduced until two years later.

Old Battle-ax Hits the Bars

CARRY NATION HURLS HATCHET "TO SAVE MEN FROM A DRUNKARD'S FATE"

The drinkers in Dobson's Saloon on June 7, 1900, hardly had time to duck as Carry Nation entered, shouting: "I have come to save you from a drunkard's fate!" Although she became famous for battering barrooms with a hatchet, on this first foray in Kiowa, Kansas, she was armed with rocks. Soon the place was a sea of broken bottles and shattered mirrors. Surveying her work with pride, Nation admonished the startled barkeep: "Now, Mr. Dobson, I have finished. God be with you."

With her buggy-load of rocks, Nation wrecked two more bars, then demanded that the local sheriff arrest her. Startled officials asked only that she leave town. Nation, president of the local Women's Christian Temperance Union chapter, had heard a voice whisper after a prayer session: "Take something in your hands and throw it at those places and smash them." Loading a wagon with rocks, she drove 20 miles from her home in Medicine Lodge to Kiowa, a town noted for its illegal taprooms (Kansas was dry).

Tracing her views on alcohol to her first husband's death from drink, Nation launched a series of well-publicized raids in Wichita and Topeka, where she first used her famous hatchet.

Conservative prohibitionists looked askance at her tactics, but soon many hatchet-wielding women were wrecking saloons across the country. Nation also went on the lecture circuit, warning audiences in America and Britain about the dreaded evils of alcohol. Still, nothing gave her more satisfaction than "hatchetation."

Yes, We Do Have Bananas

In 1900, to convince a somewhat skeptical public that bananas were not poisonous, a grocer in Stillwater, Oklahoma, asked some Oklahoma A&M students to strike a pose and take a bite. (The exotic tropical fruits had first been served in 1875 at an elegant Boston dinner party, where they were eaten daintily with knives and forks.) The grocer's advertising gimmick worked, and sweet, tasty yellow bananas—originally imported from the West Indies—have been an American favorite ever since.

But Can You Do It Without Looking?

MEMORY MASTER/CHESS CHAMP PLAYED 22 GAMES SIMULTANEOUSLY

To play 22 games of chess at the same time is hard enough, but Harry Nelson Pillsbury did it without even looking at the boards. It was easy for him; moves were communicated using an accepted chess notation, and he just remembered all the moves everybody made.

Born in Massachusetts in 1872, Pillsbury began playing chess at age 15. Seven years later, he became U.S. representative to Britain's prestigious Hastings Tournament. The older, more temperamental players resented his calm demeanor and ever-present, odorous black cigars. But by the time the last king had been tipped in checkmate, Pillsbury was in first place.

He financed his passion for chess by giving public performances that combined the game with his prodigious powers of memory. In 1902, during a day off at a German tournament, he took on 21 acknowledged masters simultaneously—without seeing a move. Although Pillsbury won only three games in this demonstration, he did manage 11 draws. That same year in Moscow, playing 22 "blindfold" matches against less awesome opponents, he lost only one.

At another performance, a pair of educated scamps gave Pillsbury a diabolical test. They supplied a 29-word list containing such tongue-twisters as Oomisillecootsi, madjesoomaloops, Piet Polgelter's Rost, and antiphlogistine. The master mnemonist merely glanced at the list, then started his chess show. A day later Pillsbury recited the list perfectly to the flabbergasted challengers; then he playfully reeled the whole thing off again—backward.

A Bronx Tale

PYGMY KEPT IN ZOO LATER ATTENDS COLLEGE

Though this incident enraged many at the turn of the 20th century, it sounds a thousand times more horrible today. For a brief time in the early 1900s, the Bronx Zoo kept a pygmy on exhibit in a cage. His name was Ota Benga (later Americanized to "Otto Bingo"), and he was one of a number of pygmies brought from Africa to be in a 1904 St. Louis Exposition freak show.

There are conflicting versions of his life. The man who brought him here, Samuel Verner, said that Benga had been rescued from headhunters and had chosen to accept Verner's offer of a trip to America. Benga reportedly said that he had been kidnapped. Verner claimed Benga didn't want to go back to Africa after the exposition, so he gave the young pygmy—whose front teeth had been filed to

Oto Benga's imprisonment caused uproars in both black and white communities.

points—to William Hornaday, the director of the Bronx Zoo. Initially, Benga wandered the zoo and was encouraged to spend time in the primate exhibit. For a brief while, he was displayed in a locked cage, where he lived along with an orangutan and a parrot.

This spectacle caused a public furor. Blacks campaigned for Benga's release; white and black clergymen, fearing that he might be used to prove Darwin's theory of evolution, raised a storm of their own. Faced with legal action, Hornaday released Benga, who strolled the zoo grounds, followed by crowds. A group of sympathetic New Jersey clergymen sent Benga to an orphanage and helped him attend college.

He eventually lived with several Virginia families and worked in a tobacco factory. When he committed suicide in 1916, it was generally acknowledged that he had never adjusted to life in America. But a cynical Hornaday saw it differently. "Evidently he felt that he would rather die than work for a living," he snorted.

Comstock's Cover-up

AMERICA'S BIGGEST PRUDE PROTECTED US FROM CHURCH RAFFLES, RUM, AND OTHER HORRORS

It was an age when bulls were called "gentlemen cows" and delicate ladies ordered turkey "bosom" for dinner. The paragon of this late-Victorian prudery was plump, pompous Anthony Comstock, a professional enemy of sin. In 1873, he organized New York's Society for the Suppression of Vice, and, as secretary of the organization until his death, he devoted 42 years to sanitizing the country of everything from rum to church raffles. His specialty was anti-lewdness, and he was proud of his work. "I have convicted persons enough to fill a passenger train of 61 coaches," he boasted in 1913, toward the end of his career. "I have destroyed 160 tons of obscene literature." And he didn't stop at dirty books.

According to a YMCA report, in little more than a year he confiscated 60,300 otherwise undefined "articles made of rubber for immoral purposes."

Comstock's campaign often exposed him to danger. Once he narrowly escaped death from a mail bomb; another time, he received a package infected with smallpox. The same zeal that helped him rid America of some of its most vicious pornographers also made him a self-righteous buffoon. He prosecuted a 19-year-old girl for distributing pamphlets for the Art Students' League and attacked demure artworks, such as Paul Chabas's "September Morn." Apparently Comstock once confused paintings from the prestigious French Académie des Beaux-Arts salon with paintings "exhibited in the Saloons of Paris."

In a disgusting display of callous arrogance, Comstock publicly expressed satisfaction at having driven 15 people to suicide. Only the 16th gave him pause. She was a deranged woman, who believed she had married an angel of God. Comstock had had her arrested when she published a book of advice for newlyweds.

It's no wonder that this bluenose reformer was vilified and lampooned in the press. One cartoon showed him in court complaining, "Your Honor, this woman gave birth to a naked child." There is, after all, something suspicious about a man whose passion for purity drives him to devote a lifetime to perusing smut.

"I have convicted persons enough to fill a passenger train of 61 coaches," Comstock boasted toward the end of his career.

A Walk on the Edge

JOURNALIST MAKES NEWS (AND SOME DOUGH) BY TAKING A LONG STROLL

Money may be the root of all evil, but as former newspaperman John Albert Krohn noted, "Most of us need the 'root.'" Krohn decided to take a walk around the perimeter of the United States, hoping he could sell the rights to the story.

Krohn set out from Portland, Maine, on June 1, 1908, his gear in a pyramid-shaped box atop a wheelbarrow. His route led west to Washington, south along the Pacific Coast, east to the Gulf, and then up the Atlantic—9,024 miles in all. Wearing out 11 pairs of shoes, 121 pairs of socks, and three rubber tires (one of which was bitten through by a giant snapping turtle), he defrayed his expenses by selling souvenir aluminum medals along the way. Response to his mission was keen. Cards and mementoes were attached to his wheelbarrow. Frequently Krohn was "arrested" and sentenced to a meal and bed at the best hotel in town.

Returning home after the 357-day trip, he wrote a book and settled into gardening—a fine activity for a man who was already familiar with wheelbarrows and liked to get to the root of things.

The Naked and the Dead

PERVERTED PREACHER GETS A BIG BREAK FROM QUAKE

Franz Edmund Creffield's Church of the Brides of Christ brought new meaning to the term "holy roller." Preaching to his female flock in the homes of Corvallis, Oregon, Creffield (who called himself "Joshua II") would close the shutters, extol the innocence of the Garden of Eden, and shout, "Vile clothes, begone!" Off came dresses, petticoats, and corsets, and the group would roll on the floor, stark naked. Joshua was looking for the girl who would become the "Second Mother of Christ," and so greater excesses followed. Comely 17-year-old Esther Mitchell got the job.

Eventually, irate husbands tarred and feathered Joshua. After doing time in prison for adultery, he reassembled a small band of followers, Mitchell among them. On April 17, 1906, he cursed Corvallis, Portland, Seattle, and San Francisco; the next day San Francisco collapsed in an earthquake. Fearing for Corvallis, some 50 women rushed to join Joshua.

Mitchell's brother shot the prophet in Seattle. After being aquitted for murder he was killed by his sister, who shot him in the exact spot where he had shot Joshua. Esther Mitchell, who never did bear the "Second Christ," was committed to a state insane asylum.

IMPROBABLE PIONEER

Joe Knowles: "Modern Primitive Man"

"I shall be entirely independent of the rest of humanity," Joe Knowles declared on a rainy August morning in 1913. At that point, he stripped down to a loincloth and moved into the Maine woods. Urban life had spawned a strong back-to-nature movement, and Knowles decided to spend two months alone to prove that man could still survive the simple life. His notes to the outside world, written on bark with burnt sticks, were picked up by a Boston reporter. Circulation soared as readers followed Knowles's progress. Despite certain discrepancies in his back-to-nature tales—was his fur cloak actually a bearskin he'd purchased for $12?—thousands cheered the "modern primitive man" when he emerged. As it turned out, Knowles's survival skills in the business world were just as keen as they were in the wild: His book, *Alone in the Wilderness,* became an instant best-seller.

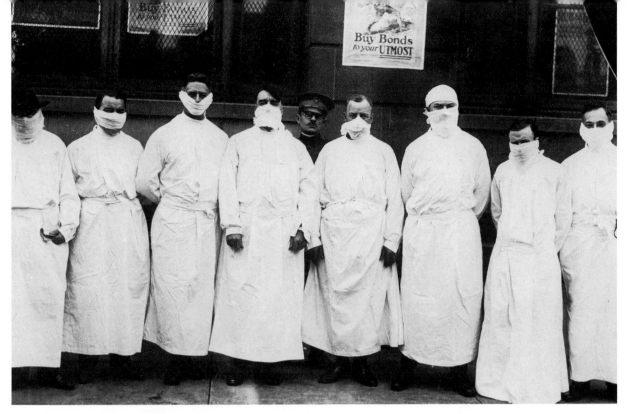

Doctors, army officers, and reporters wear surgical gowns and masks while touring a hospital to observe patients' influenza treatments. The E. M. Ashe poster behind them reads, "Buy Bonds to Your Utmost."

The Influenza Epidemic of 1918

WORLDWIDE PLAGUE KILLS MILLIONS, AND NO ONE KNOWS WHY

In August 1918, the Norwegian liner *Bergensfjord* arrived in Brooklyn. During its transatlantic voyage, 100 passengers had fallen ill, and four had died. A fifth succumbed just after docking—the first U.S. victim of a deadly form of influenza that was raging across Europe. The disease soon became the scourge of America, recalling Europe's Black Death during the Middle Ages.

At the peak of the pandemic, more than 100 people died in one day in both New York and Boston. In Philadelphia, where there were 528 victims in one 24-hour period, bodies were collected in horse-drawn carts. On Black Thursday in Chicago, almost 400 died. Schools and theaters were closed in many cities (idle chorus girls from Washington's National Burlesque worked as hospital volunteers), and folks wore face masks everywhere.

People in the prime of life were hardest hit. One in three American soldiers who caught the disease died. With flu rampant on troopships, President Woodrow Wilson considered suspending further sailings to Europe but was persuaded that they were essential to seal the Allied victory. Worldwide, about 27 million people died during the brief course of the pandemic, more than were killed in all of World War I.

Where did it all begin? Ironically, investigators now think that it probably started in the United States. They cite a March 1918 flu outbreak at an army camp in Kansas, followed by similar cases in France soon after the Kansas-based soldiers arrived there. Wartime troop movements hastened the spread of the disease, and measures taken by health authorities seem to have had no effect.

Mysteriously, the pandemic ended in early 1919. And no one yet knows why, in 1918, a mild germ turned so deadly.

The Battle of Anacostia Flats

THE BONUS MARCH ON WASHINGTON ENDS IN VIOLENCE

Top: Attorney General William Mitchell called the bonus marchers "the largest aggregation of criminals ever assembled in the city at one time." In fact, Washington's crime rate dropped during their two-month encampment. Above: A jobless Richard Barthelmess is urged to seek employment elsewhere in a scene from the 1933 film, *Heroes for Sale.*

June 17, 1932, was, according to one Washington newspaper, "the tensest day in the capital since the War." It was the depths of the Depression, and some 10,000 desperate World War I veterans were massed on the Capitol grounds. Across the Anacostia River, living in huts made of materials "dragged out of the big junk pile on the hill above the camp," were another 10,000, including wives and children. The Senate was voting on a bill, already passed by the House, to give every vet his war bonus. The bonus ($1.25 for each day overseas and $1 for every stateside day) had been awarded in 1924, but was not to be paid until 1945. The vets needed their bonus right then and had swarmed to Washington to demand it.

It was after dark when Walter Waters, leader of the so-called Bonus Expeditionary Force, emerged from the Capitol. "Prepare yourselves for a disappointment, men," he said. "The bonus has been defeated, 62 to 18." Stunned, the ragged throng stood silent. "Sing 'America,'" Waters shouted, "and go back to your billets!" Heads bared, the men sang out.

Few left Washington. They'd already been in the city nearly three weeks, camped at some 20 sites, including half-demolished government buildings, and they planned to stay. President Herbert Hoover refused to meet with them. Congress set aside $100,000 to transport them anywhere they wished to go. About 500 left; 1,000 more arrived. A silent, single-file "death march" began in front of the Capitol and lasted until July 16, when 17,000 gathered to watch Congress adjourn.

World War I veterans were supposed to receive a bonus of $1.25 for each day they spent overseas, and $1 for each stateside day.

Still the bonus marchers stayed on, and the authorities grew increasingly nervous. Finally, at 1:45 p.m. on July 28—two full months after the peaceful demonstration had begun—the spark of violence was struck. The police, ordered to clear the government buildings, met with resistance. Two officers opened fire, killing two men. By 4:45 p.m. an infantry battalion, a tank platoon, and a squadron of cavalry were on the scene. In charge was General Douglas MacArthur; his liaison with the police was Major Dwight D. Eisenhower; commanding the cavalry was Major George S. Patton Jr.

Militarily speaking, the operation was clean and swift. The infantry fixed bayonets. The cavalry, deployed along the north side of Pennsylvania Avenue, drew their sabers and charged the crowd. "Men, women and children fled shrieking across the broken ground," reported the United Press, "falling into excavations as they strove to avoid the rearing hoofs and saber points. Meantime, infantry on the south side had adjusted gas masks and were hurling tear gas bombs into the block into which they had just driven the veterans."

Within four hours, most bonus camps had been set afire, and the veterans had been driven across the Eleventh Street Bridge to the huge camp on the Anacostia Flats. By midnight those hovels, too, were ablaze. Around 4 a.m., as a light rain fell, the bonus marchers were forced across the Maryland border. They were told to keep moving to Pennsylvania. Congress finally awarded their bonus pay in 1936. The Bonus Army's lasting

continued on page 226

A Modest Beginning

First Rockefeller Center Christmas tree goes up during Depression

Happy to have jobs in 1931, New York City workmen put up a 12-foot Christmas tree amid the rubble of demolished brownstones on the future site of Rockefeller Center (St. Patrick's Cathedral is in the background). For decorations they used tin cans, paper, and tinsel. Two years later, the first official tree was festooned with 700 blue and white lights. The tradition, now grown to a nationally televised spectacular, has been observed ever since.

In 1924, an aspiring cartoonist named Harold Gray took an idea for a new comic strip to Captain J. M. Patterson, founder of the *New York Daily News*. Gray called the strip "Little Orphan Otto." But at that time, 40 other strips of the time starred boys, and Patterson thought Otto looked a little effeminate. The paper often reprinted a poem by James Whitcomb Riley called "Little Orphan Annie." "Put skirts on the kid and call her Orphan Annie," Patterson reputedly said. Gray did, and a classic comic strip was born. Gray himself drew the strip until his death, 44 years later.

accomplishment is inspiring the GI Bill of Rights, which was passed in 1944 as a result of the march. The legislation allowed World War II veterans to get government assistance and helped them assimilate back into civilian life.

Black Blizzards

IN THE DARK DAYS OF THE DEPRESSION, NATURE DEALS A SAVAGE BLOW

Sunday, April 14, 1935, began as a beautiful day on the southern plains. From southeastern Colorado clear across the Oklahoma panhandle, farm families enjoyed the fresh spring air as they went to church, praying for rain for their parched land. They had no idea that a windstorm was moving in from the Dakotas, lifting the powdery soil and swirling it into a 1,000-foot-high cloud; it was a blizzard of black dust and muddy rain hundreds of miles wide.

With winds of 60 miles per hour, the storm moved quickly, engulfing whole towns in total darkness by early afternoon. Motorists were stranded on highways; farmers were unable to find their ways home across familiar fields; families cowered in houses, watching the dust pack so thickly against windows it seemed that they were being entombed. People caught outside covered their

A farmer and his sons are caught in a dust storm in Cimmaron County, Oklahoma, in April 1936.

faces with cloth, terrified that the air would become too thick to breathe. Just a year earlier, a small boy had suffocated in a Kansas dust storm on his way home from school; such deaths were only slightly more gruesome than those from "dust pneumonia," the slow accumulation of particles in the lungs caused by months of breathing the dusty air.

NOT THE FIRST

Though probably the worst storm to sweep the Dust Bowl—an area more than twice the size of Pennsylvania, roughly centered where Colorado, New Mexico, Texas, Oklahoma, and Kansas meet—it certainly wasn't the first. Cycles of severe drought had ravaged the region since the end of the Ice Age, some 10,000 years ago. The dry spells of the 19th and early 20th centuries had ruined farms and driven settlers from the area. But back then farms were small and not much land was cultivated. Consequently, the dust storms were limited. The 1920s, however, had brought rain, new farming technology, and an influx of investors. Millions of acres of sod were plowed and planted. When the drought returned in 1931, crops failed and there was nothing to hold the vast expanses of loose soil against the blowing winds. The result was disaster, as nature added its own plague to the despair and financial failure of the Great Depression.

The unofficial beginning of the Dust Bowl occurred January 21, 1933, when the first great cloud of dust swept across the treeless plains, seeming to swallow the sun itself. Drifting dust from one storm even settled on the president's desk in Washington and was reported by ships 500 miles out to sea. In 1935 alone, the winds took an estimated 850 million tons of topsoil. And dust wasn't the only problem: Hailstones the size of baseballs rained down so hard that they killed livestock and smashed through the hoods of cars.

By the time the drought ended in 1940, the Dust Bowl had lost one-third of its population. Only concern for the land's needs and careful soil management keep disaster from happening again.

Defying superstition, Alvin "Shipwreck" Kelly spent Friday, October 13, 1939 eating doughnuts while standing on his head on a plank atop New York City's 56-story Chanin Building. He was probably 54 but claimed to be younger.

A Flagpole Sitter's Comedown

"Flagpole sitting ain't what it used to be," lamented Alvin "Shipwreck" Kelly, the master of the craft. "I thought I had a Depression-proof business, but I know better now."

Kelly had climbed his first pole for pay in 1924, to publicize a movie. He was soon a star. In 1930, after spending 49 days atop a pole at the Steel Pier in Atlantic City, he descended to the cheers of some 20,000 admirers.

But the rage faded as the Depression settled in. By 1934, Kelly was reduced to such stunts as trying to plunge off the George Washington Bridge on a greased rope, but police stopped him.

21,000 GIs Comprise Presidential Portrait

When photographer Arthur Mole assembled thousands of World War I officers and enlisted men at Camp Sherman in Chillicothe, Ohio, in 1918, he had no ordinary group portrait in mind. Instead, by arranging and rearranging 21,000 soldiers, he formed one of his most famous "living pictures": a huge portrait of President Woodrow Wilson. To shoot the picture, he had to climb a 70-foot-high tower. Then, using a megaphone to shout instructions, Mole had the men fill in a detailed outline he had created on the ground. The picture captured the patriotic fancy of America, as did many other efforts of this innovative photographer. Mole arranged thousands of troops into pictures during his career: 10,000 men into a rippling American flag, 19,000 into a profile of Uncle Sam, and 25,000 into the shape of the Liberty Bell. Some 18,000 formed the Statue of Liberty; and his biggest, the living U.S. Shield, used 30,000 people. Servicemen seemed to enjoy it; in a letter home, one of them bragged, "Hey, Mom, I was part of President Wilson's left eyebrow today."

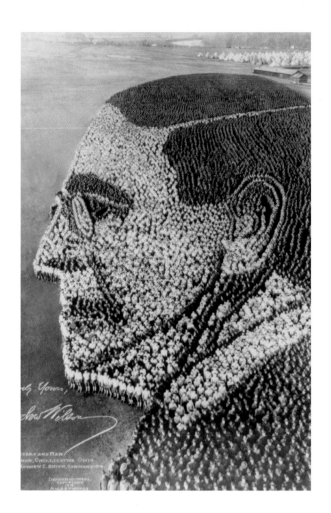

Tough Times for Temperance

A NEW NATIONAL PASTIME: GETTING AROUND THE 18TH AMENDMENT

When Representative Andrew Joseph Volstead of Minnesota pushed through the legislation that replaced bartenders with bootleggers, he sparked, quite unintentionally, the Roaring Twenties. It was a time when temperance advocates celebrated their greatest triumph, while the rest of the country seemed to go wild ignoring them.

During Prohibition—which started with the enactment of the 18th Amendment on January 16, 1920, and ended with its repeal 13 years later—you couldn't make liquor, you couldn't sell liquor, and you couldn't transport liquor within America's

Drinking liquor during prohibition wasn't illegal, but making it, selling it, and transporting it were.

borders. But that didn't stop many people from drinking liquor, for drinking in itself was not illegal. Indeed, many Americans not only made the easy move from saloon to speakeasy, they developed an almost entirely new national habit: drinking at home. Nothing prevented the trip from cup to lip; the trick was to fill the cup in the first place.

California vintners, with a little guidance from a former assistant attorney general, produced and marketed a perfectly legal grape juice, which after 60 days of loving home fermentation, became a tasty wine with a 15 percent alcohol content. The wine-makers were so successful that grape acreage in America increased sevenfold, from less than 100,000 acres in 1919 to nearly 700,000 by 1926. Before Prohibition ended, grape growing expanded even further, spurred by government loans.

Not to be outdone, beer barons offered wort, a half-brewed beer that contained no alcohol. With a little yeast and patience, the beverage could be nursed into producing its other, better half.

And the fun wasn't just in the drinking; it was in the fixing. For about $7 and a trip to the local hardware store, anyone with technological know-how could become the proud possessor of a personal still. Information on how to use the devices abounded in books and magazines; there was even a handy government pamphlet. Then, with a few potatoes, or some apples, barley, or oats, the do-it-yourselfer was ready to engage in one of our forefathers' most dearly cherished traditions: breaking a silly law. Bottoms up!

Monkeying Around with Evolutionary Law

TEACHER JOHN SCOPES WAS RECRUITED FOR THE FAMOUS TRIAL

It all began on a May afternoon in 1925 in Robinson's Drugstore in Dayton, Tennessee. Local businessman George Rappelyea argued that the state's new law—which made it a crime to teach Darwin's theory of evolution in the public schools because it challenged the biblical account of creation—offered Dayton a rare opportunity. The American Civil Liberties Union (ACLU) had offered to defend anyone willing to be prosecuted to test the law's violation of freedom of speech. Why shouldn't Dayton profit from the publicity? The drugstore group asked John Scopes, a science teacher in the local high school, to become the defendant. Dayton and Darwin were about to get their day in court.

The "Monkey Trial" captured the public's imagination, as reports were flashed across the country in the first-ever radio broadcast of a trial. The prosecution team, gathered by the World's Christian Fundamentals Association, was headed by William Jennings Bryan, three-time presidential candidate, former secretary of state, and outspoken advocate of fundamentalist teachings. For the defense, the ACLU retained Clarence Darrow, one of the century's outstanding legal minds and a self-confessed agnostic. In the press, it was a clash of titans; in reality, it was a contest between aging crusaders who had often championed the same liberal causes. Darrow had supported Bryan for president, and their mutual respect was deep.

The judge ruled that evolution was not on trial; the question was simply whether Scopes had broken the law by teaching evolution. Unable to call scientists as witnesses, a frustrated Darrow called Bryan himself, citing him as an authority on the Bible. At first Bryan parried eloquently, but as Darrow pressed, Bryan became increasingly confused and finally drew laughter from the largely fundamentalist audience.

In the end, Scopes was fined $100. The ACLU received national publicity, but failed to get a clear victory; even when the Tennessee Supreme Court overturned the conviction on a technicality, it upheld the antievolution law. William Jennings Bryan never left Dayton. Five days after the trial, he took a nap and didn't wake up.

Antievolution books were sold in Dayton, Tennessee, where John T. Scopes was on trial for teaching evolutionary theory in public school.

Edifice Complex

The world's tallest building! In the 1920s, as modern skyscrapers began to dominate the silhouette of urban America, the race was on. By 1930, New York could boast of the sleek 1,046-foot Chrysler Building. Its ornamental spire atop an Art Deco dome made it the record holder, but not for long. Not far away, the Empire State Building was rising at the astounding rate of four and a half stories a week. Though originally planned for 1,050 feet, a 200-foot mooring mast was added for dirigibles. But the builders soon recognized its disaster potential, and the mast gave way to a tower with a second observation deck. Completed in 1931, the 102-story edifice truly scraped the sky, for at 1,250 feet it was the tallest building in the world—and remained so for 42 years.

A Chilling Spectacle for a Cold Audience

SLOWLY FREEZING TO DEATH IN A KENTUCKY CAVE, FLOYD COLLINS INSPIRES A MEDIA CIRCUS

"Maddox, get me out. Why don't you take me out? Kiss me good-bye, I'm going."

Floyd Collins was delirious. On January 30, 1925, he'd been trapped about 150 feet underground in a space 8 inches high and 12 feet long and would remain trapped for about two weeks before he died. The temperature was 16°F, and water from melting mud and slime dripped constantly on his head. Up above, a raucous crowd of curiosity seekers made for a circus atmosphere.

This wasn't Collins's first trip into a cave. Eight years earlier, he had found a cavern beneath his family's farm and had turned it into a tourist attraction. Now he was in Sand Cave, on another farmer's land, hoping to make his fortune. He would get half the rights to anything he found.

Collins was headed out when his lantern failed. As he crawled on in the darkness, his foot hit a seven-ton boulder. It fell on his left leg. He was trapped, unable to turn or move in the "coffinlike straitjacket" of a dank, subterranean hell.

A SAD CIRCUS

Collins's brothers and friends tried to rescue him but couldn't. Then an eager 19-year-old reporter named "Skeets" Miller crawled into the cave for an interview; he didn't help the trapped spelunker, but a Louisville newspaper picked up the dramatic story (Miller later won the Pulitzer Prize for it), and a national obsession was born. Fifty reporters from 16 cities converged on Sand Cave, along with film crews from six studios. Regular bulletins on the new medium of radio kept the nation apprised of rescue efforts. Over the next two weeks, some 50,000 tourists bought hot dogs, balloons, and soft drinks from vendors around the cave mouth. One weekend, 4,500 cars from 20 states transformed the road to the cave into an eight-mile traffic jam. Con men and concessionaires worked the crowd. Women sent letters proposing marriage. Agents tried to book Collins for vaudeville tours.

Meanwhile Floyd Collins was dying, and rescue attempts were in chaos. A fireman proposed pulling his leg off. A college president offered to send in the school's basketball team. Collins's old business partner led 10 men into the cave, among them Everett Maddox, a tough young miner, who gave Collins his last meal. Thanks to a lightbulb and food lowered into the cave, Collins communicated with his would-be rescuers for about a week.

Then, on February 4, the entrance passage collapsed, and experts began tunneling down from above. On February 16, they found Collins's corpse. Doctors estimated that he had died about three days earlier, after two weeks of pain, terror, and freezing cold. Collins's body was put on display in a partially glass coffin at the cave on his father's land. In 1929, the corpse was stolen. When it was found nearby, one of his legs was missing.

Celebrating a Bright Idea

THE 50TH ANNIVERSARY OF EDISON'S MOST FAMOUS INVENTION WAS FRAUGHT WITH DRAMA

Half a century had passed since Thomas Edison changed the world's night life by inventing the lightbulb, and America wanted to honor the grand old man. General Electric Company officials, seeing a golden opportunity for corporate image-building, hired public relations pioneer Edward Bernays to create a gala anniversary celebration at their headquarters.

Edison was hesitant; he didn't want to be exploited by the company. Word reached Henry Ford, one of Edison's biggest fans, and a battle erupted; Ford vowed to stop the "shameful action." Finally, they reached a compromise: GE would take part in the venture, scheduled for October 21, 1929, but it would be held at Ford's Michigan reconstruction of Menlo Park, the New Jersey village where Edison had invented the incandescent bulb.

THE BIRTH OF PUBLIC RELATIONS

Bernays got straight down to business: George M. Cohan composed a theme song, "Thomas Edison, Miracle Man"; the U.S. government issued a commemorative stamp; prominent figures, including President Herbert Hoover, were invited to take part.

Ford had his own grandiose ideas. Deciding that Independence Hall would be a fine setting for the ceremony, he tried to buy the historic building from Philadelphia and move it to Michigan. The city fathers wouldn't sell it, so Ford commissioned a replica. Inside he built an Industrial Museum, filled with memorabilia from the age that Edison's invention had brought to an end. Arriving for the observance, the frail 82-year-old inventor was impressed, but his wife dismissed the project as a "plaything for Mr. Ford." That evening, 144 radio stations—the largest hookup in history—broadcast a reenactment of the moment of invention. Later that night, after giving a short speech, Edison collapsed from exhaustion. Within a week, the stock market crash smothered Bernays's carefully crafted public euphoria.

THE DAY AFTER

Recent studies of notes from Edison's lab reveal that October 21, 1879, was relatively uneventful. It was the next day that Edison managed to get an incandescent bulb to burn for 13.5 hours. Nonetheless, ever since the Golden Jubilee of Light, the 21st has been regarded as the landmark date. Edison died on October 18, 1931, and was buried on October 21, exactly two years after the jubilee. At 9:59 p.m., lights all over America were extinguished in a one-minute memorial.

"Some May Say That I Couldn't Sing, but No One Can Say That I Didn't"

Her voice was ghastly, her self-designed costumes outrageous, and her concerts ridiculous. But Florence Foster Jenkins made audiences cheer. The wealthy

heiress was 75 years old when she rented Carnegie Hall for a concert on October 25, 1944. The sold-out performance climaxed in a lively Spanish melody, during which she coyly threw flowers to the audience. The crowd demanded an encore. Out of flowers, she sent her accompanist, Cosme McMoon, to retrieve them, and she did it all over again. "She only thought of making other people happy," according to a friend, and she succeeded magnificently. The wild applause that greeted her performances was genuine, and her record album is today a collector's item.

WORLD'S FAIR
CHICAGO
1833 · A CENTURY OF PROGRESS · 1933

Light From Afar

DISTANT STAR ILLUMINATES THE 1933 WORLD'S FAIR

They called it the Century of Progress Exposition. The 1933 World's Fair, marking Chicago's 100th birthday, was supposed to brighten the gloom of the Depression, and its organizers needed a spectacular opening.

They looked to the stars. Arcturus, one of the closest, was 40 light years away. Thus, light that had left it during the Chicago exposition in 1893 would shine on the new fair. They would use that light!

The world's largest refracting telescope, at Yerkes Observatory in Wisconsin, caught the ray of starlight and focused it onto a photoelectric cell, which measured its energy and transformed it into the current needed to throw a switch at the fairgrounds. As a huge crowd watched, a red glow ran across an illuminated map high above the rostrum in the Hall of Science. Reaching Chicago, it burst into a flashing star. The switch was tripped, and a great white beam shot out from a searchlight atop the hall. As it touched one exposition building after another, they were thrown into brilliant light. And the fair was on.

FUNNY FACT

Crosby Went to the Slammer for Drinking and Driving During Prohibition

During the filming of the 1930 film, *The King of Jazz*, Bing Crosby had a minor car accident after leaving a Hollywood bash one night. A policeman smelled liquor on the crooner's breath and took him in. When, two weeks later, Crosby found himself in court, the judge asked: "Don't you know that there's a Prohibition law in the United States and liquor is forbidden?"

"Yes," Crosby replied, "but nobody pays any attention to that!"

"You'll have 30 days to pay some attention to it!" said the judge. Crosby went to the clink.

On July 1, 1946, the United States dropped a 20-kiloton atomic bomb on the deserted Bikini Atoll in the Marshall Islands. The blast, part of a nuclear weapons test, blew the socks off Pentagon brass. The bikini bathing suit—as modeled years later by Brigitte Bardot—also had a shocking effect.

The World's Smallest Bathing Suit

AN EXPLOSIVE TALE OF HOW THE "BIKINI" CAME TO BE

Two-piece bathing suits started appearing on the French Riviera in 1945. These weren't true bikinis, they were simply trunks and tops that left a band of midriff revealed. Some GIs brought the suits home to their wives and girlfriends, who were promptly thrown off local beaches.

The true bikini—two tiny cloth triangles joined at the hips, and a bra too brief to bear much more than description—was designed by French couturier Jacques Heim. He was a pioneer in bare-midriff fashions in the 1930s, who based his styles on the sultry wear of Polynesian maidens. Heim revealed his new suit at a Parisian swimming pool on July 5, 1946, and called it "*atome*—the world's smallest bathing suit."

BIKINI ATOLL

Just four days earlier, the United States had exploded an atomic bomb over a tiny Pacific island called Bikini Atoll. Throughout the early summer there had been rumors in Paris that this would be a "superbomb," and hostesses started throwing "end-of-the-world" and "Bikini" parties; so Heim's own explosive little atom came quite naturally to be dubbed a "bikini" by his competitors.

Modest as that first bikini seems today, it must have been pretty skimpy by 1940s standards. Micheline Bernardini, the woman who modeled the suit, was an experienced stage performer, but she admitted being nervous about wearing the bikini "out in the open" that July day at the pool. "All I remember are the hundreds of journalists all around me, the photographers and flashbulbs," she reminisced in 1970.

Despite the suit's explosive reception, it certainly wasn't anything new. Mosaics from the third and fourth centuries depict woman gymnasts in Roman Sicily wearing garments of much the same style.

The bikini was an immediate craze in Europe. But the suit was frowned on in America until well into the 1960s; it wasn't even manufactured in this country until 1959. Perhaps the reason was the same that *Webster's Third New International Dictionary* gives for the name of the suit: "from the comparison of the effects wrought by a scantily clad woman to the effects of an atomic bomb."

The Father, the Son, and the Holy … Bowler?

St. John the Divine in New York City, the world's largest Gothic cathedral, boasts a stained-glass window featuring a baseball player, a bowler, a cyclist, and many other sports figures. New York's Episcopal bishop's daughter came up with the idea for the intricately crafted display. Fascinated by the 1924 Olympic Games, she persuaded her father to devote an entire window to the "glory of sport." To help raise funds, famed sportswriter Grantland Rice wrote: "One of the main objects of both [sports and religion] is to build up the spirit of fair play, square dealing, and clean living." The original secular design was later changed: Modern sports figures were relegated to a small area, and such biblical athletes as Samson and Elijah took center stage. The window, dedicated to Saint Hubert, the patron saint of hunting, was installed in 1951.

Pips and Blips, Here and Then Gone

DID UFOs BUZZ WASHINGTON, D.C.?

Twice in the summer of 1952, UFOs were picked up on radar screens at Washington's National Airport and Andrews Air Force Base. They seemed to be buzzing the White House and the Capitol.

Near midnight on July 19, flight controllers at National saw "seven pips" clustered together in one corner of the radar screen. They would "loaf along" at 100 to 130 miles per hour, then suddenly accelerate to fantastic speeds—as much as 7,200 mph—before vanishing. Andrews radar technicians observed blips, too, and airline pilots saw bright lights in the sky. But when air force jets investigated at dawn, the lights had disappeared.

The press swarmed the Pentagon. Intelligence officers blamed temperature inversions, but experienced air traffic controllers asserted that the blips represented substantial objects. How else could radar have detected them?

Later that week, amber lights were seen elsewhere in the sky, including over the Guided Missile Long-Range Proving Ground in Florida. Then on July 26, more blips appeared on a Washington radar screen. A jet sent in pursuit couldn't even get close. Three days later, the air force called a press conference, its "largest and longest" since World War II. Officially, the UFOs were debunked as a weather phenomenon. Nonetheless, the eerie sightings remained a mystery to many.

Future President Spies UFO

Just after dark on a clear January 1969 evening, several members of the Lions Club of Leary, Georgia, had gathered outdoors before a meeting. Suddenly, a UFO appeared on the horizon. What was unusual about this sighting was that one of the witnesses was a future president: Jimmy Carter.

Carter, the scheduled speaker, wrote in his official report that an object "at one time, as bright as the moon" was sighted in the western sky. The men watched the phenomenon for about 10 minutes. It "seemed to move toward us from a distance," Carter continued, before it eventually departed.

He described it as "bluish at first, then reddish, luminous, not solid." Although later investigation concluded that it was probably the planet Venus (a common mistake in UFO sightings), Carter subsequently declared: "I'll never make fun of people who say they've seen unidentified objects in the sky."

On Your Mark, Get Set ...

The space age began on October 4, 1957, when the Soviet Union blasted a 184-pound artificial satellite called *Sputnik* into orbit. Foremost among those singed by the rocket's afterburners was Dr. Wernher von Braun, a German scientist who had immigrated to the United States after World War II. He could have been first.

For three years before *Sputnik*, Von Braun had tried to convince the Eisenhower administration that his research team's Redstone missile could put a satellite into orbit. In 1956 he had even demonstrated its potential, blasting a Redstone about 3,000 miles out over the Atlantic to a height of 600 miles. Had the rocket carried additional fuel instead of sand in its upper stages, it could have achieved orbit. But Von Braun's pleas for space exploration were

An illustration commemorating the 1957 launch of Sputnik I and II. The card reads: "4 October, the USSR launched Earth's first artificial satellite. 3 November, the USSR launched Earth's second artificial satellite."

ignored by Washington budget makers, lost amid demands for military rockets. Then came *Sputnik*, and the space race was on.

Where No Man Has Gone Before

ARMSTRONG WALKS ON THE MOON WITH HALF A BILLION WATCHING

While some 500 million people watched breathlessly, Neil Armstrong stepped out of his lunar module on July 20, 1969, at 10:56 p.m. EDT. Taking man's first moon walk, he said: "That's one small step for a man, one giant leap for mankind." (Static rendered the word "a" practically inaudible.)

Although Armstrong was the first man to walk on the moon, two astronauts landed in the module— the other was Buzz Aldrin. He said he was enraptured by the moon's "magnificent desolation."

As Aldrin and Armstrong prepared for the long voyage home, one of their backpacks broke a switch that controlled their module's ascent to the Apollo 11. Without some old-fashioned ingenuity, they'd

have been stuck there. Inserting a specially designed zero-gravity pen into the broken switch, they managed to flip it, and it came back alive.

Future moon walkers will find some mementos left by the astronauts: a piece of the Kitty Hawk, flown by the Wright brothers in 1903; a disc with messages from 73 important earthlings; and a memorial honoring the three Americans and two Russians who lost their lives in the space race.

The astronauts' return was "the strangest hero's welcome ever."

Since no one knew if they were contaminated, they were relegated to a quarantine trailer for 21 days. To add insult to injury, not only did they fail to receive hugs and handshakes when they arrived on the USS *Hornet*, but a man followed them around with a spray can of bug-killer.

From Fanfare to Fizzle

When Vice President Richard Nixon used an Edsel on a visit to Peru in 1958, his diplomatic mission shared a dubious distinction with the car he rode in: both failed. The Ford Motor Company announced in 1959 that, after two dismal years, "Retail sales have been particularly disappointing, and continued production of the Edsel is not justified." The car with the distinctive grill was discontinued. Thus the full-size Edsel, which had cost $250 million to produce and had been launched with great fanfare—just when the public was clamoring for smaller cars—became the automotive industry's most famous lemon.

Indecent Exposure

FAKE SOCIETY AIMS TO CLOTHE ANIMALS EVERYWHERE

"Naked animals everywhere! They are on the streets and sidewalks—a public disgrace to our children—and along the highways, causing accidents as motorists take their eyes off the road to watch nude cows and bulls. And these animals are not grazing—they are hanging their heads in shame!"

So proclaimed G. Clifford Prout Jr., president of the Society for Indecency to Naked Animals (SINA). "It should have been the Society Against Indecency to Naked Animals," he noted, but his father was "not quite of sound mind when he drew up the will." That document bequeathed $400,000 for the purpose of clothing animals everywhere, a longtime family cause. (Prout's grandfather, who fought in the Civil War "against the North and the South," had delayed Pickett's Charge as he tried to convince officers to clothe their horses.)

Clifford Prout Jr. publicized his cause on television and in newspaper articles featuring photos of well-clad animals. By 1963, the four-year-old SINA

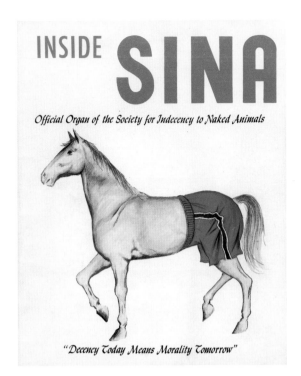

INSIDE **SINA**

Official Organ of the Society for Indecency to Naked Animals

"Decency Today Means Morality Tomorrow"

claimed a membership of 50,000, and its telephone rang constantly. Critics, of course, abounded. Wrote one: "Imagine the dog who couldn't scratch his fleas or the cat that wished to bathe herself."

It was an activist crusade. SINA supplied sympathizers with "summonses" to be issued "for appearing in public with a naked dog, cat, horse, cow, or any domestic animal." The Greyhound Bus Lines was threatened with a boycott for firing a SINA member who painted trousers on the corporate symbol. And Prout demanded that RCA's trademark dog, famous for listening to His Master's Voice, be decently covered.

But then, during a television interview, a CBS employee recognized the SINA leader as Buck Henry, a comedy writer. The truth was revealed: SINA was a hoax, the brainchild of social satirist and professional put-on artist Alan Abel. Henry would go on to stage, screen, and television fame, and Abel to such hoaxes as promoting the Sex Olympics, landing a Martian on Long Island, and writing his own premature obituary (printed in *The New York Times*). But he will probably be best remembered for getting people to put pants on pets.

Cash from the Cabbage Patch

COUNTRY GOES CRAZY FOR ONE-OF-A-KIND DOLLS

In 1983, to the utter dismay of marketers everywhere, a national craze erupted for a new line of homely dolls that didn't talk, cry, or wet their pants. Xavier Roberts, a young man from Georgia who was experimenting with soft sculpture, had drawn on Appalachian folk traditions to create his handmade dolls with yarn for hair— the antithesis of modern, high-tech toys. Roberts approached toy companies to discuss large-scale production; Coleco was interested.

Coleco's Cabbage Patch Kids were a monumental hit. Each Kid or Baby (the makers didn't call them "dolls") was unique, but all had Roberts's signature imprinted on their bottoms. "Adopted" by a child "parent," each arrived with adoption papers from the "hospital" in Cleveland, Georgia, after it had been "born" in a Cabbage Patch. Demand greatly exceeded supply, and tales of parents rioting at toy stores to get dolls were headline news in the early 1980s. Ironically, Coleco ultimately went bankrupt. Another company, Play Along, now makes the dolls.

FUNNY FACT

Where the "Beautiful People" Come From

Diana Vreeland became editor in chief of *Vogue* in 1963. It was during her tenure that she coined a phrase to describe international socialites: the "Beautiful People."

In 1620, the *Mayflower* brought English
pilgrims seeking a new life to New England.
Opposite: On June 3, 1965, Edward White
becomes the first American to walk in space.
He logged more than 6,000 miles during
his 23-minute stroll.

CHAPTER SEVEN

The Long Frontier

Wat unknown lands can we conquer? What new wonders can be found out West? America's early colonists did much to answer these questions. They set to sea, stretched their wagons westward, conceived of new religions, climbed the highest mountains, settled the widest plains, and lived with native peoples. Their successes and failures are ingrained in us; the word "American," as a result, is practically synonymous with an adventurous spirit, a curious mind, and boundless determination to see dreams come true.

As progress marches on and exploring to distant lands is as simple as booking a plane ticket (or watching a documentary on TV), only life beyond Earth holds any real mystery. Like our forefathers, we, too, wonder what new discoveries we might find "out there."

The Writing on the Wall

LOTS OF HINTS, BUT FEW SOLID ANSWERS, ABOUT OUR NATION'S FIRST EXPLORERS

Who got to the New World first: The Irish? The Welsh? The Phoenicians? The Vikings? Or some other group that we just don't know about?

In the hills of southern West Virginia are petroglyphs (rock carvings) that were long considered the work of local Indians. But lately, experts have made a convincing case that they are ancient Irish writings that may date from A.D. 500. And in New Hampshire, underground passages, stone chambers, and monoliths quarried by methods predating metal tools have led others to speculate that the Celts (or perhaps the Phoenicians) visited the spot 3,000 years ago. No wonder the site is called Mystery Hill.

A frontier tale at one time gained great popularity. In 1170, so the story goes, Prince Madoc ab Owain Gwynedd sailed west with 120 settlers, landing in Mobile Bay, Alabama. The fact that Madoc could have made the trip—Welsh ships of the time were seaworthy—was reinforced by a 17th-century clergyman who claimed to have preached in Welsh to Tuscarora Indians. But many years later, in 1792, another clergyman was sent from Wales to investigate the legends. He found no Welsh-speaking Indians, nor did Lewis and Clark.

Yet sentimental support for the story (backed by the discovery of forts in Tennessee, Georgia, and Alabama that resemble ancient Welsh construction) is strong. In 1953, a plaque was dedicated at Fort Morgan on Mobile Bay. Its inscription: "In memory of Prince Madoc, a Welsh explorer, who landed on the shores of Mobile Bay in 1170 and left behind, with the Indians, the Welsh language."

Columbus (and Company) at Sea

FAMED MARINER FUDGES BOOKS, DUELS WITH COLLEAGUE FOR GLORY

In 1492, Columbus sailed the ocean blue in the *Pinta*, the *Niña*, and the *Santa Maria*. Everyone knows that. But we might all be wrong.

The year is right, of course, and the *Pinta* and the *Niña* were there. But throughout his journal, Christopher Columbus never called his flagship *Santa Maria*, referring to it simply as *La Capitana* ("The Flagship"). The sailors called it *La Gallega* ("The Galician") after the Spanish province of Galicia, where the ship was built, but there's evidence that its real name may have been the *Mariagalante* ("flirtatious Mary")—later deemed unsuitable for the important voyage. (On his second trip to the New World, Columbus's flagship *was* called the *Santa Maria*, but he nicknamed it the *Mariagalante*.)

More important than the flagship's name was its maneuverability. The captains of the *Niña* and the *Pinta* often sailed ahead of the admiral, then waited for an embarrassed Columbus to catch up.

PINZÓN WANTS CREDIT, TOO

Martín Alonso Pinzón, commander of the *Pinta* and a master mariner in his own right, also had dreams of discovering fabulous new lands. He died two weeks after his return, but his memory was kept alive by relatives, who maintained in a lawsuit that dragged on until long after Columbus's death in 1506 that only Pinzón's influence, determination, and seamanship had made the discovery possible.

Columbus had come to Pinzón for help, they testified, and the two had struck a deal: Everything earned by the voyage would be equally divided. It was Pinzón who replaced two of Columbus's ships with the more seaworthy *Niña* and *Pinta*, and it was he who had habitually taken the lead. Had he not encouraged Columbus with the famous *Adelante!* ("Sail on!"), the disheartened admiral would have turned back. And it was Pinzón's course correction, they insisted, that led to the first landfall.

Columbus's champions argued that it was really Pinzón who wanted to turn back: "Martín Alonso, do me this favor," Columbus begged. "Stay with me this day and night, and if I don't bring you to land before day cut off my head and you shall return." Luckily, land was sighted the next day.

Columbus takes possession of the new country. The explorer landed at the island of Guanahani, West Indies, on October 12, 1492.

After the first Caribbean landfall, it had become clear that the fleet wasn't big enough for two ambitious men. While the others searched the islands for gold, Pinzón and the *Pinta* vanished for six weeks. The wayward captain later explained that he had been lured to an island called Babeque by an Indian's talk of gold. He had found none, but the side trip gave him the distinction of being the first European to sail along the shores of modern-day Haiti.

On the return voyage, Pinzón and his ship again disappeared. The admiral feared that the wanderer would return ahead of him and announce the discovery of the New World as his own, but Columbus beat him to port.

THE FRAUDULENT LOG

Columbus kept two logbooks—one public, the other private. Fearing the crew would panic if they knew how far they'd sailed, he entered reduced distances in the public log; but he overestimated his speed, so the phony log was actually more accurate than his own.

Columbus was a master sailor. Modern yachtsmen are still challenged by his times. Equally impressive was his ability to locate the same islands each time he crossed 2,500 miles of ocean.

Details of Columbus's Journal

Much has been gleaned about Columbus's voyages from Bartolomé de las Casas, the 16th-century priest who chronicled Spanish exploration. He told the world about hammocks ("very restful to sleep in") and tobacco. But it was the admiral himself who recorded the most vivid impressions of his surroundings on these shores so far from home. "Here the fishes are so unlike ours that it is marvellous," Columbus wrote. "And all the trees … as different from ours as day from night, and so the fruits, the herbage, the rocks, and all things." His descriptions set European naturalists aquiver. Among his discoveries was the delicious "pine of the Indies"—the pineapple.

Two Stitches Got 'em Grub

CABEZA DE VACA AND COMPANY SURVIVE EIGHT YEARS BY "HEALING" AMERICAN INDIANS

Knife in hand, Álvar Núñez Cabeza de Vaca knelt by the prostrate American Indian and felt around his heart, where an arrowhead had lodged long ago, causing him constant suffering. Then, intoning a prayer, he made a deep cut, probed with the flint blade, removed the foreign object, and took two stitches. The "whole town came to look" at the arrowhead, and celebrations were held, recorded the Spaniard. "The next day I cut the two stitches and the Indian was well. This cure gave us control throughout the country."

At first, when the American Indians demanded that the four Spaniards perform as healers, Cabeza de Vaca and his companions ridiculed the idea; but when the Indians withheld food, they quickly reconsidered.

Cabeza de Vaca and his three companions had become medicine men out of necessity. The sole survivors of the 300-man expedition of Pánfilo de Narváez, shipwrecked off the east Texas coast in the spring of 1528, they had been wandering through a strange, unexplored land for seven years, desperately hoping to reach a Spanish outpost. They were alive only because the native people they encountered were convinced that the explorers were sorcerers, with the ability to heal or destroy.

At first, when the American Indians demanded that the four Spaniards perform as healers, they had ridiculed the idea; but when the Indians withheld food, they quickly reconsidered. "Our method was to bless the sick, breathing upon them, and recite a Pater-noster and an Ave Maria," wrote Cabeza de Vaca. They also applied whatever they knew of European medicine. Apparently the poseurs were quite successful. The grateful native people treated them well, giving them food when they had scarcely enough for themselves.

As they struggled through the Southwest, trying to find their way to Mexico, news of Cabeza de Vaca's surgical feat preceded them, and they were received everywhere with showers of presents: 600 hearts of deer, cotton shawls, ceremonial gourd rattles, and in the Sonora River valley, coral beads and five ceremonial arrowheads of emerald (which were probably actually malachite). "Whence do these come?" asked Cabeza de Vaca. "From the high mountains to the north, where are great populous cities and tall houses," the Indians replied, referring to the pueblos of the Zunis.

In the spring of 1536, the four men, who had trudged 6,000 miles, wept with joy when they reached Culiacán, a Spanish outpost in Mexico. They told their countrymen their tale. Greed for gold fired the imagination of the Spaniards at Cabeza de Vaca's mention of the great cities to the north. For years to come, Francisco Vásquez de Coronado and others would search in vain for the Seven Cities of Cíbola, fabled for their streets of gold.

700 Pigs and Nothing to Eat

DE SOTO LEADS HOGS ON A WILD GOOSE CHASE

Power, glory, and fabulous wealth all seemed within reach for the conquistador Hernando de Soto when the king of Spain offered him the governorship of Florida (the southeastern part of the present United States) in 1537. All he had to do was to explore and settle the land—completely at his own expense. Aware that others had failed in this undertaking, he spent a year in Cuba making preparations.

In May 1539, when de Soto landed at Tampa Bay, Florida, he had with him an expeditionary force of 622 men (cavalry, footmen, and artisans), plus horses, dogs, and, as insurance against starvation, 13 Spanish hogs to breed along the way.

Heading north, the Spaniards filed through a land of plenty, but they lacked skills in foraging, hunting, and fishing. When they couldn't get food from the Indians, they were often hungry. Nevertheless de Soto, fearful of more extreme emergencies ahead, refused to allow the slaughter of pigs. When there was nothing else, the men ate dogs. In less than a year there were 300 swine, and they continued to multiply.

The expedition straggled on, periodically making monthlong stops that gave piglets time to grow so

they could hoof it with the rest. The squealing hogs had to be coaxed and herded through forests to keep them from straying to grub for nuts and roots. They were driven through bayous and canebrakes, hauled by block-and-tackle across streams, and transported across rivers on crude rafts.

Coming upon the Mississippi in May 1541, de Soto (the first white man to behold the great river) had the hogs ferried across. The swine traveled on to Oklahoma and then started back, as the explorer, who had found no treasure during his 4,000-mile march, bitterly acknowledged failure. In May 1542 he died, probably of malaria, and was interred in the river he had discovered. The hogs—by then numbering 700—were quickly auctioned off, and his men feasted on roast pork.

BRIGHT IDEA

Another Good Use for Pigs

Hogs are efficient snake killers. The pigs that Hernando de Soto took on his expedition may have served to protect his men from poisonous reptiles.

Francis Drake Claims California

BRIT IS THE SECOND MAN TO CIRCUMNAVIGATE THE GLOBE

Two centuries before the Spanish began to settle in California, an Englishman landed in a "convenient and fit harbor" along the Pacific Coast and claimed the territory for Queen Elizabeth I.

In 1577, Francis Drake, a master mariner, trader, and privateer, outfitted five ships and set out, apparently with the secret backing of the queen. His mission: to venture into the Pacific, via the Strait of

Magellan (named for the leader of the first globe-circling expedition). Once there, Drake turned north, plundering Spanish ships and settlements on the South American coast and filling his holds with treasure. He sailed as far as present-day Oregon, no doubt seeking the fabled Northwest Passage as a shortcut home.

Three of Drake's ships were lost in storms, and a fourth turned back. Only his flagship, the 100-ton *Golden Hind*, remained, and it was leaking badly when

In this late 19th-century engraving, English naval commander Sir Francis Drake is crowned the King of California.

Drake headed south again, seeking a safe harbor for repairs. On June 17, 1579, after struggling through bitter cold and "stinking fogs," he found his harbor. He spent five weeks there, on the northern California coast, while his ship lay on the beach being caulked.

The shore resembled that of his native coast, so Drake named the area Nova Albion. The Native Americans greeted the white men with friendly amazement, dubbing Drake their *hyoh* (king). He accepted the title as Elizabeth's envoy and on a brass plate nailed to a post noted "the free giving up of the province and kingdom into her Majestie's hands." Then, his ship repaired, Drake sailed off across the Pacific, returning home to glory and a knighthood. From then on, the Spanish continued to call him *El Dragón*, and Englishmen forever called him Sir.

Permanent Vacation

16TH-CENTURY PLEASURE CRUISERS RESORT TO CANNIBALISM

The New World was still very new indeed when, in 1536, sea captain Richard Hore organized the first "pleasure cruise" to its shores. Tourist cruises to warm climes were not uncommon then, though they were often disguised as pilgrimages. Hore was the first to see potential profit in the prospect of visiting the newly discovered continent. Hiring two ships and a crew of 90, he announced a sightseeing tour across the ocean. Thirty gentlemen interested in exotic adventure signed on at prices designed to make Hore a rich man.

In Newfoundland, one of the ships ran out of provisions, and the passengers began to starve. They tried to live off the land, scavenging herbs and roots. Then one man killed another and feasted on him; soon others began to disappear. Shocked, Captain Hore preached a sermon deploring cannibalism, asking everyone to abstain from it in the future.

That night, a French ship wandered into the harbor, and the Englishmen commandeered it for their trip home. None of the survivors ever explained why they couldn't have subsisted on Newfoundland's abundant fish and game, instead of each other.

Without a Trace

**COLONY OF 114 SETTLERS
DISAPPEARS FROM ROANOKE ISLAND**

One of the first serious attempts to colonize North America resulted in one of its oldest mysteries: Somehow, a colony of 114 men, women, and children disappeared without a trace.

In midsummer 1587, the expedition, financed by Sir Walter Raleigh and led by John White, landed at Roanoke Island (off the North Carolina coast in what was then Virginia) on a tide of trouble. A year earlier Raleigh had established an English garrison there to protect his title to the region; the only signs of it that the colonists could find were a ruined settlement and a single human skeleton. One man who strayed from the camp was found dead, his body abristle with 16 arrows.

Nevertheless, the new settlers remained optimistic. On August 18, 1587, Virginia Dare, White's granddaughter, became the first English child born in America. But with winter approaching and no time for planting crops, the colony was running out of supplies. Despite protests, White was chosen to return to England for help.

He arrived as the English were repelling the Spanish Armada and was unable to return to Roanoke until 1591. There was no sign of the colonists he'd left except, carved on a tree, the letters "CRO," and on a palisade post, the word "CROATOAN," which was the name of another island where the American Indians were known to be friendly. Thinking that his group had relocated there, White set out to find them, but he never did. Finally, his ship nearly destroyed by bad weather, he was forced to return to England.

Over the centuries, searches for the lost colony of Roanoke have yielded nothing but theories. Indians probably destroyed it. But what Indians, when, and how remain a mystery.

Poles Go to Polls

**PRE-*MAYFLOWER* POLISH ARTISANS GO ON
STRIKE WHEN THEIR VOTE IS TAKEN AWAY**

By the time the *Mayflower* landed at Plymouth, Massachusetts, Polish artisans had been hard at work in Jamestown, Virginia, for more than 12 years. A full year before the Puritans' arrival, the Poles had helped establish the democratic process in the New World by staging America's first labor strike.

Captain John Smith, the colony's leader, saw early on that in order to survive, Jamestown had to do more than just feed itself. It needed to produce goods that could be exported and sold at a profit. The new land had an abundance of pine trees whose sap could be tapped to produce valuable pitch, tar, resin, and turpentine. And Smith knew exactly

The construction of the settlement at Jamestown, Virginia, was largely fueled by Polish artisans who had arrived more than a decade before the *Mayflower* pilgrims.

where to find men skilled in the manufacture of these commodities; the captain had spent some time in Poland and was familiar with the flourishing pitch, tar, and glass industries there. So it was to Poland that he sent his request for artisans.

The first Polish immigrants arrived in 1608. They were probably indentured workers, which meant that in return for their passage to America, the men had agreed to work for the colony for a certain number of years.

Smith praised the Poles as hard workers and took note that two of them had saved his life when he was attacked by American Indians. The captain was probably quite surprised, then, when the hardworking Poles went on strike.

In 1619, as the colonists were preparing to elect members of the Virginia Assembly, the new governor announced that only men of English origin would be allowed to vote. The Poles, having already repaid their debt of indenture, responded to this announcement by laying down their tools. If they couldn't vote, they said, they wouldn't work. This refusal to work was the first such action in the English colonies and a bona fide American milestone.

Their startling demand was met, and a democratic precedent was set. The court record of the Virginia Company for July 21, 1619, puts it best: "Upon some dispute of the Polonians resident in Virginia, it was now agreed they shall be enfranchised and made as free as any inhabitant there whatsoever."

Morton's Merry Mount

JOLLY SETTLER IN "PARADISE" DOESN'T GO OVER WELL WITH PURITANS

Thomas Morton, an English lawyer, arrived in Massachusetts in 1625 as part of a group that settled near present-day Quincy. Their settlement was about 25 miles from Plymouth, where the Puritan Saints had landed earlier. But whereas those stern souls considered New England a "hideous and desolate wilderness, full of wild beasts and wild men," Morton saw it as a "paradise," and in his opinion the American Indians were "more full of humanity than the Christians" who had preceded him.

After their group's leader—and much of the group—took off for the milder climate of Virginia, Morton and about a dozen others threw out the lieutenant in charge, released the indentured servants, and set about the enjoyment of paradise. They renamed the plantation Ma-Re-Mount, based on the original American Indian name; it soon became Merry Mount, based on their joyous way of life.

Thomas Morton saw Merry Mount as a paradise and thought that the American Indians were "more full of humanity than the Christians" who had preceded him.

In the spring of 1627, Merry Mount instituted "revels & merriment after the old English custom." Up went an 80-foot maypole, decked out with ribbons and flowers; atop it was nailed a pair of antlers. Inviting the American Indians to join in, the colonists held a days-long fertility rite, with plenty of beer, dancing, and erotic amenities.

The Merry Mount fur trade flourished, to the dismay of the Saints, who offered the "Savages" disapproval, prayer, and violence. Fearing that contact with the natives' sensual "wickedness" might undermine their own rigid resolve— which prohibited unseemly laughter, let alone revelry—the Saints could not tolerate a neighbor like Morton.

In the spring of 1628, Captain Myles Standish invaded Merry Mount with eight armed men. They captured Morton and left him on a deserted island with nothing but his bare hands and "the thin suit" on his back to await an outbound boat to England. He was charged with selling guns and spirits to the American Indians. The English refused to prosecute, and in 1629 Morton returned to his "old nest" to resume his fur trade.

This time Puritans John Endicott and John Winthrop of the Massachusetts Bay Colony took up the cudgel. Endicott cut down the infamous maypole. Governor Winthrop hauled Morton into court, where he was sentenced to the stocks, stripped of all property, imprisoned, and finally exiled to England. As he sailed, his house was burned down.

Again, the English freed Morton. He sought legal revenge against his persecutors and almost succeeded in getting their royal charter revoked. But when he returned to Massachusetts in 1643, he was thrown into jail and kept in irons, without fire or blankets, through the harsh winter. At last, his health broken—"old and crazy," according to Winthrop—Morton was released. By 1646, he was dead.

Puritan John Endicott cuts down the maypole established at Merry Mount, which is near present-day Quincy, Massachusetts.

FUNNY FACT

There Was Once a State Named Franklin

It's a little-known fact that founding father Benjamin Franklin had a state named after him. The state of Franklin precariously survived for just four years, and its currency was so unstable that officials were paid in animal skins. Here's how it came about: As early as 1673, explorers had traveled over the Appalachian Mountains to a fertile plain crisscrossed by rivers in what is now eastern Tennessee. A ragtag assortment of colonists later moved west from Virginia and North Carolina to the banks of the Watauga and Nolichucky Rivers; in 1772, they banded together to form the Watauga Association, which established courts of justice and a militia to fend off the American Indians. During the American Revolution, many Wataugans were eager to fight the British. In a showdown at King's Mountain, South Carolina, mounted Watauga militiamen led by Colonels John Sevier and Isaac Shelby defeated the British.

In 1784, North Carolina offered to cede its Tennessee lands to the central government. Feeling abandoned, the Wataugans held a convention and voted to found Franklin. They adopted a state constitution and petitioned for recognition as the 14th state. Thomas Jefferson, who had drawn up a plan for carving new states out of the western territories, backed their request. But the support of nine of the original 13 states was required, and only seven approved. Franklin became part of the Tennessee Territory, and when that state was admitted to the Union in 1796, the citizens elected Sevier their first governor.

Twice Dead and Buried

Top: Alfred Russell's lithograph, *Sacajawea Guiding
the Lewis and Clark Expedition.* Above: Explorer
William Clark's diary contained comments and
drawings (including this
one, of a white salmon trout)
about the things that he
and Meriwether Lewis
discovered on their travels.

WHAT *REALLY* BECAME OF SACAGAWEA?

In a cemetery on the Wind River Indian Reservation near Fort
Washakie, Wyoming, stands a prominent tombstone marking the grave
of Sacagawea, the young Shoshone woman who heroically accompanied Meriwether Lewis and William Clark in 1805–06. An inscription
on the stone, erected by the Wyoming chapter of the Daughters of the
American Revolution in 1963, states that she died in 1884.

Dr. Charles Eastman, a Sioux scholar commissioned by the Bureau
of Indian Affairs to trace Sacagawea's life, found many who claimed
to remember her as an old woman. According to them, she left her
husband, the trapper Toussaint Charbonneau, after he took another
wife. Sacagawea then married a Comanche and, following his death,
rejoined the Shoshones in Wyoming. There she was reunited with
Jean Baptiste, the son born to her on the expedition.

But others contend that Sacagawea died at Fort Manuel, South
Dakota, when she was only about 25 and was buried in an unmarked
grave. On December 20, 1812, a clerk at the fort noted in his journal:
"This Evening the Wife of Charbonneau a Snake [Shoshone] Squaw,
died of a putrid fever." Unfortunately, he failed to mention which

wife. A dozen years later, however, Clark listed expedition members and their fates in a notebook; next to "Secarjaweau," he wrote, "Dead." Thus, the complete history of one of America's most celebrated women may never be known.

One Deadly Inn

MERIWETHER LEWIS'S DEATH STILL SHROUDED IN MYSTERY

At sunset on October 10, 1809, Meriwether Lewis rode up to Grinder's Stand, a lonely inn 60 miles from Nashville, Tennessee, on a wilderness trail called the Natchez Trace. He asked to stay the night. A few hours later, he died of gunshot wounds. Was it suicide? Or murder?

Lewis, whom Thomas Jefferson had appointed governor of the Upper Louisiana Territory following his expedition with William Clark, was on his way to Washington, D.C., carrying his journals of their trip. Lewis had also planned to ask the new president, James Madison, for reimbursement of his official expenditures.

The explorer and his servant, John Pernier, had left his headquarters in St. Louis by boat on September 4, 1809. Feeling ill, Lewis made a two-week stop at Fort Pickering before proceeding to the Natchez Trace. James Neelly, an agent for the Chickasaw tribe whom Lewis had met at the fort, accompanied him.

There were no eyewitnesses to what happened at the inn. Priscilla Grinder, whose husband, Robert, was reportedly away, told Neelly that the 35-year-old explorer was deranged. Neelly wrote to Jefferson: "The woman reports that about three o'clock she heard two pistols fire off in the Governors Room.... He had shot himself in the head with one pistol and a little below the breast with the other...."

But could Lewis have been murdered? Local lore holds that Robert Grinder did the job for Lewis's money. Two years later, Mrs. Grinder changed part of her story; a full 30 years later she gave a totally new version. Was she covering up for her husband?

The $120 Lewis had with him was never recovered. Neelly, who buried him, had no money at the outset of the trip, and yet he was able to give Pernier $15 to travel to Virginia to report to Jefferson. Seven months later Pernier himself died suddenly. Was it mere coincidence?

In 1848, an unfinished column was put up to mark Lewis's grave and signify his untimely death.

Portage from the Potomac

HOW A CANAL LEADS TO THE CONSTITUTION, VIA MOUNT VERNON

"The Western settlers," George Washington wrote, "stand as it were upon a pivot; the touch of a feather would turn them any way." He was referring to the pioneers who had poured into the wilderness of the post-Revolution frontier territory, that vast expanse between the well-populated Atlantic seaboard corridor and the Mississippi River.

What Washington feared was that the new settlers' isolation from the original 13 states might persuade them to direct their loyalty elsewhere. Using the Mississippi to ship their farm products and fur pelts, they could easily form alliances with the French in New Orleans or with the British along the Great Lakes.

NAVIGATING A CANAL SYSTEM

Washington believed he had found a means to turn them the right way and improve his own fortunes. He envisioned a canal system that would make the turbulent Potomac River navigable to within a short portage of the Ohio River, the main route to the new territory.

This would be a viable alternative to the Mississippi and would make it easy to move goods eastward. (And as the barges headed for Georgetown, Maryland—the port at the mouth of the river—they would pass right by Mount Vernon, the general's lovely estate on the bank of the Potomac.)

"BIND THOSE PEOPLE TO US"

Washington foresaw "an amazing increase of our exports, while we bind those people to us by a chain which never can be broken." He was not alone in seeing a need for this waterway; Thomas Jefferson wrote to him urging haste, lest New York state, planning its own canal, steal a march on the western trade. If Washington could complete the waterway, Jefferson wrote, "What a monument to your retirement it would become!"

FUNNY FACT

A Busy Week for America in 1776

Who knew? In *the same week* in 1776, the year that the Declaration of Independence was signed, Spain's flag was unfurled on the West Coast, in what was later to become San Francisco. The signing of the Declaration is celebrated on July 4, though it occurred on July 2 (see page 48); Spain's banner day was June 29.

The task of the Patowmack Company, chartered in 1785 with Washington as its head, proved daunting. Despite the general's view that navigation of the Potomac was "equal, if not superior, to any in the Union," its foaming rapids and cascading waterfalls challenged early engineering talents; it had always been a boatman's nightmare. Laborers, using black powder, had to blast passages through rock walls.

When the work was finished, the Potomac was still so unpredictable that the waterway was open to boats only 30 to 45 days a year. Yet the impact of the canal on America's history was staggering.

Under the loose union provided by the Articles of Confederation, the fledgling national government found it hard to make feuding states agree on anything. But under Washington's leadership, the delegates from Maryland and Virginia came to terms in 1785 on a way to proceed with work on the canal. The meeting was so successful that a second session was held to deal with trade problems. Representatives from five states attended, and at Alexander Hamilton's suggestion, they voted to call a convention in Philadelphia "to render the constitution of the Federal Government adequate to the exigencies of the Union."

Today the Patowmack Canal is just a weed-covered ribbon of land. But the document that delegates to the Philadelphia Convention shaped in 1787—the U.S. Constitution—is still very much alive.

Creating a Utopia

NEW SOCIETIES HAVE THEIR HEYDAY

Dreaming of a perfect society, religious leader George Rapp and, later, industrialist Robert Owen, founded frontier communities that mirrored their ideals.

Rapp arrived from Germany in 1803 and, with his flock, settled near Pittsburgh, creating a socialist commune. In 1807, he decreed that his group become celibate and give up tobacco to purify themselves in preparation for the second coming of Christ. Later, seeking new horizons, Rapp founded the town of Harmonie, Indiana. He sold that town in 1825 and moved back to Pennsylvania, where he established Economy. The Harmonists, also known as Harmonites, flourished financially and spiritually, although Rapp's teachings were a bit eccentric. When he predicted the second coming of Christ in 1829 and Christ never came, Rapp merely announced a postponement. The Harmonists survived 51 years after the death of their leader, finally dissolving in 1898.

Owen, an idealistic Englishman who believed that people were formed by their environment, bought Harmonie, Indiana, from Rapp, renamed it New

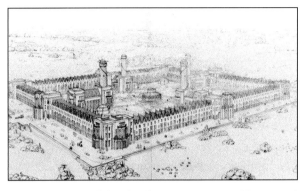

Above, a sketch of the plan for a community at Harmonie, Indiana, based on the principles advocated by Robert Owen. The city is designed to give "greater physical, moral, and intellectual advantages to every individual."

Harmony, and tried to turn it into a perfect environment. About 1,000 people joined his paradise. He promised equality to all (except "persons of color") and exhorted them to strive for "universal happiness." But from the start, there were rumbles of discontent. "The idle and industrious are neither of them satisfied," one resident wrote of the communal life that Owen proposed.

Splinter groups formed and, finances strained, Owen acquired a partner, William Maclure. The

BRIGHT IDEA

A New Way to Name Towns

Stedman Whitwell, an English architect and social reformer, went to New Harmony, Indiana, on the "Boatload of Knowledge."

Scornful of those who named one town after another for Washington, for example, or Springfield, Whitwell had a novel idea: Give each locality a name in which the letters stood for the numbers in its latitude and longitude, all keyed to a complex code of vowels and consonants. Using this method, he reasoned, every town would have a unique name and could be instantly located on any map. Applying his revolutionary system, he christened one of the New

Harmony splinter communities Feiba Peveli.

Had Whitwell prevailed, Pittsburgh would be Otfu Veitoup; New York would be Otke Notive; the nation's capital, Feili Nyvul. Ipba Venul would identify New Harmony.

Scottish geologist and businessman arrived aboard the keelboat *Philanthropist*, later known as the "Boatload of Knowledge," with scientists and educators who brought their own ideas of paradise. The town prospered, but Owen's two-year social experiment collapsed. New Harmony, now restored, has become a popular tourist attraction. It is also a living legacy of the people who came to these shores to make their dreams of paradise come true.

Christians or Devils?

ASK THE PENITENT BROTHERS: MAN IS INNATELY EVIL

Christians or devils? The Penitentes have been called both, for they create a hell on earth by pursuing absolution to rare extremes.

During the week before Easter in the remote mountain valleys of New Mexico and southern Colorado, zealots prepare to be reborn. This is the holiest season for Los Hermanos Penitentes, the Penitent Brothers, a centuries-old sect whose obscure roots trace back through the Spanish conquistadors and Franciscan missionaries to the fervent Christians of medieval Europe.

Believing that man is innately evil and that this evil can be purged only through punishment, the Penitentes have made Good Friday their most sacred holiday. The bloody rituals with which they observe this day may have developed from more benign practices introduced by the Spanish Franciscan missionaries, who occasionally practiced self-flagellation for the purification of the soul.

About 1800, the Penitentes organized into a formal fraternity with a constitution and officers. Reportedly an outgrowth of the Third Order of St. Francis, the Penitentes' Catholicism degenerated into identification of themselves with Christ through pain and penance. Originally their rituals were held in village churches. But when the Spanish were expelled, after Mexico won its independence in 1821, remote villages were abandoned by the church.

The figure of death (left) presides over the Penitentes' rituals (above). The order is noted for the extreme flagellation rituals it practiced.

Though they had no priests, the isolated parishioners tried to maintain the faith, and in the process they developed extreme practices.

In 1833, the bishop of Durango, Mexico, issued an edict condemning the brotherhood. By the middle of the 19th century their ceremonies were banned from church grounds and they were forced to meet secretly outside the villages.

PROCESSION OF BLOOD

Charles F. Lummis, a writer and ethnologist, became the first outsider to photograph the Penitentes' Easter week celebration in 1888. His record of the event remains a classic.

Easter Thursday was the culmination of preparations under way since the beginning of Lent. A flute player, his plaintive song drifting eerily over the hushed crowd, led a chorus of women in a slow and painful procession. Many of the women were hobbled by cactus stuffed tightly into their shoes.

Behind the women staggered the Brothers of Blood, each man wearing only the white pants of a penitent and a crown of thorns pressed tightly around a black cloth bag shrouding his head. These bags were worn not to conceal the brothers' identities but to protect them from the sin of vanity from glorying in their suffering before the crowd. As they walked, they lashed their own backs with whips of braided yucca studded with cactus. Their skin was beaten raw and bloody.

Then came three men, bowed under the weight of huge wooden crosses. As they struggled forward, they were viciously whipped by the Brothers of Light, the inner elite of the cult.

ATONEMENT

The next morning, Good Friday, Lummis watched in awe as a black-hooded young man, blood pouring from a wound in his right side, accepted the honor of portraying Christ. Seeing that he was to be bound to the cross, he begged for nails. But too many Christ-actors had died in that way; he was bound by ropes so tightly that his arms turned black.

Two other brothers with large bundles of cactus strapped to their backs made their way to the base of the cross. Rolling to the ground, they asked that stones be placed to drive the cactus spines more deeply into their flesh. Motionless, but in clear agony, the sufferers remained in their desperate torments for 31 minutes.

Overlooking the entire scene was a Death Cart, a two-wheeled vehicle on which sat a skeleton draped in black and lace, clutching a bow and arrow, the symbol of sudden death.

Presumably, the brotherhood's practices have become less brutal since highways opened the area in the 1920s and its residents became less isolated. In 1947 the bishop of Santa Fe declared that the Penitentes were "a pious association of men joined in charity to commemorate the Passion and death of the Redeemer" and decreed that they were part of the church. But easier access to the broader world also brought Penitente hunters and camera-wielding curiosity seekers. As a result, the order has been driven into an even deeper secrecy.

Today the remaining Penitentes meet stealthily in *moradas,* their secret churches, and observe Good Friday at night or in extremely remote locations.

Bringing Christianity West

MISSIONARIES NARCISSA WHITMAN AND ELIZA SPALDING ARE THE FIRST WHITE WOMEN TO CROSS THE CONTINENT

A tale about Northwest Coast Indians seeking the white men's Book of Heaven—the Bible—inspired 16-year-old New Yorker Narcissa Prentiss to become a missionary. Despite her fine education and deep religious commitment, her request for work in the West was denied. She was told that no single women were needed in Oregon.

When she was in her mid-twenties, Narcissa met Dr. Marcus Whitman. He shared her religious zeal, and his application to work as a medical missionary in Oregon was accepted. They married on February 18, 1836. With an agent for the Oregon mission, Rev. Henry Spalding and his wife, Eliza, they joined a caravan heading west. The new bride (who called Marcus "one of the kindest husbands") described the trek in her spirited journal: "Our fuel for cooking has been dried buffalo dung. Harriet [a sister left behind] will make a face at this, but she would be glad to have her supper cooked." The caravan crossed the Continental Divide on July 4 and soon came upon an annual rendezvous of American

Indians and fur trappers. The tribesmen looked "with wonder and astonishment" upon Narcissa and Eliza, the first white women they had ever seen.

The mountainous trail from here on was barely passable. But fortunately for Mrs. Whitman, who was now pregnant, Spalding had brought a wagon for the women. (The vehicle was left at Fort Boise, farther west than a wagon had ever been.)

The Whitmans arrived at Fort Walla Walla, Washington, on September 1, and on March 14, 1837, Narcissa Whitman gave birth to the first child born to white parents in the Northwest. A local tribal chief welcomed the baby as a "Cayuse girl," because she was born on Cayuse land.

FULFILLMENT AND TRAGEDY

The missionaries spent 11 years with the Cayuses—some happy, others not. The Whitmans' first misfortune was their daughter's accidental drowning. Although Whitman was never to have another child, she was soon raising 11 adopted youngsters. Then relations with the people they had come to serve deteriorated; their pride made the Cayuses slow to accept the white men's ways and religion. As more settlers arrived, the tribe saw its freedom and traditions endangered. Even medicines were suspect. When an epidemic of measles struck and Whitman was unable to save the lives of many tribe members, rumors circulated that he was poisoning his Indian patients.

In November 1847, a group of firebrands (led by the same chief who had welcomed the Whitmans'

Narcissa Whitman tends to a sick Cayuse Indian at the Whitman Mission, about seven miles west of present-day Walla Walla, Washington.

daughter) attacked their house. When the smoke cleared, 13 people had been massacred, among them Marcus and Narcissa Whitman. Sadly, the dream of Christian service had ended in martyrdom.

Promised Land Trial and Error

MORMONS' CITY OF GOD NOT IN OHIO, MISSOURI, ILLINOIS, OR NEBRASKA

Based on the visions of Joseph Smith, the Church of Jesus Christ of Latter Day Saints—whose followers are also known as Mormons—was founded in 1830 in New York but soon moved to Ohio. Not that they ever considered Ohio the promised land; Prophet Smith decreed that the city of God lay in Missouri.

Converts flocked to Independence, Missouri, in the early 1830s, but skirmishes broke out wherever the Mormons settled in that state. In 1838, the governor decreed that all Mormons "must be exterminated or driven from the state." Many people believed that the Mormons were trying to establish a religious dictatorship, or theocracy. Finally, in 1839, the Saints—as they called themselves—retreated from

Missouri, leaving a bloody trail of murdered martyrs behind.

The group migrated to an Illinois bog on the Mississippi River. Though it was still not Zion, they thought no one would fight them for the mosquito-infested land. Their numbers grew, and the city of Nauvoo soon rivaled the size of Chicago. But resentment against the Mormons flared again, fanned by their practice of polygamy. In 1844, Smith decided to run for president of the United States. A local newspaper criticized his platform and revealed the church's endorsement of polygamy, prompting the Mormon-run city council to ban the newspaper and Smith to order the destruction of the paper's presses. The governor of Illinois then ordered Smith's arrest. Smith and his brother, Hyrum, turned themselves in, and an angry mob broke into the jail and shot them dead. Six months later, Illinois revoked Nauvoo's charter, and the new Mormon

In 1838, the governor of Missouri decreed that all Mormons "must be exterminated or driven from the state."

leader, Brigham Young, declared that the sect would move farther west. In 1846 the Saints, forced from their homes, made for Nebraska, where their winter encampment has been compared to Valley Forge. In the spring they moved on, and after much hardship, they reached the Salt Lake Valley in Utah, where Young planned a separate Mormon nation called Deseret.

Salt Lake City and its environs grew quickly. From across the country and around the world, Mormons moved to the new land. Farms and mines were started, the terrain was mapped, and Las Vegas (among other outlying communities) was founded as a Mormon colony. But the great Deseret dream faded when Congress declared Utah a U.S. territory. There would be other problems, including court fights that eventually ended the legal practice of polygamy. But this time the Saints had found their Zion and remain there to this day.

King of Beaver Island

Farm boy turns Mormon monarch

On his 19th birthday, a New York farm boy confided an extraordinary dream to his diary: He hoped "to rival Cesar [sic] or Napoleon." James Jesse Strang got closer to that dream than might have seemed possible when he wrote those words in 1832. From 1850 to 1856, Strang was the monarch of 13-mile-long Beaver Island in Lake Michigan. His subjects? Over 2,500 Mormons who believed that he, not Brigham Young, was the true head of their church.

When Young led the faithful to Utah, Strang's group went to

Wisconsin. But in the face of growing hostility, they retreated to Beaver Island. It proved an ideal site on which to establish the kingdom that had been revealed to Strang on sacred brass tablets (claimed by Young's supporters to be the melted remains of a kettle). By the time Strang was crowned in 1850, he had created his own nobility, anointing followers with dabs of oil that produced an eerie glow. (Phosphorescence, it seems, had been added.)

Strang opposed polygamy, endorsed by Young, until he met 18-year-old Elvira Eliza Field.

Already married with four children, he took Elvira as his second bride, persuading her to dress as his nephew. After declaring polygamy acceptable, he took four more brides; all four of his new wives were pregnant when, on June 16, 1856, Strang was shot to death by former supporters.

Following his death, mainland mobs chased the colonists away. But Beaver Island still bears a trace of its regal past. The chief thoroughfare is called by the name Strang gave it: King's Highway.

Running for His Life

**JOHN COLTER'S INCREDIBLE
300-MILE NAKED EXPEDITION**

Trapper, adventurer, woodsman, explorer, and the first of this nation's great mountain men, John Colter was one of the West's mythic figures. In the fall of 1808, his fame was assured by a daring and near-miraculous run from the tribe of Blackfoot Indians.

Following three years of hazardous duty as a member of Lewis and Clark's expedition, Colter turned to trapping beaver in the Three Forks area of the Missouri River, deep in Blackfoot territory.

NATIVE ATTACK

One day Colter was inspecting traps by canoe with John Potts, another veteran of the Lewis and Clark expedition. Suddenly the two men found themselves flanked on both banks by Blackfoot braves. Potts was killed as he tried to escape, but Colter was captured and became sport for the tribe. Stripped of all his clothing, including his shoes, the adventurer was led 400 yards out onto the prairie; then the chief let out a war whoop and sent several hundred braves in hot pursuit.

Sprinting painfully across the prickly brush, Colter headed for the Jefferson Fork, some six miles away. He outdistanced all but one spear-carrying Blackfoot, whom he finally turned to face. He killed the pursuer with his own spear. On the verge of collapse, Colter dove into the bitterly cold Jefferson River, where he hid under a pile of timbers until nightfall. He then swam away, drifted downstream, and stumbled ashore.

ASTOUNDING ARRIVAL

What followed was a legendary, 11-day overland trek. Traveling day and night—without a stitch of clothing—Colter climbed mountains, scurried across fields, and tramped through woods, covering an unbelievable 300 miles. When he reached Manuel's Fort on the Big Horn River, he was bearded, bleeding, and barely recognizable. His astonishing journey guaranteed him a place in the pantheon of America's frontier heroes.

A Gift to the Morning Star

**HUMAN SACRIFICE ONCE COMMON
AMONG NATIVE TRIBES**

At one time human sacrifice was quite common in Nebraska. The Skidi Pawnee, a local Indian tribe, believed that if humans were occasionally offered up to a deity called the Morning Star, crops would be abundant, hunting good, and the general well-being of the community assured. In 1827, Indian agent John Dougherty decided put an end to the practice.

Local fur traders alerted Dougherty that a Pawnee raiding party had captured a Cheyenne woman, intending to offer her as a sacrifice— although the tribe had promised years before to give up the custom. Dougherty resolved to visit the tribal chiefs and try to hold them to their word. The agent put together a small party of soldiers and, on April 4, set out for a chat with the chiefs.

THE MORNING STAR CEREMONY

When the band arrived at the Pawnee village, the five-day ritual was under way. One of the tribal chiefs asked Dougherty and his group to dine with him. (Since there were six chiefs altogether, the white men each devoured half a dozen meals before the evening was over—they didn't want to insult anyone at the start of such delicate negotiations.)

Afterward, the ceremony of the sacred Morning Star sacrifice was described to them: The victim would be tied to a scaffold and offered to the Morning Star; after torture by fire, she would die from an arrow through the heart. Then the victim's chest would be cut open and the blood smeared on one of the Indian priests. After further ritual and celebration, her body was to be left on the open plain, an offering to the animals and the elements.

The next day, Dougherty made an eloquent plea for the woman's life, implying that trade items such as gunpowder and flints could be withheld by the government. An Indian priest consulted Tirawahat, the Master of Life who brought the Skidi universe into existence, and announced that there was no need for a sacrifice. Finally the chiefs agreed to release the Cheyenne woman to Dougherty.

> In the sacrifice, the victim would be tied to a scaffold and offered to the Morning Star; after torture by fire, she would die from an arrow through the heart.

The agent and his party hoped to leave early the next morning, while the village was asleep. But by the time they were ready to go, the entire population was awake and waiting. Some wanted to see them off safely, but others had different intentions.

"A HORRID SIGHT"

A Skidi faction believed that to rob the Morning Star of its sacrifice would be to bring ruin to the village and vowed that the prisoner would never leave alive. As the Cheyenne woman rode her horse past the assemblage, a warrior shot her with an arrow. The crowd went wild, and a heated battle erupted. Dougherty tried desperately to restore order, but by the time he did, it was too late. The woman was dead, her corpse hacked to pieces—"a horrid sight," the agent later reported. But he found some consolation in the fact that the small band of soldiers had "prevented her being tortured to death with firebrands … [an] abominable custom."

"I, Only an Indian Woman"

SARAH WINNEMUCCA FIGHTS FOR HER TRIBE'S SURVIVAL

Fed up with how poor and degraded members of her Pauite tribe were in the mid-1860s, Sarah Winnemucca gave them some tough advice: Take your cues from the white people and learn to work for a living!

Winnemucca, who was then about 21 years old, was impressed by the whites. She had been living with them in California and had attended a convent school at the insistence of her grandfather, Chief Truckee. A guide for the explorer John C. Frémont in the 1840s, the chief had great admiration for the European settlers.

But Winnemucca's people were bitter. After the great silver strike of 1859, whites had swarmed into western Nevada, the Paiutes' territory, grabbing up their land and depriving the tribe of its livelihood. In 1860, a war blazed between whites and Indians; afterward, the Paiutes were driven onto Pyramid Lake Reservation, where they could find little food. Starving, many crept back to the white settlements to accept handouts, take menial jobs, or steal.

POLITE INDIFFERENCE

A high-spirited, precocious young woman, Sarah Winnemucca was proud of being a Paiute. Her father, Chief Winnemucca, was too ineffectual to lead, so she stepped forward to solicit the help of white officials. Exasperated by the white men's polite indifference, she joined her brother, Natchez, on the reservation.

There she was outraged by the corruption of the Indian agent in charge, who leased reservation land to white ranchers and sold government provisions that were intended for the Paiutes, leaving them to starve. After the Indians retaliated for the killing of one of their own, the agent asked the commander of Fort McDermitt to send troops to punish them.

Instead, the commander summoned Winnemucca and her brother to hear their side of the story.

"We went like the wind," she recalled. Impassioned and eloquent, she described the Paiutes' plight. At once the commander dispatched supplies and canvas tents. He even offered the Paiutes the fort as a refuge from the whites. Before long, 900 Paiutes were living there.

CRUEL TREATMENT

All went well until the sympathetic commander was transferred; his replacement cut off the Indians' food rations, and the hungry Paiutes returned to Pyramid Lake Reservation. Realizing that her people needed a permanent home and farming skills, Winnemucca repeatedly asked the commissioner of Indian Affairs in Washington, D.C., for assistance.

In 1875, Winnemucca led many Paiutes north to Oregon's Malheur Reservation, where she was hired as interpreter for agent Sam Parrish. Unlike most Indian agents, Parrish did all he could for the tribe. When he was replaced by a cruel man named William Rinehart, the Indians suffered helplessly. In 1878, the desperate Paiutes collected $29.65 to send Winnemucca to the nation's capital to plead their case. She started out on June 8 for Silver City, Idaho. From there she planned to take the Union Pacific Railroad.

A DANGEROUS MISSION

As they rumbled toward Silver City, a U.S. Army detachment halted them. Winnemucca learned that the Bannocks, an Idaho tribe, were leading a great Indian uprising and had kidnapped part of her peaceful tribe, including her father.

The army, worried that the Paiutes might join forces with the Bannocks, needed someone to steal into the enemy encampment and help them escape to Fort Lyon. Winnemucca undertook the dangerous mission. Riding day and night, she covered 223 miles, accompanied by two Paiute men. "I, only an Indian woman, went and saved my father and his people," she declared.

At the end of the three-month Bannock War, during which Winnemucca was an interpreter for

Wearing a beaded buckskin tunic and red leather leggings, Chief Sarah Winnemucca drew big crowds to lectures in Boston and San Francisco. Speaking from the heart, she moved audiences to tears.

General O. O. Howard, the Paiutes named her a chief, an honor never before accorded a woman. The federal government awarded Winnemucca $500 but ignored a promise to her that the Paiutes could return to their ancestral lands.

Instead, the tribe was force-marched—in the dead of winter—to a desolate reservation in Yakima, Washington. After more than a month's trek, during which many tribe members froze to death, 543 Snake and Paiute Indians arrived at Yakima and were herded into an unheated shed. The Paiutes accused Sarah of having been duped by the white men she had trusted. She was devastated.

Chief Sarah made a bold move: She went to San Francisco to give lectures on the plight of her tribe. "If your people will help us ... I will promise to educate my people and make them law-abiding citizens of the United States," she told applauding audiences.

Alarmed by the surge of sympathy for Winnemucca, the Bureau of Indian Affairs invited her to Washington to meet Secretary of the Interior Carl Schurz and President Rutherford B. Hayes. Schurz issued an order freeing the Paiutes from the reservation, guaranteeing them land allotments. But when Winnemucca triumphantly presented the order to the Indian agent at Yakima, he ignored it. It was not, he said, addressed to him.

In 1883, Sarah Winnemucca gained further attention for her cause by writing her autobiography, *Life Among the Paiutes: Their Wrongs and Claims*. It was the first book in English by an American Indian. The next year she was invited to testify before a congressional committee, and Congress quickly passed a bill allowing the Paiutes to leave Yakima. This time it was Secretary Schurz who ignored it.

His betrayal was a blow from which Winnemucca never recovered. In 1887, after the death of her husband (her second white spouse), she grew despondent and went to visit her sister in Montana. There she died in 1891, apparently of tuberculosis.

Scalped!

Frontier doc aids victim of hair-raising, life-threatening scare

A doctor who practiced medicine on America's western frontier in the mid-1800s had to be prepared for almost anything. Yet in August 1867, when Omaha doctor Richard Moore was confronted by a man carrying his scalp in a bucket of water, all of his medical talents—as well as his constitution—were put to the test. For here on his doorstep was a patient who had barely escaped with his life, let alone his hair.

The scalping victim was William Thompson, a repairman for the Union Pacific Railroad who had been sent out to fix a break in a telegraph line. On the

way, he was set upon by a band of Cheyenne Indians in a sudden, vicious attack. They took his scalp, but one of the tribesmen accidentally dropped it as he mounted his steed. Though, as he later said, "it just felt as if the whole head was taken right off," Thompson managed to retrieve the scalp.

After struggling some 15 miles to the nearest railway station, the victim was taken to Omaha, where Moore assessed his pitiful pate. "The scalp was entirely removed from a space measuring nine inches by seven," he later reported. "The denuded surface extended from one inch above the left eyebrow backwards." Thompson's hope of having his scalp restored was dashed when he was told it simply could not be sewn back in place. With time and care, however, his head healed.

Before returning to his native England, Thompson gave the scalp, now tanned and preserved, to Moore, who eventually presented it to the Omaha Public Library Museum for display.

A circa-1875 engraving depicts new railroads stretching across the Great Plains.

Guarding the Iron Horse

"BAREBACK" PAWNEE TRIBESMEN PROTECT THE U.S. RAILROAD

As the Union Pacific workers on the transcontinental railroad moved west from Omaha, they quickly found themselves attacked by the Sioux and Cheyenne tribes, whose hunting grounds they had invaded. The U.S. Army was supposed to provide protection for the railroad, but post-Civil War budget cuts had thinned its ranks; only about 200 cavalrymen and 600 infantrymen were on duty between Omaha and the Colorado border, some 500 miles away. Fort Kearny, Nebraska, for example, had a garrison of 12 infantrymen and a small marching band.

The railroad finally got able defenders when Major Frank North recruited Pawnee Indians to patrol the tracks. The Pawnees had been farmers in Texas until the Spanish introduced horses; then they became nomads whose buffalo hunts made them enemies of the Sioux and Cheyennes. Outfitted with regulation uniforms, the Pawnee scouts outraged spit-and-polish officers by cutting the seats from their trousers and riding bare-bottomed into action.

> Outfitted with regulation uniforms, Pawnee scouts cut the seats from their trousers and rode bare-bottomed into action.

Their effectiveness, however, was undeniable. When Chief Turkey Leg's Cheyennes derailed a freight train near Plum Creek, Nebraska, in 1867, North's Pawnees were more than 200 miles away. They reached Plum Creek the next day and, without a pause, took after the Cheyennes, killing 17 of them. There were no more Indian raids in Nebraska that year.

First Wagon Train to California

MISSOURIANS HEAD WEST TO "PARADISE"

The Western Immigration Society: It was a pretentious name for a group who, like most Americans, knew little about the far side of an untamed continent. Missourian John Bidwell, who had heard in late 1840 that California was a paradise, signed up for a westward trek—and so did 500 other families. By spring, however, the group's enthusiasm had waned. On May 9, 1841, the day the group was scheduled to depart, only one wagon—and Bidwell—showed up. Undaunted, Bidwell waited until 68 people had straggled in.

A man named John Bartleson was elected captain of the group; he had a crude map and a letter from a Dr. Marsh in California that contained the only clues to the path they were to follow (he also showed up with eight men in tow). Talbot Green, carrying a cache of lead bars, was named president. Bidwell was made secretary, and soon they were all off. They slowed only to allow a party of missionaries to catch up, because the missionaries had with them a guide, Thomas "Broken Hand" Fitzpatrick. Fitzpatrick was a mountain man who knew the route at least as far as his destination: Soda Springs, Idaho.

After encountering endless herds of buffalo and a near-catastrophic waterspout, the group reached Soda Springs and parted ways. California was to the west; even Fitzpatrick knew little more than that. By now, only 32 people retained their resolve to continue. While some men rode on in search of a new guide, the rest of the group headed for the Great Salt Lake. But before they reached it, their scouts returned. They could find no guide, but they'd been given advice: not to venture south into the desert, nor too far north, lest they get lost amid steep canyons.

As the wagon train pushed west, the way became increasingly impassable. No longer able to carry sufficient food, the group traded with local Indians for berries and a sweet honey ball they favored (until,

that is, they realized that its main ingredient was mashed insects). In the toughest part of the journey, the emigrants virtually clawed their way across the Sierras. Before they reached the other side, Indians had stolen their remaining mounts. Along the way, they were forced to eat crows, wildcats, and whatever they could find. And then they came to a valley ripe with wild grapes, deer, and antelope. Surprisingly, at the end of that valley lay the farm of Dr. Marsh, whose letter they carried. It was November 4, 1841, and they'd reached California's San Joaquin Valley.

In a trek marked by dogged determination and incredible good luck, one woman and 31 men had made the historic journey to "paradise."

Bartleson faded into the haze of history. Bidwell made a fortune in the 1849 gold rush and even ran for president. And Green turned out to be an embezzler—his lead bars were really made of gold.

IMPROBABLE PIONEER

Ezra Meeker: Father of the Oregon Trail

Regarding the Oregon Trail as "sacred to the memories of the pioneers," Ezra Meeker retraced his travels along the famous route four times—the first at age 75.

In 1852, he had gone west with his family, settling in Washington, where he lived for the next 53 years. Then, "to mark it for all time for the children of the pioneers who blazed it," he returned to the trail in 1906 and 1910 by wagon. In 1915, he went by car. And in 1924, at the age of 93, he got a bird's-eye view, following its course for 1,300 miles by plane.

Dead Man Leads Wagon Train

A DEVOTED FATHER KEEPS A PROMISE TO HIS SON

To William Keil, a promise was a sacred thing. In 1855, he promised his 19-year-old son, Willie, that he could lead their wagon train west. Not even Willie's sudden death could prevent his father from honoring his word; Keil had his son's body placed in a lead-lined casket and preserved in alcohol. And when the wagons started rolling westward, Willie led the way.

Keil, a German immigrant, was a tailor, medical practitioner, and Methodist-turned-mystic. His powerful personality and strong religious conviction readily attracted followers. Though he was barely literate, Keil succeeded in establishing a colony in 1844 at Bethel, Missouri. He was, of course, its leader.

Comprising mostly German immigrants, the Bethel Colony had distinguished itself from most other utopian experiments by its relative success. Despite this success, Keil felt crowded by secular society. After sending scouts to the Washington Territory to stake out claims, he decided to move part of the colony there.

The group intended to set out in May 1855. Willie's death from malaria delayed those plans, but not for long. Though deeply saddened, Keil did not preserve and transport the body out of sentiment. He carried the corpse across a continent to prove to his followers how strong was the bond of a man's word.

The expedition must have been a bizarre sight: Keil, a bearded, heavy-set man, would give a blast on a trumpet to signal the start of each day's march. Willie's coffin led the cortege. The colonists followed, singing German funeral hymns. And the

BRIGHT IDEA

Wind Wagons

In 1830, a wind-driven car set sail on the Baltimore & Ohio Railroad. Doomed to failure, the *Aeolus* proved how difficult it was to handle when it sailed off the end of the track, smack into an embankment.

In 1853, Tom "Windwagon" Smith was confident that his vehicle could "fly over the plains." But his enormous Conestoga-style wagon, complete with a 20-foot mast flying a huge sail, got caught in a crosswind and careened in a circle—and his investors abandoned ship.

On a sunny spring day in 1860, as a wind wagon sailed into Denver, "everyone crossed the street to get a sight of this new-fangled frigate." Who made this particular wagon? We're not absolutely certain, but evidence points to A. J. "Andy" Dawson, from Oskaloosa, Kansas. His contraption had a boatlike mast and sail and had a crank, so the vehicle could be propeled, if need be. The wind wagon was alleged to have arrived in Denver from Kansas in about 20 days.

Indians, respectful, fearful, and at least a little awed, left them alone.

Upon reaching the Willapa Valley in October, Keil was disappointed to find the site unsuitable for settlement. Short of money but not of spunk, he resolved to push farther north into the Oregon Territory, where he eventually founded the colony of Aurora.

But first his group took time out for a long-overdue ceremony: Willie's burial. Willapa was their original destination and only 20 miles from the Pacific Ocean. Keil had kept his promise: Willie had led them across the continent.

Sam Houston Makes a Bad Love Connection

THE TENNESSEE GOVERNOR WAS ON THE PATH TO THE PRESIDENCY—THAT IS, UNTIL HE MARRIED ELIZA ALLEN

A hero of the War of 1812, a congressman, and governor of Tennessee—all before his 35th birthday—Sam Houston seemed destined for the White House. When he married the 18-year-old socialite Eliza Allen in 1829, the match seemed a perfect one, in spite of their 17-year age difference.

After less than three months of marriage, Eliza fled back to her childhood home. Neither spouse would reveal why. There were hints of unfaithfulness, but the only tantalizing glimpse of their marital problems is a letter Houston sent Eliza's father, begging for her return. "She was cold to me and I thought did not love me," he confessed, insisting that "I ... do love Eliza."

But there was no reply, and rumors that Houston had mistreated his bride were rampant. So hostile was public opinion that when the distraught governor sought religious solace, a minister refused to baptize him—his reputation, it seems, was too tarnished.

Only a week after the scandal erupted, Houston resigned the governorship and left for Arkansas, seeking out the Cherokee tribe with whom he had spent three years as a teenager. Without divorcing Eliza, Houston took a Cherokee wife, but he continued to wear Eliza's engagement ring in a pouch around his neck. And he drowned his misery in alcohol with such regularity that the tribesmen called him "the Big Drunk."

Not until 1833, after leaving the tribe and settling in Texas, did Houston divorce Eliza. And in 1840, at the age of 47, he wooed and won 21-year-old Margaret Lea. This happy union produced eight children and lasted until Houston's death at the age of 70.

Not even wedded bliss, however, could make Houston break his silence. Once, when he arrived at a friend's home drunk, his host thought Houston's condition would make it easy to pry the truth out of him. But when he asked what had happened with Eliza, Houston simply jumped on his horse and rode off into the night.

Eliza, who also remarried, was no more forthcoming, though various relatives have claimed to know the truth. One story was that Eliza loved another man, but her parents, blinded by Houston's great reputation, forced her to marry him. Others reported that a jealous Houston locked Eliza in her room when he left her alone, while some maintained that an unhealed wound he had received in combat so revolted the sensitive young woman that she refused all physical contact. (Houston's relatives, citing a medical history compiled during his lifetime, denied this.)

Whatever the cause of the couple's unhappiness, it may well have been on Eliza's mind as she lay dying. She ordered that all pictures of her be burned, and so no image remains of the fair-haired girl who changed Sam Houston's life.

How a Whale Destroyed the *Essex* and Changed Literature Forever

MOBY-DICK LOOSELY BASED ON A TRUE STORY

For hardy whalers, no ocean was too wide to cross in pursuit of their prizes. In 1819, more than a dozen ships were launched from Nantucket, Massachusetts, all headed for distant hunting grounds in the Pacific. One, the three-masted *Essex*, suffered such a calamity that it inspired a classic American novel.

For months the ship had survived the hazards of whaling around Cape Horn. On November 20, 1820, however, a mammoth sperm whale turned the tables on the *Essex*, ramming it head on. Then the leviathan passed under the vessel, turned, and attacked again. He hit, as first mate Owen Chase recalled, "with ten-fold fury and vengeance." The crew abandoned ship and from their whaleboats watched in horror as the *Essex* slid into the sea.

A month went by before the survivors—in three small boats, far from land—were roused from their stupor by the sight of a South Pacific islet (known today as Henderson Island). But after six days there, lack of food drove them back to the sea. As one crew member after another succumbed, those left behind decided to eat the remains of the dead. After 83 desperate days at sea, Chase and a few companions were

This 19th-century wood engraving is the only known picture of Moby-Dick drawn during Herman Melville's lifetime.

rescued by a British brig. All returned to Nantucket, Chase forever haunted by the "horrid aspect and malignancy of the whale." The harrowing experience inspired Herman Melville's *Moby-Dick*.

FUNNY FACT

James Fenimore Cooper Starts Writing Novels on a Dare

It's hard to believe, but gentleman farmer James Fenimore Cooper wrote his first novel on a dare from his wife. His second book brought him such literary acclaim that he changed his vocation.

Cooper published his first novel, *Precaution* (1820), after his wife had challenged him to improve on the dull English novel he was reading aloud to her. Unlike *Precaution*, Cooper's second book, *The Spy*, was an immediate success when it came out in 1821. The adventure story about a double agent during the Revolutionary War captivated readers. His next work, *The Pioneers* (1823), introduced readers to Cooper's most endearing character, Natty Bumppo, the ideal frontiersman who would appear in all five Leatherstocking Tales, for which Cooper is best known. He wrote 39 novels in all, including *The Last of the Mohicans* (1826) and *The Deerslayer* (1841), before he died in 1851.

Lending a Hand (and Some Long Johns)

HOW UNDERWEAR SAVED JOHN WESLEY POWELL FROM FALLING TO HIS DEATH

Explorer John Wesley Powell lost his right arm in the Battle of Shiloh. Almost seven years later, that loss nearly cost him his life. The near-fatal mishap occurred in 1869, while he was scaling a sheer rock wall that towered more than 800 feet above the Green River in Utah.

Powell, a largely self-trained geologist and naturalist, was leading a nine-man party down the Colorado River and its tributaries; the party would be the first to travel through the Grand Canyon. As he and a companion, George Bradley, inched along a treacherous rock face, he saw a promising foothold, made a short leap and found himself trapped. He was what rock climbers call "rimmed," unable to move without risk of falling.

Powell shouted to Bradley, who was able to climb to a ledge above him but was still too far away to reach his arm. Bradley searched for a branch to stretch down; finding none, he tried the barometer case they carried for scientific observations. But the case was too thick for Powell to grasp securely with his one hand.

By this time, Powell's legs were about to give out. "My muscles begin to tremble," he recalled in his diary. "If I lose my hold, I shall fall to the bottom." Just then Bradley had an inspiration. He quickly stripped off his long underwear and extended the dangling legs down toward Powell. With his heart in his throat, the trapped explorer loosed his grip on the rock and made a life-or-death grab for the waving cloth. It worked. The underwear held, and Bradley was able to lift Powell high enough to grasp his wrist and pull him to safety.

Bradley's inspired use of his own underwear proved a boon to American science. Powell went on to chart the Grand Canyon and head both the U.S. Geological Survey and the Bureau of American Ethnology. In his day, he was America's most important scientific administrator and a strong advocate of government-funded research.

John Wesley Powell's diary, as illustrated above, never explained how Bradley shed his long johns while remaining clothed.

A Cross-Country Connubial Campaign

MERCER BRINGS A BOATLOAD OF BRIDES TO WASHINGTON TERRITORY

Asa Shinn Mercer knew exactly what Washington Territory needed most: women!

The adventurous men who had migrated to the Pacific Northwest in the mid-19th century were very lonely. Stories of miners traveling the entire day simply to gaze from afar at a female face were common.

To young Mercer, who was by his mid-20s already a founder and the first president of the territory's new university, the solution to the problem seemed clear, if difficult: New England, its male population decimated by the Civil War, had a surplus of women. The task was simply to bring the supply to the demand.

Early in 1865, Mercer placed an advertisement in a Seattle newspaper, promising to find a wife for every man who subscribed $300 toward the cost of bringing her from the East. Reaction was predictably enthusiastic. Seattle even held a band concert in Mercer's honor the day he left on his cross-country connubial campaign.

Although one New York magazine approvingly wrote of him as a modern Moses leading an exodus to the West, hoots of disbelief greeted his assurances that the girls would be employed only as schoolmistresses of the greatest propriety. Skeptics wondered how there could be any children to teach in Washington if so few women resided there. Rumors arose of more tainted intentions, and Mercer was accused of "seeking to carry off young girls for the benefit of miserable old bachelors." Nonetheless, plenty of adventuresome young women saw the logic of his transcontinental plan, and he jubilantly wrote home to Seattle that he had 300 recruits.

Then his troubles began. By the time he was able to get passage for the "Mercer girls" on January 16, 1866, his flock had dwindled to a mere 100. The four-month trip around Cape Horn took a further toll—not in seasickness, but in lovesickness. Predictably, despite warnings from both Mercer and the captain, romance blossomed between the ship's passengers and its crew.

But even shipboard dalliance paled when compared with the enthusiastic welcome the ladies found in Lota, Chile, where they were courted by that outpost's military officers. One of Mercer's belles rode a spirited horse with such style that she received 17 proposals right then and there. Many others wanted to stay with their Chilean suitors, forcing the ship's captain to sneak out of port at night to prevent his precious cargo from escaping. Later, 11 stayed behind in San Francisco.

Excitement to meet the young women ran so high as the ship docked in Seattle that Mercer had to go ashore first to warn eager suitors to mind their manners if they wanted a bride.

Subscribers to the original fund soon discovered that their $300 outlay gave them no added

TRUTH OR RUMOR?

Is it true that Daniel Boone was killed by a bear, and that he never really wore coonskin caps?

No, and yes. In his long and active life, Daniel Boone (below) achieved worldwide fame as America's quintessential frontiersman. The grandson of an English Quaker, Boone never wore a coonskin, preferring the broad-brimmed beaver hat that was a family tradition.

As for his demise, it wasn't the great outdoors that did him in. In 1820, at the age of 85, it seems he overindulged in one of his favorite dishes, baked sweet potatoes, and died of indigestion.

Boone was laid to rest in Missouri beside his wife, Rebecca. In 1845, Kentucky reclaimed its famous son, and their bodies were reburied there. Modern research suggests, however, that the grave next to Rebecca's may contain the remains of a slave originally buried beside her, and that Boone still rests on a scenic hilltop in Missouri.

advantage in securing a wife. One man, who had given Mercer money to bring back a particular lady with whom he had corresponded, found instead a different woman of the same name. Making the best of it, he gallantly proposed: "All I want is a wife, and if you are willin' I would as soon take you as the other woman." But this Mercer girl had not come so far to be second best. "I do not wish to marry, sir," came the reply.

Not all newcomers were so unyielding. Among the first marriages after the long-awaited ship reached Seattle was that of Miss Annie Stephens, formerly of Baltimore, to Asa Shinn Mercer.

The "Kansas Fever" Exodus

IN A PHENOMENAL MIGRATION, THOUSANDS OF BLACKS—CALLED EXODUSTERS—STREAMED WEST SEEKING A BETTER LIFE

Eager to escape post-slavery laws requiring passes, harsh sharecropper contracts, imprisonment, and murder, thousands of African Americans were beset with "Kansas fever," and in 1879 the "Exodusters" set off for the promised land, where slavery had never existed. Many who poured off southern plantations onto steamboats were nearly destitute, few knew anything about Kansas, and most had been duped by promises of free transportation and land.

The first boatload landed in St. Louis in "utter want." Local blacks opened their churches as dormitories and collected money to send the throngs on to Kansas. But Kansas City refused to allow blacks to settle there, so they moved to tiny Wyandotte, which shortly "looked like the almshouses of the Mississippi Valley had been searched to get them together."

Southern whites blamed the exodus on fraudulent handbills and railroad promotions. But blacks had been leaving the South for years—ever since it became clear that Reconstruction promises would not be fulfilled. The National Colonization Council had plans to send émigrés to Liberia, but in

> A cabinetmaker named "Pap" Singleton claimed to be the Father of the Colored Exodus. In 1879, Singleton Colony was incorporated near present-day Emporia, Kansas.

1879, Kansas fever even overshadowed the attractions of Africa.

A steamboat strike, though finally settled, slowed the migration, and by 1881 the flood of Exodusters was reduced to a trickle.

BRIGHT IDEA

Hiding in Plain Sight Aboard a Whaling Ship

Help aboard ship was scarce during the Civil War. John Luce, captain of the whaler *America*, felt lucky to add a newcomer to his crew: a sailor who signed on as George Weldon. The new sailor could pull an oar, climb the rigging, and dance a jig with the best of them.

But when Weldon was ordered flogged because he had attacked the second mate, all were astonished to find bound breasts beneath "his" shirt. The "sailor" was a Confederate cavalry colonel's missing child, a young woman named Georgiana Leonard. Needless to say, she didn't get the flogging she was due.

In an entry in his log, the captain noted: "This day found out George Weldon to be a woman, the first I ever suspected of such a thing."

Insatiable Insects

SWARMS OF LOCUSTS LEAVE MANY 19TH-CENTURY SETTLERS DESTITUTE

The most amazing thing about the insect onslaughts was the suddenness with which they occurred: Farm families first noticed a thick gray cloud approaching. Then they heard the beating of wings, a sound like a cascading waterfall. All at once, there would descend a swarm of 120 billion grasshoppers—a mile high, 100 miles wide, and up to 300 miles long.

The locusts plunged down, and the munching noises of their feasting echoed across the land. First they'd devour the crops, then they'd go after tools and harnesses. In desperation, people hit at the hungry insects—sometimes four deep on the ground—with whatever they could wield. But no matter how many were killed, others took their places. They ate through cloth hastily thrown over crops, survived fires, and ignored smudge pots. (One farmer claimed they would warm their legs by his fire.) "Hopperdozers" were used; the insects were forced into a pan of sticky tar, then thrown into a fire.

The ravenous creatures also invaded homes and stores, consuming clothing, curtains, and food. Then, after a few days, they went on to ruin some other area, leaving wells and streams polluted with their corpses. People whose existences were already spare were reduced to destitution.

The insects were Rocky Mountain locusts. They normally bred in the foothills of Montana and Wyoming, but in dry weather, such as the summers from 1874 to 1878, they swarmed more fertile lands.

In 1874, a Nebraska farmer swings in vain at the locusts that descend upon his land.

Frontier farmers were a hearty lot, but this plague discouraged hundreds of them; giving up the fight, they went back east. Others hung on. They appointed committees to go east for supplies, some counties voted relief bonds to aid the destitute, and affected states provided aid. In 1875, Congress appropriated $30,000 for seeds. Meanwhile, settlers continued to be lured west by free or cheap land. They knew they faced the risk of being wiped out by storms, drought, or locusts, but these optimists contended that "things will be better this year." And, for some, they were.

The Irish Angel

NELLIE CASHMAN BRINGS HOSPITALITY AND HEALTH TO MINING TOWNS

At 16, Nellie Cashman, a tiny, dark-eyed brunette with a brogue and a hearty laugh, came to America from Ireland with her sister, Fannie. The pair settled in San Francisco. Though times were hard, Fannie Cashman married and had seven children. In 1877 Nellie Cashman set out for Alaska, where gold had been discovered near Juneau.

According to Nellie Cashman, she journeyed north with a party of 200 miners, then "alternately mined and kept a boardinghouse." That fall, when an outbreak of scurvy threatened lives in the camp, Cashman and six men traveled 77 days in arctic weather to bring in 1,500 pounds of vegetables and other supplies from Victoria; although they were literally worth their weight in gold, she gave potatoes away to anyone who needed them.

Cashman next moved to Virginia City, Nevada, and Tucson, Arizona, where she opened the first of her many restaurants. But brand-new Tombstone, Arizona, the site of huge silver strikes, beckoned. In 1880, she opened the Nevada Cash Store, selling fruit, provisions, gents' furnishings, dry goods, and children's shoes. Then came the Russ House, a hotel and restaurant. Miners flocked there. "If a fellow has no money, Miss Nellie gives him board and lodging until he makes a stake," one of them wrote.

Tombstone was a boomtown, full of gamblers, prostitutes, and such legendary gunfighters as Wyatt Earp and Doc Holliday. Yet Cashman went calmly about, doing good. She built a Catholic church and was treasurer of the Irish National Land League. She wrote an eloquent newspaper plea for aid for "our less favored kindred in the unequal contest they are waging against … want."

In 1884, five men were to be hanged for murder. They were upset because bleachers were being built to make their execution a public spectacle, and because their bodies were to be denied burial and given to medical students for dissection. The night before the execution, Cashman led a midnight party of miners to destroy the bleachers. Then, for 10 nights afterward, two prospectors guarded the murderers' graves.

After 20 years in Tombstone, interspersed by mining expeditions to Baja California, New Mexico, and the Arizona Territory, Nellie Cashman returned to Alaska, where she mined and ran a store for the next quarter-century. She ignored friends' requests that she slow down. "I've suffered trials and hardships in the frozen plains of Alaska and on the deserts of Arizona, but I have been happy and healthy," she declared. Her last mining camp was inside the Arctic Circle. As her health failed, she went to St. Joseph's Hospital in Victoria, a hospital she had helped fund almost 40 years earlier. She died there in 1925 at nearly 80 years old from double pneumonia she had contracted after flying in a mail plane.

TRUTH OR RUMOR?

Is it true that Oklahoma's state name has something to do with a bird?

No—unless you subscribe to the adage, "The early bird catches the worm." When large parts of the Oklahoma district were opened for free settlement in 1889, tens of thousands thronged to the borders to await the starting gun at noon on April 22. But some sneaked in sooner to stake their claims, even lathering their horses with soap to make them look as if they had just arrived. They were derisively called Sooners, but the term later became respectable; today Oklahoma's nickname is the Sooner State.

From Slumming to Farming

CHILDREN'S AID SOCIETY SENDS URCHINS WEST

They were called "street arabs"— ragged children who roamed the streets of New York City. By day they were newsboys, bootblacks, beggars, and thieves; by night they slept in barges on the river or in alleyways. In 19th-century New York only a few overcrowded orphanages offered an alternative, until 1854, when Charles Brace founded the Children's Aid Society. He  proposed a novel plan: Send these children west, to America's wholesome heartland.

From 1854 to 1929, the Children's Aid Society rescued children from institutions and from parents who could not afford to keep them. Each child was given a bath and fresh clothes, and put on an orphan train to find a new home with a family out West.

The orphan train's arrival was exciting. The train would pull into a small farming community, where hundreds of couples from miles around waited anxiously. The children were brought and perused by the locals, who would help their new offspring into the family buggy and go home.

By modern standards such methods seem primitive, even cruel. But life in the city streets offered nothing better, and the society did have some striking successes. A 1917 study showed that thousands of professionals had gotten their start on orphan trains. Even two future governors—Andrew Burke of North Dakota and John Brady of the Alaska Territory—were taken from a Randall's Island orphanage and sent west on the same train.

Early in the 20th century, social workers began finding ways to keep families together; foster homes and modern methods of adoption brought an end to the orphan trains.

A great cattle baron in his later years, with a herd of 100,000, Charlie Goodnight (right) did much to establish respect for the law among ranchers, who saw nothing wrong with stealing unbranded stock.

Herds Go West

GOODNIGHT AND LOVING BLAZE A NEW CATTLE ROUTE

Most Texas cattlemen drove their great herds of long-horns north to the stockyards in Missouri or Kansas, but not Charlie Goodnight. In the spring of 1866, he planned to blaze a new westward trail to Colorado. There were plenty of good ranges there and lots of money because of the new silver mines.

Outfitting for his first drive, the 30-year-old Goodnight, a former Texas ranger and an experienced woodsman, bought a government wagon with strong iron axles, equipped it with a chuckbox, and stocked it with sourdough starter and other provisions, thus creating the first chuck wagon. He was nearly ready to depart when he met Oliver Loving, another pioneer cattleman. The two agreed to join forces and set out with 2,000 longhorns and 18 cowboys.

Goodnight took a route that went through New Mexico to avoid dangerous Comanche country, but he still encountered a host of new problems. From Fort Belknap in the Texas panhandle they would take the old stage-coach-rutted Butterfield Mail Route to the Middle Concho River and follow it to its headwaters; from there they would have to cross 80 miles of waterless plain to the Pecos River. Continuing up the Pecos, their course would parallel the Rockies north to Denver.

On June 6, Goodnight and Loving pointed their cattle westward. Reaching the headwaters of the Concho, they filled their water barrels and let the cattle drink. Then they headed into the setting sun to cross the dreaded plain. By the end of the second day, the cattle were too thirsty to bed down, and so they stumbled on. For three days and nights the men rode without sleep, driving cattle that bawled constantly for water. More than 300 animals died, their carcasses left to mark the trail.

Smelling water when it was still miles away, the crazed beasts made a mad dash and, at the end of the stampede, catapulted over the river's steep banks. Many drowned. Others were mired in quicksand.

Some drank from alkali holes (pools of water with a poisonous concentration of alkaline salt scoured up by the river) and dropped dead in their tracks.

Rounding up the survivors, Goodnight and Loving pushed north along the Pecos through desolate rattlesnake country. By then, many cows were dropping calves. Hundreds of newborns had to be shot while the cows, bawling until they were hoarse, milled about trying to find their offspring.

Around July 1, they reached Fort Sumner, where the army had in its charge several thousand starving Indians. The military bought part of the herd for eight cents a pound on the hoof—a total of $12,000 in gold. Overjoyed, Loving pressed on to Colorado to sell the rest, while Goodnight backtracked to Texas to bring up a second herd before winter set in.

This time, crossing the arid plain, Goodnight let the cattle graze at sunup and sundown and trailed them in between. Using this system, he never lost another head. In years to follow, millions of hoofs would pound the Goodnight-Loving Trail.

Calamity Jane

FOUL-MOUTHED AND ROUGH AROUND THE EDGES, WHO KNEW THAT SHE WAS ALSO A NOTED NURSE?

While drinking in a Montana bar near the end of her life, the notorious "Calamity Jane" turned to her friend, a cowhand named Teddy Blue, and remarked: "I want to be left alone to go to Hell in my own way. I want to be with you boys, that's the only life I know." They were drinking on money Blue had paid back for a kindness she had done him years before.

Much maligned by a host of tall tales and long-remembered legends, Calamity Jane—born Martha Jane Canary—was basically a loner, given to bragging, brawling, and hanging around with some pretty rough characters. But, as it turns out, she was also a woman of great compassion who gave money to hungry cowhands, treated children gently, and tended the sick wherever she happened to be.

SMALLPOX STRIKES

The two sides of her character were never more evident than in Deadwood, South Dakota, during the smallpox epidemic of 1878.

The smallpox victims, relegated by terrified residents to a little shack outside town, were cared for by Deadwood's lone physician, Lyman Babcock. One day he was startled to find Calamity waiting for him in front of the modest cabin. When he asked her what she was doing there, the tall, scruffy-looking woman replied, "Well, Doc, somebody's got to take care of them."

CALAMITY'S HUMANITY

After entering the shack, she ordered the doctor to tell her just what to do. And then she proceeded to do it. Her nursing abilities had already been praised in a newspaper account: "There's a lot of humanity in Calamity."

Jane stayed at the remote pesthouse (as it was called) caring for patients until the epidemic finally ended. C. H. Robinson, who was a small boy at the time, recalled "Old Calam" as a devoted nurse who was given to growling orders like, "Here, you little bastard, drink this soup."

A story that some view as doubtful, but that might just be typical, has Jane taking sacks of groceries out of a Deadwood store. When the owner pointed out that she had failed to pay, she drew her six-gun and said, "Don't worry about your damned bill. I'll pay for it when the boys get better."

Whether Calamity Jane was the romantic figure of western legend or a violent, hard-drinking slattern, it is clear she could be counted on to pitch in when help was needed. The only time she was ever tried for a crime, it turned out that the money she had stolen had been contributed to a hospital for the care of a sick prostitute.

Calamity Jane died in 1903 and was buried in Deadwood. The undertaker, who had been one of her smallpox patients, donated a coffin. And the rector of the cemetery, who sealed her coffin and lowered her into the grave, was none other than C. H. Robinson, who had been so gruffly nursed back to health by Calamity Jane in the pesthouse during the epidemic of '78.

Calamity Jane—born Martha Jane Canary—visits the grave of her good friend, Wild Bill Hickok, who was murdered by Jack McCall while playing poker in 1876. At her request, Jane was buried beside Hickok after her death in 1903.

Killed by a Broken Heart

INCONSOLABLE LOVER DIGS HIS OWN GRAVE ... AND JUMPS IN

High on Brown Mountain, near the town of Silver Plume in the Colorado Rockies, stands a 15-foot granite obelisk with an unlikely inscription: "Clifford Griffin ... of Brand Hall, Shropshire, England ... buried near this spot."

Brothers Heneage and Clifford Griffin immigrated to America and became miners. But though they grew rich on silver and gold, Clifford remained disconsolate. His fiancée had died just before their wedding. Every evening he would stand outside and play his violin, while other miners listened, far below.

Legend has it that Griffin gouged out a grave from the solid rock of the mines and that one June evening in 1887, he finished playing, walked to his tomb, and shot himself. Mysteriously, although 120 years have passed, the remote mountain obelisk is still scrupulously kept up and is a popular destination for hikers.

Zachary Taylor's Dead Letter

EXORBITANT POSTAL CHARGES ALMOST PREVENT HIS PRESIDENCY

The view that "the mail must get through" had, it seems, a rather shaky start. True, the Constitution empowered Congress to "establish Post Offices and Post Roads." But for 50 years after the Constitution was ratified, if you wanted to send mail, you just folded the letter over, sealed it with wax, and gave it to a stagecoach driver. To receive the letter, the addressee had to go to his local post office and pay the charges. When some local letter carriers started working in 1825, their wages were the fees received from addressees. If you weren't home to pay, you didn't get your letter.

AN "ODIOUS MONOPOLY"

Although envelopes first appeared in 1839, the stamp problem remained. So did the delivery problem. Roads could be impassable for weeks at a time, holding up all mail. As railroads began to snake across the land in the 1830s and 1840s, delivery in a few areas improved, but overall service was

> In 1825, letter carriers' wages were collected from addressees. If you weren't home to pay, you didn't get your mail. More than 20 years passed before the first stamps were used.

so expensive and haphazard that many people wanted to abolish the post office.

In 1845, Congress legislated cheaper postage. At first postmasters printed their own stamps and cancellations, adding to the general chaos. Finally, a couple of years later, the Post Office Department came through with official postage; the first stamps bore portraits of George Washington and Benjamin Franklin.

ECONOMICAL, COMICAL ZACH

Paying postage still got a letter only as far as the addressee's post office, and he was obliged to bail out his mail with his own cash. Zachary "Old Rough-and-Ready" Taylor, popular hero of the Mexican War, received pounds of mail but wouldn't spend the money to get it out of the Baton Rouge post office; he had the postmaster send all collect letters to the dead letter office. When the Whig Party nominated Taylor for president in 1848, officials wrote to tell him so. The announcement also landed in the dead letter office, with 10 cents postage due.

It was weeks before the worried Whigs discovered what had happened. They sent another missive (prepaid, this time), and Taylor's acceptance arrived by return mail. The incident provided fodder for campaign claims: The Whigs cited him as a model of frugality, while the Democrats made fun of "economical, comical old Zach." But Taylor won—he was the last Whig ever elected.

Even when Post Office mailmen started getting paid in 1863, mail was still delivered only in cities. It was 1896 before farmers enjoyed the "luxury" of Rural Free Delivery.

BRIGHT IDEA

Dogs That Deliver Mail

Fenton Whiting proved that many modern mail carriers are wrong: A dog can be the postman's best friend.

In the winter of 1858 he hitched some mongrels to a $75 sled and brought the mail through California's deep Sierra Nevada snow by dog team. His canine couriers lasted until 1865, when sleigh runners were put on stagecoaches and horses were fitted with snowshoes for the winter runs.

Overnight? Not Quite.

THE PONY EXPRESS AND RAILROADS PROPEL AMERICA'S MAIL OUT WEST

Shortly after gold was discovered in California in 1848, the Post Office Department awarded a contract to the Pacific Mail Steamship Company. Eastern mail took a month to reach San Francisco by way of Panama, where it crossed the isthmus by rail. Mail was left unsorted and undelivered. Miners had to travel to the Post Office and paw through mountains of letters. In typical gold-rush spirit, entrepreneurs quickly took advantage of this chaos: For an ounce of gold dust (about $16), Alexander Todd would find a letter on the West Coast and deliver it to miners in the field. Other express services soon sprang up, and by 1852, Wells Fargo & Company had begun private mail delivery.

Above: A Pony Express rider as depicted on a 1960 U.S. stamp. Right: An undated advertisement for the service promised that mail would amazingly take only "10 Days to San Francisco!"

OVERLAND ROUTES AND THE PONY EXPRESS

In 1856, more than 75,000 Californians petitioned for overland transcontinental delivery. The postmaster general awarded the $600,000 annual contract to John Butterfield's 2,800-mile Oxbow Route through the Southwest. Butterfield promised delivery in 25 days and, to skeptics' astonishment, he kept his word. On September 16, 1858, a stagecoach left Tipton, Missouri, reaching San Francisco only 23 days, 23 hours later. "A glorious triumph for civilization and the Union," gushed President James Buchanan.

In April 1860, the Pony Express cut the time to 10 days or less. Its founder, William H. Russell, won the federal contract by recruiting the right kind of riders: "Wanted: Young, skinny, wiry fellows not over 18. Must be expert riders willing to risk death daily. Orphans preferred." Although the service lasted less than 19 months, the Pony Express carried 34,753 pieces of mail over the 1,966 miles between St. Joseph, Missouri, and Sacramento, California, losing only one mail sack. The record time of 7 days, 17 hours was set delivering Lincoln's 1861 inaugural address to California. But in October of that year, the transcontinental telegraph line was completed, putting an end to the Pony Express.

END OF AN ERA

Horse-and-wagon delivery was quickly replaced by the transcontinental railway, which was completed on May 10, 1869. Mail had been sorted in railroad cars since 1862 on runs between Hannibal and St. Joseph, Missouri, where it was shifted to westbound stagecoaches. In 1864, the railroad post office began, and with transcontinental railroads, mail arrived in California presorted. By 1930, the railway mail service, a branch of the U.S. Post Office, was using more than 10,000 trains to deliver mail to every crossroads town in the country.

The Father of Western Botany

THOMAS "OLD CURIOUS" NUTTALL EXPANDS SCIENCE'S FRONTIER

Many explorers went west before Thomas Nuttall set out in April 1810, but none of them really saw it—at least not the way he did. Arriving in America from England at age 22, he got his big break two years later when Dr. Benjamin Smith Barton, a prominent Philadelphia academic, offered to outfit him for a one-man scientific wilderness expedition. Certainly the kind doctor, who fiercely desired scientific acclaim for himself, understood the dangers and the way he was exploiting Nuttall's youthful enthusiasm. "Should his life be spared," wrote Barton with astounding smugness, "he will add much to our knowledge."

Nuttall's Lesser-Marsh Wren **by John James Audubon.**

Nuttall not only survived, he thrived on the two-year trek from Philadelphia that took him as far west as the upper Missouri. Because of Nuttall's fanatic devotion to collecting plant specimens, American Indians thought him insane and treated him as a holy man. And indeed, Nuttall's behavior verged on bizarre. Once, enraptured by nature's bounty, he wandered 100 miles, finally collapsing from exhaustion. An Indian found him and saved his life.

After several more trips to the Northeast and the Midwest, Nuttall became curator of the botanical gardens at Harvard University. The reclusive botanist had a trapdoor built in his boardinghouse living quarters, so that he could avoid encountering other residents. In 1834, he decided that Harvard was a waste of his time, so he and a protégé, ornithologist John K. Townsend, joined a fur-trading expedition to the Pacific Coast. Their collection of western wildlife became a landmark of 19th-century research. Sailing home, Nuttall was nicknamed "Old Curious" by the ship's crew. When he went to the ship owner's Boston office to pay his bill, the tough-minded merchant told him the passage was free, since he had traveled "not for his own amusement, but for the benefit of mankind."

FUNNY FACT

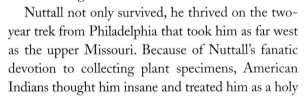

Artist John Audubon Was Once Jailed

Naturalist John James Audubon is world famous for his realistic bird portraits. But when it came to business, the budding artist's grasp of reality was much more tenuous.

While in his early thirties, Audubon and his brother-in-law built a steam grist and lumber mill in Henderson, Kentucky. The enterprise failed in 1819, and Audubon was jailed in Louisville for debt. He was released only after he had declared bankruptcy. "With nothing left to [him] but [his] humble talents," Audubon supported his family as a portraitist and pursued his passion of observing and recording the birds of America's wilderness. His endeavor eventually took flight into a profitable enterprise: In 1827, the first folios of his famous *Birds of America* were published.

Cold Case

CHARLES HALL MYSTERIOUSLY POISONED EN ROUTE TO THE NORTH POLE

"I am on a mission of love … ready to do or die," Charles Hall rhapsodized in his diary. The former blacksmith and engraver had never before been north of Vermont. But when he first read of Sir John Franklin's 1847 disappearance on his third Arctic expedition, Hall suddenly saw his mission in life: He, too, would be an explorer, and he would find out what had happened to the renowned English explorer and his men.

The novice sailor set out in May 1860 aboard a whaling ship with a pitiful $980 worth of supplies. He reached Frobisher Bay, where he settled down to live with the Eskimos for the next two years. Hall learned the Eskimo dialects, ate the local food (including seal's blood), and allowed the shamans to treat his maladies.

Although he gleaned no information about the Franklin expedition, Hall returned to the United States rich in experience and, with his usual determination, began raising funds for another Arctic journey. This time, he did find relics of the Franklin voyage. And although Hall's bullying and inability to pay his crew almost caused a mutiny, the second expedition established his reputation as an explorer. In 1871, Congress appropriated $50,000 to fund what Hall regarded as his ultimate mission: to sail to the North Pole.

Hall left Connecticut in July aboard the *Polaris*. Always single-minded, he paid no attention to the simmering stockpot of personalities he'd assembled. The chief scientific officer, Dr. Emil Bessels, showed open contempt for Hall's scientific qualifications. The sailing master, Sidney Budington, constantly raided the ship's alcohol supply. Ethnic tensions, too, flared among the crew.

For a while the men made progress, reaching a point of 82°11' North—the farthest north a ship had ever sailed. Then winds and ice-clogged seas pushed the *Polaris* south. Hall decided to take refuge for the winter in an inlet he dubbed Thank God Bay, ignoring vehement objections from Bessels and Budington.

The days turned colder and soon became months. Rations dwindled. Hall set out for a two-week probe of the area. When he returned, he asked for a cup of coffee. Shortly after drinking it, he complained of "a foul stomach." A few days later he was delirious. Sure that Bessels was poisoning him, Hall refused the doctor's medication. Finally, he died. Dr. Bessels's diagnosis: "Apoplexy."

A naval commission later exonerated Bessels and Budington of murder. But in 1968, two scholars exhumed Hall's frozen body. Analysis of hair and fingernails confirmed their suspicions: Hall had been poisoned with arsenic. But the murderers would never be found. Hall, who tried so hard to solve the mystery of an explorer's death, is himself a murder mystery.

American explorer Captain Charles Francis Hall's steamship, *Polaris*, and the expedition's transport ship, *Congress*, at a Danish settlement off the coast of Greenland.

Charles Wilkes's sketch of man's first landing on the Antarctic continent was later made into a painting and illustrates that the voyage was a feat not only of exploration and navigation but of survival. The men's clothes, as Wilkes wrote, were "entirely unworthy in the service, and inferior in every way."

An Expedition to Antarctica

EXPLORER CHARLES WILKES CHARTS THE UNKNOWN CONTINENT

The expedition was controversial from the start. Fishing interests lobbied the U.S. government for accurate charts of the lucrative but dangerous Antarctic waters, while other powerful factions opposed public funding. After the government finally appropriated $300,000 for the task, several politically astute naval officers declined to command the expedition. But Charles Wilkes, never one to let caution stand in the way of duty, accepted; in August 1838, his six wooden ships began what would be a four-year journey to the bottom of the world.

It seemed as if everything conceivable was against them. On the first foray into far southern waters, beset by pack ice and racked by gales, one ship sank. Denying defeat, Wilkes sailed into the South Pacific and spent several months mapping the islands of Hawaii, Tahiti, and Samoa. After docking in Sydney, Australia, for repairs, Wilkes sailed south once more on December 26, 1839, leading the way in his ship, the *Vincennes*. A month later, he spied an Antarctic continent. Wilkes sailed along the unknown coast for hundreds of miles, making charts as he went. In February, he rendezvoused with his other ships and led them home.

Upon his return to the United States in 1842, Wilkes was outraged that other explorers had challenged his findings. Englishman James Ross, sailing by charts Wilkes had sent him in Australia, claimed to have sailed across areas Wilkes had marked as land. A French captain, Dumont d'Urville, claimed to have found Antarctica a day before Wilkes did.

Later studies did reveal some inaccuracies in Wilkes's charts—probably because the reflective qualities of the Antarctic atmosphere can distort the proximity of land—but most were astonishingly accurate. D'Urville's ship's log showed that he had failed to allow for the international dateline; Wilkes's sighting had preceded the Frenchman's by 10 hours. Today a vast expanse of the continent he explored at such risk honors the intrepid American's achievement: Wilkes Land's 1,500-mile coastline is about one-fifth of Antarctica's shore.

Sourdoughs Rise to the Top

NATIVE ALASKANS SCOFF AT OUTSIDERS AND CLIMB McKINLEY IN RECORD TIME

One day in 1909, a group of Alaskan miners, popularly called Sourdoughs, were sitting in a saloon in Fairbanks talking about outsiders (like Dr. Frederick Cook) climbing "their" Mount McKinley. Convinced that Cook's ascent had never been made, some of the boys decided to prove it the only way they knew how: by doing it themselves. Enthusiasm in Fairbanks ran high. "Our boys will show up Dr. Cook and other 'outside' doctors and expeditions," the Fairbanks *Times* declared.

Four Sourdoughs—Tom Lloyd, Billy Taylor, Pete Anderson, and Charlie McGonagall—set out in December 1909. For climbing shoes, they strapped spikes on their moccasins. They used hooked poles to balance themselves. In March they reached a ridge 11,000 feet up, and on April 3, carrying a 14-foot wooden flagpole, some doughnuts, and thermoses of hot chocolate, three miners raced for the North Peak. Taylor and Anderson won.

> It took the Sourdoughs only 18 hours to complete a trip that would later take professional climbers two weeks.

Just as simply as they had gone up, the Sourdoughs returned to camp, in an incredible 18 hours (the ascent would later take professional climbers two weeks). But when Lloyd got back to Fairbanks, few believed his outrageous story, and nobody could see the flagpole.

The first professional climbers to scale Mount McKinley reached the South Peak in June 1913. To their complete amazement, standing proudly on the North Peak, only 850 feet below, was the flagpole left by the Sourdoughs.

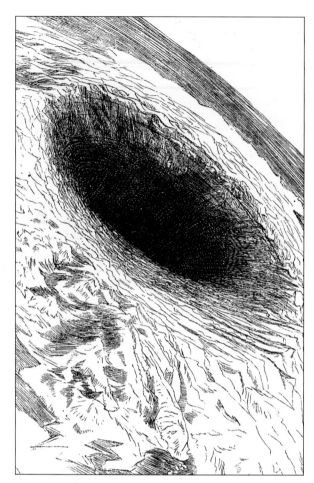

John Symmes's hollow earth theory posited that one could reach the center of the earth by sailing over the rim of a polar hole.

Holes in the Poles?

"I ask 100 brave companions … to start from Siberia.… I engage we find a warm and rich land, stocked with thrifty vegetables and animals … northward of latitude 82." John Symmes, a hero of the War of 1812, was convinced that he could easily sail over the curved rim of a polar hole and into a hollow earth. Attempts by like-minded congressmen to fund Symmes's journey failed in 1823, but public lectures by a Hollow Earth disciple, Jeremiah Reynolds, stressed the commercial potential of the bizarre crusade and helped win support for the Wilkes expedition to Antarctica 15 years later.

Cook Cooks Up Tall Arctic Tale

**EXPLORER FALSELY CLAIMS LANDING
ON NORTH POLE AND MOUNT McKINLEY**

On September 6, 1909, a weary, triumphant Robert Peary wired from Labrador: "Stars and Stripes nailed to the pole Peary." The 53-year-old explorer had spent nearly 23 years pursuing his goal, but his cable was too late. Five days earlier, Dr. Frederick Cook had wired from the Shetland Islands that he had beaten Peary by a year. Commander Peary, a proud and forthright man, told the press that Cook was a liar: It was impossible to reach the pole with only two Eskimos and two sledges. Cook may have been away from his Greenland base for 14 months, but he'd either been hunting or gotten lost.

The controversy was among the most vicious in the history of exploration. Peary spoke to Cook's Eskimo companions, who said that they had gone "no distance north and not out of sight of land." Peary's own claim was supported by Matthew Henson, his longtime aide. But Henson was black, and many people would not take his word. Instead, they believed the handsome and charming Dr. Cook; a bona fide explorer, he had scaled Denali (Mount McKinley), Alaska's highest peak, and brought back a photograph of the view.

But on the day Cook received the keys to New York City, the man who had climbed McKinley with him said they had never been near the 20,320-foot peak. The Explorer's Club investigated and found that the "summit" picture had been taken from a 5,300-foot ridge. Next, an astronomer proved that Cook had fabricated the date and latitude on which he claimed to have seen the midnight sun.

Nevertheless, much of the public still found Cook too charming to disbelieve, and Peary grew increasingly bitter; after he retired from the navy in 1911, he often refused to discuss the North Pole. In 1918, two years before Peary's death, Cook's "North Pole" photographs were discredited. The plausible doctor later served four years in Fort Leavenworth for promoting stock in a company owning oil he had "discovered" in Wyoming.

Frederick Cook surveys an Arctic horizon in one of the faked photographs that dazzled the public.

Young Daredevil

19-YEAR-OLD CROMWELL DIXON IS FIRST TO FLY ACROSS THE CONTINENTAL DIVIDE

As a child in Ohio, Cromwell Dixon dreamed of flying to Mars. He even drew blueprints for a manned rocket—quite a feat for a boy born in 1892. At 14, he designed a "sky bicycle," a 32-foot, silk, hot-air balloon on a wooden frame connected to a propeller driven by bicycle pedals and a rudder. Dixon persuaded his mother to sell some jewelry to raise $500 to build it, and for the next three years the boy pedaled his contraption at county fairs. By 1911, Dixon was ready for bigger things. After only three days at the Curtiss Aviation School in Hammondsport, New York, he soloed in a biplane. When the Aero Club of America gave him pilot's license No. 43, he was, at 19, the youngest pilot in the country.

Ever supportive, Dixon's mother signed a contract with Curtiss so that the underage boy could fly in air shows. After he developed the Dixon corkscrew dive, a spiral from 8,000 feet that leveled off just above the ground, his weekly pay jumped from $1,500 to $2,000.

After only three days in aviation school, the young daredevil soloed a biplane. Soon he was making $2,000 a week— a fortune at the time.

Dixon decided that he wanted to be first to fly over the Rocky Mountains. Little was known of mountain flying at the time; several previous attempts had been ended by treacherous downdrafts. To encourage the feat, a consortium that included showman John Ringling and the president of the Great Northern Railway had put up a $10,000 purse.

On September 30, 1911, Dixon took off from the Montana state fairgrounds in Helena. He spent 15 minutes reaching an altitude of 7,000 feet—only 800 feet higher than the mountains he intended to cross— then headed for Blossburg, just over the Continental Divide. To provide a landmark, his friends lit a bonfire on a high peak near the town. When Dixon landed, he said, "Boys, I knew I could do it," and wired Curtiss. Tragically, a few days later, Dixon was killed at Spokane, Washington, when a sudden air current slammed his plane into the ground, crushing him under the engine.

First U.S. Woman in Flight

HARRIET QUIMBY ALSO FIRST FEMALE TO FLY ACROSS ENGLISH CHANNEL

Harriet Quimby was the first woman in America— and the second in the world—to earn a pilot's license. A successful New York journalist, Quimby became intrigued by airplanes after covering a flying meet in 1910.

When reporters quizzed her about taking flying lessons, she replied, "There is no more risk in an airplane than a high-speed automobile, and a lot more fun. Why shouldn't we have some good American women pilots?"

Quimby passed the test for her pilot's license in a Blériot monoplane. America was plane crazy, and there was good money in air shows. The aviatrix toured the East and Mexico with the Moisant International Aviators troupe. Then she decided she would be the first woman to fly across the English Channel.

She took off in a biplane on April 16, 1912, sitting in a wicker basket seat in the open fuselage and keeping her bearings in dense fog with only a compass. Finally she risked dropping to 1,000 feet—and emerged into bright sunlight over a French beach. Alas, the sinking of the *Titanic* robbed the pilot of her headlines; and a *New York Times* editorial huffed that her feat "proves ability and capacity, but it doesn't prove equality."

In July, Quimby went to attack the world speed record at the Harvard-Boston Aviation Meet. Although the Blériot was thought to be unstable with a passenger, she took the air-show manager for a spin over Boston Harbor. Suddenly the plane's nose dropped sharply. The pilot managed to right it, but, as horrified spectators watched, the plane flipped into another nosedive and crashed into the harbor. Harriet Quimby was dead at 37.

BRIGHT IDEA

Person-Powered Plane

The first successful person-powered plane was launched in 1977. Two years later, the pedal-driven *Gossamer Albatross* successfully flew 22 miles to cross the English Channel. Although the plane weighs only 71 pounds, its 94-foot wingspan is longer than that of a DC-9.

Post Office Takes to the Skies

CHARLES LINDBERGH AMONG FIRST AIRMAIL PILOTS

May 15, 1918, simply wasn't Lieutenant George Boyle's day. He had been chosen to pilot the first leg of the first scheduled airmail flight, from Washington, D.C., to New York City. Curious spectators, among them President Woodrow Wilson, were gathered to witness the historic takeoff of the modified JN-4H biplane (the "flying Jenny"). But the Jenny seemed to be rooted to the ground, its 150-horsepower Hispano-Suiza engine silent. Boyle sat in the cockpit shouting "Contact" while mechanics desperately spun the propeller—until the awful truth struck them: The plane's gas tank was empty.

Fueled at last, the Jenny rose skyward. But instead of heading north, Boyle circled the field and flew south. An hour later Captain Benjamin Lipsner, coordinator of the U.S. Post Office's new airmail service, got a phone call from the embarrassed pilot. Explaining that his "compass had gotten a little mixed up," Boyle confessed he had just crashed, and

his plane was upside-down in a Maryland cornfield. Lipsner sent a car to recover the pilot and the three sacks of mail.

Some months later, military fliers were replaced by a small corps of intrepid airmen, whose skills became legendary. Without cockpit navigational aids, they kept on course by following highways, railroad tracks, and riverbeds. For the first nighttime transcontinental mail flight, residents of small Nebraska towns lit bonfires to help pilot Jack Knight find his way.

Not all pilots made it to their destinations safely. Of the original 50, 32 pilots died in crashes. And others had so many near misses, they lost count. One young pilot on the St. Louis to Chicago run, Charles Lindbergh, twice bailed out of his crippled plane safely, earning the nickname "Lucky Lindy." Lindbergh, who joined the

Charles Lindbergh (left), attempted a nonstop flight to Paris in his Ryan monoplane, *The Spirit of St. Louis* (top) while on leave from flying the mail. Above: Lieutenant George Boyle (left), pictured here with the major in charge of the airplane service, piloted the first airmail flight in 1918.

service in 1926, was on leave of absence from the Post Office when he made his historic transatlantic flight the following year. Before he realized that fame would make a return to his old job impossible, Lindbergh confidently told reporters: "I am an airmail pilot and expect to fly the mail again."

The 6,000-mile Space Walk

THE ASTRONAUT WHO WOULDN'T COME BACK TO EARTH

It was the longest space mission up to that time: a mind-boggling 66 orbits around 1,906,684 miles of the earth. But what captured the imagination of people all over the world—and caused quite a bit of concern for the National Aeronautics and Space Administration (NASA)—was the first American to walk in space.

On June 3, 1965, astronaut Ed White, wearing a $31\frac{1}{4}$-pound space suit that cost $26,000, opened the hatch of the *Gemini 4* space capsule at 3:41 p.m. EDT and floated out. He was 135 miles above Earth, a slender 30-foot lifeline his only link to the rest of humanity.

The mission plan called for a 12-minute space walk. But White started having so much fun "walking" on top of the world while traveling at 17,500 miles an hour that he decided not to come in.

"They [the earthbound controllers at NASA] want you to get back in now," Jim McDivitt, White's partner back inside *Gemini 4*, told him at the appropriate moment. "I'm not coming in ... this is fun," the space walker responded.

"Come in," McDivitt ordered.

Ground control soon informed the astronauts that they had about four more minutes until they reached Bermuda and darkness on the other side of Earth. But White was still happily afloat at the end of his tether.

"Come on. Let's get back in here before it gets dark," McDivitt pleaded.

"It's the saddest moment of my life," said White.

"Well, you're going to find that it's sadder when we have to come down with this thing."

At this point an exasperated ground control still couldn't believe that White wasn't back inside. "*Gemini 4. Gemini 4.* Get back in.... You getting him back in?"

FUNNY FACT

Astronaut Submits Travel Expenses to NASA

Michael Collins (below) got to walk in space twice during the 1966 *Gemini 10* mission. After returning to Earth, the astronaut put in

his travel voucher for the flight. At $8 per day, the total for three days came to $24 (as much of a bargain for NASA, no doubt, as Manhattan Island had been for Peter Minuit more than three centuries earlier).

About eight years after his mission, Collins acknowledged in his autobiography that he should have claimed seven cents a mile on that voucher, which would have entitled him to $80,000 for the trip. He didn't attempt it, though, because one of the original *Mercury* astronauts had already tried that stunt and in return had received a bill "for a couple of million dollars" for the nonreusable rocket that had catapulted him into space.

McDivitt answered: "He's standing in the seat now and his legs are below the instrument panel." A sigh of relief went up all along the NASA control panel at Houston. "OK," NASA said. "Get him back in. You're going to have Bermuda in about 20 seconds."

White had set a record by walking through space for a very long 21 minutes. He had strolled across 6,000 miles of the earth before giving in to the more routine (but no less spectacular) experience of whizzing around the planet in a space capsule.

Extraordinary Heroes

Top: The explosion of space shuttle *Challenger* claimed the lives of seven crew members on January 28, 1986. Above: The *Challenger* crew. Left to right, front row: Astronauts Michael Smith, Francis "Dick" Scobee, and Ronald McNair. Back frow: Ellison Onizuka, Sharon Christa McAuliffe, Gregory Jarvis, and Judith Resnick.

CHALLENGER AND *COLUMBIA* CREWS
LOST IN FATAL SPACE SHUTTLE ACCIDENTS

In 1986, one of the darkest days that this generation can remember was caused by the malfunction of a simple gasket.

America's space program suffered a heartbreaking setback on January 28, when the space shuttle *Challenger* disintegrated in a fireball 73 seconds after liftoff. On board was a crew of seven, including civilian Christa McAuliffe, a New Hampshire high school teacher who had been chosen in a nationwide search.

It was America's worst space disaster to date. Although three astronauts had burned to death during a simulation in 1967, none had ever died on an actual space flight, and the entire country mourned. In one of the most eloquent addresses of his presidency, Ronald Reagan comforted the nation. The seven *Challenger* astronauts, he said, had "slipped the surly bonds of Earth to touch the face of God."

A special commission later traced the explosion to the spacecraft's right rocket booster and a simple O-ring gasket. Design errors and atypically low temperatures on the morning of the launch had combined to weaken the seal. As the *Challenger* ascended, flames leaked from the booster, burning into the shuttle's main fuel tank like a match held to dynamite. The tank exploded, pulling the *Challenger* apart.

The disaster might have been prevented. For seven successive launches, engineers had known about the gasket problem, only to have the information lost somewhere in NASA's chain of command. American astronauts would not return to space for nearly three years.

TRAGEDY STRIKES AGAIN

On February 1, 2003, America was again devastated by a space shuttle disaster. On that day, seven astronauts—six Americans, plus Israel's first astronaut, Ilan Ramon—perished aboard the shuttle *Columbia*. The shuttle broke up over Texas, almost 40 miles above the Earth, on its way back home after a 17-day mission. It was due to land at Florida's Kennedy Space Center just 15 minutes after the accident.

Sadly, a seemingly minor occurrence—a piece of insulating foam that came off the external tank during the shuttle's launch—was again at the root of the tragedy. The foam separated from the shuttle's exterior and hit the left wing, causing a breach in the shuttle's thermal protection system. On reentering the atmosphere, this breach allowed very hot air to penetrate *Columbia*'s insulation, which melted the aluminum in the left wing. This structural damage caused a loss of control and the eventual breakup of the orbiter.

"The cause in which they died will continue," said President George W. Bush in an address to the nation that day. "Mankind is led into the darkness beyond our world by the inspiration of discovery and the longing to understand. Our journey into space will go on."

America's journey into space *did* go on, but not without an overhaul of the space agency's culture and procedures. Just two weeks after the disaster, President George W. Bush announced a new vision for NASA, which included spending $12 billion over five years on the program and returning humans to the moon by 2020. Seven months later, the panel that investigated the accident called for sweeping changes, including better protection for the public during shuttle launch and reentry, as well as improving NASA managers' "practices detrimental to safety."

After the 2003 shuttle tragedy, President George W. Bush said in a speech to the nation: "The same creator who names the stars also knows the names of the seven souls we mourn today. The crew of the shuttle *Columbia* did not return safely to Earth, yet we can pray that all are safely home." Below: The *Columbia* crew. Seated, left to right: Rick Husband, Kalpana Chawla, and William McCool. Standing, left to right: David Brown, Laurel Clark, Michael Anderson, and Ilan Ramon. Bottom: After the explosion, firefighters from Oregon and California search Texas fields for *Columbia* debris.

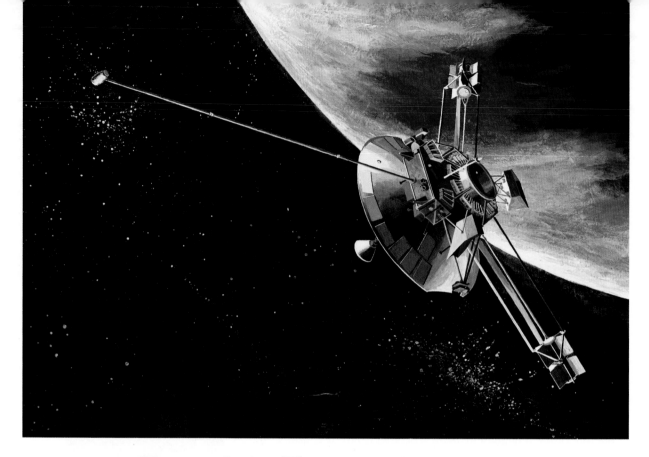

Beyond the Terrestrial Frontier

SPEEDING TOWARD THE MYSTERIOUS
WORLD OF DISTANT STARS AND GALAXIES

Speeding out of our solar system, the appropriately named *Pioneer 10* spacecraft was launched in March 1972, carrying America's exploration to incredibly distant frontiers.

The primary mission of *Pioneer 10* was an encounter with Jupiter in December 1973, 21 months after its launch from Cape Canaveral. As fascinated earthlings looked on, *Pioneer*'s equipment sent back photographic transmissions of Jupiter's amazing Great Red Spot and detailed images of its satellites. The spacecraft also discovered that Jupiter is a mammoth, liquid hydrogen planet with no solid surface beneath the thick clouds that envelop it.

The record-setting *Pioneer 10* was the first man-made object to navigate the main asteroid belt (discovering that it presents no great hazard to spacecraft), the first to confront Jupiter and its powerful radiation belts, and the first to cross the

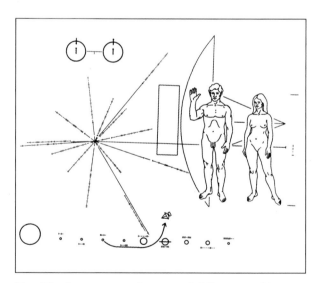

Top: The first unmanned spacecraft fully powered by nuclear energy, *Pioneer 10* sped past Jupiter on its interstellar flight. On June 13, 1983, it became the first probe to leave the solar system. Above: detail of the plaque placed inside the *Pioneer 10* space probe prior to launch. It indicates, among other things, the location of the planet Earth in relation to the sun.

orbits of Uranus, Pluto, and Neptune. Since moving beyond the solar system, the craft has investigated the mysteries of the sun's atmosphere (the heliosphere).

Launched more than a year after its sister spacecraft, *Pioneer 11* provided the first close-up observations of Saturn's stupendous network of rings as well as its magnetic field, satellites, radiation belts, and atmosphere. It also paved the way for the more sophisticated *Voyager* probe, four years later. (The two *Voyager* spacecraft transmitted the spectacular photos showing details of Saturn's rings.)

As both *Pioneer* craft wander into unknown interstellar regions, they carry identical six- by nine-inch plaques. Each plaque, created to show any intelligent aliens who might intercept it where it comes from and who sent it, bears a simple diagram of Earth and the solar system, a drawing of a woman and a man, and some basic scientific symbols. Scientists have noted that the *Pioneer* plaques represent "a mark of humanity which might survive the solar system itself." Surely the plaques, and the vehicles that carry them, push America's frontiers beyond the wildest imaginings of those who struggled across the continent in covered wagons not much more than a century ago.

The last weak signal was received from *Pioneer 10* in 2003. *Pioneer 11*'s generator began declining in 1985, and its routine daily mission operations and communications ceased a decade later.

The next phase of the *Pioneer* launched in 1978 with *Pioneer 12* and later *13* headed for Venus. *Pioneer 12* continued to orbit Venus until it ran out of propellant and burned in Venus's atmosphere in 1992. *Pioneer 13* dropped four probes into Venus's atmosphere. The bus and three of the probes burned up upon entry into the atmosphere, but the smallest probe survived the heat long enough to transmit radio signals for about an hour.

RC   PIONEER 10   UNIV A
2965000 KM PHASE: 28.7   LCM2:
RECEIVED 1 DEC 22:17:08 TO 1 DEC 22:
LOR SECTOR 154 - 441 B 06/11/74

In the latest iteration of unmanned space exploration, the twin Mars exploration rovers are getting smarter as they get older. Launched in 2003, *Spirit* began its fourth year of roving Mars's surface on January 3, 2007, and *Opportunity* followed on January 24. Thanks to computer uploads of new software, the rovers are able to make smarter decisions about what photographs to transmit, what objects to reach for, and what course to follow.

Imagine what Christopher Columbus and other early explorers could have discovered with a little help from a computer.

Thomas Alva Edison, in 1911, listens to a phonograph. Opposite: Apple CEO Steve Jobs shows off a new iPod shuffle digital music player at the 2005 Macworld Expo.

CHAPTER EIGHT

Innovations and Inspirations

C all it American ingenuity, Yankee know-how, or just plain brilliance. Whatever name it goes by, the fact is, our nation has been at the forefront of medical, technological, and other advancements since—well, since we've been on these shores.

These next pages chronicle some of America's most significant feats of invention including electricity, the television, the phonograph, and other marvels. Here, too, are some less heralded brainstorms that were submitted to the U.S. patent office, but never quite got off the ground. Some famous names—Thomas Edison, Benjamin Franklin, and Alexander Graham Bell among them—you'll recognize, but others (who the heck was Nathan Stubblefield?) are probably news to you.

From genius to gonzo, from accidentally discovered to methodically tested, one thing is for sure: America is not short on brainpower!

A 1752 Currier & Ives lithograph shows Benjamin Franklin and his son, William, using a kite and key during a storm, to prove that lightning was electricity.

An American Genius

BENJAMIN FRANKLIN INVENTS LIGHTNING ROD, BIFOCALS, AND OTHER REVOLUTIONARY THINGS

Printer, author, scientist, diplomat, statesman, "damned revolutionary" (according to George III), and Constitution framer: Benjamin Franklin was all of these and more. Throughout his long life, he never stopped inventing things. Fed by an insatiable curiosity and a fertile imagination, his restless mind ranged far and wide in search of solutions to common and complex problems. And if a solution didn't exist, he'd invent it.

In 1723, when he was 17, Franklin left Boston to pursue a career as a printer in Philadelphia. Eventually he published *Poor Richard's Almanack*, the book of wit and wisdom that included many of his now-famous maxims, among them, "God helps those who help themselves."

Later, Franklin became intrigued with a budding discipline, science, which led to some of his best-known inventions. One of his first innovations was the Pennsylvania fireplace (known today as the Franklin stove). It would, its inventor claimed, make a room "twice as warm with a quarter the wood."

What really captivated Franklin was an electrical demonstration he witnessed in 1746. He is the one who came up with the concepts of positive and negative charges and showed that electricity could be stored in a device he called an electrical battery. When his published conclusions were read before the Royal Society in England, Franklin's scientific reputation was assured.

Franklin's most fabled experiment took place in 1752: He proved that lightning is an electrical phenomenon. While there is some debate as to whether Franklin himself participated in the experiment, his description of drawing electricity from lightning with a metal-pointed kite—"to be raised when a thunder-gust appears"—is definitive. And there is no doubt that Franklin was responsible for the lightning rod. (Even the British royal palace installed this safety device!)

Franklin's inventiveness was not limited to electricity. He perfected the rocking chair, and at the age of 77, troubled by failing eyesight, he took time out from negotiating the Treaty of Paris—the treaty that ended the Revolutionary War—to design the first pair of bifocal eyeglasses. For his own enjoyment, he devised the armonica, a musical instrument played by rubbing fingers against rotating glass globes. Franklin called its tones "incomparably sweet," and Mozart and Beethoven evidently agreed; both of them composed for it.

Franklin created the odometer; he also conceived of a clock that told the hours, minutes, and seconds by means of a simple movement. And generations of students can trace their school desk, a combined chair and table, to Franklin's 1800 design.

The inventor didn't usually patent his brainstorms. Expressing his firm belief in the free exchange of ideas, Franklin wrote: "As we enjoy great advantages from the inventions of others, we should be glad of an opportunity to serve others by an invention of ours."

Native Tongue

SEQUOYAH DEVELOPS CHEROKEES' WRITTEN LANGUAGE

Though he never learned to read and write English, Sequoyah single-handedly brought literacy to the Cherokees. Fascinated by white men's books, this son of an Indian woman and a white trader dreamed of creating a written language. He divided all Cherokee sounds into 86 syllables, devising a symbol to represent each one. Inspired by the script in missionary Bibles, Sequoyah used it as the basis for his new alphabet, turning letters upside down or on their sides, sometimes adding curlicues. Sequoyah taught his five-year-old daughter to read in less than a week. In 1821, a group of skeptical tribal chiefs also mastered the alphabet in seven days and then gave Sequoyah permission to teach the language to the whole tribe.

After his death in 1843, this Cherokee chieftain was honored in a way that made his name known far and wide: The towering redwood trees of California were named Sequoias.

Turn-of-the-Century Ingenuity

From the Files of the U.S. Patent Office

Rolling Privy with Removable Vault
Patent No. 334,151 (Jan. 12, 1886)
Inventor: Philip Anthony, Cleveland, Ohio

"In some rural districts, where, from the primitive habits of the people, there is but little call for a privy, except for an occasional visitor, and where a hole in the ground serves as a privy-vault to meet the requirements for a generation or two, there would be but little call for my valuable improvement.... [However] in the larger towns and cities ... perhaps half of the expense and much of the annoyance [of cleaning privy vaults] may be saved."

Method of Preserving the Dead
Patent No. 748,284 (Dec. 29, 1903)
Inventor: Joseph Karwowski, Herkimer, New York

"I ... a subject of the Czar of Russia, residing at Herkimer ... have invented certain new and useful Improvements in Methods of Preserving the Dead ... whereby a corpse may be hermetically incased within a block of transparent glass [and] maintained for an indefinite period in a perfect and life-like condition.

"I first surround the corpse 1 with a thick layer 2 of sodium silicate or water-glass. After the corpse has been thus inclosed ... it is allowed to remain for a short time within a compartment or chamber having a dry heated temperature ... to evaporate the water from this incasing layer, after which molten glass is applied to the desired thickness. Cylindrical or other forms may be substituted for the rectangular block. The head alone may be preserved in this manner, if preferred. It will be at once noted that a body preserved in this way may be kept indefinitely.... The glass surrounding the corpse being transparent, the body will be at all times visible."

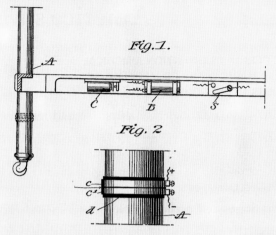

Fig. 1.

Fig. 2

Fig. 2.

Electrical Bedbug Exterminator

Patent No. 616,049 (Dec. 13, 1898)
Inventor: Frank M. Archer, New York, New York

"This invention ... consists of electrical devices applied to bedsteads in such a manner that currents of electricity will be sent through the bodies of the bugs, which will either kill them or startle them, so that they will leave the bedstead.... I place pairs of metallic contacts ... so close together that an insect in passing from one to the other must necessarily ... close the circuit through its own body, and thus receive a current of electricity ... which will either terminate its career at once or make it seek other locations. In like manner contact-strips ... may be located ... on the bedstead or on the bedsprings, which will so harass the bugs as to cause them to shun the bed entirely."

America's First Quack

WAS DR. PERKINS'S INVENTION A MEDICAL MARVEL, A MAGIC WAND, OR MERELY A SET OF USELESS METAL RODS?

Born in 1741 to a distinguished physician and his wife in Norwich, Connecticut, Elisha Perkins started his career honorably enough. He became a doctor, built a decent practice, and was a founding member of the state medical society.

Perkins desperately needed supplemental income, however, to support his wife and 10 children. Inspired by the new theory of animal electricity, he began selling pairs of metal rods; drawn across an afflicted area of the body, he claimed, they would relieve pain or any other ill.

Perkins took out a patent on these amazing "Metallic Tractors" and marketed them for a whopping $25 a pair. The Connecticut Medical Society promptly expelled him, but many distinguished patients, including Chief Justice Oliver Ellsworth,

Perkins's wands wouldn't work when he needed them most: He caught yellow fever and died.

several congressmen, and, it is said, George Washington, continued to use the magic wands.

Though often called a quack (his "treatment" was the subject of a scathing poem titled "Terrible Tractoration!!"), Perkins really believed in his invention. In 1799, the good doctor went to New York to "venture his life" during a yellow fever epidemic. Neither his Tractors nor his highly touted antiseptic (made of vinegar and sodium chloride) worked; Perkins caught the fever and died.

But the Metallic Tractors continued to sell. In Denmark, a scientific committee pronounced them highly effective, and in London there flourished a Perkinean Institution (formed by Perkins's son, Benjamin, who proceeded to get rich selling his father's devices). Only after a test proved that wooden bars apparently worked just as well as the metal rods—a triumph of the power of suggestion—were Perkins's Tractors finally discarded.

Twins or Tumor?

19TH-CENTURY DOC REMOVES 22.5-POUND OVARIAN GROWTH

At a time when scarcely one American doctor in 10 had formal training, Ephraim McDowell was unusual: Apprenticed to a doctor in Virginia, he had pursued further study in surgery in Scotland. No wonder that, in 1809, two local practitioners summoned him from his office in Danville, Kentucky, to assist with the delivery of overdue twins. But when Dr. McDowell arrived at Jane Crawford's backwoods cabin, his examination showed that she was not in labor at all; she was suffering from a massive ovarian tumor.

The doctor's diagnosis presented a dilemma: without surgery to remove the growth, the patient would die. According to prevailing wisdom, the operation itself would surely kill her. Still, McDowell held out a slim chance. Crawford understood the odds and chose to risk it. On the day of the surgery, local citizens, outraged at the proposed operation, tried to beat down the door of the doctor's office. It was much calmer inside. Crawford, her senses perhaps dulled somewhat by the standard tranquilizers of the period—alcohol or opium—sang hymns to take her mind off the pain while McDowell removed a 22.5-pound tumor. The operation was a complete success; 25 days after the surgery, the doctor pronounced the patient "perfectly well." And so she was: Crawford lived another 32 years.

Although most doctors of the time criticized McDowell's operations, the University of Maryland gave him an honorary degree in 1825, and his pioneering techniques paved the way for modern abdominal surgery. He died at 58 of what experts now believe was appendicitis.

As Ephraim McDowell performed the first ovariotomy in 1809, an angry mob besieged his office. McDowell is honored today as the pioneer of abdominal surgery.

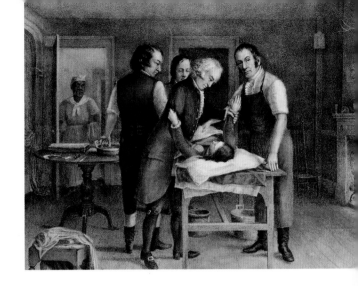

New Procedures, New Remedies

Since the mid-1800s, America has been making significant strides in medicine. Here are a few medical milestones that show just how far we've come in 160 years.

1842 Dr. Crawford W. Long uses ether as a surgical anesthetic for the first time.

1844 The American Psychiatric Association is founded.

1847 The American Medical Association is established.

1855 The nation's first permanent state board of health is created in Louisiana.

1890 Dr. William Stewart Halsted uses rubber gloves in surgery for the first time.

1893 Dr. Daniel Hale Williams performs the world's first open-heart surgery.

1902 Surgeon Alexis Carrel develops sutures to close incisions in blood vessels, thus aiding healing and helping to prevent infection.

1912 Casimir Funk suggests that certain diseases, such as scurvy and rickets, are due to dietary deficiencies in nutrients that he called "vitamines."

1923 George N. Papanicolaou develops the Pap test, a lifesaving procedure for the early detection of uterine cancer.

1943 Biologist Selman A. Waksman discovers the antibiotic streptomycin, which helps eradicate tuberculosis.

1953 American James D. Watson and Briton Francis H. Crick decode the structure of the genetic material DNA.

1954 John F. Enders, a virologist, and Thomas Peebles, a pediatrician, develop a vaccine to prevent measles.

1957 Clarence W. Lillehei, a physician, builds the first pacemaker to stabilize an irregular heartbeat.

1973 Michael S. Brown and Joseph L. Goldstein discover how cholesterol is transported through the body, advancing the treatment of cardiovascular diseases.

1981 The U.S. Centers for Disease Control and Prevention first recognizes AIDS.

2003 The Human Genome Project is completed in the United States, mapping out all the genes in human DNA.

2006 The human papillomavirus (HPV) vaccine, developed by researchers in the United States and Australia, is approved to prevent certain sexually transmitted diseases that can cause cervical cancer.

A Wound with a View

By using an open wound in a man's abdomen as a peephole of sorts, pioneering medical researcher Dr. William A. Beaumont discovered much of what we know about the human digestive system.

Beaumont's research began in 1822, when he was an army surgeon in Michigan. A young Canadian trapper, Alexis St. Martin, was accidentally shot in the side. Dr. Beaumont thought St. Martin was a goner; his wound was so large that a man could put his hand through it. But the doctor treated him, and St. Martin survived. The hole in his side, however, never closed. A two-and-a-half-inch opening remained, and a skin flap formed that could be lifted to inspect the man's insides.

"I can look directly into the cavity of the Stomach," Beaumont wrote, "observe its motion, and almost see the process of digestion." As a result, the doctor found out a great deal more about how the digestive tract works than anyone had ever known before. His book on the subject, published in 1833, put Beaumont in the scientific spotlight—even though he'd never gone to medical school. Incredibly, 90 percent of his observations are still valid.

Beaumont had taken the pauperized St. Martin in and saw to it for about a decade that his experimental subject was well taken care of.

When St. Martin died—he outlived his doctor by 20 years—he was buried eight feet below ground to ensure that no scientific curiosity-seekers would try to dig him up.

Laughing Away the Pain

Well into the 19th century, surgery was crude and painful—an absolute last resort for those in unbearable agony. Only a swift surgeon's hand limited the torture that patients had to endure. This all changed in 1842, when Crawford Long, a physician in rural Jefferson, Georgia, attended an "ether party."

In those days, itinerant performers toured America demonstrating the silly side effects of nitrous oxide, or laughing gas. When his friends asked Long to make them some nitrous oxide for their own frolic, the doctors suggested that they try sulfuric ether instead—it was a compound that he himself had found suitably diverting. Thus began a series of parties in which the Georgians chuckled in blissful oblivion at their own bruising stumbles and falls.

Intrigued that the merrymakers felt no pain, Long convinced fellow partygoer James Venable to sniff ether before having a tumor removed; on March 30, 1842, the operation was performed painlessly. The world, however, would have to wait for this breakthrough; not fully convinced of his success, the doctor delayed publishing his findings.

> Intrigued that partygoers felt no pain, Dr. Long convinced one of them to sniff ether before having a tumor removed.

Two years later, Horace Wells, a dentist in Connecticut, attended a laughing gas show, recognized nitrous oxide's anesthetic potential, and took his discovery to Boston's Massachusetts General Hospital. When the demonstration went awry, Wells was ridiculed and dismissed as a fraud.

It was left to Dr. William Morton, who had once practiced dentistry with Wells, to bring anesthesia to the world. Morton learned of ether's numbing properties from Charles Jackson, a Boston chemist, and soon he was trying it on patients

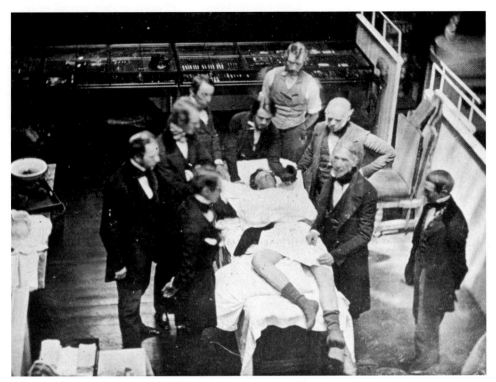

Dr. John Collins Warren (second from left) treats a surgery patient under ether. Behind him is the physician and poet Oliver Wendell Holmes, the father of the Supreme Court justice.

himself. Then, disguising the common chemical with aromatic oils and a new name, he, too, approached Massachusetts General with his wonder drug. In the fall of 1846, the hospital's chief of surgery used ether in the removal of a huge neck tumor and in a leg amputation. The age of anesthetics had begun.

Years of bitter controversy followed concerning who actually made the discovery. Morton's voice was loudest—he had patented his compound and hoped to make a fortune. Visiting New York in 1868 to defend his position against Jackson's supporters,

Morton had a seizure and died. Jackson fared little better. After seeing the tombstone that gave the credit to Morton, Jackson went insane; he spent the rest of his life in an asylum.

Saddest of all was Wells, who became addicted to chloroform and slowly destroyed his mind. Confined to a New York City jail, he soaked a cloth in the drug, painlessly severed an artery, and bled to death.

Long, who'd been too timid to publish, continued as a successful general practitioner in Georgia until 1878, when he died while making a house call.

Purity, Pre-Pasteur

GAIL BORDEN DEVELOPS CONDENSED MILK

For Texan Gail Borden, preserving food wasn't a pastime, it was a passion. He'd seen children die from drinking spoiled milk.

The great-great-great-grandson of Roger Williams (who had founded Rhode Island), Borden moved to Texas, took part in the revolution against Mexico, and then settled down to experiment with

condensed food. At one memorable dinner party, he served concentrated soup and fruit, testing both the palates and the politeness of his guests.

Later, Borden developed the "meat biscuit," a dried meat extract much like Indian pemmican. Returning from London in 1851, where he received an award for the biscuits, he had the experience that shaped the rest of his life.

SICK COWS, SUFFERING CHILDREN

Cows, taken on ship to provide food, sickened during the voyage; children either went hungry or became ill from tainted milk. Some babies died. In an age before refrigeration, Borden vowed to find some way of keeping milk fresh.

At first he tried boiling the milk, but this left a burnt taste. Then he remembered the Shakers—the religious sect from New Lebanon, New York—who concentrated fruit juice with vacuum pans they had developed. The pans sealed out air, thus allowing the liquid to evaporate at a lower temperature. Moving to the Shaker village, Borden experimented for months, finally finding a method that left condensed milk tasty and unspoiled for more than two days.

As a business venture, Borden's idea failed. Customers in New York City preferred the taste they were used to: watered "swill milk," which contained chalk to make it white and molasses to make it

The Borden Co. pavilion at the 1939 World's Fair was designed to demonstrate the cleanliness and efficiency of its advanced milking methods.

creamy. Borden tried again in 1858, and this time his condensed milk caught on.

In fact, what Borden had developed was a way of purifying milk, 11 years before Louis Pasteur revolutionized biology with his discovery of germs.

Brain Drain

HOW A LITTLE-KNOWN PATHOLOGIST CAME TO POSSESS EINSTEIN'S GRAY MATTER

When he died on April 18, 1955, Albert Einstein's remains were cremated—except for his brain. Einstein died at Princeton Hospital; the facility subsequently announced that they'd do a study to determine whether the scientist's genius was the result of unusual brain features. Dr. Thomas Harvey, a former pathologist who had performed the autopsy, kept the brain, apparently without permission from Einstein's family. Princeton later dismissed Harvey. No one knew his secret until 1978, when a reporter traced the brain back to Harvey.

Harvey (who had long since moved to Wichita) said that he was hiding Einstein's brain in jars, in a box behind a beer cooler in his office. He explained that Einstein's son had let him keep the brain for the study, but people who knew the unassuming Einstein doubted that he would have countenanced such a thing. Though he kept the brain for decades, the

never published the results of his study. In 1998, Harvey returned the remaining brain to Dr. Elliot Krauss, chief pathologist at Princeton Hospital.

There are now at least three published papers about Einstein's brain: Researcher Marian Diamond discovered that Einstein had measurably more glial cells, which supply nourishment to the brain, than the average person. But she emphasized that this overabundance alone could not account for Einstein's genius. The second paper, published in 1996, revealed that Einstein's brain weighed less than the average adult male brain, and the cerebral cortex was thinner than others in the study, but the density of neurons in Einstein's brain was greater.

A third study, published in England in 1999, reported that Einstein's brain had an unusual pattern of grooves on the lobes. Modern scientists believe that the great man's gray matter has been afloat in chemicals for so long that neither Harvey nor other researchers will ever learn very much from it.

And Suddenly, the World Shrinks

CYRUS FIELD'S CABLE CROSSES THE ATLANTIC

By 1854, a message could be sent from Maine to New Orleans in minutes. But 2,000 miles of storm-tossed ocean separated America from Europe; messages from the United States might take two weeks to reach London. To shorten the time would require laying a cable across the Atlantic, a feat that everyone knew was impossible—everyone, that is, except Cyrus Field.

A SHORT-LIVED TRIUMPH

Field, a New York paper merchant, had already retired with a fortune at the age of 34, when he conceived the plan of a transatlantic cable. The idea was feasible: The wire could rest on a submerged plateau between Newfoundland and Ireland. Encouraged, Field formed the Atlantic Telegraph Company in 1856. Soon ideas from the public began flooding in. One proposed suspending the cable by underwater balloons; another suggested floating call boxes for the benefit of passing ships.

Fancy schemes, however, soon gave way to harsh realities. The technical problems were mammoth; the open ocean was brutal to both men and equipment. Although the 2,500-mile-long cable weighed a ton per mile, it snapped in the rolling sea. Storms, cable partings, and other setbacks led to two years of delays. It was not until August 1858 that a cable was successfully laid, and the continents were electronically connected.

But the triumph was short-lived. Following an inaugural greeting from Queen Victoria to President James Buchanan, the cable went dead, much to the delight of Perry McDonough Collins.

THE PACIFIC CONNECTION

Collins had a different plan. He approached Western Union and proposed to run a cable north to Alaska, under the narrow Bering Strait, and then across Siberia to the wires of Europe. In 1864, Western Union agreed. Meanwhile, Field had secured

The American ship *Niagara* lays the last kilometer of the transatlantic telegraph cable in August 1858.

299

backing for a second transatlantic attempt, and the race was on.

On July 27, 1866, despite serious setbacks along the way, Field's ship steamed into Heart's Content, Newfoundland, trailing its massive cable behind. This time, the cable worked perfectly; 12 years after he had begun the project, the Atlantic was bridged. Although it was the death knell for the Siberian route, communications were so bad that it took almost a year before crews in Alaska learned of the Atlantic success.

Collins's effort was abandoned; but all was not for naught. The diplomatic connections that had been developed with Russia bore fruit a year later, when America bought Alaska from the Russians for the bargain price of $7.2 million.

Crossed Lines on Telephone Patent

ANTONIO MEUCCI INVENTS PHONE LONG BEFORE BELL

Before 1876, few people shared Alexander Graham Bell's vision of the power of the telephone as vividly as Antonio Meucci (right), a theatrical set designer from Staten Island, New York, whom Bell didn't even know. Born in Florence, Italy, in 1808, Meucci had studied drawing and mechanical engineering before becoming a set designer for the theater and opera in Florence. Moving to Cuba, he became superintendent of mechanics at Havana's Tacon Opera House.

A VOICE THROUGH THE WIRE

While pursuing his more artistic calling, Meucci also experimented with electricity, established his own electroplating business, and used electrotherapy to treat rheumatism. During one of these treatments, he heard, over the wires he was using, the voice of a speaker three rooms away. He later learned how to amplify voices by attaching a paper cone to the wires.

When he left Cuba in 1850 and settled on Staten Island, he continued his experiments with the *teletrofono*. By the mid-1850s, the inventor was using it to speak to his wife on the third floor from his basement workshop. By 1857, Meucci had developed a working model; he demonstrated it to potential investors three years later, but failed to win their financial backing. This marked the beginning of a long series of disappointments. Over the next 10 years, Meucci worked on other inventions and obtained patents for a canal steamer, a marine telegraph, and a device that measured humidity. Unfortunately, the patents were registered under the

names of his investors, and Meucci did not share in the financial rewards.

Seriously injured in an explosion on a New York Harbor ferry, Meucci was bedridden for five months. His wife was forced to sell his best telephone models to a junkman to raise desperately needed cash.

PATENTS BEFORE BELL

The inventor remained determined to produce a telephone. He took drawings and a detailed description to the patent office and received a caveat, or temporary patent, in December 1871, a full five years before Bell was to receive a patent for his own telephone. Meucci renewed the caveat the following two years but let it lapse in 1874 because he couldn't afford the fees.

In desperation, Meucci offered his telephone plans to a local Western Union official, who held the designs and models for almost two years and then lost them. A few months later Bell received his patent, a process that took only three weeks. Subsequent legal appeals by Meucci failed. He died in 1889, a poor and heartbroken man.

Gray Versus Bell

WHO GETS OFFICIAL CREDIT FOR THE TELEPHONE?

As an inventor, Elisha Gray was a consummate professional. He got his first patent for an automatic telegraph relay in 1867, at the age of 32. Later, when Western Union bought his printer (it translated Morse code into type), he used the profit to form Gray & Barton, a partnership that was later to become Western Electric.

In the early 1870s, Gray turned his attention to an urgent problem: how to send several simultaneous signals over one telegraph wire. Whoever created such a "multiplex" system would reap a rich reward. Gray's idea—to use a different musical tone for each message—was fairly simple in terms of transmission; the difficulty lay in creating a receiver capable of sorting out the tones. Attacking the challenge in his usual methodical way, Gray designed prototype after prototype and then tinkered with them, learning from each mistake.

AN ODD SIDE EFFECT

In the process, it became clear that such a receiver could also reproduce the tones of the human voice, if an adequate transmitter could be developed. Gray thought he knew how to do that, but the multiplex telegraph took priority.

Meanwhile a young amateur named Alexander Graham Bell was working on the same problem, and competition between the two grew fierce. A teacher of speech to the deaf, Bell understood the mechanics of speech and was trying to apply similar principles to a multiplex telegraph. He, too, realized the potential for sending speech over a wire.

"Bell seems to be spending all his energies in [the] talking telegraph," Gray wrote to his attorney. "While this is very interesting scientifically, it has no commercial value. I don't want at present to spend my time and money for that which will bring no reward."

Nonetheless, on Valentine's Day 1876, Gray filed a caveat (a description of a new device, not yet perfected) with the U.S. Patent Office for a talking

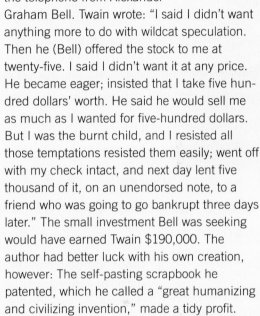

Mark Twain Dials the Wrong Number

America's foremost humorist was a bit of a sucker when it came to investing in other people's inventions, but he somehow managed to turn down a stock offering in the telephone from Alexander Graham Bell. Twain wrote: "I said I didn't want anything more to do with wildcat speculation. Then he (Bell) offered the stock to me at twenty-five. I said I didn't want it at any price. He became eager; insisted that I take five hundred dollars' worth. He said he would sell me as much as I wanted for five-hundred dollars. But I was the burnt child, and I resisted all those temptations resisted them easily; went off with my check intact, and next day lent five thousand of it, on an unendorsed note, to a friend who was going to go bankrupt three days later." The small investment Bell was seeking would have earned Twain $190,000. The author had better luck with his own creation, however: The self-pasting scrapbook he patented, which he called a "great humanizing and civilizing invention," made a tidy profit.

telegraph. He was too late. A few hours earlier, Bell had applied for a patent on his telephone, even though it, too, was not yet perfected. Gray's lawyer said that he could block Bell's patent by filing a full application, but Gray saw no reason to waste time and money on a "toy." He wanted to display a working model of his multiplex at the Centennial Exhibition in Philadelphia that summer.

Bell knew the telephone was no toy. "The whole thing is mine," he wrote his father, "and I am sure of fame, fortune, and success."

HISTORIC ACCIDENT

On March 10, 1876, Bell accidentally spilled acid on his clothes and shouted to his assistant, "Mr. Watson, come here. I want you!" Watson, in another room, heard the words over the telephone.

Both Gray and Bell displayed their inventions at the Centennial Exhibition in June. The judges were amazed when Gray's multiplex received eight messages at once from New York, but they awarded first prize for scientific achievement to Bell.

Bell offered to sell his patents to Western Union for $100,000 and was turned down. Instead, the company bought Gray's patents and sued Bell for infringement. The case was finally settled in the courts, leaving Bell in sole possession of the telephone.

Elisha Gray was not satisfied. He spent the rest of his life trying to prove that he, not his younger rival, had invented the telephone.

Meanwhile, Bell went on teaching the deaf (Helen Keller became a close friend). In 1879, he created the audiometer, which detected hearing loss. As a result of his work, degrees of loudness came to be measured in bels or decibels.

> As a result of Bell's work with the deaf, degrees of loudness came to be measured in bels or decibels.

AN ECLECTIC GENIUS

Bell's imagination knew few limits. After his newborn son died of respiratory failure in 1881, he developed a "vacuum jacket," which was a precursor to the iron lung. His graphophone improved on Edison's phonograph by recording on wax cylinders rather than on tinfoil. Bell's solar still used the sun to condense pure water from saltwater.

In the 1890s, fascinated by the prospect of manned flight, Bell experimented with rockets, rotors, aerofoils, and huge kites. After the Wright brothers' flight at Kitty Hawk, he organized the Aerial Experiment Association to further the development of controlled, powered flight.

Almon Brown Strowger: The Undertaker Who Did Away with Phone Operators

Almon Brown Strowger, a Kansas City undertaker, was losing business. He blamed the local switchboard operator who had failed to notify him of his close friend's death; a competing undertaker got the work. Strowger decided to create a telephone system that didn't rely on an operator.

The undertaker made a rough model from a paper-collar box, 100 straight pins, and a pencil. Then, with the help of his nephew, Walter, and a Wichita jeweler, he designed a more sophisticated model; on March 12, 1889, he filed for a patent on his Automatic Telephone Exchange. Further refinements earned more patents. In November 1892, La Porte, Indiana, became the first city to replace operators with automation.

He experimented in genetics, trying to develop four-nippled sheep that would bear twins and give enough milk to feed them.

During World War I, Bell worked on "water ears," an early form of submarine detection, and developed a hydrofoil craft to serve as a high-speed submarine chaser.

The Lost Genius

RADIO'S TRUE INVENTOR
HAD NO HEAD FOR BUSINESS

Nathan Stubblefield was a lonely, impoverished hermit when he was found starved to death in a shack near his hometown of Murray, Kentucky, in 1928. He was buried in an unmarked grave. The world had forgotten Stubblefield, though he had invented radio.

Around 1890, when the Italian wizard Guglielmo Marconi was still in his teens, Stubblefield demonstrated his wireless telephone for a few friends on his farm. He filed no patent then, just went on tinkering. Finally, on January 1, 1902, less than a month after Marconi had transmitted the letter S across the Atlantic in Morse code, the Kentuckian got around to a public demonstration. About 1,000 friends and neighbors watched in amazement as, speaking softly into a two-foot-square box, he was heard at half a dozen listening posts around town. Then his 14-year-old son, Bernard, whistled and played the harmonica.

Nathan Stubblefield patented both the wireless telephone and radios for horseless carriages.

Later that year, Stubblefield gave a more impressive—and better publicized—demonstration in Washington, D.C., from a steam launch on the Potomac River.

At this point, the inventor should have capitalized on his ingenuity. He did patent his wireless telephone and form a company to promote it, but it never did anything more than sell stock. Marconi, who is known today as the father of radio, actually pioneered wireless telegraphy, which was the transmission of Morse code. Stubblefield sent voices and music over the air. In a 1908 patent, the Kentuckian described how to put radios in horseless carriages, making him the father of the car radio—another invention that did not make him rich. In fact, none of his inventions, including a battery for radios, made much money.

Stubblefield's marriage later broke up, his house burned down, and his spirit withered. Still, he continued to work on new inventions. Shortly before his death, he destroyed them all and burned their plans.

A Visionary Inventor

MAN BEHIND THE TV TOLD TO DO
"SOMETHING MORE USEFUL" WITH HIS TIME

If it weren't for a fellow named Vladimir Zworykin who immigrated to America, the world might not be watching television today. The Russian engineer's lifelong interest in electronics began when he pushed a buzzer on his father's steamboat; a sailor responded promptly, and the five-year-old was hooked. He became an electrical engineer, and by 1919 he had moved to the United States, landing a job as a research engineer at the Westinghouse Electric Corporation.

At the company's Pittsburgh laboratory, Zworykin invented the iconoscope (electronic camera) and the kinescope (picture tube). Then, in 1923, he proudly demonstrated his most enduring invention: television—in this case, a cloudy image of boats on the river outside his lab appeared on the screen. His employers, however, were not impressed. Zworykin was urged, he later said, "to spend my time on something more useful."

By 1929, Zworykin had obtained the first patent for color television. David Sarnoff, founder of the Radio Corporation of America (RCA), asked what it would take to develop TV for commercial use.

continued on page 308

The Sound Writer

EDISON'S PHONOGRAPH GAINS POPULARITY IN RECORD TIME

Thomas Alva Edison (above), circa 1929. Top: a model of the inventor's original phonograph, circa 1877.

Since the dawn of time, sounds have been as fleetingly ephemeral as dreams; even the most exquisite vanish as they occur, leaving only a memory. In 1877, Thomas Edison finally captured this elusive element, giving it a permanence that art and writing had achieved millennia earlier. So new was his invention, so different from anything anyone had ever conceived, that the patent was approved in just seven weeks. But at first no one, not even Edison, foresaw the revolution the phonograph would create.

The idea for recording the human voice came to Edison while he worked on a new telephone transmitter, which used a needle instead of a tuning fork to pick up sound vibrations. "I was singing to the mouthpiece of a telephone when the vibrations of the voice sent the fine steel point into my finger," he wrote. "If I could record the actions of the point ... I saw no reason why the thing would not talk."

A friend bet him a barrel of apples that he'd never get his talking machine to work. But within weeks Edison had developed a device with which the voice literally drew a picture of itself: a stylus, jiggled by sound vibrations, inscribed a pattern on a sheet of tinfoil as it rotated on a metal cylinder. Aptly, he named the invention the phonograph, or sound writer. And he won the apples.

Originally little more than a novelty, the phonograph caused a sensation everywhere it was demonstrated. In one week in Boston, people paid more than $1,800 in admissions to hear it cough, bark, crow, and speak French.

Now that the phonograph existed, the question was how to use it. Edison thought it would serve the telephone, which he believed would be too expensive for most Americans to own. As a former telegraph operator, the inventor foresaw central stations at which people would record their messages on his "telephone repeater." The messages would then be transmitted over phone lines to another office at which recipients could listen to them in the senders' own voices.

It took more than a decade for the phonograph to emerge as a machine for home entertainment. By then it had become one of Edison's favorite inventions, and he went on to a 40-year career as a recording producer.

Although partially deaf, Edison had perfect pitch; he personally supervised auditions, and he certainly knew what he liked. In the early 1920s the Russian composer Sergei Rachmaninoff came to his studio to make a trial record. After only a few bars, Edison interrupted with: "Who told you you're a piano player? You're a pounder—that's what you are, a pounder!" Rachmaninoff put on his hat and walked out.

Edison's fascination with the sound machine lasted a lifetime. In 1927, at the age of 80, he developed a double-sided, 80-rpm, 10-inch LP that played for 40 minutes. Ahead of its time, the record was a commercial failure; nonetheless, the phonograph was already creating one of the world's most prosperous industries.

"Who told you you're a piano player? You're a pounder—that's what you are, a pounder!"

—**THOMAS EDISON** to composer Sergei Rachmaninoff, during one of the Russian's recording sessions

continued on page 306

Is it true that Thomas Edison was a mind reader?

No, but he did try to invent a machine that did just this. It failed.

Thomas Edison theorized that memory was composed of electronlike particles hurtling through space, bringing otherworldly knowledge to certain people. He believed the particles never died; they simply left the body of the dying to search for another friendly human host.

Henry Ford introduced the inventor to a medium, Bert Reese, whose telepathic experiments Edison tried to duplicate by using electric coils wound around the head. "Four of us gathered at one time in four different rooms, each wearing the apparatus." But, the inventor admitted, "We achieved no results in mind reading."

Edison Goes Broke

By the age of 43, Thomas Edison was wealthy, and restless. "I'm going to do something now," he told a friend, "so different ... that people will forget that my name ever was connected with anything electrical!"

The scheme was a new kind of iron mining. In the early 1890s, the price of iron ore had skyrocketed. Edison purchased 19,000 acres near Ogdensburg, New Jersey, that had been mined but still contained an estimated 2 billion tons of low-grade iron ore. There he built an entire village, complete with a stone quarry and a seven-story ore separator of his own design. At its heart were 480 magnets to remove the ore from the stone.

The machines were a marvel, but they were plagued by major problems. Edison was forced to rebuild the entire plant when its foundations began to crumble. Then the Depression of 1893 stilled production as new orders ceased to come in. When rich iron deposits were discovered in Minnesota's Mesabi Range, the price of ore plummeted from $7.50 a ton to $2.65.

With more than $2 million invested in the project, Edison was nearly bankrupt by 1899. "It's all gone," he said, "but we had a hell of a time spending it."

The Invention Factory

EDISON CALLED "THE WIZARD OF MENLO PARK"

Thomas Edison had no formal scientific training and no time for "theoretical scientists." He thought of himself as an entrepreneur who was in "the invention business"; only projects with a marketable outcome interested him. It was typical, therefore, that in 1876 he created perhaps his greatest invention—the world's first "invention factory." He moved his staff of 15 to a large, new building in rural Menlo Park, New Jersey. Edison boldly proclaimed that this industrial research laboratory would produce "a minor invention every ten days and a big thing every six months or so." Just 10 years later the research facility had grown into a full-fledged village. Edison had been granted 420 patents, including those for the phonograph and the incandescent lightbulb.

These achievements earned the inventor the nickname, "Wizard of Menlo Park," but Edison knew there was no magic to it. He is often credited with the expression: "Genius is two percent inspiration and ninety-eight percent perspiration." And his own appetite for work was unmatched. The town of Menlo Park reflected his philosophy, offering few diversions to fill leisure time. One day, to help alleviate Mrs. Edison's boredom, her husband converted a telephone receiver into a loudspeaker and, by means of his private phone line to

Western Union headquarters in New York City, let her listen to a concert taking place 23 miles away.

Edison abandoned Menlo Park in 1886 for larger facilities in West Orange. The work in that New Jersey pasture signaled the end of an age when "pure" scientists looked down on such "practical" scientists as Edison, who invented for money.

The Executioner's Choice

ELECTRIC CHAIR BECOMES A GRISLY SHOWCASE IN THE RIVALRY BETWEEN EDISON AND WESTINGHOUSE

The competition between Thomas Edison's direct current (DC) and George Westinghouse's alternating current (AC) heated up in the late 1880s. AC was cheaper to transmit, but DC was thought to be safer. When Harold P. Brown, a self-taught electrical consultant, joined this "battle of the currents" in 1888, the rivalry took on a macabre twist.

Brown, an advocate of Edison's DC because of its supposed safety, tortured animals to determine how much of each current they could survive. At a public demonstration at Columbia University, he exposed a caged dog to 300 volts of DC (about the level of AC the animal could withstand). Then, as the dog howled in agony, he increased the charge to 400, 500, and finally 1,000 volts.

Observers were sickened, but Brown's timing was perfect. New York State had recently formed a commission to investigate alternatives to hanging as a method of capital punishment. Electrocution had been considered, and the commissioners asked Edison for his opinion. The inventor was opposed to execution; but if it must take place, he said, using Westinghouse's lethal AC would be the most humane way.

On January 1, 1889, New York became the first state to adopt electrical execution. Needing an expert to manage the project, officials hired none other than Brown, who invented the electric chair. Brown powered his device with a Westinghouse dynamo, hoping to malign AC as the "executioner's current." AC eventually triumphed in the marketplace because of its lower distribution costs. Properly insulated and applied, it soon became the national standard.

> New York became the first state to adopt electrical execution on January 1, 1889.

Zworykin, who really had no idea, answered with assurance: a year and a half, and $100,000. Sarnoff hired him; later he delighted in pointing out that it had really taken 20 years and $50 million.

Zworykin worked on many other inventions while at RCA, among them the electron microscope (developed in an amazing three months, before the company's budget office even knew about it) and "electric eye" infrared tubes, the first sniperscopes in World War II.

Despite the fact that he lived to see his most famous invention flourish—he died in 1982, at age 92—Zworykin rejected what TV had become. As he told a reporter: "The technique is wonderful. It is beyond my expectation. But the programs! I would never let my children even come close to this thing."

Chicken Salad Ushers in Computer Age

LADIES AT "STATISTICAL PIANOS" TABULATE 1890 CENSUS

As rows of young women tabulated the U.S. population for the 1890 census by pounding away on "statistical pianos," they unknowingly marked the beginning of an era: The machines they operated were calculators invented by 30-year-old Herman Hollerith. His devices heralded the dawn of the computer age.

When Hollerith was asked how he came to invent his machines, his reply was: "Chicken salad." A dance partner had invited him to her home to enjoy his favorite dish. There he met her father, head of the Division of Vital Statistics for the 1880 census, who suggested that a machine using notched cards could tabulate census statistics, which were still counted by hand.

Intrigued, Hollerith recalled a train ticket with his description punched out in a "punch photograph." With this as the starting point, he devised a machine that used the punch card to record information and other machinery to electrically "read" and tabulate it.

In a test against two hand methods, the machines proved twice as fast, and Hollerith won the contract for the 1890 census. (Alexander Graham Bell, who had invented another card-sorting machine, abandoned his project.)

The census office rented 56 of Hollerith's machines. They were powered by batteries recharged from the brand-new Edison electrical circuits. Wires ran to an airy room where "nice-looking girls in cool

A newspaper observed that the statistical piano's inventor "will not likely get very rich." In 1924, Herman Hollerith's Tabulating Machine Co. changed its name to IBM.

white dresses" sat at what looked like upright pianos, punching hundreds of cards a day. "Women are better adapted for this particular work than men," wrote the *New York Sun*. (A night shift of men confused the system and was soon eliminated, but while it lasted, the two shifts exchanged flirtatious notes.)

Since one operator could count some 80,000 people a day, the entire population—62,622,250—was added up in only six weeks. The census superintendent was delighted. "The bright young women and the sturdy young men of our Population Division," he enthused, "could run through the entire population of the earth ... estimated at 1,300,000,000, in less than 200 days."

From Seed to Orchard

COLLEGE DROPOUTS DESIGN APPLE COMPUTERS

Working in a Cupertino, California, garage, whiz kids Steven Jobs (right) and Stephen Wozniak—neither of whom ever finished college—put together their first microprocessor computer board. Unlike other microprocessors, their device was relatively cheap and uncomplicated, and it was hooked up directly to a video monitor.

In 1976, Jobs and Wozniak formed the Apple Computer Company. They had a product and a company, but no cash to get started. Jobs sold his van and Wozniak parted with his programmable calculator, and with a loan of $5,000 from a friend—and a 30-day line of credit at an electronics company—they hired two firms to make the boards. They ended up selling about 175 Apple I microprocessors.

Sparked by their modest success, Wozniak designed a more sophisticated version of their computer, the Apple II. By April 1977, it was on the

To raise funds for their company, Jobs sold his van and Wozniak parted with his programmable calculator.

market. Although primitive by today's standards (it used audiotapes for data storage and an ordinary television set for a screen), Wozniak's machine became an instant hit. In the next three years the pair sold 130,000 Apple II's at a price of just $1,298—a mere fraction of the cost of a bulky mainframe computer.

Four years later, computer giant IBM introduced its first desktop computer, the IBM PC, and by the end of the decade, microcomputers had become an everyday part of life in businesses, schools, and homes across America. So momentous was the personal computer revolution that, in 1983, *Time* magazine named the computer the "Man of the Year."

TRUTH OR RUMOR?

Is it true that an early computer once predicted the outcome of a presidential election?

It would have, but for the fault of its operators. On election night in November 1952, the special guest star for the election's television coverage was UNIVAC, a $600,000 electronic computer.

The UNIVAC, short for "universal automatic computer," was to forecast the results of the election long before the final tally. Stuffed with figures from the 1944 and 1948 elections, the computer was programmed to compare the early returns in each state with the early returns from the previous two presidential elections.

That evening, with less than 7 percent of the votes in, the computer predicted a landslide victory for Dwight Eisenhower, over Adlai Stevenson. Statisticians were shocked—politicos had predicted a very close race. After reprogramming the machine, technicians reported that UNIVAC was calling the race a toss-up. When the election was over, the popular and electoral vote totals came close to UNIVAC's original prediction. Eisenhower did, indeed, win the presidency by a landslide. "The trouble with machines," concluded CBS broadcaster Edward R. Murrow, "is people."

Underwater Warriors

INVENTING AND REVISING THE FIRST SUBMARINES

It was after midnight on a September evening in 1776. The powerful British fleet sat anchored off Staten Island, poised to attack General George Washington's beleaguered army on Manhattan. Confident of their superiority, the British were unaware that a deadly new weapon was aimed at their admiral's flagship, the *Eagle*.

Bobbing just beneath the choppy waves, an odd, egg-shaped craft proceeded ponderously but steadily, powered by the furious cranking and peddling of Sergeant Ezra Lee, Connecticut Militia. His mission: To get under the *Eagle*, attach a mine, and blow the British vessel to smithereens.

Lee's assault, the first submarine attack in naval history, was David Bushnell's idea. Four years earlier, while spending his inheritance to attend Yale as a 30-year-old undergraduate, Bushnell had shown that gunpowder could be ignited underwater in a sealed container. He developed the submarine as a stealthy means of attaching these submerged bombs to their targets.

The attack by the *Turtle* (as the world's first workable sub was called) failed because Lee was unable to screw the bomb onto its target, despite three dogged attempts directly below the *Eagle*'s hull. The new weapon did, however, capture the military's attention.

David Bushnell's *Turtle* was a hand- and foot-powered vessel. It may have been primitive, but it had a propeller for forward motion, water tanks for ballast, and a conning tower for vision, all of which are used in modern submarines.

THE PERIPATETIC COFFIN

It was not until the Civil War that a submarine succeeded in battle. Desperate for a way to break the Union Navy's blockade of Southern ports, the

Pre-Steamboat Success, Fulton Dabbled in Subs

Before his steamboat made him famous, Robert Fulton experimented with submarines and tried to sell them to Napoleon as the antidote to Britain's dominance at seas. The emperor was intrigued by the prototype; in 1801, he proposed to test the weapon by offering its inventor up to 400,000 francs for any British vessels he sank. But despite a summer of eager hunting, Fulton and his two-man crew were unable to bomb any ships, and the French lost interest. Ever the entrepreneur, Fulton then offered his craft to the British, but they, too, let the project sink.

Confederacy developed the *Hunley*, a sub made from a boiler tank about 25 feet long, propelled by eight men pumping a hand crank. Three crews drowned during tests, and the ship was morbidly nicknamed the "Peripatetic Coffin." Nonetheless, on February 17, 1864, the *Hunley* rammed and sank the Union sloop *Housatonic* in Charleston Harbor. It was a Pyrrhic victory; the Hunley's entire crew drowned.

THE FIRST MODERN SUBS

The modern submarine was made possible by two key inventions: the electric engine for submerged cruising and the self-propelled torpedo. Among the first to use them successfully was John P. Holland. After the U.S. Navy rejected his submarine in 1875, Holland threw in with the Fenian Society, a group of Irish radicals committed to their country's independence. Although this association was short-lived, Holland's *Fenian Ram* presaged the design of submarines used until the advent of nuclear power.

The *Holland VI*, purchased by the U.S. Navy in 1900, beat out a submarine designed by another American, Simon Lake, who is noted for his work developing periscopes. Lake had proposed a sub that crept along the ocean floor on wheels. Undaunted by rejection, he went on to sell the craft to the Russians.

FUNNY FACT

American Invents Amphibious Automobile

Oliver Evans not only built the first steam-driven dredge ever used in this country, he also built America's first automobile—in fact, they were the very same machine. Christening it the *Orukter Amphibolos* (Amphibious Digger), he drove it from his workshop to the river in 1805.

To convince the public that his engine "could propel both land and water carriages," Evans added wheels to the board of health's dredging scow. The prototype *Orukter* steamed through the heart of Philadelphia before plunging into the Schuylkill River; once in the water, it easily outdistanced all other river craft. Sadly, this impressive debut failed to earn Evans enough financial backing to go on producing his land carriages. But he remained confident that the automobile would prevail one day. "The time will come," he wrote, "when people will travel in stages [coaches] moved by steam engines from one city to another almost as fast as birds can fly—15 to 20 miles an hour."

Three Is the Magic Number

FITCH, RUMSEY, THEN FULTON PIONEER THE STEAMBOAT

The Constitution wasn't the only American institution launched in Philadelphia in 1787. On August 22, members of the federal convention gathered at the Delaware River to witness the trial voyage of the nation's first practical steamboat. Designed by John Fitch, an itinerant brass worker from New Jersey, the ship was propelled by 12 steam-driven paddles, six to a side. To some observers it looked like a giant bug walking across the water.

Inspired by the publicity surrounding Fitch's vessel, Virginian James Rumsey launched a steamboat on the Potomac River three months later. Rumsey's craft, which he had been working on secretly for two years, was a kind of jet boat, propelled by streams of water forced out through the stern by a steam-driven pump.

Neither Fitch nor Rumsey was financially successful; America wasn't ready for steam travel. In later years, Fitch wrote: "The day will come when some more powerful man will get fame and riches from my invention." That man was to be Robert Fulton, whose *Clermont* churned up and down the Hudson River on August 17, 1807.

An 1860 locomotive boasted many improvements, among them a bright headlight, a steam whistle, a flexible front section that helped it cling to curves, and a new cowcatcher.

Basic "Train"-ing

INNOVATIONS MAKE RAILROADS FASTER AND SAFER

In the early days of railroading, trains averaged speeds of only 10 miles per hour. There were no brakes, no lights, and no whistles. Engineers had to stop to chase animals off the tracks, and derailments were commonplace. To improve the lives of trainmen and passengers alike, a lot of innovating needed to be done. American ingenuity rose to the challenge.

BUMPS IN THE ROAD

The first rails were L-shaped iron strips bolted to wooden planks. Too much speed on a curve, a stone on the track, or a broken rail, and the train derailed. In 1830, Robert L. Stevens and his brother Edwin

A. Stevens, sons of famed inventor-engineer John Stevens, founded New Jersey's Camden & Amboy Railroad. The next year, on his way to England to buy an engine, Robert Stevens whittled a model of a T-shaped track that could be spiked to a wooden crosstie on both sides. Upon his arrival, he persuaded skeptical ironmongers to cast his "utterly insane" designs. (The T-rail is still standard worldwide.)

When Stevens's new locomotive, the John Bull, arrived in Philadelphia in pieces, Isaac Dripps (who'd never seen one before) put it together. To enable it to navigate curves more easily, he replaced the huge front wheels with two small ones that held a V-shaped shield—the first cowcatcher.

MOVING RIGHT ALONG

John Jervis improved Dripps's design with a swiveling, four-wheeled truck on his engine's front end. With it, the boiler became a counterweight on curves. Meanwhile, Matthias Baldwin designed a steam-tight, high-pressure boiler that enabled his train to reach an unheard-of 80 miles an hour!

High speed spawned numerous safety devices. The first locomotive headlight was an enlarged oil-burning ship's lantern mounted above the cowcatcher. With a series of reflectors behind its foot-high lens, it could beam a light as far as 100 feet ahead. And, as an engineer pulled a cord to open a valve, the first locomotive steam whistle wailed across the land.

REPORTING BY WIRE

After the innovative 1830s, the pace of invention abated a bit. The telegraph was first used on the Erie Railroad in 1851, when the superintendent of the line took the throttle from a nervous engineer and chugged west on a single track, relying on tele-graphed reports that the eastbound train was delayed. As late as 1871, though, an express plowed into a local in Massachusetts because the line still depended on railroad timetables.

> It wasn't until 1893 that President Benjamin Harrison signed a bill requiring air brakes on all locomotives.

The air brake was a boon to the perilous life of brakemen. Patented by George Westinghouse in 1869, it meant that there was no longer any need to crawl atop moving cars to stop each one by hand or to worry about collisions when trains couldn't stop.

CUTTING CASUALTIES

Still, it took a 20-year crusade to force railroads to adopt the system. It was not until 1893 that President Benjamin Harrison signed a bill requiring air brakes (and automatic couplers) on all locomotives. By 1894, casualties had dropped 60 percent.

The Vertical Railway

OTIS'S ELEVATOR CHANGES AMERICA'S SKYLINE

The setting was the dazzling 1854 Crystal Palace Exposition in New York City. On display was an intriguing sight: On a hoist platform, surrounded by barrels and packing cases, stood a handsome gentle-man in his early forties; he was lifted to the hoist's highest point, some 30 feet above the assembled spectators. Then Elisha Graves Otis, the man on the platform, gave orders to cut the hoisting rope. The crowd gasped, but Otis calmly doffed his elegant top hat, bowed from the waist, and said: "All safe, gentle-men, all safe!" For the motionless platform and its inventor were in absolutely no danger.

Hoists had been used since antiquity. Otis's insight wasn't in how to get things up, but in how to keep them from falling down unexpectedly.

SAFETY TEETH

Thus was born the modern elevator, a hoist safe enough for people to ride in. Otis had built his first lift in 1852, to carry bedsteads to the second story of the New York factory where he worked. Such machines were relatively common, but none could boast Otis's safety device: two metal hooks at the sides of the car, attached by a springline to the hoist cable. If the cable broke or tension was released, the hooks immediately sprang out, catching in teeth that were cut into the guide rails in the elevator shaft. Descent was stopped at once.

At first Otis didn't think his invention was worth much; he dreamed of going to California to try his luck at panning gold. Then he received two orders for his safety lift, and suddenly it seemed wiser to seek his fortune at home.

The *New York Tribune* called Otis's Crystal Palace feat "daring" and "sensational," but it would be three years before a New York department store dared to install an Otis elevator to lift its passengers five stories. At a speed of 40 feet per minute, the lift was hardly faster than walking the stairs. (At that speed, it would take an elevator 36 minutes to reach the top of Chicago's Sears Tower.)

ARCHITECTURE LOOKS UP

By the early 1870s, the elevator had begun to change skylines all across America. Architects started looking up, rather than out. From a limit of five stories (the most that people could reasonably be expected to climb), buildings soon grew to 12 stories tall.

In 1904, the Otis Company, then directed by Elisha Otis's two sons, pioneered the gearless traction elevator. An innovative element in the creation of the skyscraper, it was used in New York's 41-story Singer Building in 1907 and again, in 1932, in the 102-story Empire State Building.

For years, the top speed for elevators traveling to the tops of tall buildings was a rate of about 1,800 feet per minute (about 20.5 miles per hour). That began changing in the late 20th century, as technology rapidly improved. The Taipei 101 building, completed in 2004, currently holds the record, with an elevator that services its 89-floor observation deck at peak speeds of 3,314 feet per minute.

Oddly enough, it's not technology that limits speed; it's human frailties. Rapid ascension and descension play havoc with people's equilibrium, and the potential noise could be deafening. Thanks to technology, new elevators are aerodynamically designed and equipped with sound insulators and air pressure control systems. Elisha Otis would've been impressed.

The First Airplanes

AFTER LANGLEY'S FOLLY FALTERS, NO ONE PAYS WRIGHTS ANY MIND

"Will man ever fly?" The debate raged into the 20th century, with scientists lining up on both sides of the question. The highly respected Simon Newcomb of Johns Hopkins University wrote articles proving definitively that the feat was impossible. And even if a man managed to get a machine in the air, he wrote in 1903, "Once he slackens his speed, down he begins to fall.... Once he stops he falls a dead mass. How shall he reach the ground without destroying his delicate machinery?"

Meanwhile, Samuel Pierpont Langley, secretary of the Smithsonian Institution and the nation's unofficial chief scientist, had staked his reputation on proving that it could be done. He was already a celebrity; he had flown two unmanned steam-powered models as far as 4,200 feet in 1896. When the Spanish-American War broke out in 1898, the War Department gave Langley $50,000 to develop a manned motor-driven flying machine. He added another $20,000 of Smithsonian funds, and on December 8, 1903, he was ready.

His machine, the *Great Aerodrome*, was mounted atop a houseboat anchored in Washington's Potomac River. Charles Manly, the Smithsonian's chief aeronautical assistant, stripped to his union suit, twisted himself into the cockpit and was catapulted down a

The failure of Langley's *Great Aerodrome* was seen as proof that manned flight was impossible. Hence, few believed in the Wrights' success nine days later.

60-foot track. A throng of news reporters watched as the *Great Aerodrome* turned an awkward flip and splashed down flat on its back. Manly, and a workman who plunged in to rescue him, were fished out of the water.

Newspapers had a field day ridiculing "Langley's Folly." The public was outraged, the House of Representatives debated the foolish expenditure of government funds, and the Senate threatened an investigation.

The next day a young bicycle mechanic named Orville Wright left Dayton, Ohio, on a train bound for Kitty Hawk, a remote fishing village in North Carolina. He chose Kitty Hawk because it had ample winds blowing off the Atlantic, plenty of sand, and a sparse but helpful population. Eight days later, on December 17, Wright and his brother, Wilbur, became the first to achieve powered flight, after three years of work at their own expense.

Although the Wrights had notified newspapers of their plans, no reporters came to watch. The *New York Daily Tribune* noted the flight with a short item

The First Fatal Air Crash

As 2,000 people watched, Orville Wright and Lieutenant Thomas E. Selfridge soared 150 feet over Fort Myer, Virginia. It was September 17, 1908. Wright was demonstrating his latest airplane for the army as Selfridge, cofounder of the Aerial Experiment Association, assessed its military value. During the fourth and final lap, a guy wire broke loose and fouled a propeller. The plane, said one eyewitness, "came down like a bird shot dead in full flight." Orville's left leg and hip were smashed; Selfridge, his skull fractured, died that night.

on the sports page. "Dayton Boys Fly Airship," bragged the *Dayton Evening Herald*. But there was no fanfare when the "Dayton boys" came home. For one thing, nobody understood what they'd done; an "airship" could be a balloon. Nor was the rest of America impressed. The great Langley had failed; how could two bicycle mechanics do it? The first magazine to tell the story was *Gleanings in Bee Culture*, in its March 1904 issue.

The Wrights began sustaining flight by making wide circles over a pasture near Dayton. Again, no one paid any attention. One farmer saw the machine fly 24 miles in 38 minutes, but kept right on plowing.

Ultimately the Wrights offered their patents to the U.S. government. But, still smarting over the Langley affair, the War Department would take no action until a machine "by actual operation is shown to be able to produce horizontal flight and to carry an operator."

Meanwhile, Langley's successor at the Smithsonian spearheaded efforts to prove that the *Great Aerodrome* had really been the first airplane. The machine was later put on exhibit there; miffed, Orville Wright sent the original *Wright Flyer* to the Science Museum in London. Not until December 17, 1948—11 months after Orville's death—did this priceless American treasure receive its place of honor in the Smithsonian.

Flights of Fancy

DESPITE HIGH EXPECTATIONS, THE CAR-PLANE COMBO NEVER GETS OFF THE GROUND

Thousands of planes zoom over a city, piloted by shoppers going to the mall, businesspeople headed for three-martini lunches, and carpool drivers getting their kids from school. An air controller's nightmare? On the contrary, this astounding prospect—the dream of the personal plane—was an American fantasy even before the Wright brothers got us off the ground in 1903.

Within a decade of that historic flight, the dream was real for a few wealthy daredevils, who used seaplanes to commute from country estates to waterfront hangars in downtown New York and Chicago. But these audacious aircraft were dangerous and expensive: far from personal planes for Everyman. At a time when Henry Ford's assembly line had lowered the cost of a car to about $850, these planes sold for $7,000.

Ford, who made a fortune democratizing the roads with his modestly priced Model T, had visions of doing it all over again in the sky. The experiments he started in 1926 ended in disaster two years later, when a friend was killed in Ford's prototype plane at Miami Beach. By 1930, the auto magnate was out of the airplane business completely.

Others, however, were eager to take his place, especially after the federal government began supporting the quest for a "poor man's plane" that would be both as safe and as cheap as the family car. Some of the backyard inventors of these "foolproof" flying machines showed real genius. One of them,

Fred Weick, developed the anti-tailspin design and three-wheel landing gear that are standard on modern planes.

By the mid-1930s combination car-planes, suitable for both the skyways and the highways, were making their way off the drawing boards, down the road, and into the air. In August 1936, test pilot John Ray astonished Washington, D.C., as he landed a forerunner of the helicopter in a city park. Folding the gangling overhead blades, he then drove the prototype to the Department of Commerce, where he presented it to government officials. When the ceremony was over, Ray took off again, but in mid-flight his craft's oil pressure suddenly dropped dangerously. Spotting a near-empty roadway, the pilot landed, pulled into a gas station, and replenished his oil supply. Within minutes, he was back in the air.

After World War II, people expected the personal plane to really take off. Towns built airfields, high schools offered flying lessons, and car dealers prepared to add aircraft to their showrooms. Even Macy's department store was selling planes. A small flock of flying cars again fluttered across technology's horizon. One, the *Airphibian*, was featured in *Life* magazine when its inventor piloted it to New York for an evening at the theater. But these hybrids neither flew as well as small planes nor cruised the highways with the ease and comfort of the family car.

On the Aircar's third trip aloft (top) it ran out of gas and crashed (above). The pilot was not injured, but the project never really recovered.

"Nothing Has Come Along to Beat the Horse"

AS FAR AS J. P. MORGAN WAS CONCERNED, THE AUTOMOBILE HAD NO FUTURE

As the 19th century gave way to the 20th, many investors shared the opinion of Senator Chauncey Depew, whose faith in four-footed transportation was unshakable. "Nothing has come along to beat the horse," he counseled. "Keep your money." And no one agreed with him more than J. P. Morgan, who had made millions from shrewd industrial investments. But when it came to gauging the potential of the vehicle that would change American life, he was way off base.

THE FIRST AUTO COMPANIES

Morgan's opportunity to get into the automobile business came in 1908, when William Crapo Durant approached him for a loan. Durant and Benjamin Briscoe proposed a merger with two other auto manufacturers, Henry Ford and Ransom Olds; but Ford (who was just about to introduce the Model T) wanted a total of $3 million, making the deal much too expensive. Now the pair were seeking Morgan's capital to combine their own firms, Buick and Maxwell-Briscoe.

When Durant confidently predicted that annual auto sales would someday reach 500,000, he was laughed out of the room. "If he has any sense," snorted one of Morgan's partners, "he'll keep such notions to himself."

A FAMILIAR NAME

Briscoe went out on his own, but his company failed. Durant, meanwhile, without the backing of the financiers, went ahead and formed a holding company with $2,000. He named it General Motors.

By 1910, Durant was faltering and received help from some of Morgan's competitors. A decade later, however, the House of Morgan had another chance to get into the car business. With a total of $30 million in debts, General Motors was in deep trouble. To forestall bankruptcy, Durant turned to two financial giants: J. P. Morgan and Co. and Pierre du Pont. They saved the company, but at a tremendous cost. Du Pont took over as president, and Durant was out.

The First Assembly Line

CAR PRODUCER INSPIRED BY MIDWESTERN SLAUGHTERHOUSES

Henry Ford, credited with creating the modern assembly line, said that the "idea came in a general way from the overhead trolley that the Chicago packers use in dressing beef."

That may be where he got the idea, but the Chicagoans got it from Cincinnati.

In the 1850s, some 400,000 pigs per year were being herded through Cincinnati's streets. The city was, said a British visitor, "a monster piggery … Alive and dead, whole and divided into portions, their outsides and their insides, their grunts and their squeals, meet you at every moment."

The scene inside a slaughterhouse was, according to landscape architect Frederick L. Olmsted, "a sort of human chopping machine.... By a skilled sleight-of-hand, hams, shoulders, clear, mess and prime fly off.... Amazed, we took out our watches and counted thirty-five seconds, from the moment when one hog touched the table until the next occupied its place." In the 1860s, Wilson, Eggleston & Company installed an overhead track to speed things up even more.

Meanwhile, the meat-packing industry was centralizing in Chicago. The pork business left Cincinnati to join it, taking along the idea and technology of the overhead conveyor. And so, when Henry Ford needed inspiration, he got it in Chicago, not Cincinnati, where the "disassembly" line was born.

A Tank Full of Miracles

CON MAN TAKES HENRY FORD FOR A RIDE

Cheap, efficient, and readily available, Louis Enricht's chemical mixture was a gasoline substitute that could transform the automobile industry. At least that's what Enricht claimed in 1916, when he insisted that his mystery formula would run any car for about a penny a gallon. Always ready to prove his point, he'd brandish a vial of green liquid, mix it with water, and pour it in the dry gas tank of any car handy. The engine would promptly start up.

Seeking cheaper fuel for his Tin Lizzies, Henry Ford felt that there was substance to the man's claim. Even after Enricht's participation in shady land deals and questionable stock transactions was revealed, the auto pioneer gave the con man $1,000 in cash and a car on which he could continue to test the amazing elixir.

When the rights to Enricht's discovery were apparently sold to another company for $1 million, Ford canceled the deal, suing Enricht for the return of his Model T. In a comedy of errors, the auto was returned without the motor. So by the time Ford pulled out of the deal, he'd lost $1,000—and his car engine.

While no one ever discovered what exactly was in Enricht's potion, experts theorize that he used acetone. Added to water, it could indeed run a car. But the subsequent corrosion would ruin the motor.

What Has Five Wheels and Practically Parks Itself?

The Parccar! Invented by San Francisco lumberman Brooks Walker in the early 1950s, the Parccar featured a fifth wheel that occupied most of the trunk of a Cadillac. To park Walker's car (above), the driver simply put the front wheels into the curb, lowered the fifth wheel to the ground (raising the two rear wheels), and then swung the back end of the car into the parking space. With this device, a 12-foot car could park in a 13-foot space in nine seconds.

In 2006, luxury automaker Lexus took the "self-park" concept one step further, installing a parallel parking "intelligent park assist" option on its top models. The car uses a sonar sensor to measure the size of the parking space and your distance from the other cars; it then steers itself backward into the spot. All the driver has to do is put the car in "drive" and square the car, if necessary, in the space. Lexus, though, doesn't need a fifth wheel.

Great Strides in Transportation

From the Files of the U.S. Patent Office

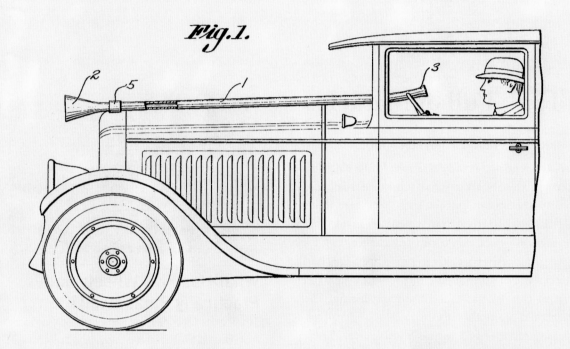

Fig.1.

Automobile Attachment

Patent No. 1,744,727 (Jan. 28, 1930)
Inventor: Eugene L. Baker, Taunton, Massachusetts

"This invention relates to an attachment for automobiles and more especially for closed vehicles ... to provide a simple and efficient device by means of which the driver of the vehicle can speak to persons in front thereof, thereby to facilitate traffic.

"Referring to the figures by character of reference 1 designates a tube arranged longitudinally of the hood of a vehicle. This tube is provided at one end with a small megaphone which can consist of a flared extension 2 of the tube. The other end of the tube is extended into the vehicle to a point close to the driver where it is provided with a mouth-piece into which the driver can easily speak."

Flying Apparatus

Patent No. 132,022 (Oct. 8, 1872)
Inventor: Watson F. Quinby, Wilmington, Delaware

"This invention relates to a new apparatus for enabling men to fly with the use of side and dorsal wings, which are connected with the extremities for operation. The chief object of the present invention is to support the flying

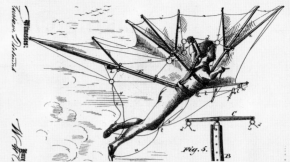

apparatus entirely on the trunk of the operator, and remove all weight from the arms and legs, so that they will be free to give their entire strength to the operation.... The weight of the whole machine need not exceed 15 pounds. It is constructed inside of a semicircle, all the points touching the periphery.

"In order to make a beginning one foot is disengaged from the stirrup, when, by raising the other foot and pushing the hands upward and forward the wings are raised. The actions are intended to be natural, resembling those of swimming in water."

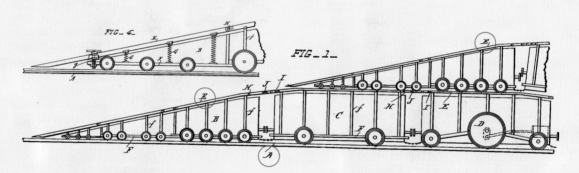

New, Useful Railroad-Trains

Patent No. 536,360 (March 26, 1895)
Inventor: Henry Latimer Simmons, Wickes, Mont.

"This invention ... consists in the novel construction and combination of parts ... whereby one train may pass over another train which it meets or overtakes upon the same track....

"When one train meets or overtakes another train, one train will run up the rails E carried by the other train, and will run along the rails E and descend onto the rails A at the other end of the lower train as shown in Fig. 1.

"The trains have the inclined lower ends of their rails E adjusted at different distances from the rails A in a prearranged manner.... The train having the ends of its rails E higher above the rails A than those of the train it meets will rise up on the rails E of the other train."

Shaking Out the Wash

When David Parker, a Shaker from Canterbury, New Hampshire, saw how much energy was expended by doing laundry, he created a new washing machine. Shaker sisters were jubilant, and the washers, patented in 1858, made a splash in the commercial market as well. Hotels—from the Parker House in Boston to the Tremont in Chicago—clamored for them; one Philadelphia hotel fired 14 laundresses after the machines took over their work.

"Zip 'er Up! Zip 'er Down!"

EITHER WAY, THE SLIDE FASTENER GOT OFF TO A SHAKY START

One of industrial America's most successful products, the zipper took two decades of trial, error, and frustration to perfect the marvel that everyone takes for granted today.

In 1891, Chicago resident Whitcomb Judson assured his place in history when he applied for a patent on a "Clasp Locker or Unlocker for Shoes." Since the patent office had nothing on file remotely resembling Judson's device, he was free to proceed with his project.

The only person who appreciated the slide fastener was a lawyer, Colonel Lewis Walker, who set up the Universal Fastener Company in 1894 to manufacture it. He and Judson then put fasteners on their shoes to advertise their practicality, but they still needed a machine for quantity production. They successfully tested one in 1905. To celebrate, Walker ordered a keg of beer and scheduled a demonstration, but nothing happened. The machine had quit.

Walker's faith was unbounded. Reorganizing the company, he had Judson simplify his invention; the result was called the C-Curity fastener. Ads proclaimed: "A Pull and It's Done! No More Open Skirts … Ask the Girl."

That last sentence proved to be the company's undoing; the fasteners, with a tendency to pop open at inopportune moments, soon became a joke.

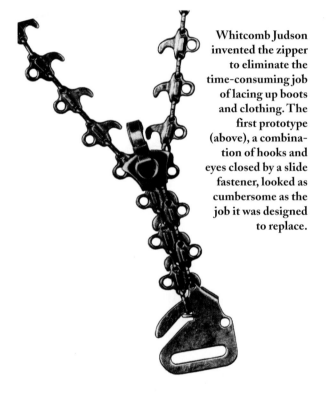

Whitcomb Judson invented the zipper to eliminate the time-consuming job of lacing up boots and clothing. The first prototype (above), a combination of hooks and eyes closed by a slide fastener, looked as cumbersome as the job it was designed to replace.

This humiliation was too much for Judson, but Walker continued to work on the device; to make ends meet, he had to go back to his "day job" practicing law. (He was once forced to settle a grocery bill with worthless shares of stock; eventually, the grocer made a fortune.) Walker's faith finally paid off when the prototype for the modern zipper was perfected in 1913.

But people hadn't forgotten the C-Curity fiasco. For years the new fasteners were considered mere novelty items; only actors used them regularly to make quick costume changes. It wasn't until 1917, when an itinerant tailor used the fasteners on money belts for sailors, that Walker's company took off.

In 1923, the name "zipper" was first used when B. F. Goodrich Co. put fasteners on galoshes. The company president himself promoted the product, urging people to "Zip 'er up! Zip 'er down!" "Zippers" was the trademark for the galoshes. But the public remembered zippers long after the overshoes were forgotten.

Walker laughed all the way to the bank. He was the president of his original company—later renamed Talon—until 1938, when he died at age 83.

Boardwalk Babies

SAVING PREEMIES' LIVES, WITH A SHOW-BIZ TOUCH

In the early decades of the 20th century, the best treatment for dangerously frail premature infants could be found in a very unlikely place: on the midway at Coney Island. That's where Dr. Martin Couney demonstrated the lifesaving benefits of the infant incubator, a device new to (and scorned by) the medical community. Audiences willingly paid admission to marvel at incredibly tiny babies, each nestled snugly in an incubator inside a glass-enclosed nursery. As the tots put on enough weight to leave Couney's pavilion, he would replace them with new preemies struggling for survival.

Couney's show-business career began in 1896, quite by accident, when he was a young doctor at the French maternity hospital where incubators were developed. He was asked to demonstrate the new device at an international exposition in Berlin. The exhibit, complete with premature babies who had been supplied by German hospitals, was such a success (as was the technology) that Couney followed with exhibitions in London and Paris.

HOPE FOR AMERICAN PREEMIES

In 1901, Couney brought his touring incubator show to the United States for the Pan-American Exposition in Buffalo; the preemies proved to be such a popular attraction that the doctor decided to remain

"Don't pass the babies by!" At the Coney Island display of thriving premature infants, one of the barkers was an unknown English actor, Archibald Leach, who moved to Hollywood. There he acquired a new name: Cary Grant.

in America. Two years later, he built an ornate baby palace on Coney Island's boardwalk and hired handsome young barkers to hustle the crowd through the turnstiles.

Once inside, the spectators were often given powerful proof of just how small the preemies were: Couney's chief nurse (there was a full professional staff in attendance at all times) would remove a ring from her finger and easily slip it over the wrist of one of the tiny tots.

The good doctor profited from the demonstrations, taking in $72,000 for a 10-month stay at a San Francisco exposition alone. At the Chicago World's Fair in 1933–34, Couney's pavilion was next to fan dancer Sally Rand's; when police came to arrest the stripper, she protested that at least she wore more clothes than her tiny neighbors.

BELATED RECOGNITION

It took the medical profession decades to catch on: for nearly 40 years Couney toured the country, publicizing incubators. Then, in belated recognition of his work, the New York Medical Society presented him with a platinum watch in 1937. Ironically, his fellow doctors' acceptance is what spelled the end for Couney's sideshow. As hospitals finally began to establish units to treat premature babies, attendance declined. In the mid-1940s, almost half a century after he had begun his combined career as a neonatal pediatrician and show-business entrepreneur, Couney closed the Coney Island pavilion for good. Of the 8,000 premature babies he had treated, Couney maintained that an astonishing 6,500 had survived. "I made my propaganda for the preemie," he explained. "My work is done."

Silly Putty's Surprising Start

RUBBERY GOO A BIG HIT WITH KIDS

During World War II, General Electric engineer James Wright was trying to develop a rubber substitute when he came up with some gooey stuff that, to his surprise, bounced when he dropped it.

Although it had no practical use, everyone found it fascinating. It stretched, it snapped, it shattered when hit with a hammer, and when pressed against newsprint, it picked up the ink, colors and all. Not practical, but certainly a lot of fun to have around.

It owes its name and fame, however, to Peter Hodgson, who dubbed it Silly Putty, included it in the 1949 catalog of the toy store owner who'd told him about it, and created a best-seller. Hodgson (who thought it was more than just a passing fancy) borrowed $147, packed Silly Putty into egg cartons

Silly Putty (above) can be serious stuff: It's been used for strengthening hands, taking lint off clothes, and fastening down weightless tools on space missions

from a local poultry association, went on the road, and proved its continuing popularity. After almost 60 years, its popularity persists.

Soap Floats

IVORY BECOMES FAMOUS BY ACCIDENT

Harley Procter was proud. In 1878, his company had come up with a soap bar as fine as the finest imported castile soaps but much less expensive. Indeed, a chemist's report confirmed that Procter & Gamble's White Soap (the original name for what later became known as Ivory soap) was 99 and 44/100 percent pure. It was only by sheer accident that the soap acquired its most singular feature.

One day, a factory worker forgot to shut off the soap-making machine when he went out to lunch. While he was away, so much air was worked into the mixture that it turned light and frothy. The worker decided not to discard the soap and shipped it out anyway. After all, the ingredients were the same. Who'd notice?

Well, customers *did*—and deluged the company with requests for its unique "soap that floats." After some hasty detective work, Procter found out that P&G had inadvertently created a floating gold mine.

The soap boasted of its purity and lightness well into the 20th century with the familiar slogan, "Ivory: 99 and 44/100% pure—it floats."

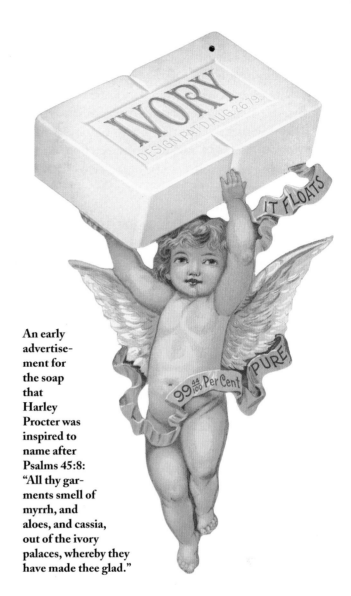

An early advertisement for the soap that Harley Procter was inspired to name after Psalms 45:8: "All thy garments smell of myrrh, and aloes, and cassia, out of the ivory palaces, whereby they have made thee glad."

Godfather of Glamour

MAX FACTOR TAKES GOOP OFF STAGE, MAKES MAKEUP ACCESSIBLE TO ALL WOMEN

Max Factor started out as a makeup artist for the theater and movies and went on to virtually create the modern cosmetics industry. He pulled glamour off the stage and put it within reach of every American woman. His role was so fundamental, he even popularized the word "makeup."

After working as a makeup artist for the Russian Royal Ballet, Factor came to America in 1904. He settled in St. Louis and opened a concession selling beauty aids at that year's world's fair. Within four years, he had started a theatrical makeup store in Los Angeles. There he found that traditional stick greasepaint was too thick and garish for use in the movies; in 1914, he introduced a thinner cream greasepaint in more precise skin tones.

Makeup wasn't his last contribution to movie magic. Factor also created the first human-hair wig used in a movie; in 1918 he made the first false eyelashes, for actress Phyllis Haver. Lip gloss, developed in 1930 for use under film lights, was also his idea.

But it was the special requirements of color film that led to Factor's best-known invention—pancake makeup. The flat cake of transparent makeup in its little pan, applied with a sponge, was introduced in 1938 and was soon used off the screen by models and actresses, because of the natural-looking sheen it gave their faces. Women everywhere quickly followed suit. When Factor started his business, few American women used makeup; today many don't leave home without it.

Max Factor was often seen on movie sets applying his makeup to such beautiful actresses as Josephine Dunn.

The Birth of the Bra

MARY JACOB BROKE THE BINDS OF WOMANHOOD

"When I made my debut, girlish figures were being enclosed in a sort of boxlike armor of whalebone and pink cordage. This contraption ran upward from the knee to under the armpit.... They were hellishly binding." So wrote Mary Phelps Jacob, a free-spirited American socialite who was never one to be tightly bound. In her late twenties, Jacob fled her proper marriage for a European tryst with playboy Harry Crosby, then changed her first name to Caresse, rode an elephant naked through the streets of Paris, and founded an avant-garde publishing house that brought out works by such "pornographers" as James Joyce, D. H. Lawrence, and Ezra Pound.

Years earlier, as a teenager in 1913, Jacob had for all intents and purposes invented the bra. One evening she wanted to wear a rose-garlanded dress to a party but was concerned by the way her corset cover "kept peeping through the roses around my bosom." So she ordered her maid to bring her two handkerchiefs, pinned them together, and tied the ends behind her back. "The result was delicious," she wrote. "I could move much more freely, a nearly naked feeling."

Jacob sold the patent for her "backless brassiere" to the Warner Brothers Corset Company of Bridgeport, Connecticut, for $1,500. And the bra as we know it was born.

A hosiery factory chemist submits stockings to a waterproofing test in 1938.

Professor Nylon

CHEMIST CREATOR DIDN'T LIVE TO SEE MATERIAL'S LEGGY SUCCESS

A distinguished chemistry professor at Harvard University, Wallace H. Carothers was hired by DuPont chemical company in 1928 to head a laboratory research team. The offer was especially attractive because, as he wrote to a friend: "Nobody asks any questions as to how I am spending my time." It was a situation a researcher dreams of: being paid to do his work, unfettered by commercial concerns.

Carothers specialized in synthetic materials. In 1930, he and his team invented neoprene, a synthetic rubber that brought DuPont healthy profits. But Carothers's professional paradise was not to last; it came to an end when the Great Depression caused DuPont to change its research policy. Profit now took precedence over pure science, and the dedicated chemist despaired at the loss of his integrity. Although he and his team did perfect a synthetic fiber—nylon—he saw himself as a failed scientist.

Carothers became severely depressed. Alone in a hotel room on April 29, 1937, just three weeks after he had been awarded the patent for nylon, he swallowed a fatal dose of cyanide. He was 41.

Inside Jobs

A NEW ROUTE FOR RHINOPLASTY

It sounds like torture, but it was a major medical advance. Prior to 1887, "nose jobs" were performed by cutting through the skin on the outside of the nose to get at the bony deformities and excessive tissue below. This method left bad scars, which often were greater psychological burdens than the deformed nose had been. In 1887 Dr. John Orlando Roe, a nose and throat specialist from Rochester, New York, invented a new approach. Using cocaine as an anesthetic, he cut the flesh inside the nose and pried the skin back from the underlying bone. Then he inserted a tiny saw he had designed for sculpting the distorted cartilage without scarring the face. As primitive as the procedure was, Roe's results were miraculous. His surgery became the basis for modern rhinoplasty.

Beauty and Health Breakthroughs

From the Files of the U.S. Patent Office

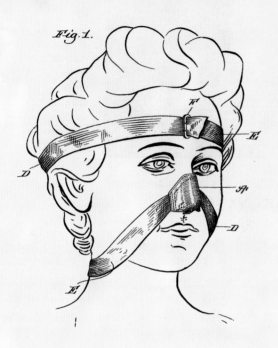

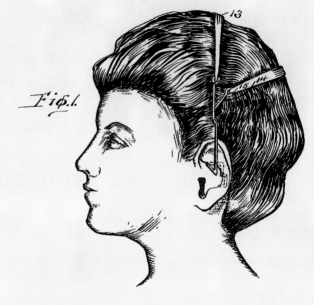

Nose Shaper

Patent No. 850,978 (April 23, 1907)
Inventor: Ignatius Nathaniel Soares
Framingham, Massachusetts

"The noses of a great many persons are slightly deformed and therefore … the appearance of the … face is more or less disfigured. Such deformity can frequently be remedied by a gentle but continuous pressure in a way that shall be painless to the individual."

Wrinkle Remover

Patent No. 1,062,399 (May 20, 1913)
Inventors: Abbie Hess and Alfred Lee Tibbals,
Kansas City, Kansas

"A pair of engaging members may be inserted in the ears of a wearer for exerting an upward and rearward pull thereon. [The device] prevents contraction [of the ears] so as to relieve partial deafness, and so as to prevent the forming of wrinkles in the skin, and the growth of a double-chin."

Dimple Maker
Patent No. 560,351 (May 19, 1896)
Inventor: Martin Goetze, Berlin, Germany

"In order to make the body susceptible to the production of artistic dimples, it is necessary that the cellular tissues surrounding the spot should be made susceptible to its production by means of massage. The knob [of the device's] arm must be set on the selected spot. The cylinder serves to ... make the spot where the dimple is to be produced malleable."

Tapeworm Trap
Patent No. 11,942 (Nov. 14, 1854)
Inventor: Apheus Myers, Logansport, Indiana

"The object of my invention is to effect the removal of worms from the system, without employing medicines, and thereby causing much injury. My invention consists in a trap which is baited, attached to a string, and swallowed by the patient after a fast of suitable duration to make the worm hungry. The worm seizes the bait, and its head is caught in the trap, which is then withdrawn from the patients stomach by the string which has been left hanging from the mouth, dragging after it the whole length of the worm."

The trap could be baited with "any nutritious substance." But the overzealous were warned that "in constructing the trap, care should be taken that the spring is only strong enough to hold the worm, and not strong enough to cause his head to be cut off."

American naval officer John Paul Jones captures the HMS *Serapis* in 1779. Opposite: A Gulf War soldier in Saudi Arabia is outfitted in chemical warfare gear.

CHAPTER NINE

A Call to Arms

The author H. G. Wells once said, "If we don't end war, war will end us," and it was an idea so poignant that President Kennedy paraphrased him a few decades later. But knowing war's possible effects hasn't changed our behavior much. From the moments that we touched down on these shores, Americans have been engaged in conflict—for defending our liberties, our lands, then the liberties and lands of others.

Names like Bull Run, the Alamo, Midway, Pearl Harbor, Omaha Beach, and Iraq are etched in our minds. They are just a few of the places where generations of Americans have served and sacrificed. What follows are stories of valor and terror, ruses and glories, heroism and ignominy. They are true tales of American men and women who bravely answered their country's call to arms.

John Trumbull's 1786 painting, *The Death of General Warren at the Battle of Bunker Hill.*

The Battle of Bunker Hill

"YANKEE DOODLE" MEANING GOES FROM INSULTING TO TRIUMPHANT

Boston was a powder keg in April 1775, with tensions rising between the colonists and the British. But General Thomas Gage and his seasoned British regulars were confident they could put down any uprising of farmers and shopkeepers. And the redcoats didn't keep their disdain to themselves. As they marched, they sang a sarcastic song that mocked Americans as rustic buffoons. The song was "Yankee Doodle."

On the night of April 18, however, the British weren't singing. They were marching stealthily westward to destroy a rebel arsenal at Concord and arrest John Adams and John Hancock. Outside Lexington, they captured a night rider named Paul Revere. They didn't consider him worth arresting; they just took his horse and set him free. Revere walked to where

Adams and Hancock were staying and helped them escape. Other riders made for Concord.

The cocky British were met the next morning at Concord's North Bridge by militia from all the surrounding towns—and the farmers routed them.

BIG GUNS

As the New England patriots plotted their next moves, one thing was certain: They would need cannon. A captain of the Connecticut Militia named Benedict Arnold knew where to get them. British-held Fort Ticonderoga in upstate New York had plenty, he said, and only a token force to guard it. Arnold himself offered to lead the attack. En route he ran into Colonel Ethan Allen and his Green Mountain Boys, who had the same idea. The backwoods Vermonters, who had been formed into a crack guerrilla unit five years earlier—not to fight the British but to settle a land dispute with neighboring New York—proved too much even for Arnold's ego, and the outraged future traitor was forced to take a backseat to Allen's rowdy troops.

Fort Ticonderoga and its cannon were captured on May 10, without a single casualty. Allen, with Arnold at his side, rapped on the fort's main door at dawn and demanded the garrison's immediate surrender. The British officer who answered the knock had his pants draped over his arm. He listened politely to the Americans, and then decided they really would have to speak to Ticonderoga's commander. Allen did, and the fort surrendered.

WRONG HILL, RIGHT SPIRIT

Once the colonials had cannon, Gage knew his position in Boston was vulnerable. If the rebels could occupy the strategic heights outside the city, their big guns would control the harbor. Even though Ticonderoga was 300 miles away and the Americans would have to wait until winter before they could transport the heavy cannon by sled through the rugged back-country, the general resolved to strike quickly.

Colonial spies learned his plans, and the Americans moved into action. Rebel leaders ordered the militia to occupy Bunker Hill above Charlestown, but the militia's own commanders occupied Breed's Hill, some 2,000 feet away instead. The reasons for the confused orders still baffle historians, but the fact is that the famous Battle of Bunker Hill took place on Breed's.

Gage played into the colonials' hands by ordering a frontal assault. Instead of fleeing as expected, the Americans cut the enemy down with disciplined fire from behind hastily constructed bulwarks. More than half of the 2,000 redcoats were killed or wounded; the Americans suffered about 450 casualties.

The British technically won the battle because the undersupplied rebels ran out of ammunition.

After these hard-fought conflicts, the British started singing a different tune, and the patriots took up choruses of "Yankee Doodle" with an inspired sarcasm the redcoats had never imagined.

FUNNY FACT

In Painting, Washington Crosses Rhine, Not Delaware

The famous depiction of George Washington crossing the Delaware was actually painted in Germany in 1851 by Emanuel Leutze, who used American tourists as models but patterned the river on the Rhine. The boats, the flag, the dress, and the ice are inaccurate; nonetheless, Leutze vividly captured the drama of the Christmas 1776 assault.

Only a second version of Leutze's painting (right) made it to the United States. The original, which had been damaged by fire at his studio, hung in Bremen, Germany, until September 5, 1942, when it was destroyed in an Allied bombing raid.

Getting the Word Out

**FEARLESS RIDERS BRING GOOD TIDINGS
AND BAD DURING AMERICAN REVOLUTION**

The poet Henry Wadsworth Longfellow invited readers: "Listen, my children, and you shall hear of the midnight ride of Paul Revere." But who ever heard of Jack Jouett, or Tench Tilghman, or Israel Bissel? These heroes also leaped to their saddles for American liberty.

JEFFERSON'S CLOSE CALL

On the night of June 3–4, 1781, Jouett, a captain in the Virginia Militia, saved Thomas Jefferson (and the entire Virginia Assembly) from 250 British troops who had been sent to Charlottesville to capture them. The 27-year-old colonial spied the red-coated dragoons at Cuckoo Tavern in Louisa County and took off into the night.

Unlike Revere's ride along well-traveled roads, Jouett's 40-mile trek took him through wilderness, where riding was slow by day and potentially deadly in darkness. When the captain reached Jefferson's home at dawn, his face was swollen and bleeding from being lashed by branches. By the time the British arrived, the Americans had fled.

Tench Tilghman made his trip four months later, this time bearing good news rather than warnings. As General Washington's aide-de-camp, he sped to Philadelphia to announce to Congress the British surrender at Yorktown. Traveling from Virginia by boat and horseback, it took him five days to complete the 200-mile journey.

THE LONGEST RIDE

But no messenger can match Israel Bissel, a humble post rider on the Boston–New York route. After the Battle of Lexington and Concord on April 19, 1775, Bissel was ordered to raise the alarm by carrying the news to New Haven, Connecticut. He reached

Paul Revere (above) made his famous ride on April 18, 1775, to warn Samuel Adams and John Hancock that British officers were coming to arrest them.

Worcester, Massachusetts, normally a day's ride, in two hours. Then his horse promptly dropped dead. Pausing only to get another mount, Bissel pressed on and, by April 22, reached New Haven. In two more days, he was in New York; by April 25, Philadelphia. His 125-hour, 345-mile ride sparked anti-British riots and signaled American militia units throughout the Northeast to mobilize for war.

IMPROBABLE PIONEER

George Rogers Clark: Frontier Securer

A bold, shrewd strategist, George Rogers Clark had succeeded in securing America's frontier territory—and all without bloodshed.

At dawn on July 4, 1778, the inhabitants of the British post of Kaskaskia, near the Mississippi River in present-day southern Illinois, awoke to find the streets guarded by 178 ragged, bearded men who ordered them to stay in their homes. Clark, commander of this motley force, made the villagers sit indoors for hours. Under cover of darkness Clark's men had surrounded Kaskaskia, lukewarmly defended by the French militia in the absence of the British, without firing a single shot. When one resident finally ventured out, Clark assured him that the Americans were not "plunderers and barbarians." Clark told them they could keep their possessions in return for a pledge of allegiance to his country, and soon the streets were full of celebrating people.

But Clark was in a tight spot. Almost half of his troops insisted on going home, so his men were outnumbered 25 to 1 by the American Indian allies of the British. Clark called a peace conference and, bluffing all the way, he offered the Indians a peace belt and a war belt, claiming that he didn't care which one they chose. His audacity so impressed the Indians that they took the peace belt, and within five weeks Clark had won pledges of good behavior from almost a dozen tribes.

Traitor and Mrs. Traitor

HOW BENEDICT ARNOLD AND HIS WIFE ESCAPED HANGING

Benedict Arnold is America's most famous traitor. But did he win that dubious distinction on his own? Probably not, because he was married to the indomitable Peggy Shippen Arnold, who dreamed that her husband's treason would enable her to return one day to the subdued colonies as Lady Arnold. And they were but two corners of a treacherous triangle that included Major John André, adjutant general of the British Army in North America—and Peggy's ex-boyfriend.

Arnold had his own reasons to defect to the British. Despite the fact that he was a great general and a hero on the field of battle, a cloud hung over him: word of shady financial dealings had led to his court-martial. Although he was found innocent of some charges, the military court insisted that General George Washington reprimand him.

Arnold's bitterness against the Revolutionary government was deeply ingrained by the time he met 18-year-old Peggy Shippen, his future second wife, in Philadelphia in 1778. They married the next year, but before Arnold's arrival, Shippen had been the belle of the British social scene, often seen in the company of the dashing Major André.

When Arnold started negotiating the sale of West Point, he dealt with André in New York. Using the code name "Monk," Arnold sent secret messages and pleas for money to André. Peggy, too, corresponded with her old flame, attempting to ease the difficult negotiations.

Then, on the morning of September 25, 1780, Washington stopped to have breakfast with the Arnolds on his way to West Point. Upon his arrival he was disappointed to discover that Arnold had just rushed to the fort and that Mrs. Arnold was ill. Washington became even more annoyed when he arrived at West Point to learn that Arnold hadn't even shown up there that morning. A stickler for protocol, he was deeply offended that one of his favorite generals would so rudely snub him.

The reason for the snub was soon clear: That very morning, after his first face-to-face meeting with Arnold, André had been arrested on his way back to British lines. Even though he was wearing a disguise, he had been picked up, and evidence of the plot was found in his stocking. Just before Washington showed up, word of the arrest reached Arnold, and he barely escaped.

Mrs. Arnold remained behind in her room and, at about the time that the stunned Washington heard the report of Arnold's treason, she conveniently went mad. "As the lovely lady raved and gestured," one historian later observed of Peggy's dramatic command performance before the general, "her clothes sometimes parted to reveal charms that should have been hidden."

The act worked. Washington refused to believe that Mrs. Arnold—whom Alexander Hamilton described as possessing "all the sweetness of beauty, all the loveliness of innocence"—could be involved in such a heinous crime.

Mrs. Arnold's old friend André, who was caught red-handed, was hanged as a spy eight days later. (Washington suggested "a handsome gratuity" for André's captors, John Paulding, Isaac Van Wert, and David Williams. Congress voted each of them a lifetime pension and ordered medallions struck in their honor.) Recovering in remarkably short order, Mrs. Arnold was reunited with her husband. Ultimately, after Arnold led a force of Loyalists and

IMPROBABLE PIONEER

Private Peter Francisco: Revolutionary War Soldier

As dawn broke over Camden, South Carolina, on August 16, 1780, General Charles Cornwallis's seasoned British troops launched a sudden attack on an American force made up of inexperienced Virginia and North Carolina militiamen. It quickly became a rout.

They say that 19-year-old Private Peter Francisco lifted an abandoned 1,100-pound cannon and carried it to a secure position at the rear of the Continental Army lines. Then Francisco—who was six-foot-six and 260 pounds and said to be the strongest man in the colonies—shot a grenadier threatening his commanding officer, Colonel William Mayo. Ordered by a British cavalryman to drop his musket, he used the bayonet to lift the hapless horseman from the saddle and, wearing his victim's headgear, rode among the enemy yelling, "Yonder go the damned rebels!" When he saw Mayo being led away, a prisoner, he cut the British captor down, gave the officer the horse, and saw him safely on his way. Though young, Francisco had already been at war for three years. Now long forgotten, he was called "the most famous private soldier of the Revolutionary War."

deserters in a series of raids against American troops in Virginia, the two moved to England where, comfortably supported by pensions, they spent most of the rest of their lives.

The Private Private

ROBERT SHURTLEFF HAS A BIG SECRET

During a skirmish at East Chester, New York, Private Robert Shurtleff took a musket ball in the thigh. Rejecting medical help, the young soldier crawled into the woods and hid until the wound healed over. Then, rejoining the 4th Massachusetts Regiment, Shurtleff

marched into the Adirondack Mountains to battle Mohawk Indians.

Later, serving as a clerk to General John Paterson in Philadelphia, Shurtleff fell ill with "malignant fever" (probably influenza) and was taken to a hospital. This time, there was no escape; a doctor named

Barnabas Binney was amazed to discover that his delirious patient was a woman!

Deborah Sampson, descended from Pilgrims, had first enlisted under the name Timothy Thayer. But using her bounty money to celebrate at a local tavern, she all too clearly revealed her identity. Her church excommunicated her for wearing men's clothes and behaving "very loose and un-Christian-like." The army bounced her.

Walking 75 miles to Worcester, Sampson enlisted again as Robert Shurtleff. This was in May 1782, six months after the surrender at Yorktown, but there was still plenty of fighting going on. Guerrilla bands, known as "cowboys," raped and pillaged at will in a no-man's-land between the British lines at Yonkers, New York, and the American lines at Peekskill, New York; Sampson's regiment was sent to fight them.

> Deborah Sampson was excommunicated for wearing men's clothes and behaving "very loose and un-Christian-like."

In her first skirmish, Sampson took a saber slash to the left cheek. Recovering with only a scar, she wrote home that she was working in a "large but well-regulated family." It was in her next battle that she got the musket wound.

The kindly Dr. Binney kept Deborah's secret for a time. But when his niece fell in love with the "handsome young soldier," he told General Paterson, who told George Washington. On October 23, 1783, Sampson was honorably discharged. When, clad in a dress, she watched her old regiment pass in review, no one recognized her.

Deborah Sampson enlisted in the army twice under false names: First she was Timothy Thayer, then Robert Shurtleff. After she was discharged, members of her old regiment didn't recognize her when they saw her in female garb.

John Trumbull's *Surrender of Lord Cornwallis* is a moving but incorrect depiction of the Revolution's end: In reality, General Cornwallis boycotted the formal surrender ceremony.

Surrender at Yorktown

A VICTORY MARKED BY SUBTERFUGE AND A BREACH OF ETIQUETTE

During the summer of 1781, General George Washington couldn't decide whether to mount an attack against the British garrison in New York City or against General Charles Cornwallis in the South. As a result, his English counterpart, Sir Henry Clinton, was kept guessing. And after Colonel Alexander Hamilton—while telling a known British double agent that the target would be Virginia—let the man catch sight of a marked map of New York, Clinton was sure that the northern city was the real objective.

Meanwhile a French fleet, under François Joseph Paul, Comte de Grasse, drove British warships from the Virginia coast. American and French troops, meeting near New York, started south. On September 28, more than 16,000 of them laid siege to Cornwallis's stronghold at Yorktown. For a week, beginning on October 9, as de Grasse prevented escape or reinforcement by sea, the Virginia town was pounded by artillery, in the heaviest barrage laid down to that time

in the Western Hemisphere. Cornwallis, expecting a fleet from the north, held on.

American victory seemed assured until October 16, when de Grasse told Washington that the French fleet must leave within 48 hours. A ruse was needed, or the siege would have to be lifted. Again, Hamilton played a gambit superbly: Under a flag of truce, he let it be known that an assault was imminent and that American troops were "so exasperated at the Conduct of the British to the Southward, that they could not be restrained by authority and Discipline." An immediate surrender, he suggested, would save much bloodshed.

The next morning a message from Cornwallis asked for "a cessation of hostilities for twenty-four hours" while terms of surrender were discussed. Washington, with an anxious eye toward the sea, agreed to only two hours. Terms were arrived at, and at 2 p.m. on October 19, 1781, in a formal ceremony that Cornwallis boycotted, the last major battle of the American Revolution came to an official end.

Mother Nature Visits the Capital

HOW A HURRICANE SAVED WASHINGTON FROM BRITISH FORCES

"Clear out, clear out!" President James Madison's servant galloped to the Executive Mansion with frightening news of the battle at Bladensburg, Maryland. American militia were in disarray. Madison himself had witnessed the debacle and sent word to his wife, Dolley, to flee. The fall of the nation's capital was imminent.

Eight days earlier 4,000 British troops, fresh from fighting Napoleon, had begun a whirlwind sweep through the Chesapeake Capes. The Americans, ill-led and ill-trained, could muster little effective defense. Now, on August 24, 1814, civilians and soldiers alike were fleeing Washington in a panicked melee. It was the beginning of a national humiliation that would become surreal, even for the conquerors.

When the British marched into the city that evening, it was nearly deserted. The only resistance they encountered was a single volley of musket fire, which killed one redcoat, wounded three others, and shot the horse from under their commander, Major General Robert Ross.

The invaders moved quickly to the Capitol, where they feared the Americans might make a defiant last stand. After shooting rockets through the windows, an assault party stormed the entrance, broke down the door, and was greeted by silence. Soon both the Senate and House chambers were ablaze. Before the night was over, the White House and Treasury were also in flames.

The soldiers roamed the city like tourists. At the abandoned office of the *National Intelligencer*, General Ross picked up a copy of the newspaper's last issue, the one that had assured Washingtonians their city was safe. He tried to stuff it into his coat, but failed. "Damn it," he cried, "my pocket is full of old Madison's love letters." The British general had taken them earlier as souvenirs from the White House.

The next morning, Dr. William Thornton, superintendent of the Patent Office, returned to his office to retrieve a violin and found British soldiers preparing to burn the building. If they did so, he scolded, they would be equated with the barbarians who had destroyed the ancient library at Alexandria. The argument worked; the Patent Office was spared.

Then the British encountered their first setback. While they were destroying 150 barrels of gunpowder at a deserted American fort, the barrels exploded. Some 30 redcoats died from the blast; 44 were wounded. Shortly thereafter, the storm clouds that had threatened all day released a torrential hurricane. Ross's troops and lines of communication were thrown into confusion; the general ordered a retreat to the ships. It was as if nature had saved the city in the absence of human defenders.

Ironically, although the hurricane quenched many of the fires the British had set, it blew the roof off the Patent Office, which Thornton just that morning had so luckily preserved.

BRIGHT IDEA

The Purple Heart

The Purple Heart was the first medal "for military merit" ever given to enlisted men. George Washington created the award in 1782, after which it lapsed into disuse for 150 years. Reinstated to honor Washington's 200th birthday, it is today given to anyone wounded in action.

A Family Squabble

POCAHONTAS'S SON FIGHTS HIS MOTHER'S PEOPLE

Thomas Rolfe could have been an Indian chief. Instead, the son of Pocahontas and Jamestown planter John Rolfe became a wealthy landowner, inheriting his father's 400-acre plantation plus thousands of acres from his grandfather, Chief Powhatan (his real name was Wahunsunacock, but because he was chief of the Powhatans, the English called him Chief Powhatan). When the time came to make a choice between his two heritages, he donned an English uniform and helped to wipe out his mother's tribe.

Raised by an uncle in England after Pocahontas died there in 1617, the young man returned to his Virginia birthplace around 1635. Relations had been tense between colonists and Indians since 1622, when the Powhatan tribe—led by Pocahontas's uncle, the war chief Opechancanough—had massacred 347 people, including John Rolfe.

> Thomas Rolfe was the only child of Pocahontas and Jamestown settler John Rolfe, both of whom died when Thomas was very young.

Colonists were forbidden to "speak or parley" with the tribesmen, but young Rolfe petitioned the governor in 1641 "to let him go to see Opachankeno to whom he is allied and Cleopatra, his mother's sister." No record of the meeting exists; we must imagine the confrontation between the Anglicized 26-year-old, hearing his mother's tongue spoken for the first time in his adult life, and the Indians, gazing at a face that bore a striking resemblance to that of their beloved lost princess.

In 1644, Opechancanough, who was said to be over 100 years old, mounted another assault. Carried on a litter, he led his warriors in raids that killed more than 400 Virginians. The colonists, among them Lieutenant Thomas Rolfe, fought back. Opechancanough was captured and killed. By 1646, the General Assembly reported that the American Indians were "so routed and dispersed they are no longer a nation."

King Philip's War

THE PURITANS FACE OFF AGAINST THE AMERICAN INDIANS

Metacom, also known as Philip, was only 24 when he became chief, or king, of the Wampanoags in 1662, succeeding his brother, Alexander. (Chief Massasoit, who had befriended the Pilgrims in 1621, gave all his sons English names.) Claiming that an English doctor had poisoned his brother, King Philip vowed vengeance.

For 13 years, Philip swallowed his hatred. Meanwhile the Puritans, favoring so-called "praying" or converted Indians, took more and more land from his people; they even confiscated the tribe's guns, forcing them to relearn how to hunt with bows and arrows.

In 1675, after the Puritans tried and executed three Indians who, on Philip's orders, had killed a Harvard-educated praying Indian as an English spy, the Wampanoags and some allied tribes began to raid villages, burning and killing all the way. They were opposed by a mixed troop of whites and Indians led by a 35-year-old carpenter named Benjamin Church. As expert a swamp fighter as Philip himself, Church tracked his quarry relentlessly, but the elusive Philip reveled in a prophecy that he would never die at English hands. After one bloody battle, Church captured Philip's wife and son, who wound up among the many Indians sold into slavery by the Puritans. Philip's hatred burned brighter.

One day, Philip killed one of his own warriors with a tomahawk—just because that warrior suggested that the chief consider peace. The man's brother, Alderman, defected and led Church to Philip's camp. That night, August 12, 1676, Philip woke once, saying that he had dreamed of being captured. Aroused at dawn by shots, he leaped from the flat rock that had been his bed and, gun in hand, fled into the swamp. There he was shot through the heart by Alderman. Philip's head was impaled on a pole, his body quartered and hung from trees. One hand went to Alderman, who kept it in a bucket of rum, exhibiting it for money.

Metacom, chief of the Wampanoag tribe, was shot through the heart on August 12, 1676, and was dismembered shortly thereafter.

England and Spain Spar in America's South

HOW A MUMMIFIED EAR SPARKED THE BLOODY MARSH BATTLE

In 1739, a shaky peace between England and Spain flared into war. Commercial interests in the West Indies lay at the heart of the dispute, but Robert Jenkins's ear touched the whole thing off.

Jenkins had been master of the English merchant ship *Rebecca* in 1731, when it was stopped and boarded by a Spanish coast guard vessel whose captain not only stripped the *Rebecca* of its cargo, but cut off Jenkins's ear. Seven years later, when the English Parliament thought that Spanish depredations had gone too far, someone remembered Jenkins and called him to testify. The mariner not only told the story of his capture and mutilation, but produced his mummified ear. The ghoulish symbol became the rallying point for war. Among the most enthusiastic hawks was James Oglethorpe, a veteran soldier and philanthropist who, in 1732, had founded the colony of Georgia as a place where debtors released from prison could start new lives. Oglethorpe had lobbied Parliament long and hard for help in containing attacks on Georgia from Spanish Florida. Now he saw an opportunity to do something about the situation.

In the spring of 1740, he led a combined group of Georgians, South Carolinians, and friendly American Indians in a successful attack on several Spanish outposts near St. Augustine. But an ensuing assault on the Spanish stronghold itself failed, and Oglethorpe was forced to retreat with his fever-ridden army to the strategic border town of Frederica.

There, in July 1742, the Spanish made a play for English Georgia by attacking Frederica with a large sea and land force. Oglethorpe had been expecting them. Though his troops were severely outnumbered, they ambushed the invaders in a battle so fierce it earned the name Bloody Marsh.

The Spanish were about to retreat when a Frenchman who'd been fighting with Oglethorpe deserted and revealed how weak the colonists' forces really were. Heartened, the Spanish prepared a counterattack but then fell prey to an ingenious bit of deception. Upon hearing of the Frenchman's treachery, Oglethorpe released one of his Spanish prisoners and sent him back to the enemy with a "secret" message for the deserter, designed to make him look like a double agent: He was to go ahead with the prearranged plan to lure the Spaniards into a trap.

The Spanish commander packed up his men and ships and sailed away. The War of Jenkins's Ear and the battle of Bloody Marsh ended forever the Spanish threat against England's southern colonies.

Germ Warfare, Colonial Style

HOW A NATIVE TRIBE WAS KILLED OFF WITH TWO BLANKETS AND A HANKY

Lord Jeffrey Amherst was a seasoned soldier, the shining hero of the French and Indian War, and the commander in chief of British troops in North America. Despite this, he had little personal experience fighting American Indians, and some of the tales he heard about the way they battled made him sick. Supposedly one captured British officer had been boiled and eaten. Another officer had been killed while on a peace mission; it was said that the Indians mutilated his body and ate his heart.

FUNNY FACT

Stewart Film Based on True Story

In 1892, ex-Indian agent Tom Jeffords became a recluse near Tucson, Arizona. A tough, hard-drinking bachelor, he was the unlikely model for the romantic figure played by Jimmy Stewart in the 1950 film, *Broken Arrow*. Jeffords had gained fame in the 1860s and 1870s by befriending Apache Chief Cochise. The two had brokered peace between the white men and native tribes; Jeffords was replaced in 1876, two years after Cochise had died. The new apache chief, Geronimo, and Jeffords didn't get along quite as well.

Amherst was fed up, and in his anger he resorted to barbaric tactics.

"I wish to hear of no prisoners," he wrote to Colonel Henry Bouquet, the man he put in charge of rescuing beleaguered Fort Pitt, on the site of modern Pittsburgh. "Could it not be contrived to send the smallpox among those disaffected tribes of Indians?" Bouquet replied that he would try.

A few months later, on June 24, 1763, Captain Simeon Ecuyer, the commander at Fort Pitt, wrote in his diary of a meeting with Turtle's Heart, a leader of the attacking Delaware Indians. It seems that Turtle's Heart had come to the fort to try his hand at a little psychological warfare.

Expressing concern for the defenders' safety, Turtle's Heart told them that a vast army of six united tribes had already overwhelmed the entire countryside, but the Delawares could offer protection if the settlers would give up the fort at once and flee. Captain Ecuyer thanked the Indians profusely for their concern; then "out of our regard to them we gave them two blankets and a handkerchief out of the Small Pox Hospital. I hope it will have the desired effect."

It did. Before long, a lethal smallpox epidemic raged through the tribal camps, killing warriors and their families alike.

Brothers Tenskwatawa and Tecumseh headquartered their new tribal nation at Tippecanoe in 1808. Three years later, on November 7, 1811, General William Henry Harrison led an army of about 1,000 men who destroyed the town.

The Prophet and His Brother

TENSKWATAWA AND TECUMSEH PLAN FOR A UNIFIED TRIBAL NATION

His was a dissolute, misspent youth: Laulewasika, the younger brother of the great Shawnee leader Tecumseh, even lost an eye during one of his drunken brawls. Then one day, while casually lighting his pipe, he suddenly collapsed, apparently dead. Tribe members were astonished when, as they were making burial arrangements, he awoke and calmly announced that he had returned from the Master of Life and was now a prophet named Tenskwatawa.

The message the prophet preached was really an American Indian version of fundamentalism—he'd probably adapted it from sermons he heard in a nearby Shaker community. Indians, he insisted, had to return to the ancient ways of the Master of Life and renounce all of the white man's influences and customs, particularly religion and liquor. In addition, Tenskwatawa claimed to have received the power to heal all diseases and stop the white man's bullets.

This religious message fit in perfectly with his brother's plans to create a confederation of all Indian tribes to fight white settlers in the Old Northwest.

Indeed, the two brothers often traveled together visiting various tribes. Tecumseh would galvanize the crowd with his eloquent political appeal, then

Tenskwatawa would finish them off with his missionary revivalism.

The combination alarmed the territorial governor of Indiana, William Henry Harrison, who challenged Tenskwatawa to perform a miracle. "If he is really a prophet," the governor declared, "ask him to cause the sun to stand still, the moon to alter its course, the rivers to cease to flow. If he does these things, you may then believe he has been sent from God."

As if in reply to this challenge, on the morning of June 16, 1806, the prophet arrived at an Indian gathering in a long black robe and pointed at the sun, which obediently disappeared. As darkness fell, the Indians cowered in terror. Tenskwatawa asked the Master of Life to bring back the sun, and it reappeared. There was no doubt that Tenskwatawa had the crowd completely under his spell. (As it turns out, it was not the prophet's magic, but an eclipse he knew was coming, that caused the sudden darkness.)

The brothers eventually set up headquarters for their new tribal nation at a town they called Tippecanoe, or Prophetstown, in 1808. Three years later, while Tecumseh was assembling an army to battle the Americans, he left Tenskwatawa in charge of Tippecanoe with specific instructions not to get into a fight until he returned.

But Tenskwatawa, a better prophet than politician, bowed to the demands of the militant Indians who wanted to attack Harrison immediately. First he had the warriors touch his "bean belt" to make them immune to bullets and then dip their weapons in his "magic bowl" to ensure victory.

Neither belt nor bowl was effective. The Indians were routed at the Battle of Tippecanoe, and the town was burned to the ground. The surviving warriors were so incensed at being duped by Tenskwatawa that they were ready to kill him on the spot. But glib as ever, he was able to talk them out of it by claiming that the presence of his squaw at the magic bowl had ruined all the spells.

Tecumseh returned home to find Tenskwatawa's credibility demolished, Prophetstown lost, and his grand plans for a unified resistance destroyed. He fought on gallantly against the invaders, joining the British during the War of 1812, but was shot dead on the battlefield in 1813. Years later, Harrison, of course, won the 1840 presidential election, only to die a month into his term.

Indian Messiah

THE GHOST DANCERS' HOPE ENDED IN TRAGEDY

Although it lasted only two years, by the time the Ghost Dance movement was over, Sitting Bull was dead, and more than 200 Sioux (mostly women and children) and 25 U.S. soldiers had been killed at Wounded Knee Creek in South Dakota. Yet the Ghost Dance began as a kind of Christianity that expressed the Indians' longing to return to their past.

Ghost Dancing had occurred before among the Plains tribes. But it emerged anew early in 1889, when a Nevada Paiute holy man named Wovoka—who had been raised by a white family after his father's death—had a vision. In it, God assured him that Christ's second coming was at hand, and the prophet learned a sacred dance, which the Indians should perform to hasten the new age. When the messiah came, the dancers would be lifted into the air as a bountiful land slid into place beneath them, burying the old corrupt world. Indians who had died would be resurrected to join their descendants on earth, which may be why the dance was called the "Ghost Dance."

Although the peaceful message encouraged only trancelike dancing, white Indian agents were frightened. They feared they were losing control of the tribes. Reports of Ghost Shirts, which the Indians believed to be impervious to bullets, only heightened their alarm.

In December 1890, the government tried to arrest Sitting Bull, whom they thought was inciting the

Ghost Dancers. He resisted and was murdered. A few days later, Big Foot, another Sioux chief, learned that his own arrest had been ordered. When he and his people slipped away, the 7th Cavalry—General George Armstrong Custer's old regiment, which the Sioux had massacred at the Little Bighorn—was sent to bring them back.

On December 28, the soldiers intercepted Big Foot, who was dying of pneumonia, and about 350 of his followers. The Indians were moved out peacefully to a camp at Wounded Knee Creek, where the braves were told to surrender their weapons. Reports vary, but it's certain that someone fired a shot, and the nervous, tired, and freezing troops who surrounded the camp opened fire.

The terrified Indians discovered that their Ghost Shirts were worthless. Some fought back, but many of the women, children, and elderly fled, and as they ran they were slaughtered. Corpses were recovered miles from the camp. One baby, half frozen, was found sheltered desperately in its dead mother's arms, still nursing at her breast.

This was the last "battle" the army fought against the Indians. It ended forever the Ghost Dance and the dream of an Indian messiah.

The Ghost Dance (above) was not a war dance. But most whites didn't understand this and were frightened by the Indians' belief that their Ghost Shirts could not be penetrated by bullets.

Sitting Bull's Murder

As the winter dawn broke over South Dakota on Monday,  December 15, 1890, 43 blue-uniformed American Indian police crossed the Standing Rock Reservation, heading toward the house of the powerful Hunkpapa Sioux medicine man Sitting Bull. Fearing that white soldiers were after their powerful leader, the tribal police attempted a preemptive arrest. As they dragged the Sioux leader from his cabin, his teenage son, Crow Foot, awoke and joined about 150 Hunkpapas who had gathered outside. Sitting Bull refused to go. One of his supporters fired at the policemen, hitting their leader, Lieutenant Bull Head. As the lieutenant fell, he fired into Sitting Bull's chest. Another policeman shot him in the back of the head, killing him instantly.

Pandemonium erupted. Shouts and bullets sounded everywhere. Crow Foot was killed. Cued by the gunshots, Sitting Bull's trained horse, whom he had ridden in Buffalo Bill Cody's Wild West Show, started his trick routine; to him the bloodbath—in which 15 people died—was just one more show. But to the awestruck Indians it was as if Sitting Bull's spirit had entered the horse, who now danced to hasten the coming messiah.

The Heroic Men of Missouri

**TROOPS HERALDED FOR THEIR GREAT
(AND GRUELING) MARCH TO MEXICO**

They traveled 3,600 miles by land and 2,000 miles by water. They had no orders from Washington, no supplies, and no pay, so they lived off the land, fought with ammunition captured from the enemy, and left a trail of victories. That's what made this trek the greatest long march in U.S. military history.

The commander of the 1st Regiment of Missouri Mounted Volunteers was Colonel Alexander Doniphan. When the Mexican War broke out in 1846, he organized a force, mostly of spirited farm boys, and joined General Stephen Kearny's victorious expedition to New Mexico.

From Santa Fe, Doniphan prepared to join General J. E. Wool's men, who were headed south for Chihuahua, 600 miles away. Christmas found the volunteers 30 miles from El Paso at Brazito, where a Mexican force ambushed them and demanded surrender. Doniphan promptly attacked; in half an hour, the Mexicans fled.

Word reached Doniphan in El Paso that General Wool's orders had been changed; he was to join General Zachary Taylor. With no instructions from his superiors, Doniphan decided to continue on to Chihuahua. At Rio Sacramento (18 miles from their destination) his troops confronted a Mexican army of 4,000. Doniphan had fewer than 900 men, but they overran the fortifications, and the enemy scattered. When the tattered Missourians finally swarmed into Chihuahua, they looked more like bandits than the conquerors they were.

From Chihuahua, the men marched an amazing 700 miles to join General Taylor at Saltillo, where victory again was theirs. Continuing to the Rio Grande, they set sail, adding 2,000 water miles as they headed for New Orleans. There the men were greeted as heroes, fed well, paid for their exemplary service, and sent home. The Show-Me State gave them another rousing welcome, as cheering crowds, parades, and fireworks honored the incredible trek of these men from Missouri.

How the War Cry, "Remember the Alamo!" Came About

America didn't have the best luck against Mexico's Antonio López de Santa Anna in the siege on the Alamo that began on February 23, 1836. Under Colonel William Travis, Texans and American volunteers defended the fortress against Santa Anna's forces, but in the end, the Mexicans slaughtered all 189 Alamo defenders. The incident did inspire General Sam Houston's army a couple of months later, though; the small Alamo group had managed to kill more than 600 Mexicans. On April 21, Houston's army cried, "Remember the Alamo!" as they shattered the Mexican army at San Jacinto and won Texas's independence from Mexico.

Is it true that the Army once had an outfit of camels—and if so, why?

Yes. In 1855, U.S. Secretary of War Jefferson Davis (later president of the Confederacy) pushed through an appropriation of $30,000 for 32 Egyptian camels. The officer in charge was so impressed that he sent for more.

Lieutenant Edward Beale, a former naval officer, used 25 of the camels to survey a route from Fort Defiance, New Mexico, to eastern California, trailblazing part of what became the famous U.S. Highway 66. He, too, was impressed—the camels were strong and fast.

The camel project ended in 1863. The animals were auctioned, many of them ending up in circuses or carrying freight for mining companies. Others "escaped" into the wild and became legends. Among them was the Red Ghost, a camel that first appeared in the Arizona Territory in 1883, when he trampled a woman to death. Only later was the source of the animal's fear of people discovered: A human corpse was lashed to his back. The Red Ghost raged through Arizona for a decade, until he was shot.

Diplomat Nicholas Philip Trist masterminded the Treaty of Guadalupe Hidalgo, which called for Mexico to cede present-day Arizona, California, New Mexico, and parts of Colorado, Nevada, and Utah. In exchange, the United States would compensate Mexico $15 million for war-related damage to Mexican property.

A Long, Fast Ride

When 600 Mexican troops surrounded 50 Americans in Los Angeles in 1846, it was Juan Flaco who made the 500-mile dash for help on horseback. Carrying messages with Captain Archibald Gillespie's seal and the words "Believe the bearer," Flaco sped to Monterey to seek out Commodore Robert Stockton.

The journey was harrowing. At one point Flaco, whose first horse was shot out from under him, was forced to run 27 miles. Then, on another horse, he negotiated treacherous mountains and a rugged coastline. He reached Monterey in four days only to find that Stockton was anchored in San Francisco harbor. Flaco pressed on. Responding to the plea, Stockton dispatched his ship and its crew to southern California, but rough weather delayed the vessel.

Trist's Treaty

PRESIDENT POLK FIRES DIPLOMAT WHO WINS WEST FOR UNITED STATES

Nicholas P. Trist negotiated the treaty that ended the Mexican War and added California, Nevada, Arizona, New Mexico, Utah, and parts of Colorado and Wyoming to America's expanding territory, finally stretching the nation from sea to sea. It was the most bizarre diplomatic achievement in U.S. history. And it ruined his life.

Trist arrived in Mexico in May 1847 as a special envoy from President James K. Polk. His job was to offer the Mexicans, who were being badly beaten, terms for surrender. But blunders and bickering led to confusion. Polk lost faith in his emissary and in October had him recalled.

Defying the president's order, Trist stayed on and continued his negotiations without official authority. He was finally making progress. By January 25, 1848, he had an agreement: Mexico would accept

$15 million for the land it ceded to the United States. The Treaty of Guadalupe Hidalgo was signed a week later, and in the spring the Senate approved it. But Polk remained furious about Trist's insubordination and fired him.

The diplomat spent much of the rest of his life working not in politics, but as a menial railroad clerk. It was not until 1870, 23 years after his success in Mexico, that he was officially recognized for his achievement. By then, of course, the West was a thriving part of the United States, due largely to the discovery of gold in California on January 24, 1848—just one day before Trist had persuaded the Mexicans to sell the territory.

IMPROBABLE PIONEER

William Walker: The Only Native-Born American to Become President of Another Country

In 1855, a 31-year-old adventurer named William Walker was hired by an American investor to provide Nicaragua with a mercenary army. Walker landed in Nicaragua on June 16, 1855, at the head of a tough band of 58 fighting men drawn from daredevils and soldiers-for-hire. They called themselves the Immortals.

The country they found was in revolution; there had been 15 presidents in six years. The Nicaraguans quickly realized that Walker was a dangerous man. In less than five months, Walker's mercenaries captured the enemy faction's capital of Granada. From that point, Walker was the power in Nicaragua. The newspaper he founded touted the 120-pound man as "the gray-eyed man of destiny," foretold by Indian legends, who would lead the nation. After ruling through a puppet government, he took the oath as president on July 12, 1856, and remained president until

General William Walker, the former president of Nicaragua, with a priest before being executed in 1860.

May 1, 1857, when he was sent back to the United States.

Continuing to claim the presidency of Nicaragua, Walker tried several times to return. He was executed in Honduras in September 1860. To this day he is remembered by Latin Americans as a hated symbol of Yankee imperialism.

Bleeding Kansas

BATTLES AND BLOODSHED
FORESHADOW THE CIVIL WAR

For Senator Stephen A. Douglas, slavery was nothing to get excited about. What really excited him was his plan to organize the sprawling Nebraska Territory so that a railroad could be built through it from Chicago to the Pacific. And if, in so doing, he upset the razor-thin balance between the nation's pro- and anti-slavery forces, he could ride out the storm. It would blow over in time, he was sure. He was tragically mistaken.

Southerners in Congress, fearing a new Northern state, had defeated every bill to organize the territory, in which slavery was barred by the long-revered Missouri Compromise. To win them over, Douglas proposed dividing the territory into Kansas and Nebraska and letting the settlers of each decide upon the issue of slavery or freedom. His Kansas-Nebraska Act of 1854 repealed the Missouri Compromise. And the storm it brewed not only wrecked Douglas's chances of ever becoming president, but also pushed the nation a bloody step toward civil war.

Determined to control Kansas, pro-slavers poured in to build the towns of Leavenworth and Atchison. Free-staters challenged them by founding Lawrence and Topeka. Guerrilla warfare flashed across the land, fueled by such supporters as the abolitionist minister Henry Ward Beecher, whose Brooklyn congregation sent crates of Sharps rifles marked "Farming Implements." (The weapons were soon known as "Beecher's Bibles.") Livestock was stolen or slaughtered, crops and homes were burned, and captives were shot dead.

In a year's time, at least 200 people were killed, and many more were wounded. Raiders from Missouri gutted Lawrence in 1856; John Brown and his followers struck back by murdering five pro-slavers at Pottawatomie, Kansas. One abolitionist minister,

TRUTH OR RUMOR?

Is it true that the song "John Brown's Body" was about the infamous abolitionist?

No. John Brown (right) had "a little touch of insanity about his glittering gray-blue eyes," and he hacked five pro-slavers to death in Kansas. He seized a federal arsenal at Harpers Ferry, Virginia, in 1859, taking George Washington's great-grandnephew hostage. Robert E. Lee captured him. Stonewall Jackson and John Wilkes Booth watched him hang. But, oddly enough, the song "John Brown's Body" had nothing to do with him: The men of a Massachusetts volunteer regiment first sang it in 1861, to taunt a messmate named Sergeant John Brown.

facing a noose for his views, was spared when a pro-slaver argued that the cause would be sullied by hanging a man of the cloth. He was tarred and feathered instead.

When an election was called to choose a territorial legislature, Senator David Rice Atchison of Missouri sent hundreds of pro-slavers into Kansas to intimidate voters and stuff ballot boxes for "a dollar a day and free whiskey." Their side won and wrote a constitution in 1857. It was voted down in an 1858 referendum. The next year, another convention adopted a new constitution flatly barring slavery; in 1861, after 11 Southern states had seceded from the Union, a free Kansas became the 34th state.

History will long remember its violent beginnings as Bleeding Kansas—the first unofficial battlefield of the Civil War.

The first shots of the Civil War broke out at Fort Sumter, in Charleston, South Carolina, on April 12, 1861.

Sunrise at Fort Sumter

SOUTH CAROLINA SEES THE FIRST SHOT OF THE CIVIL WAR

Early in 1861, all eyes were on Charleston, South Carolina, where the Civil War was sure to begin—if it was to begin at all.

U.S. troops held the "impregnable" Fort Sumter, at the entrance to Charleston Harbor. The Confederacy, deeming them a foreign force, wanted them out. President Abraham Lincoln promised to "hold, occupy, and possess" the fort no matter what. But if it came to war, he was determined that the United States not fire the first shot.

"Under no circumstances," Confederacy President Jefferson Davis wired General P. G. T. Beauregard, "are you to allow provisions to be sent to Fort Sumter." On April 10, another wire ordered the general to ensure the fort's evacuation or "reduce it."

At 4:30 a.m. on April 12, Lieutenant Henry S. Farley lobbed a signal shell that burst 100 feet above the fort, and firing on the fort began. In his diary, Edmund Ruffin wrote that "by order of General Beauregard" he'd been given the "compliment" of firing the first shot. Ruffin was an ardent secessionist whose teachings on crop rotation had virtually saved the Southern economy decades before. Not until 7 a.m. did Captain Abner Doubleday order a reply. The first Union shot "bounded off the sloping roof of the battery opposite without producing any apparent effect," he later recalled.

Ruffin survived the war but, mourning the demise of his beloved South, committed suicide on June 18, 1865. Doubleday, who lived until 1893, mentioned Fort Sumter in his memoirs but made no reference to ever having invented the game of baseball.

A Skirmish on San Juan Island

BRITAIN AND AMERICA ALMOST COME TO BLOWS OVER A DEAD PIG

According to the Oregon Treaty of 1846, the strait between Vancouver Island and the mainland was the boundary between British and American territories. But there were two straits, and San Juan Island was between them. Britain and America both claimed it, and settlers from each country took up residence.

When America tried to tax British produce, farmer Charles John Griffin refused to pay, insisting that he was not subject to American taxation. Then in 1859 one of his pigs got loose and began rooting around in the potato patch of American Lyman Cutlar, who promptly shot it. Livid, Griffin went to the local British magistrate, demanding a payment of $100 for the pig. Cutlar refused to pay, insisting that he was not subject to British law. Tempers flared.

Americans petitioned their government for protection. Soon Captain George Pickett—later to lead a famous charge at Gettysburg—arrived with troops. British Columbia sent warships to rout them. But each side waited for the other to fire the first shot. Finally, General Winfield Scott came from Washington to propose that the standoff be institutionalized: Each country would station 100 men on San Juan Island until an accord could be reached. The British accepted.

Meanwhile the Civil War occurred, and it was 12 years before the matter was submitted to German emperor Wilhelm I for binding arbitration. He ruled in favor of America in 1872.

Lincoln's General Problems

THE PRESIDENT HAS A TOUGH TIME ROUNDING UP A UNION LEADER

When Abraham Lincoln became president, one of his greatest challenges in preserving the Union was finding a general competent enough to take control of it. His only authentic military star at the onset of war was 75-year-old General Winfield Scott, hero of the War of 1812 and the Mexican War, who became the first commander of the Union Army. Declining health and old age forced the diligent general into retirement within months.

LEE'S CRISIS OF CONSCIENCE

Before the war broke out, General Scott reportedly pleaded with Lieutenant Colonel Robert E. Lee not to join the secession. Scott hinted that Lee, while nominally serving under him, would in fact

> One Union general, Fighting Joe Hooker, was infamous for his bizarre attitudes and behavior. Allegedly, his camp was so filled with prostitutes that the ladies acquired a new name: "hookers."

command the Union armies in the field, since Scott himself was too old. Soon the offer was official. But Lee declined, not because he supported slavery, but because of loyalty to Virginia, whose history had been shaped by his ancestors for generations.

When Lee informed Scott of his decision, the aged general remarked, "Lee, you have made the greatest mistake of your life; but I feared it would be so." Virginia officially proposed secession on April 17, 1861. On the 20th, Lee resigned from the U.S. Army. Three days later he was named commander of Virginia's armed forces.

McCLELLAN'S CIGARS

From there the Union course was downhill. General George McClellan, who virtually built the Union

Army from scratch, saw himself as a young Napoleon and referred to Lincoln as "the Gorilla." Despite his arrogance, McClellan, and most other Union generals, suffered from what Lincoln called "the slows."

In September 1862, Lee invaded Maryland and split his army into two sections to secure his supply routes. McClellan is said to have received advance word of Lee's plans when a Union soldier in Frederick, Maryland, stooped to pick up three Virginia cigars that had dropped in the street. The cigars were wrapped in a copy of the Southern general's orders to his field commanders. McClellan was ecstatic; his larger army now had a perfect opportunity to surprise and overwhelm the divided Confederate troops. But McClellan's advance was so slow that

Lee was able to regroup his army at Antietam. The battle there, on September 17, was one of the bloodiest of the war. Although McClellan reported it as a great victory, it is often cited as one of his major blunders. He outnumbered Lee's force almost two-to-one; indecisiveness prevented him from destroying the Southern army and ending the war. Lee escaped with his forces intact as McClellan found excuses to delay pursuit.

GARIBALDI'S TERMS

The paucity of Northern leadership had been apparent from the beginning. It drove Lincoln to attempt to enlist Giuseppe Garibaldi, the hero of Italian unification, as early as 1861. But talks broke down when Garibaldi, who had fought against slavery in South America, wanted a promise that American slaves would be freed. Even well into the war, Lincoln doubted that he could make this commitment and still preserve the Union.

The president's problem would continue until Lieutenant General Ulysses S. Grant forcefully took control of both the army and the war in March 1864.

Battle of the Bands

MUSICIANS KEEP UNION AND CONFEDERATE SOLDIERS' EMOTIONS HIGH

Requisite for a good battle in the Civil War were opposing soldiers, sufficient weapons, and at least two brass bands. During nearly every major battle, music urged the troops onward, and military units hotly competed for talented musicians. At Fort Sumter, a Federal band mournfully accompanied the surrender. Selections from *Il Trovatore* were stirringly played at Shiloh by a band stationed right at the front. During the Battle of Gettysburg, the musical aggregations of the 11th and 26th North Carolina regiments got so loud they were shot at by irked Union soldiers.

By the summer of 1862, there were an estimated 618 bands in the service of the Union, at a cost of $4 million. This averaged out to one musician for every 41 soldiers. The underfunded Confederacy had fewer and smaller musical ensembles. The 2nd Virginia Regiment, however, did manage to form a band with instruments taken from a New York unit after a battle.

During the siege of Atlanta, a Georgia cornet player gave suppertime concerts at the front. One night the fighting was so heavy he didn't show up, and there was a flood of protest from angry Northern soldiers who had looked forward to his performance. A short ceasefire was worked out so that the cornetist's melodies could drift through the evening. After each selection, both sides applauded wildly. But as soon as his concert had ended, the bloody shooting resumed.

Stonewall Jackson's Two Graves

THE DISTINGUISHED GENERAL WAS SHOT BY HIS OWN MEN

Thomas Jonathan Jackson had been a professor of philosophy and artillery tactics at Virginia Military Institute in 1861. As a Confederate officer in the Civil War, he practiced what he preached.

Jackson distinguished himself early in the war. At the First Battle of Bull Run, in July 1861, Union troops had shattered the Confederate line until the men under his command shored the breach. "See, there is Jackson standing like a stone wall!" cried General Bernard E. Bee. Bee soon fell in the fighting, but the nickname stuck to Jackson.

Stonewall Jackson's favorite meal? Raspberries, bread, and milk, oddly enough.

"Stonewall" Jackson's severe but inspiring military bearing may have been caused by a touch of hypochondria. Jackson never ate pepper, claiming it weakened his left leg; raspberries, bread, and milk were his preferred meal. He was comfortable only in a stiff, upright position, with his organs set "naturally"

Thaddeus Lowe: Hot Air Balloonist

At 3:30 a.m. on April 20, 1861, Thaddeus Lowe set out from Cincinnati on a test flight of his 20,000-cubic-foot balloon, *Enterprise*. After traveling at more than 100 miles per hour, he was deflected from his course by crosswinds. He landed in South Carolina, expecting a hero's welcome. But Fort Sumter had fallen just six days earlier, and Lowe was arrested as a Federal spy. Only after local professors vouched for his purely scientific interests was he released. The audacious aeronaut simply hadn't realized how close America was to civil war. Lowe later became leader of the Aeronautic Corps of the Army of the Potomac, a group composed primarily of civilian balloonists who made reconnaissance missions from moored balloons, so that the aeronauts could direct ground artillery and transmit information about enemy troop movements.

Stonewall Jackson, left, was wounded during the battle of Chancellorsville, Virginia (above). The battle took place on May 2, 1863; he died of pneumonia a week later.

on top of each other. In this erect posture astride his mount, one arm outstretched, he led his men to combat.

Jackson took a bullet in his upraised hand at Bull Run. His doctor insisted that an injured finger be amputated, but as he turned to fetch his instruments, the general got up and quickly rode away. It was one of the few times Jackson—who often exhorted his troops, "The Stonewall Brigade never retreats"—took to his heels himself.

Victory followed victory, until Jackson's greatest triumph turned out to be his last. In the spring of 1863, his troops soundly thrashed the Union forces of General Joseph Hooker at Chancellorsville, Virginia, forcing them into retreat. The next evening, as

Jackson returned from a risky scouting mission, he was fired upon by his own troops, who in the darkness were unaware of his identity. Two bullets shattered his left arm, and this time he could not escape the surgeon. The arm was immediately amputated. Jackson might have recovered had he not ordered a servant to place cold towels on his body to lower his fever. The general contracted pneumonia and died a week later.

The amputated arm was given its own formal military burial near Chancellorsville in a properly marked grave. The inscription reads simply: "Arm of Stonewall Jackson. May 3, 1863." The rest of the general is buried more than 100 miles away at Lexington, Virginia.

Heroines of Espionage

FEMALE SPIES SERVED UNION AND CONFEDERACY BRAVELY

The First Battle of Bull Run might not have been such a smashing Confederate victory without the flowing curls of a blushing Southern belle. On July 9, 1861, Rose Greenhow hid a ciphered message in the tresses of one of her lovely couriers. When the girl combed out her hair for Rebel officers, they learned that Union troops were about to march on Richmond. A second message, a week later, contained the invaders' exact strength and marching orders.

"WITHIN RIFLE RANGE OF THE WHITE HOUSE"

The victorious Confederate general, P. G. T. Beauregard, later noted with pride that the woman who provided this crucial intelligence "lived in a house within rifle range of the White House." That house on 16th Street became the heart of a Rebel spy network as Greenhow took full advantage of her position as one of Washington's most alluring hostesses. At the height of her activities, she directed more than 50 agents—48 of them women—who worked in five states, including far-off Texas. Many an official panicked when detective Allan Pinkerton arrested her for espionage in August 1861.

Even while jailed, Greenhow somehow smuggled secrets about the Union Army to Richmond. A loyal southerner to the end, she died while trying to run a Federal blockade off the North Carolina coast in 1864.

CRAZY BET

Greenhow may have lived near the White House, but Union spy Elizabeth Van Lew was even more daring—she placed a servant right in the home of Jefferson Davis, the president of the Confederacy. Although Van Lew came from one of Richmond's wealthiest families, her Northern schooling had made her a fervent abolitionist. Dressing in rags and feigning madness, she visited captured Union soldiers at

Confederate spy Rose Greenhow (right) with her daughter in the courtyard of Old Capitol Prison in Washington, D.C.

Libby Prison to gather and disperse information. Neighbors in the Confederate capital dismissed her as Crazy Bet. But, as she said, "It helps me in my work."

Van Lew was anything but crazy. Not only did she provide military intelligence, she also hid Union soldiers who had escaped from Confederate prisons in a secret room in her house. Once she even masterminded a scheme to smuggle the corpse of a Union officer through Confederate lines to get him a decent burial.

More prudent than Greenhow, Van Lew was a Union agent in the heart of Dixie during the entire war. As Richmond fell, she raised the first Stars and Stripes over the city. Later, General Ulysses S. Grant visited her personally; he considered Crazy Bet one of his most valuable spies.

THE JOAN OF ARC OF THE CONFEDERACY

Belle Boyd was only 17 years old on July 4, 1861, when Federal soldiers, drunk from celebrating, began looting houses and insulting residents in her home-town of Martinsburg (in present-day West Virginia). One tipsy soldier threatened to raise a Union flag over the Boyds' house. When Belle's mother protested, the soldier responded abusively, and Belle shot him dead.

Soon she was riding all over the Shenandoah Valley gathering information for the Confederacy. Her most daring exploit took place at Front Royal, Virginia, where she learned that retreating Yankee soldiers planned to burn the town's bridges as they fled. She dashed past Union pickets, dodging their rifle fire as she sped across the open field to General Stonewall Jackson and his attacking Southern troops. Jackson took the bridges before they could be destroyed.

Often arrested, Boyd was just as often released, sometimes in prisoner exchanges, until she became famous as the Joan of Arc of the Confederacy. On her last mission in 1864, she was carrying letters from Davis to agents in England when the blockade runner on which she traveled was seized by a Union warship. Once again her charm and spunk didn't fail her. The Yankee commander asked her to marry him. She was not yet 20 years old.

McLean's Real Estate

CIVIL WAR FOLLOWS GROCER WHEREVER HE GOES

Virginia grocer Wilmer McLean had a nose for history if not for real estate. During the First Battle of Bull Run, Confederate General P. G. T. Beauregard commandeered McLean's house for his headquarters. A Union cannonball crashed through the kitchen. A year later, after the Second Battle of Bull Run once more ravaged his land, McLean moved on.

He settled in a farmhouse in the backwater town of Appomattox Court House, Virginia. But the war followed him. On April 9, 1865, Robert E. Lee sent Colonel Charles Marshall to find an appropriate site for a conference with Ulysses S. Grant. The first person Marshall asked about possible places was McLean, who took him to a deserted house without furniture. Marshall rejected it. Sensing the inevitable, he offered his own home for the meeting.

The surrender, signed by Lee and Grant that afternoon in McLean's parlor, ended the war and ravaged McLean's home. General Edward O. C. Ord paid him $40 for the table at which Grant had sat, and another Union general got Lee's table for $25. McLean refused to sell the rest of his furniture, but souvenir hunters reduced the parlor to shambles.

The Northernmost Rebel Raid

HOW THE CIVIL WAR REACHED VERMONT

They swooped down out of Canada—20 cavalrymen organized by Confederate agent George Sanders and led by Lieutenant Bennett Young—and laid siege to St. Albans, Vermont. With his gun drawn, Young mounted the steps of a hotel and shouted: "This city is now in the possession of the Confederate States of America."

It was October 19, 1864, and the Civil War battlefields suddenly didn't seem so far from the village, which hugs the scenic Lake Champlain shoreline. The citizens of the tiny town near the Canadian border had become victims of a Rebel raid.

Shock and confusion followed as gun-toting horsemen galloped down Main Street, herding terrorized townfolk onto the village green. The raiders then turned their attention to robbing the local banks. Even though the Confederates dropped much of their loot in the confusion of escape, they still made off with about $200,000. As a final humiliation, they tried to burn down the town. But success eluded them; only a woodshed was destroyed by the flames.

It was as long as half an hour before St. Albans residents could organize a pursuit party, and by that time the Rebel-yelling marauders were well on their way back toward the Canadian border. The hit-and-run raid had lasted about 30 minutes.

TRUTH OR RUMOR?

Is it true that the Confederacy burned down New York City during the Civil War?

They tried. By November 1864, Southern troops were on the defensive everywhere. In a desperate attempt to force the North to negotiate, Confederate agents based in Canada devised a scheme to burn the entire city of New York. They struck the city on November 25.

Carrying small glass bombs of an incendiary fluid called Greek fire in a valise, agents would check into hotels, set their rooms ablaze, and leave. The city was soon in a panic. But the Greek fire didn't work very well, and the fire department acted quickly. Although flames broke out in 12 hotels, no serious damage was done. Two arsonists were captured, including Captain Robert Cobb Kennedy, who became the last Confederate soldier to be hanged before the Civil War ended.

Victories at Sea

THE CIVIL WAR TAKES TO THE WATER

Skeptics called it "Ericsson's Folly" (after its stubborn Swedish inventor) or the "cheesebox on a raft." But its real name was the *Monitor*, for the large revolving gun turret, or monitor, atop its flat deck. It was the Union's representative in the world's first battle between iron-clad warships.

The Confederacy had rescued the Union frigate *Merrimack* from the bottom of a Norfolk harbor and plated it with iron to serve as a ram. It was rechristened the *Virginia*, but the old name stuck. When the two met head-on it was the beginning of the end for the proud reign of wooden warships.

CLANGOROUS CONFRONTATION

On March 8, 1862, the *Merrimack* sank one Union sloop and crippled a frigate, part of a blockading squadron at Hampton Roads, Virginia. But when it returned on March 9 to finish the job, the ship's captain was astonished to see the Yankee cheesebox come at him out of the mist. A four-hour slugging match ensued.

Like two boxers, the ships circled each other. The *Monitor*'s turret was hard to control, so its crew just let it revolve; but then messengers had to tell the gunners if they'd hit anything. As shot upon shot bounced noisily off iron plating, the metal monsters bumped at least five times.

When the *Monitor* backed off because its captain was blinded by a powder burst, the *Merrimack*'s captain apparently thought his adversary was retreating. His ship had sprung a leak anyway, so he left. Both sides claimed victory.

FAR-RANGING FIGHTER

Not all sea combat took place close to home. In 1865, a Confederate captain sailed his armored clipper ship on a mission all the way to the Pacific Ocean.

The *Shenandoah*'s assignment was to cripple the Northern economy by attacking whaling ships.

> Four months after the end of the Civil War, Waddell asked a passing British ship for news of the war. "What war?" was the reply.

The vessel reached Australia, then headed north, with Captain James Waddell and his crew burning or scuttling ships as they went. The startled skipper of one whaler, brandishing a newspaper account of the surrender at Appomattox Court House, told Waddell that the war was over. Undeterred, the captain fought on. In the ice-clogged Bering Strait off the coast of Siberia, he came upon a cluster of American whalers. He burned eight of them.

A full four months after the surrender, Waddell asked a passing British ship for news of the war. "What war?" came the reply. Convinced at last, the Confederate raider set sail for England.

In its 13-month, 60,000-mile, globe-circling trip, the *Shenandoah* had seized 38 ships. And the shot that it had fired at the whalers in the Bering Strait was the last one of the Civil War.

The Union vessel, *Monitor,* and the Confederate frigate, *Merrimack,* face off at Hampton Roads in Virginia.

Saluting Those Who Surrendered

GALLANT UNION LEADER PAYS HOMAGE TO CONFEDERACY

On the morning of April 12, 1865—exactly four years after the Civil War had begun at Fort Sumter—Major General John Gordon paraded his men down the main street of Appomattox Court House. Robert E. Lee had chosen him, because of his unswerving valor, to lead his brigade first to the the formal surrender of the Army of Northern Virginia.

Union soldiers lined the street, commanded by Major General Joshua Chamberlain. As the Confederate troops came abreast, Chamberlain, in an unheard-of show of respect, ordered his men to salute. At first Gordon was too dejected to be aware of the tribute; but when he heard the Union troops shifting their guns, he responded in kind. Wheeling to face Chamberlain, he spurred his horse to its hind legs, raised his sword, and lowered it to his toe. Then, head held high, he ordered his men to return the Union salute. In silence, Americans who had fought and suffered bitterly now honored each other's courage.

Historical artist Mort Künstler's *Salute of Honor* depicts the Union's show of respect for the Confederate soldiers on April 12, 1865.

After the war, Chamberlain, who was awarded the Medal of Honor for his heroism at Gettysburg, was elected governor of Maine. He later became president of Bowdoin College. For the rest of his life, he carried a souvenir of the Civil War—a silver tube in his abdomen to drain a wound that never healed and eventually killed him.

TRUTH OR RUMOR?

Is it true that Jefferson Davis wore his wife's dress to elude Union troops during the Civil War?

Though a May 1865 report in the *New York Herald* claimed that Jefferson had "slipped into his wife's petticoats, crinoline, and dress, but in his hurry he forgot to put on her stockings and shoes," it's simply not true. When Davis tried to escape an attack one evening in Georgia, it is true that he grabbed his wife's cloak by mistake instead of his own; she threw a shawl over his shoulders. When the War Department asked that Davis's "dress" be turned over, the only items received were the cloak and shawl. They were locked away in an office safe, where they stayed until 1945.

Wagging the Dog

HEARST STARTS HIS OWN WAR AND SELLS MORE NEWSPAPERS

They say that soon after illustrator Frederic Remington arrived in Cuba to cover the revolution against Spain for the *New York Journal,* he asked to return home because there was no war. But his boss, press lord William Randolph Hearst (below), fired off a message: "Please remain," he wired. "You furnish the pictures; I'll furnish the war."

The story may be apocryphal, but it could have happened. Hearst needed a war in the worst way. He was embroiled in a circulation battle with Joseph Pulitzer's *New York World,* and he knew that there was nothing like a war to grab the readers' attention.

The only problem was getting hostilities cranked up. A tiny band of Cubans were in rebellion against the autocratic Spanish rule, but the "unkempt mob of brave but disorganized bushwhackers" (according to one Hearst biographer) didn't stand a chance unless they could get American troops to do their fighting for them. This was where Hearst cheerfully stepped in, printing any item of rebel propaganda as gospel truth.

Getting caught by the truth was merely a temporary setback for Hearst. When Evangelina Cosio y Cisneros was arrested for trying to help her rebel father break out of jail, Hearst's imaginative reporters claimed that her only crime had been defending her chastity against a lustful Spanish colonel. "We've got Spain now," Hearst boasted. He managed to have "the Cuban Joan of Arc" liberated in a dramatic prison break, then brought her to New York for a tumultuous heroine's welcome and a new round of hysterical headlines.

The deception was so great that Spain began to fear America's newspapers more than its government. Unable to stand up to the more powerful nation, Spain did everything to soothe the situation, even granting autonomy to Cuba.

Then on February 15, 1898, the U.S. battleship *Maine* blew up in Havana harbor (from causes unknown to this day), and Hearst finally got his war. "THE WHOLE COUNTRY THRILLS WITH WAR FEVER," the *Journal* declared on February 18, blaming the explosion on Spain. Hearst even offered readers a card game called "War with Spain."

President McKinley opposed the war—according to Teddy Roosevelt, he had "no more backbone than a chocolate eclair"—but was swept along and asked Congress to declare war on Spain. And Hearst wouldn't let anybody forget who had started it all. "HOW DO YOU LIKE THE JOURNAL'S WAR?" a headline immodestly asked.

"You furnish the pictures;
I'll furnish the war."
—WILLIAM RANDOLPH HEARST

Teddy Roosevelt and his Rough Riders in 1898, after capturing Cuba's San Juan Hill.

The Hero of Kettle Hill

WHY ROOSEVELT NEVER GOT HIS MEDAL

In the sweltering Cuban heat of July 1898, Lieutenant Colonel Theodore Roosevelt, commander of a volunteer cavalry regiment called the Rough Riders, was ready for the most crucial battle of the Spanish-American War: the attack on heavily fortified San Juan Heights. But the orders never arrived. Illness had intervened, and while the American chain of command stumbled, Roosevelt fumed.

It was bad enough his cavalrymen had to fight on foot, for all horses except officers' mounts had been ordered left in Florida. Now, as they moved to the right of the attack line and waited, they found a hill laced with Spanish gunmen who cut them to shreds with deadly accurate rifle fire.

Finally, Roosevelt advanced his troops to the foot of the hill (called Kettle Hill, for a huge caldron on top that was used to process sugar cane). There he encountered elements of the 9th U.S. Cavalry (Colored) and ordered their white captain to charge the hill. When the officer refused, questioning Roosevelt's authority to give such a command, the future president bellowed: "Then let my men through!"

The African American soldiers, despite their officer, stood up against the killing fusillade, flattened a barbed wire fence with their bodies, and joined in the heroic charge. Astride his horse Little Texas, Roosevelt ignored the bullets that flew past with a sound "like the ripping of a silk dress."

They took the hill and, seeing that the main attack had begun on San Juan Hill some 700 yards away, set up a fusillade of their own against the defending Spaniards. Then Roosevelt decided to join the attack but forgot to order his men to follow. Finding himself almost alone partway down the far slope of Kettle Hill, he ran back, yelled, "Forward, march!" and made it to the top of San Juan Hill in time to participate in the final victory.

Roosevelt was recommended for the Medal of Honor, but because of politics, he never got it. At the end of the three-month war, the Americans who remained in Cuba were being decimated by malaria, but Secretary of War Russell Alger failed to move them to a healthier climate. Roosevelt and other senior officers sent a letter to the press describing the emergency. The outcry was a factor in Alger's forced resignation, and there is evidence that before leaving office Alger saw to it that Roosevelt's medal would be denied. Roosevelt was crushed.

During Teddy Roosevelt's presidency, an act was passed listing the rules that make the Medal of Honor a true symbol of heroism. And it was his cousin, Franklin Delano Roosevelt, who bestowed the medal posthumously on Theodore Roosevelt Jr. during World War II.

Panama Gets Out from Under Colombia

U.S. ENCOURAGES INSURRECTION TO HASTEN BUILDING OF CANAL

The Spanish–American War left the United States with new territories to protect in the Pacific and the Caribbean. Such responsibilities made President Theodore Roosevelt eager to build a canal across the narrow Isthmus of Panama, thereby providing a shortcut between the Atlantic Ocean and Pacific Ocean.

Standing in the way was Colombia, which owned Panama and was reluctant to give up any of its territory. U.S. and Colombian officials negotiated a long-term treaty that would have allowed the United States to lease a 10-mile-wide strip of land across Panama in return for a fee of $10 million, plus annual payments of $250,000. The Colombian senate refused to ratify the treaty. By the summer of 1903, all hope for the canal seemed lost.

Meanwhile, behind the scenes, plans were being hatched for a Panamanian revolt against Colombia. A major instigator was Philippe Bunau-Varilla, a former director of a French company that had earlier tried without success to build a Panama canal. Although Panamanian businessmen supported the insurrection, it probably would never have occurred without the tacit approval of the United States, which sent three naval vessels to the area with instructions to land troops if necessary. The revolution came on November 3, 1903. Discouraged by the American presence on land and sea, Colombia made little effort to regain control. Three days later, the United States recognized the new Republic of Panama.

"Shoot Him Again, Tougher"

HOW PANCHO VILLA HELD UP HOLLYWOOD

Mexican bandit and revolutionary Pancho Villa became the Robin Hood of his country when his well-armed men defeated Mexico's federal troops in 1913. But perhaps his greatest scheme for robbing the rich to pay the poor was the deal he cut with a Hollywood studio to star in a movie about his exploits.

On January 3, 1914, Villa signed a contract with the Mutual Film Corporation giving him a $25,000 advance and 50 percent of all profits. In return, if Villa was victorious in a battle, Mutual would own the right to show the film of the fighting in the areas his troops had conquered and throughout the United States and Canada. Camera crews were invited to join Villa's army as it swept across Mexico, and the fiery revolutionary agreed to stage his raids during daylight hours to facilitate filming. In fact, the contract even required Villa to reenact battles for the cameramen if the footage they had shot wasn't sufficiently "realistic."

Top: Pancho Villa with his troops in 1914, the same year in which the bandit inked a Hollywood deal. The general, above, was required by his film contract to reshoot battle scenes when the studio deemed it necessary.

The resulting film, *The Life of General Villa*, was a military voyeur's delight. On May 5, 1914, a critic from the *New York World* stated: "There is thunder and gore from beginning to end. Marvelous pictures of the fighting at Torreón are woven clearly into the drama of Villa's life.... The whole is so realistic that it is almost as good as being on the scene, and far much safer."

Minister Without Portfolio

THE CASE OF THE SPY ON THE NEW YORK SUBWAY

World War I was raging in Europe, but the United States was keeping its distance. Even after 124 Americans went down with the torpedoed *Lusitania* in May 1915, isolationist sentiment remained strong. An absentminded German spy master helped change that.

Heinrich Albert, officially a commercial attaché at the German Embassy, kept meticulous records on his highly sophisticated espionage ring, operating all across America. And these details were in his briefcase when he boarded the Sixth Avenue subway in New York City on July 24, 1915. But he forgot his precious cargo on the train, and Secret Service Agent Frank Burke, who was tailing him, pounced on it, ran off the train, and dashed down to the street. With Albert in hot pursuit, Burke hopped on a streetcar and told the conductor that he was being chased by a madman. To avoid a scene, the motorman bypassed the next stop leaving the panting, half-crazed German stranded.

In Albert's briefcase, officials found schemes for buying all of America's chlorine (used in poison gas) and toluol (for TNT) to prevent their sale to Britain and France. But in their most enterprising plot, the Germans had set up a munitions factory, planning to take huge orders from Britain and France and never to deliver them. They also hoped to buy so much incendiary powder that it would be impossible for other companies to fill orders.

U.S. authorities made the skulduggery public (without admitting the briefcase theft) by leaking the story to the *New York World* on the promise that the paper would not reveal its source. The ensuing hue and cry helped persuade Americans that Germany was a menace. And the escapade gave Albert a new title; he became known as Minister without Portfolio.

Allen Dulles's Date

YOUNG CIA AGENT REFUSES RENDEZVOUS
WITH LENIN BECAUSE HE HAD BIGGER PLANS

Allen Dulles was looking forward to the night of April 11, 1917, because he had a date with Helene Herzog, whom he'd been wild about since he was 15 years old, when he studied French with her family. Herzog had spurned his schoolboy advances. But now he was 24, World War I was raging, and he worked in the American legation in Berne, Switzerland. He figured his chances were better.

Although the office was closed, Dulles was working late that afternoon when the phone rang. His heart sank. The caller was a Russian revolutionary living in exile in Switzerland. He declared that he was coming to Berne with important information

After becoming head of the CIA, Dulles repeated the surprising story as a warning to new agents.

and needed to talk with someone in the American legation immediately.

Since nobody else was around, that meant Dulles. But Dulles had a date, so he told his caller that he would have to come by the next morning. The man was adamant that tomorrow would be too late, and Dulles was just as adamant about Herzog.

History doesn't tell us how the date went, but it does record that later that evening Vladimir Ilyich Lenin boarded a train in Switzerland and was allowed passage across Germany to Sweden. Within days he was in Moscow, the revolution had started, and Russia was pulling out of the war with Germany, abandoning the Allied cause. Apparently, Lenin had been trying to alert President Woodrow Wilson to the scheme in advance. But Wilson learned the news with the rest of the world, all because Dulles had a date.

Breaking the Code

A CRUCIAL CABLE FANS THE WINDS OF WAR

It was not on the field of battle that the Germans committed their worst blunder during World War I. The site was, instead, a Western Union telegraph office.

In 1917, Germany's submarine fleet was capable of cutting Britain's lifeline of shipping from Canada and the United States, which supplied oil, food, and raw materials. The only hope for the British seemed to lie with the United States entering the war on the side of the Allies; but President Woodrow Wilson refused to abandon his neutral position, declaring that to enter the war would be a "crime against civilization." His stand led Germany to resume submarine warfare against all vessels bound for Britain.

Even so, on January 16, German foreign secretary Arthur Zimmermann sent an odd cable to his minister in Washington, by way of the U.S. diplomatic line—which Wilson allowed Germany to use to send peace proposals to Britain. Western Union relayed the message to the German legation in Mexico, and from there it was delivered to Mexico's president.

The carefully coded message proposed that if U.S. neutrality could not be maintained, Mexico should enter the war on the side of Germany in exchange for "generous financial support" and reclamation of "lost territory" in the Southwest. To make sure the message got through, it was also sent by wireless and through a Swedish diplomatic channel.

Favoritism from Uncle Sam: A circa-1917 Navy recruiting poster tries to hurry would-be soldiers to enlist.

Indomitable as ever, British intelligence intercepted all three messages and broke the "unbreakable" German code. One problem remained: how to use the information without revealing the decoding. First the British waited to see if renewed submarine warfare would push Wilson into the war.

It didn't. Finally, they gave him the message with the cover story that one of their spies had stolen it from the Germans in Mexico.

Wilson was livid; Germany had used America's own cable against it. But many citizens believed the message was fake. How could its authenticity be proven without jeopardizing the code breakers?

Remarkably, Western Union resolved the dilemma. Breaking its own rules, it released a copy of the telegram. Zimmermann then admitted sending it. With America itself a target, all chances for neutrality were gone, and on April 6 the United States entered the war.

This 1929 portrait shows the survivors of the "lost battalion," the 77th Division A.E.F., which was commanded by Major Charles Whittlesey. The soldiers were cut off by German forces in the Argonne Forest in October 1918; they defended themselves until they were rescued five days later.

The Lost Battalion

DOOMED HEROES IN A BLEAK AND BRUTAL WAR

Neither lost nor a battalion, they were 550 stalwart soldiers, the tattered remnants of New York's famed 77th "Statue of Liberty" Division, fighting their way through France. Commanding them was a bespectacled Wall Street lawyer, Major Charles Whittlesey, who won the Medal of Honor for his deeds.

When Allied forces began the 1918 drive that would end World War I, the 77th faced the Argonne Forest, a formidable German stronghold. Whittlesey's exhausted troops had been fighting steadily for weeks; nonetheless, General John J. "Black Jack" Pershing ordered the Americans to advance "without regard of losses." When the major's protest was refused, he responded: "I'll attack, but whether you'll hear from me again, I don't know."

SURROUNDED BY THE ENEMY

On October 2, Whittlesey led his men through a steep ravine dotted with enemy gunners. Withering fire came from the left side, but the troops made it up and over the right side of the ravine. They reached the high ground easily, but they were alone. Certain that the group was spearheading a massive attack, the Germans rushed reinforcements into the area, and the major and his men were cut off. A few carrier pigeons brought along in a cage were their only means of communication. Of the four companies sent as Allied reinforcements, just one got through. "Our mission is to hold this position at all costs," the steadfast Whittlesey told his men. "No falling back."

A third of the force became casualties of an attack the next day, and there was neither food nor medical supplies. On October 4, a misguided Allied artillery barrage hit Whittlesey's men. The major wrote a message pinpointing their position and pleading: "For heaven's sake, stop it." His last pigeon, Cher Ami, flew through enemy fire to deliver it, and two hours later the shelling stopped. After an airlift failed (the hungry men watched supplies fall behind

German lines), the "Lost Battalion" became nation-wide news. Embarrassed, General Pershing ordered a rescue effort. It, too, failed.

Although Whittlesey's force was too weak to bury its dead, when the Germans suggested surrender, the major didn't even reply. Not until five harrowing days had passed did relief get through. Only 194 Americans survived the living nightmare.

Three years later, the highly decorated Whittlesey also became a casualty. Unable to come to terms with the disparity between his celebrity and the ordeal of his men, he committed suicide.

Premature Peace

REPORTS OF WAR'S END A HOAX, CAUSING GREAT HUMILIATION FOR NEWSPAPER PUBLISHER

Just before noon on November 7, 1918, the New York headquarters of United Press received a cable from its president, Roy Howard. It read: "Urgent. Armistice allies Germans signed 11 smorning hostilities ceased two safternoon."

The news, which bannered the nation's midday papers, set off celebrations across America. Everywhere people poured into the streets, laughing and crying; in New York City, delirious crowds cheered one of the largest ticker-tape parades in history.

Howard was thrilled with his scoop. Through a series of coincidences, he had gotten the armistice report from none other than the American naval commander in French waters, Admiral Henry B. Wilson. Rushing to the offices of a Brest newspaper and using its machinery, he had managed to slip his wire past French censorship and through to UP headquarters in New York. At the same time, Admiral Wilson had released the joyous news in Brest.

That evening, Howard went with a few friends to a bar in town to celebrate. In the midst of the uproar a coded message was quietly delivered to an officer in his party. Deciphering it, he handed it to Howard: "Armistice report untrue. War Ministry issues absolute denial and declares enemy plenipotentiaries to be still on way through lines.... Wire full details of local hoax immediately."

The celebration came to a halt, and Howard turned white. Clearly, he and the United Press were

How the Tomb of the Unknowns Came to Be

On October 22, 1921, four bodies were exhumed at four cemeteries in France, near sites where American soldiers were known to have fallen in the War to End All Wars.

Those selecting the remains had to make sure they were indeed Americans but were otherwise truly unidentifiable, with no clues as to name, rank, or service. For evidence they relied upon the location of the original burial, gunshot wounds, and fragments of uniform. The bodies were embalmed, placed in similar coffins, and taken to the city hall at Chalons-sur-Marne.

In a simple ceremony on the morning of October 24, Sergeant Edward S. Younger, a soldier decorated for heroism in the war, entered the chapel, circled the four caskets, and choosing at random placed a spray of white roses on the second from the right. The chosen soldier was interred at Arlington National Cemetery on Armistice Day. On his white marble tomb appears this inscription: "Here Rests in Honored Glory an American Soldier Known but to God."

doomed. Admiral Wilson exonerated him, however, by publicly taking the blame for the false news, apparently the work of German spies. Four days later, peace was officially declared.

The USS *Shaw* explodes during the December 7, 1941, attack on Pearl Harbor. Right: The Japanese attack makes headline news in the local Honolulu paper and in papers worldwide.

The Surprise at Pearl Harbor

DID THE JAPANESE GET STRATEGY IDEAS FROM A BRITISH BOOK PUBLISHED 15 YEARS BEFORE THE ATTACK?

The surprise attack on Pearl Harbor should not have been a surprise to U.S. military officials—at least, not if they had paid attention as the Japanese had to a book published in America in 1925. Its title? *The Great Pacific War*. Written by Hector C. Bywater, a British naval intelligence agent and military correspondent, it vividly foretold the strategy the Japanese would employ in a war against America.

The Japanese ambition, Bywater wrote, was to conquer China and Korea for raw materials. But to achieve its goal, Japan would first have to cripple American forces in the Pacific. Japan would do so in a series of precision strikes, Bywater said; he went on to predict that the war would begin with a devastating sneak air attack on U.S. naval forces. The first target, he thought, would be Manila Bay. He was wrong about the target but uncannily accurate otherwise.

Did the Japanese in fact use Bywater's book as a blueprint for their assault? At the time it was published, Isoroku Yamamoto, Japan's brilliant commander in World War II, was stationed in Washington, D.C., as naval attaché. Fluent in English, he could hardly have missed the book, which was featured on the front page of *The New York Times Book Review*.

Also, both *The Great Pacific War* and Bywater's 1921 study, *Sea Power in the Pacific*, were pirated in Japan and circulated among its officers. Years later Mitsuo Fuchida, a prominent Japanese military historian, admitted that when he attended the Japanese Naval War College in 1936, both works were studied.

By then students taking final exams at the Japanese naval academy were routinely asked: "How would you attack Pearl Harbor?" America may have helped answer that question, too! In 1932, war games conducted by Admiral Harry Yarnell in Hawaiian waters revealed Pearl Harbor's vulnerability to a surprise predawn aerial attack launched from aircraft carriers. The results of the games were widely publicized.

Yet to what extent, if any, Admiral Yamamoto was seriously influenced by Bywater is hard to say. Bywater had also predicted the ultimate destruction of the Imperial Navy and the bombing of Tokyo.

Sending the Wrong Message

AMERICANS RETALIATE AT MIDWAY

The Battle of Midway, the decisive turning point of World War II in the Pacific, would have been a disaster had it not been for Commander Joseph J. Rochefort Jr., who in 1940 had helped break the top Japanese naval code known as the JN-25.

Following the Pearl Harbor disaster, America anxiously wondered where and when the Japanese would strike again. (On December 7, 1941, knowledge of the code had done no good because the Japanese had maintained radio silence prior to the attack.) Then, in the spring of 1942, Rochefort's intelligence unit in Hawaii started picking up an unusual volume of coded radio traffic from the Japanese fleet. What they read was ominous. Admiral Isoroku Yamamoto was pulling together a huge fleet for an assault on a target

> "In attempting surprise," said Admiral Nimitz, "the Japanese were themselves surprised."

called "AF." It was believed the letters were coded map coordinates for Midway, but Admiral Chester Nimitz could take no chances. He had to be sure.

Rochefort proposed a ruse. He sent a coded message to Midway telling the Americans to return a bogus message, uncoded, that the island's water distillation system had broken down. The trick worked. A few days later the Japanese code reported that "AF" was short on water.

With this information, Nimitz rushed to position the U.S. fleet on the flank of the Japanese, who thought it was 1,300 miles away in Hawaii. When the Japanese launched their attack, they were dumbfounded by an American counterattack that sank four of their aircraft carriers and ended their ability to take the offensive. "In attempting surprise," said Nimitz, "the Japanese were themselves surprised."

Kamikaze Bats and Balloon Bombs

AMERICAN AND JAPANESE SECRET WEAPONS FIZZLE

A Pennsylvania dentist, Lytle S. Adams, was driving home from Carlsbad Caverns in New Mexico when he heard about the Pearl Harbor attack. Remembering the millions of bats in the caverns, Adams wondered why they couldn't be armed with tiny incendiary bombs. He sent his idea to President Franklin D. Roosevelt, who agreed to give it a shot. The army and the navy spent 27 months of research and $2 million on what came to be called Operation X-ray.

The plan was simple enough: Hundreds of thousands of bats would be captured and stored, asleep, in freezers. A one-ounce bomb would be attached to the loose skin on each one's chest. The bats were to be dropped from a plane over Japan in containers that would open at 1,000 feet. Startled, the bats would head for the nearest cracks and crevices of buildings and chew off the bombs, which would explode, shooting a two-foot-high flame into the air for eight minutes.

Early testing at an army air force base in California had mixed results: Some bats slept through free fall and dropped like rocks; others escaped and set the entire base on fire, including a general's car. The army then passed Operation X-ray on to the navy. But the project came to an abrupt halt in 1944, as the military worked on a bomb far more powerful than anything a bat could deliver.

CRANES AND SYMPATHY

Meanwhile, the Japanese were working on Operation Fu-Go, a plan to wreak havoc in America with balloons towing incendiary bombs. Made of rice paper and inflated with hydrogen, the balloons measured 33 feet in diameter. Toward the end of 1944, more than 300 of them sailed the jet stream across the Pacific to the West Coast.

In May 1945, one of the balloon bombs exploded in Oregon, killing a woman and five children on a picnic—the war's only casualties in continental America. In 1987, several of the Japanese women who had made that balloon sent notes of sympathy to the victims' families, along with 1,000 folded paper cranes, a Japanese symbol of peace.

IMPROBABLE PIONEER

Ernie Pyle: The GI's Reporter

During the World War II battle for Cherbourg, the crew of an American tank, hit by a German shell, scrambled to a nearby doorway for cover.

There they met a small, balding man with sad eyes who was also ducking bullets. They asked for his autograph.

That wasn't unusual. The man was Ernie Pyle, the GI's reporter. He shared the fears, the pain, and the suffering of the men "who do the dying." And in his column, which ran in 700 publications with a combined circulation of 14 million, he made sure that the folks back home knew exactly what their fighting men were going through.

Pyle, who described himself as a "talker to obscure people," took no notes for his stories except the names and addresses of the men with whom he spoke. By 1945, he was earning a six-figure income. But he couldn't desert the men whose stories needed telling, so he headed to the Pacific for the invasion of Okinawa. On April 18, hit by Japanese machine-gun fire on Ie Shima, he died instantly. He was 44.

Phantoms of the Army

603RD'S DECEPTION DEFLATED—
AND DEFEATED—THE ENEMY

The 603rd Engineer Camouflage Battalion almost blew its cover one morning in 1944 when two French cyclists watched four soldiers pick up a huge tank and turn it around. The tank was inflated rubber, and the 603rd was just doing its job: fooling the Germans.

Deception has been part of warfare at least since the Trojan horse; during World War II it became high art. In fact, the members of the 603rd were artists. They included fashion designer Bill Blass and painter Ellsworth Kelly, as well as a Hollywood set designer and assorted illustrators and photographers.

The special weapons of the battalion (which belonged to the 23rd Headquarters Special Troops) were dummy planes, tanks, and antiaircraft guns; amplified recordings that created war sounds; flash canisters for gunfire; and fake shoulder patches. To enable a combat unit to change positions or to attack while the Germans thought it hadn't moved at all, the 1,800 men of the 23rd impersonated entire divisions. They would move in at night, change insignias, and inflate their rubber dummies. Meanwhile, the troops they were replacing sneaked away. Though inflated tanks and planes might suddenly spring leaks or burst when the sun expanded the pumped-in air, by and large the artifice worked. Their impersonation of tank and field artillery battalions once fooled not only the 38,000 Germans holding the French port of Brest, but nearby Allied troops as well.

The 23rd hit the beaches at Normandy a few days after D-Day, an invasion that itself was made possible, in part, by an entire ghost army—the First United States Army Group (FUSAG) that helped divert enemy troops before, during, and after the onslaught. Supposedly stationed in England, FUSAG faked radio communications and planted intelligence messages with double agents to convince the Germans that it was going to attack at Pas de Calais and that the Normandy invasion was a mere diversion. A series of distinguished real generals, including George S. Patton, did stints as FUSAG commanders.

When the 9th Army was trying to cross the Rhine in March 1945, the 23rd created the illusion of a huge buildup at Viersen; "divisions" paraded about, hundreds of rubber vehicles and planes and elaborate bridging equipment were displayed, and entire field hospitals were built. The real crossing took the Germans completely by surprise. It was the 23rd's last work of artifice. In May the hostilities in Europe ended, and in September the battalion was sent home.

BRIGHT IDEA

Spam: Great War Fare

Minnesota meatpacker George Hormel perfected a new product in 1937. Made of pork shoulder, ham, salt, water, sugar, and sodium nitrate, it was originally called spiced ham. Hormel offered a $100 reward in a naming contest. The winner was the brother of a company executive, and with the help of a high-powered ad campaign, an American phenomenon was born.

But it was during World War II that Spam really came into its own. "Without Spam," Nikita Khrushchev later wrote, "we wouldn't have been able to feed our army."

"I ate my share of Spam along with millions of other soldiers," Dwight D. Eisenhower once said. "I will even confess to a few unkind words about it."

An Offer They Couldn't Refuse

**NAVY USES, THEN COVERS UP, CONNECTION
WITH MAFIA TO SECURE ISLAND**

Treacherously mined harbors. Booby-trapped beaches. Rocky terrain. More than 400,000 enemy troops. As the Allies zeroed in on Sicily in 1943, the strategic island threatened to be a costly prize. Yet casualties were remarkably light, and Sicily was captured in 39 days.

A growing enmity between the Germans and Italians was partly responsible for the swiftness of the victory. But there were other factors. The U.S. Navy had solicited help from a most unlikely source: the American underworld.

The navy lacked an effective intelligence network in Sicily. As part of its jury-rigged effort to gather information, it turned to Charles "Lucky" Luciano, the Mafia chieftain and big-time purveyor of prostitutes who was serving a 30- to 50-year prison sentence.

Luciano, a poor Sicilian immigrant turned organized crime kingpin, was reluctant at first but finally agreed to lend the navy his Mafia contacts. Lucky was a powerful crime leader both in the United States and in Sicily, where the organization controlled most local governments. His influence (combined with an ongoing feud between the Mafia

On July 22, 1943, cheering residents greeted the men of General George S. Patton's forces (above) as they rolled through the streets of Palermo, Sicily's capital. It was just 12 days after the Allies had landed on the beaches of the big island off the toe of Italy's boot.

and Mussolini's Fascists) attracted hundreds of informants. With their help, intelligence officers penetrated Italian naval headquarters, filching vital maps and documents. Mafia members even acted as guides for advance units and "persuaded" Italian soldiers not to fight.

After the war, the navy moved quickly to cover up its Mafia connections. And although Luciano had not been promised a deal for his cooperation, the gangster was released from prison and deported to Italy in 1946, after serving 10 years of his sentence.

IMPROBABLE PIONEERS

The Four Chaplains Aboard the S.S. *Dorchester*

In January 1943, 903 GIs and four chaplains—George Fox, Clark Poling, Alexander Goode, and Johnny Washington— boarded the S.S. *Dorchester*. On February 3, a German torpedo ripped into the ship. "She's going down!" the men cried, scrambling for lifeboats. When one GI told the clergymen that he had lost his life jacket, the chaplain gave his up, saying, "I'm staying. I won't need it." One by one, the other three also gave up their life jackets. The chaplains, arms linked and heads raised in prayer, stood on deck as the *Dorchester* slipped beneath the waves. They were among 678 men lost that night.

President Harry Truman later praised the four: "I don't think in the history of the world that there has been anything in heroism equal to this. It was the greatest sermon that was ever preached."

The Ordeal of the *Indianapolis*

CRUISER SINKS, AND SAILORS SET ADRIFT WITHOUT ASSISTANCE

A little before midnight on Sunday, July 29, 1945, the heavy cruiser *Indianapolis* was returning from a secret mission to the Pacific atoll of Tinian. It had delivered parts for the atomic bomb that would be dropped on Hiroshima eight days later. Headed toward Leyte in the Philippines, the vessel was ripped by torpedoes from a Japanese submarine. Within 15 minutes, it had vanished beneath the surface, the last American ship sunk by the enemy in World War II. For its survivors, the most desperate days of the war were about to begin.

The ship sank so quickly that of the 1,199 crewmen, only about 850, including Captain Charles McVay, escaped. In the confusion, they had released a mere dozen life rafts and six flotation nets, and the captain had been unable to send an SOS. But the survivors weren't even aware of their greatest catastrophe. An earlier message giving the ship's estimated arrival time had been garbled in transmission

Rescuers were aghast at the suffering of the *Indianapolis*'s survivors. Of the 1,199 crewmen on board, only about 850 escaped before the ship sank. Of that number, just 316 survived the four-day ordeal aboard the life rafts.

so that it couldn't be decoded, and no one at Leyte had asked for a retransmission. The terrifying truth was that it would take days for the U.S. naval command to discover that the *Indianapolis* was missing.

D-Day's Disastrous DD Tanks

This was the weapon that would win the war: a 32-ton Sherman tank with a seven-foot canvas collar folded accordion-like against its sides.

The brainchild of Nicholas Straussler, a Hungarian immigrant in England, the "bloomers" could float the tank on water, where it was driven by two rear-mounted propellers powered by the same engine that drove it on land—hence the invention's name, the Duplex

Drive (DD) Tank. Developed by the British, the tanks quickly gained enthusiastic support.

The DDs were first demonstrated to Allied supreme commander General Dwight D. Eisenhower on a small English lake. Unfortunately, the English Channel around Normandy on June 6, 1944, was nothing like that quiet lake. It was still wild from the storm that had forced cancellation of an invasion attempt just the day before.

At Utah Beach, all 28 of the DDs actually put in the water at Utah made it ashore, guns blazing. This was the floating tank's greatest success. Omaha Beach, however, was a tragedy. As the canvas flotation "bloomers" collapsed in the choppy seas, the DDs sank, one after another, like stones. The men atop the tanks struggled to break through the seven-foot collars. But the soldiers inside never had a chance.

Its survivors were alone and unnoticed, except by the sharks.

As morning dawned on Monday, July 30, ominous fins sliced the water: 88 men were attacked and killed in the largest group of survivors; 25 more in another. One sailor had his legs bitten off; becoming top-heavy in his life vest, he tipped upside down and drowned. The sharks continued to feed intermittently for days.

The effects of exposure and lack of fresh water were less gruesome but even more deadly. Sunburn became lethal; men went blind. Those who drank seawater got salt poisoning; those who abstained succumbed to dehydration. Sailors started hallucinating. After 48 hours in the sea, the kapok life jackets became waterlogged and began dragging men under.

But, extraordinarily, many of the survivors maintained hope, even when planes flew overhead without seeing them. Finally, at five minutes past noon on Thursday, August 2, they were spotted.

> The *Indianapolis* survivors in life rafts had to deal with shark attacks, deadly sunburn, salt poisoning, and other horrors.

Lieutenant W. Charles Gwinn, a navy pilot on a routine flight, had given in to mild curiosity and dipped his PV-1 Ventura aircraft to inspect what he thought was an oil slick.

Rescue ships arrived around midnight. By then the crew of the *Indianapolis* had been in the water for four full days—96 desperately terrifying hours. Only 316 men survived, and for one of them, Captain McVay, the ordeal was not yet over.

In a move apparently aimed at appeasing public outrage, McVay was court-martialed, the only U.S. Navy captain in World War II to face trial for losing a ship. Many of his crew believed he had been made a scapegoat for naval brass, who by failing to keep track of the ship's location had botched the rescue. As expected, the captain was found guilty, but within a year the navy remitted his sentence.

D-Day Double "Cross"?

In the five weeks prior to the invasion of Normandy, London's *Daily Telegraph* published five crossword puzzles containing top-secret D-Day code words. "Utah," "Omaha," "Mulberry," and "Neptune" appeared as solutions during May. But the biggest blow came on June 2, just four days before the invasion, when "Overlord," the code name for the entire operation, was given as the answer to 11 across.

Soon, Leonard Dawe, the bespectacled 54-year-old physics teacher who had compiled the *Daily Telegraph* puzzles for more than 20 years, found himself being grilled by Scotland Yard. But it was all just an amazing coincidence. The suspicious crosswords were not a double-cross, and the Germans remained puzzled about the time and location of the D-Day invasion.

The Power of Words

THE AGE OF ATOMIC WARFARE MAY HAVE BEEN STARTED BY A CONFUSING TRANSLATION FROM THE JAPANESE

Daily air raids were taking a heavy toll on Japan during the summer of 1945; defeat seemed imminent. On July 26, Allied leaders issued the Potsdam Agreement: "We call upon the government of Japan to proclaim now the unconditional surrender of all Japanese armed forces. The alternative for Japan is prompt and utter destruction." But the offer was also in some ways generous; it allowed Japanese soldiers to return home without imprisonment.

Emperor Hirohito believed the Potsdam peace terms "were the most reasonable to be expected." But Prime Minister Kantaro Suzuki disagreed; he felt Japan still had some negotiating leverage with the Russians. Soon, Suzuki was telling reporters that Japan must *mokusatsu* the Allied offer.

Mokusatsu literally means "to kill with silence." Suzuki later claimed he had meant "no comment." But the Japanese news agency, Domei, quickly translated

the word as "ignore." With this, the bombing of Hiroshima and Nagasaki was virtually inevitable.

Just a week later, on August 6, 1945, the *Enola Gay* took off on its fateful mission. At 8:15 a.m., bombadier Major Thomas Ferebee had his target in his sights: the Aioi Bridge crossing the Ota River in Hiroshima.

About half a mile from his target, the crew of the *Lonesome Lady*, which had been shot down just 10 days earlier, were being held as war prisoners along with fliers from two other American planes—at least 10 GIs in all.

Although the solid brick of their cells managed to withstand the awesome initial blast, only three of these prisoners are known to have survived the explosion. Navy pilot Normand Brissette and the *Lonesome Lady*'s gunner, Ralph Neal, stayed nose-deep in a cesspool until the flames died down. As soon as they emerged, they were recaptured by the Japanese. During the next days each suffered acutely with oozing sores and constant vomiting, the result of radiation exposure. Both men died slow and horrible deaths.

The third American who survived the explosion died as a scapegoat for the bombing. History

One second after the atomic bomb's explosion at Hiroshima, a fireball 650 feet wide scorched everything in its path. Shock waves destroyed brick buildings within a mile of the bomb site; wooden buildings were simply obliterated. Half an hour later, a firestorm was sweeping the city. This was followed by a muddy, chilling rain, which poured radioactivity. About 80,000 people were dead by mid-afternoon; another 120,000 were dying. For more than a mile from the bomb's point of impact, the once thriving city was ashes.

doesn't record his name, but an eyewitness called him "the handsomest boy I ever saw." He was tied to the remains of the Aioi Bridge with a placard that said: "Beat This American Soldier Before You Pass." Besides these military prisoners, more than 3,000 Japanese-American civilians were stranded in Hiroshima when the war began. Of those who survived the blast, perhaps 1,000 returned to the United States.

The story of any single person who endured the atomic attack on Japan is appalling. If we then consider statistics in light of these scenes of individual agony, the extent of human suffering begins to stagger the mind: the two bomb blasts at Hiroshima and Nagasaki killed 300,000 people.

This News Just In

MacARTHUR LEARNS HE'S BEEN DUMPED BY TRUMAN ON THE RADIO

General Douglas MacArthur had brilliantly routed the North Koreans at Inchon in September 1950 and pursued them into North Korea. But the offensive backfired. MacArthur's soldiers were ambushed by Chinese Communists, and the general pressed President Harry Truman for permission to attack inside China. But Truman refused, loath to start a major conflict so soon after World War II.

MacArthur found Truman's position incomprehensible and repeatedly made his unhappiness known to the press. The president saw this as gross insubordination for which there was only one solution: MacArthur must go, and Truman wanted the satisfaction of firing him.

To forestall the great general's resignation, the White House announced his dismissal in a hastily called press conference at 1 a.m. on April 11, 1951. Halfway around the world, an officer at MacArthur's headquarters informed the 71-year-old general that he'd been dumped. The officer had heard the news

President Harry S. Truman with General Douglas MacArthur, circa 1950. MacArthur learned shortly thereafter that Truman was firing him for insubordination.

on the radio. MacArthur's firing created a predictable uproar, and everywhere he went well-wishers greeted him. Jokes ridiculing the president became popular, among them one about a Truman beer: just like any other beer, but without a head.

Bombs Over Albuquerque

THE DAY NEW MEXICO WAS NEARLY NUKED

It weighed 42,000 pounds. It was one of the nation's most powerful hydrogen bombs, and in May 1957, it fell on New Mexico.

The Mark 17, as this monster armament was called, is cited in the Nuclear Weapons Databook as "the first droppable thermonuclear bomb to be tested." But this "test" most definitely went awry. A safety-release lever was in the wrong position, causing the Mark 17 to rip away the bomb-bay door and fall from the plane. Although its nonnuclear explosives blasted a 25-foot-wide crater in the desert, its

10-megaton nuclear charge miraculously wasn't set off, narrowly averting horror for New Mexico. The bomb was hundreds of times more powerful than the one that had leveled Hiroshima.

In 1981, the government issued a noncommittal report about the accident. Five years later, the *Albuquerque Journal* used the Freedom of Information Act to dig up further documentation. When the truth came out, a Defense Department spokesman tried hard to look on the bright side: The nuclear bomb's failure to explode, he pointed out, "confirms the efficacy of the safety devices."

Remembering the Vietnam War

MEMORIAL INSPIRES CONTROVERSY, JUST AS WAR DID

One of the most moving monuments in the nation's capital, the Vietnam Veterans Memorial consists of two polished black granite walls engraved with the names of more than 58,000 dead or missing American servicemen and women of the Vietnam War. It was dedicated in November 1982, culminating a successful three-year campaign by a group of veterans that raised $8.4 million in private donations. In 1980 the Vietnam Veterans Memorial Fund offered a $50,000 prize to the winner of a design competition. Of 1,421 designs submitted in the competition, the one selected was by a 21-year-old architecture student named Maya Ying Lin. Her design was highly controversial, called by some a "black gash of shame."

Designed by 21-year-old Maya Ying Lin, the Vietnam Veterans Memorial is engraved with the names of more than 58,000 dead or missing American service members.

The nation had been deeply divided by the Vietnam War, which ended in 1975; the war's veterans had not had the hero's welcome accorded to the GIs returning from World War II. With this tangible public recognition, America at last honored the sacrifices of the war's fallen. At the monument's 1982 dedication, one veteran gave voice to the others' sentiments: "We waited 15 years to get here, man. But it's not too late."

Thousands of visitors file by the monument every day to touch the names of loved ones, make a wall rubbing, or leave gifts or cards. "Tomorrow is your birthday," said one letter. "The only present I can give you is to have your family come to this memorial ... and to remember you." Mementos are not discarded—the National Parks Service keeps them.

Operation Desert Storm

Operation Desert Storm began on the evening of January 16, 1991, with a massive aerial bombardment of Baghdad and Iraqi positions inside occupied Kuwait. The air strikes began the U.S. air and land operations in the Gulf War, a conflict between Iraq and a United Nations coalition force led by the United States to liberate Kuwait. It would be the first real test of America's new arsenal of computer-aided weaponry. Over the next month, living rooms across the United States glowed with taped news footage interspersed with live war broadcasts. Americans watched in awe as radar-dodging stealth aircraft delivered payloads of laser-guided bombs, and Patriot missiles snatched Iraqi scuds right out of the air.

When the ground offensive began on February 24, it seemed almost anticlimactic. Iraqi leader Saddam Hussein's pledge to fight "the mother of all battles" failed to materialize. The Iraqi threat to use chemical weapons proved just that—a threat—and coalition forces met only minimal resistance as they advanced to Kuwait City. On February 26, Hussein announced a "victorious" retreat, but he was too late; weighted down with booty, Iraqi forces had begun to flee Kuwait City the day before, only to be caught in a merciless air attack on the road to the border.

In just 100 hours, the ground conflict was over. On February 28, declaring that the 28-nation coalition had achieved the liberation of Kuwait, President George H. W. Bush announced an end to the offensive. By the time Iraq formally accepted the terms of a U.N. cease-fire on April 6, some 200,000 American troops were on their way home. In all, the coalition forces had suffered just 343 combat deaths, 146 of them American. As many as 100,000 Iraqis were killed. Saddam Hussein remained in power, but for taking a stand against him, George H. W. Bush saw his approval rating soar to 83 percent—making him, for a brief moment, the most popular president of modern times.

Nearly a decade later, after the September 11, 2001, terrorism attacks on the United States, Bush's son, President George W. Bush, announced a "war on terrorism" that two years later led to another war against Iraq. The 2003 invasion was ordered on the grounds that Iraq had violated the U.N. resolution on "weapons of mass destruction." No weapons were ever found, but U.S. troops and 20 coalition allied forces captured Saddam Hussein on December 13, 2003. Nearly three years later he was tried by the Iraqi interim government, and on December 30, 2006, he was executed. This, too, was viewed by many Americans, this time in the form of private pictures and videotapes relayed around the world using the Internet.

In Kuwait, an American soldier standing night guard watches as oil wells burn in the distance. The wells were burned as acts of sabotage by Iraqi soldiers pulling out of Kuwait at the close of the Persian Gulf War.

Mission Accomplished?

**HOW A SIMPLE BANNER CAME TO SYMBOLIZE
IRAQ WAR BLUNDERS AND MISJUDGMENTS**

Late into the evening of March 20, 2003, American missiles hit targets in Baghdad, the capital of Iraq, marking the beginning of a U.S.-led military campaign to oust Iraqi leader Saddam Hussein. The legality of invading Iraq was hotly debated in the United Nations and in homes around the world. But at the time, polls show that a majority of Americans believed that it was the right thing to do for U.S. and global safety.

American forces, together with a coalition of armies from around the world, easily took control of several Iraqi cities, and on April 9, 2003, the troops overpowered the Iraqi army and advanced into central Baghdad. In a symbolic gesture, U.S. troops helped Iraqi citizens topple a 40-foot statue of Saddam Hussein in the city.

On May 1, President George W. Bush landed in a fighter plane on the deck of the USS *Abraham Lincoln*, which was returning from a 10-month mission in Afghanistan and Iraq. The troops on board cheered as President Bush stood under a bright, red, white, and blue banner that read, "Mission Accomplished." The president declared that "major combat operations in Iraq have ended."

American confidence in the mission in Iraq was buoyed by the speech, but it was grossly premature. In the weeks and months after the event, an Iraqi insurgency grew stronger. Thousands of U.S. soldiers and tens of thousands of Iraqi civilians have been killed in Iraq since "major combat operations ended." And the mystery of the banner came to symbolize a greater mismanagement of the war.

WHO MADE THE BANNER,
AND WHAT DID IT MEAN?

Within months of President Bush's landing on board the *Lincoln*, with U.S. casualty figures in Iraq growing, the American media began to question the theatricality surrounding the speech. The "Mission Accomplished" banner, in particular, became the center of intrigue—and the infighting between the press offices of the White House and the navy.

Back in May 2003, the White House told reporters that the navy had hung the sign, but it emerged that White House aides had actually put it up, strategically positioning it behind the president. Still, the White House insisted that the navy had made the banner. Not so, said navy officials. Finally, the White House admitted that its aides had made and hung the banner—at the navy's request. Things became even more confusing when the White House suggested that the phrase "Mission Accomplished" had nothing to do with the war in Iraq but instead referred to the successful completion of the ship's 290-day deployment.

Critics of the Bush administration claimed that the U.S. public was fooled by the event, and the term "mission accomplished" came to symbolize not only the orchestration of White House media events, but also the underestimation of the Iraq insurgency and America's poor planning in dealing with post-war Iraq.

As this book goes to print, nearly four years since the start of military operations in Iraq, U.S. troop levels in the country are increasing, as is the rate of casualties. There is still no exit strategy for Americans or a clear future for Iraqis.

President George W. Bush arrives on the U.S.S. *Abraham Lincoln*, **off the West Coast near San Diego, on May 1, 2003. On board, President Bush declared the combat phase of the war in Iraq over, in a nationally televised speech to the nation.**

A Treasury of Amazing Facts

PRESIDENTS OF THE UNITED STATES OF AMERICA

~ ONE ~
GEORGE WASHINGTON

1732–99

The only president who did not live in Washington, D.C., he was also the first and only president to be unanimously elected.

Years in Office: 1789–97
Political Party: Federalist
Home State: Virginia
Opposing Candidate: None
Vice President: John Adams
First Lady: Martha Dandridge Custis

~ TWO ~
JOHN ADAMS

1735–1826

He died at the age of 90 on the same day as his successor, Thomas Jefferson—July 4, 1826.

Years in Office: 1797–1801
Political Party: Federalist
Home State: Massachusetts
Opposing Candidate: Thomas Jefferson (1796)
Vice President: Thomas Jefferson
First Lady: Abigail Smith

~ THREE ~
THOMAS JEFFERSON

1743–1826

Jefferson was an architect as well as a president. He used his talent to design the University of Virginia, a school he also founded.

Years in Office: 1801–9
Political Party: Democratic-Republican
Home State: Virginia
Opposing Candidates: Aaron Burr (1800); Charles Pinckney (1804)
Vice Presidents: Aaron Burr, George Clinton
Married: Martha Wayles Skelton (died 1782)

~ FOUR ~
JAMES MADISON

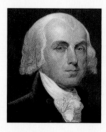

1751–1836

The first president to involve the nation in war (1812), he was the last surviving signer of the Constitution.

Years in Office: 1809–17
Political Party: Republican
Home State: Virginia
Opposing Candidates: Charles Pinckney (1808); DeWitt Clinton (1812)
Vice Presidents: George Clinton, Elbridge Gerry
First Lady: Dolley Dandridge Payne Todd

FIVE
JAMES MONROE

1758–1831

He was the first president to have a daughter marry in the White House.

Years in Office: 1817–25
Political Party: Republican
Home State: Virginia
Opposing Candidates: Rufus King (1816); John Q. Adams (1820)
Vice President: Daniel Tompkins
First Lady: Elizabeth Kortright

SIX
JOHN QUINCY ADAMS

1767–1848

In 1848, he collapsed on the floor of the House from a stroke. He died two days later.

Years in Office: 1825–9
Political Party: Democratic-Republican
Home State: Massachusetts
Opposing Candidates: Andrew Jackson, Henry Clay, William H. Crawford (1824); Andrew Jackson (1828)
Vice President: John C. Calhoun
First Lady: Louisa Johnson

SEVEN
ANDREW JACKSON

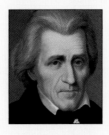

1767–1845

In his first run for president, in 1824, Jackson captured the most votes but lost the election; because he did not win a clear majority, the House of Representatives chose John Q. Adams.

Years in Office: 1829–37
Political Party: Democratic
Home State: Tennessee
Opposing Candidates: John Q. Adams (1828); Henry Clay (1832)
Vice Presidents: John C. Calhoun, Martin Van Buren
Married: Rachel Donelson (died 1828)

EIGHT
MARTIN VAN BUREN

1782–1862

Van Buren was the first president not born under British colonial rule.

Years in Office: 1837–41
Political Party: Democratic
Home State: New York
Opposing Candidate: William H. Harrison (1836)
Vice President: Richard M. Johnson
Married: Hannah Hoes (died 1819)

NINE
WILLIAM HENRY HARRISON

1773–1841

The first president to die in office, he gave the longest presidential address (one hour, forty minutes), but served the shortest term as president (one month).

Years in Office: 1841
Political Party: Whig
Home State: Ohio
Opposing Candidate: Martin Van Buren (1840)
Vice President: John Tyler
First Lady: Anna Tuthill Symmes

TEN
JOHN TYLER

1790–1862

The first vice president to become president because of the death of a chief executive, he was also the first president to be married while in office.

Years in Office: 1841–5
Political Party: Whig, Democratic
Home State: Virginia
Opposing Candidate: None
Vice President: None
First Ladies: Letitia Christian (died 1842), Julia Gardiner

~ ELEVEN ~
JAMES K. POLK

1795–1849

Staunch moralists, President and Mrs. Polk banned card playing, alcohol drinking, and dancing in the White House.

Years in Office: 1845–9
Political Party: Democratic
Home State: Tennessee
Opposing Candidate: Henry Clay (1844)
Vice President: George M. Dallas
First Lady: Sarah Childress

~ TWELVE ~
ZACHARY TAYLOR

1784–1850

A career officer, he was the first president with no prior political experience.

Years in Office: 1849–50
Political Party: Whig
Home State: Louisiana
Opposing Candidates: Lewis Cass, Martin Van Buren (1848)
Vice President: Millard Fillmore
First Lady: Margaret Mackall Smith

~ THIRTEEN ~
MILLARD FILLMORE

1800–74

Using a congressional allowance of $250, Fillmore created the first White House library.

Years in Office: 1850–3
Political Party: Whig
Home State: New York
Opposing Candidate: None
Vice President: None
First Lady: Abigail Powers

~ FOURTEEN ~
FRANKLIN PIERCE

1804–69

Pierce delivered his inaugural address from memory. He was the only president to seek renomination but be rejected by his party for a second term.

Years in Office: 1853–7
Political Party: Democratic
Home State: New Hampshire
Opposing Candidate: Winfield Scott (1852)
Vice President: William R. King
First Lady: Jane Means Appleton

~ FIFTEEN ~
JAMES BUCHANAN

1791–1868

He was the first president who never married.

Years in Office: 1857–61
Political Party: Democratic
Home State: Pennsylvania
Opposing Candidates: John C. Fremont, Millard Fillmore (1856)
Vice President: John Breckinridge
First Lady: None

~ SIXTEEN ~
ABRAHAM LINCOLN

1809–65

The first president born outside of the original 13 states, he was also the first president to be assassinated.

Years in Office: 1861–5
Political Party: Republican
Home State: Illinois
Opposing Candidates: Stephen A. Douglas, John C. Breckinridge, John Bell (1860); George McClellan (1864)
Vice Presidents: Hannibal Hamlin, Andrew Johnson
First Lady: Mary Todd

SEVENTEEN
ANDREW JOHNSON

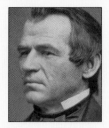

1808–75

The first president who did not have legal or military experience, he was also the first president to be impeached. (He was acquitted.)

Years in Office: 1865–9
Political Party: Democratic
Home State: Tennessee
Opposing Candidate: None
Vice President: None
First Lady: Eliza McCardle

EIGHTEEN
ULYSSES S. GRANT

1822–85

Grant was the first president whose administration was involved in major financial scandal.

Years in Office: 1869–77
Political Party: Republican
Home State: Illinois
Opposing Candidates: Horatio Seymour (1868); Horace Greeley (1872)
Vice Presidents: Schuyler Colfax, Henry Wilson
First Lady: Julia Boggs Dent

NINETEEN
RUTHERFORD B. HAYES

1822–93

Hayes was the first president to have a telephone at the White House.

Years in Office: 1877–81
Political Party: Republican
Home State: Ohio
Opposing Candidate: Samuel J. Tilden (1876)
Vice President: William A. Wheeler
First Lady: Lucy Ware Webb

TWENTY
JAMES A. GARFIELD

1831–81

In 1880 Garfield was eligible for three federal posts at the same time. He was a congressman as well as a senator-elect and president-elect. He gave up his senatorial seat and resigned from the House before his inauguration.

Years in Office: 1881
Political Party: Republican
Home State: Ohio
Opposing Candidate: Winfield S. Hancock (1880)
Vice President: Chester A. Arthur
First Lady: Lucretia Rudolph

TWENTY-ONE
CHESTER A. ARTHUR

1829–86

Arthur was the last of four presidents who did not give an inaugural address (Tyler, Fillmore, and Andrew Johnson were the other three).

Years in Office: 1881–5
Political Party: Republican
Home State: New York
Opposing Candidate: None
Vice President: None
Married: Ellen Lewis Herndon (died 1880)

TWENTY-TWO
GROVER CLEVELAND

1837-1908

Cleveland was the only president to get married in the White House.

Years in Office: 1885–9
Political Party: Democratic
Home State: New York
Opposing Candidate: James G. Blaine (1884)
Vice President: Thomas A. Hendricks
First Lady: Frances Folsom

~ TWENTY-THREE ~
BENJAMIN HARRISON

1833–1901

Harrison was the only grandson of a president (William Henry Harrison) to also become president.

Years in Office: 1889–93
Political Party: Republican
Home State: Indiana
Opposing Candidate: Grover Cleveland (1888)
Vice President: Levi P. Morton
First Lady: Caroline Lavinia Scott (died 1892)

~ TWENTY-FOUR ~
GROVER CLEVELAND
(see # 22)

The only president to serve two non-consecutive terms, Cleveland was also the first president to have a child born at the White House.

Years in Office: 1893–7
Opposing Candidates: Benjamin Harrison, James Weaver (1892)
Vice President: Adlai E. Stevenson

~ TWENTY-FIVE ~
WILLIAM McKINLEY

1843–1901

McKinley was the first president to use the telephone for presidential campaigning.

Years in Office: 1897–1901
Political Party: Republican
Home State: Ohio
Opposing Candidates: William J. Bryan (1896); William J. Bryan (1900)
Vice Presidents: Garret A. Hobart, Theodore Roosevelt
First Lady: Ida Saxton

~ TWENTY-SIX ~
THEODORE ROOSEVELT

1858–1919

The youngest president to take office, he was the first president to win a Nobel Peace Prize, to travel in a submarine, and to visit a foreign country while in office.

Years in Office: 1901–9
Political Party: Republican
Home State: New York
Opposing Candidate: Alton B. Parker (1904)
Vice President: Charles W. Fairbanks
First Lady: Edith Kermit Carow

~ TWENTY-SEVEN ~
WILLIAM H. TAFT

1857–1930

Taft was the only president later to become chief justice of the U.S. Supreme Court.

Years in Office: 1909–13
Political Party: Republican
Home State: Ohio
Opposing Candidate: William J. Bryan (1908)
Vice President: James S. Sherman
First Lady: Helen Herron

~ TWENTY-EIGHT ~
WOODROW WILSON

1856–1924

Within two and a half years, Wilson went from having never held public office to being president of the United States.

Years in Office: 1913–21
Political Party: Democratic
Home State: New Jersey
Opposing Candidates: Theodore Roosevelt, William H. Taft (1912); Charles E. Hughes (1916)
Vice President: Thomas R. Marshall
First Ladies: Ellen Louise Axson (died 1914), Edith Bolling Galt

⌐ TWENTY-NINE ⌐
WARREN G. HARDING

1865–1923

Harding was the first president to make a speech over the radio.

Years in Office: 1921–23
Political Party: Republican
Home State: Ohio
Opposing Candidate: James M. Cox (1920)
Vice President: Calvin Coolidge
First Lady: Florence Kling De Wolfe

⌐ THIRTY ⌐
CALVIN COOLIDGE

1872–1933

The only president sworn in by his father (who was a justice of the peace), Coolidge was also the first president whose oath was administered by a former president (Chief Justice William Howard Taft).

Years in Office: 1923–9
Political Party: Republican
Home State: Massachusetts
Opposing Candidates: John W. Davis, Robert M. La Follette (1924)
Vice President: Charles G. Dawes
First Lady: Grace Anna Goodhue

⌐ THIRTY-ONE ⌐
HERBERT C. HOOVER

1874–1964

The first president born west of the Mississippi River, he held more than 75 honorary degrees from American and foreign universities.

Years in Office: 1929–33
Political Party: Republican
Home State: California
Opposing Candidate: Alfred E. Smith (1928)
Vice President: Charles Curtis
First Lady: Lou Henry

⌐ THIRTY-TWO ⌐
FRANKLIN D. ROOSEVELT

1882–1945

FDR was the only president elected to four terms.

Years in Office: 1933–45
Political Party: Democratic
Home State: New York
Opposing Candidates: William Lemke, Alfred Landon (1936); Wendell Willkie (1940); Thomas E. Dewey (1944)
Vice Presidents: John Nance Garner, Henry Wallace, Harry S. Truman
First Lady: (Anna) Eleanor Roosevelt

⌐ THIRTY-THREE ⌐
HARRY S. TRUMAN

1884–1972

Truman gave the first presidential address telecast from the White House.

Years in Office: 1945–53
Political Party: Democratic
Home State: Missouri
Opposing Candidates: Thomas E. Dewey, James Strom Thurmond, Henry A. Wallace (1948)
Vice President: Alben W. Barkley
First Lady: Elizabeth "Bess" Virginia Wallace

⌐ THIRTY-FOUR ⌐
DWIGHT D. EISENHOWER

1890–1969

Eisenhower held the first presidential news conference covered by newsreels and television.

Years in Office: 1953–61
Political Party: Republican
Home State: New York
Opposing Candidates: Adlai E. Stevenson (1952 and 1956)
Vice President: Richard M. Nixon
First Lady: Mamie Geneva Doud

~ THIRTY-FIVE ~
JOHN F. KENNEDY

1917–63

The first president born in the 20th century, Kennedy was also the first Roman Catholic president.

Years in Office: 1961–3
Political Party: Democratic
Home State: Massachusetts
Opposing Candidate: Richard M. Nixon (1960)
Vice President: Lyndon B. Johnson
First Lady: Jacqueline Lee Bouvier

~ THIRTY-SIX ~
LYNDON B. JOHNSON

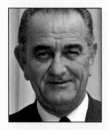

1908–73

Johnson was the first president sworn in by a woman, and he was the second president named Johnson to become president after the death of the incumbent.

Years in Office: 1963–9
Political Party: Democratic
Home State: Texas
Opposing Candidate: Barry M. Goldwater (1964)
Vice President: Hubert H. Humphrey
First Lady: Claudia Alta "Lady Bird" Taylor

~ THIRTY-SEVEN ~
RICHARD M. NIXON

1913–94

Nixon was first president to choose a vice presidential running mate under the 25th Amendment and the first president to resign.

Years in Office: 1969–74
Political Party: Republican
Home State: California
Opposing Candidates: Hubert H. Humphrey, George C. Wallace (1968); George S. McGovern (1972)
Vice Presidents: Spiro T. Agnew, Gerald Ford
First Lady: Thelma Catherine "Pat" Ryan

~ THIRTY-EIGHT ~
GERALD R. FORD

1913–2006

Ford became vice president, and then president, without having been elected to either office.

Years in Office: 1974–7
Political Party: Republican
Home State: Michigan
Opposing Candidate: None
Vice President: Nelson A. Rockefeller
First Lady: Elizabeth "Betty" Anne Bloomer Warren

~ THIRTY-NINE ~
JIMMY CARTER

1924–

Carter was the first president sworn in using his nickname and the first to assign three women to cabinet posts.

Years in Office: 1977–81
Political Party: Democratic
Home State: Georgia
Opposing Candidate: Gerald R. Ford (1976)
Vice President: Walter F. Mondale
First Lady: Rosalynn Smith

~ FORTY ~
RONALD REAGAN

1911–2004

Reagan was the first divorced president and the oldest president to take office.

Years in Office: 1981–89
Political Party: Republican
Home State: California
Opposing Candidates: Jimmy Carter, John B. Anderson, Ed Clark (1980); Walter F. Mondale (1984)
Vice President: George H. W. Bush
Married: Jane Wyman (divorced 1949)
First Lady: Nancy Davis

~ FORTY-ONE ~
GEORGE H. W. BUSH

1924–

Bush was the first president who had earlier served as Ambassador to the United Nations and head of the CIA.

Years in Office: 1989–93

Political Party: Republican

Home State: Texas

Opposing Candidate: Michael S. Dukakis (1988)

Vice President: J. Danforth Quayle

First Lady: Barbara Pierce

~ FORTY-TWO ~
WILLIAM J. CLINTON

1946–

Elected at age 46, along with 44-year-old Al Gore, he headed the youngest president-vice president ticket ever.

Years in Office: 1993–2001

Political Party: Democratic

Home State: Arkansas

Opposing Candidates: George H. W. Bush, H. Ross Perot (1992); Bob Dole, H. Ross Perot (1996)

Vice President: Albert Gore Jr.

First Lady: Hillary Rodham

~ FORTY-THREE ~
GEORGE W. BUSH

1946–

Bush is the only president whose father attended his inauguration as a former president.

Years in Office: 2001–

Political Party: Republican

Home State: Texas

Opposing Candidates: Albert Gore Jr., Ralph Nader (2000); John Kerry, Ralph Nader (2004)

Vice President: Richard Cheney

First Lady: Laura Welch

THE UNITED STATES OF AMERICA

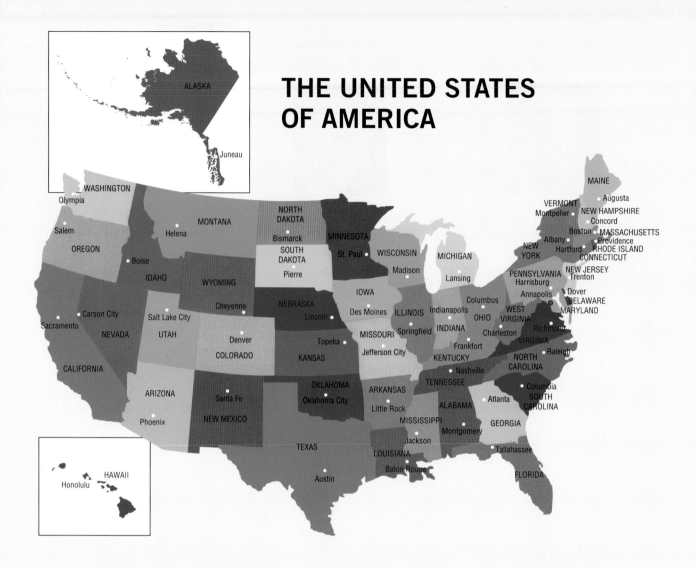

Capital: Washington, D.C.

Area: 3,787,319 sq. mi.

Population: 301,486,823

Population Density: 76 per sq. mi.

Population Growth Rate: 0.91%

Life Expectancy: 77.85 years

Languages Spoken: English (82.1%), Spanish (10.7%), other (7.2%)

Adult Literacy Rate: 99%

Currency: U.S. dollar

GDP: $13.22 trillion

GDP Per Head: $43,500

ALABAMA

Heart of Dixie, Camellia State

Capital: Montgomery

Admission to Union: Dec. 14, 1819

Total Area: 51,705 sq. mi.

Rank in Size: 29

Flower: Camellia

Tree: Southern pine

Bird: Yellowhammer

Famous Residents: Tallulah Bankhead, Nat "King" Cole, Helen Keller, Willie Mays, Rosa Parks

ALASKA

Land of the Midnight Sun

Capital: Juneau

Admission to Union: Jan. 3, 1959

Total Area: 591,004 sq. mi.

Rank in Size: 1

Flower: Forget-me-not

Tree: Sitka spruce

Bird: Willow ptarmigan

Famous Residents: Susan Butcher, Joe Juneau, Chief Katlian

ARIZONA
Grand Canyon State

Capital: Phoenix
Admission to Union: Feb. 14, 1912
Total Area: 114,000 sq. mi.
Rank in Size: 6
Flower: Saguaro
Tree: Paloverde
Bird: Cactus wren
Famous Residents: Cochise, Geronimo, Barry Goldwater, Sandra Day O'Connor

ARKANSAS
Land of Opportunity

Capital: Little Rock
Admission to Union: June 15, 1836
Total Area: 53,187 sq. mi.
Rank in Size: 27
Flower: Apple blossom
Tree: Pine
Bird: Mockingbird
Famous Residents: Helen Gurley Brown, Johnny Cash, J. William Fulbright, Tess Harper, Douglas MacArthur, Edward Durell Stone

CALIFORNIA
Golden State

Capital: Sacramento
Admission to Union: Sept. 9, 1850
Total Area: 158,706 sq. mi.
Rank in Size: 3
Flower: Golden poppy
Tree: California redwood
Bird: California valley quail
Famous Residents: Joe DiMaggio, Isadora Duncan, William Randolph Hearst, Jack London, George S. Patton Jr., John Steinbeck

COLORADO
Centennial State, Rocky Mountain State

Capital: Denver
Admission to Union: Aug. 1, 1876
Total Area: 104,091 sq. mi.
Rank in Size: 8
Flower: Rocky Mountain columbine
Tree: Colorado blue spruce
Bird: Lark bunting
Famous Residents: Molly Brown, M. Scott Carpenter, Jack Dempsey

CONNECTICUT
Constitution State, Nutmeg State

Capital: Hartford
Admission to Union: Jan. 9, 1788
Total Area: 5,018 sq. mi.
Rank in Size: 48
Flower: Mountain laurel
Tree: White oak
Bird: American robin
Famous Residents: Katharine Hepburn, Harriet Beecher Stowe, Noah Webster

DELAWARE
First State, Diamond State

Capital: Dover
Admission to Union: Dec. 7, 1787
Total Area: 2,045 sq. mi.
Rank in Size: 49
Flower: Peach blossom
Tree: American holly
Bird: Blue hen chicken
Famous Residents: Thomas Francis Bayard, Annie Jump Cannon, E. I. Du Pont

FLORIDA
Sunshine State

Capital: Tallahassee
Admission to Union: March 3, 1845
Total Area: 58,664 sq. mi.
Rank in Size: 22
Flower: Orange blossom
Tree: Sabal palm
Bird: Mockingbird
Famous Residents: Marjorie Kinnan Rawlings, Janet Reno, Joseph W. Stilwell

GEORGIA
Empire State of the South, Peach State

Capital: Atlanta
Admission to Union: Jan. 2, 1788
Total Area: 58,876 sq. mi.
Rank in Size: 21
Flower: Cherokee rose
Tree: Live oak
Bird: Brown thrasher
Famous Residents: Martin Luther King Jr., Margaret Mitchell, Flannery O'Connor, Jackie Robinson

HAWAII
Aloha State

Capital: Honolulu
Admission to Union: Aug. 21, 1959
Total Area: 6,471 sq. mi.
Rank in Size: 47
Flower: Hibiscus
Tree: Candlenut
Bird: Hawaiian goose (nene)
Famous Residents: Sanford B. Dole, Daniel K. Inouye, Kamehameha I, Queen Liliuokalani

IDAHO
Gem State

Capital: Boise

Admission to Union: July 3, 1890

Total Area: 83,564 sq. mi.

Rank in Size: 13

Flower: Syringa

Tree: Western white pine

Bird: Mountain bluebird

Famous Residents: Gutzon Borglum, Ezra Pound, Sacagawea

ILLINOIS
Prairie State

Capital: Springfield

Admission to Union: Dec. 3, 1818

Total Area: 56,345 sq. mi.

Rank in Size: 24

Flower: Native violet

Tree: White oak

Bird: Cardinal

Famous Residents: Jane Addams, Jack Benny, Walt Disney, Benny Goodman, Ernest Hemingway, Carl Sandburg

INDIANA
Hoosier State

Capital: Indianapolis

Admission to Union: Dec. 11, 1816

Total Area: 36,185 sq. mi.

Rank in Size: 38

Flower: Peony

Tree: Tulip poplar

Bird: Cardinal

Famous Residents: James Dean, Theodore Dreiser, Jane Pauley, Cole Porter, Ernie Pyle, Knute Rockne, Red Skelton, Kurt Vonnegut Jr.,

IOWA
Hawkeye State

Capital: Des Moines

Admission to Union: Dec. 28, 1846

Total Area: 56,275 sq. mi.

Rank in Size: 25

Flower: Wild rose

Tree: Oak

Bird: Eastern goldfinch

Famous Residents: Bix Beiderbecke, Buffalo Bill Cody, Glenn Miller, Lillian Russell, John Wayne, Grant Wood

KANSAS
Sunflower State

Capital: Topeka

Admission to Union: Jan. 29, 1861

Total Area: 81,781 sq. mi.

Rank in Size: 14

Flower: Sunflower

Tree: Cottonwood

Bird: Western meadowlark

Famous Residents: Amelia Earhart, Buster Keaton, Edgar Lee Masters, Charlie Parker, Damon Runyon

KENTUCKY
Bluegrass State

Capital: Frankfort

Admission to Union: June 1, 1792

Total Area: 40,409 sq. mi.

Rank in Size: 37

Flower: Goldenrod

Tree: Kentucky coffee tree

Bird: Cardinal

Famous Residents: Muhammad Ali, D. W. Griffith, Loretta Lynn, Carrie Nation

LOUISIANA
Pelican State

Capital: Baton Rouge

Admission to Union: April 30, 1812

Total Area: 47,752 sq. mi.

Rank in Size: 31

Flower: Magnolia

Tree: Bald cypress

Bird: Brown pelican

Famous Residents: Louis Armstrong, Truman Capote, Lillian Hellman, "Jelly Roll" Morton

MAINE
Pine Tree State

Capital: Augusta

Admission to Union: March 14, 1820

Total Area: 33,265 sq. mi.

Rank in Size: 39

Flower: White pine cone and tassel

Tree: White pine

Bird: Chickadee

Famous Residents: Dorothea Dix, Henry Wadsworth Longfellow, Edna St. Vincent Millay

MARYLAND
Old Line State, Free State

Capital: Annapolis

Admission to Union: April 28, 1788

Total Area: 10,460 sq. mi.

Rank in Size: 42

Flower: Black-eyed Susan

Tree: White oak

Bird: Baltimore oriole

Famous Residents: Benjamin Banneker, William Halsted, Billie Holiday, Babe Ruth, Harriet Tubman

MASSACHUSETTS

Bay State, Old Colony State

Capital: Boston
Admission to Union: Feb. 6, 1788
Total Area: 8,284 sq. mi.
Rank in Size: 45
Flower: Mayflower
Tree: American elm
Bird: Chickadee
Famous Residents: Susan B. Anthony, Clara Barton, W. E. B. Dubois, Emily Dickinson, Robert Goddard, Nathaniel Hawthorne

MICHIGAN

Great Lakes State, Wolverine State

Capital: Lansing
Admission to Union: Jan. 26, 1837
Total Area: 96,705 sq. mi.
Rank in Size: 11
Flower: Apple blossom
Tree: White pine
Bird: Robin
Famous Residents: Ralph Bunche, Edna Ferber, Henry Ford, Joe Louis, Diana Ross, Stevie Wonder

MINNESOTA

North Star State, Gopher State

Capital: St. Paul
Admission to Union: May 11, 1858
Total Area: 84,402 sq. mi.
Rank in Size: 12
Flower: Pink and white lady's slipper
Tree: Norway pine
Bird: Common loon
Famous Residents: Warren E. Burger, William O. Douglas, F. Scott Fitzgerald, Judy Garland, Sinclair Lewis

MISSISSIPPI

Magnolia State

Capital: Jackson
Admission to Union: Dec. 10, 1817
Total Area: 47,716 sq. mi.
Rank in Size: 32
Flower: Magnolia
Tree: Magnolia
Bird: Mockingbird
Famous Residents: William Faulkner, Elvis Presley, Leontyne Price, Tennessee Williams

MISSOURI

Show Me State

Capital: Jefferson City
Admission to Union: Aug. 10, 1821
Total Area: 69,697 sq. mi.
Rank in Size: 19
Flower: Hawthorn
Tree: Dogwood
Bird: Bluebird
Famous Residents: Maya Angelou, Josephine Baker, George Washington Carver, Walter Cronkite, Langston Hughes, Mark Twain

MONTANA

Treasure State

Capital: Helena
Admission to Union: Nov. 8, 1889
Total Area: 147,046 sq. mi.
Rank in Size: 4
Flower: Bitterroot
Tree: Ponderosa pine
Bird: Western meadowlark
Famous Residents: Gary Cooper, Chet Huntley, Myrna Loy, Jeannette Rankin

NEBRASKA

Cornhusker State

Capital: Lincoln
Admission to Union: March 1, 1867
Total Area: 77,227 sq. mi.
Rank in Size: 15
Flower: Goldenrod
Tree: Cottonwood
Bird: Western meadowlark
Famous Residents: Marlon Brando, Johnny Carson, Willa Cather, Henry Fonda, Malcolm X

NEVADA

Sagebrush State, Battle Born State, Silver State

Capital: Carson City
Admission to Union: Oct. 31, 1864
Total Area: 110,561 sq. mi.
Rank in Size: 7
Flower: Sagebrush
Tree: Single-leaf piñon
Bird: Mountain bluebird
Famous Residents: Sarah Winnemucca, Wovoka

NEW HAMPSHIRE

Granite State

Capital: Concord
Admission to Union: June 21, 1788
Total Area: 9,279 sq. mi.
Rank in Size: 44
Flower: Purple lilac
Tree: White birch
Bird: Purple finch
Famous Residents: Robert Frost, Christa McAuliffe, Jodi Picoult, Alan B. Shepard Jr., Daniel Webster

NEW JERSEY

Garden State

Capital: Trenton

Admission to Union: Dec. 18, 1787

Total Area: 7,787 sq. mi.

Rank in Size: 46

Flower: Purple violet

Tree: Red oak

Bird: Eastern goldfinch

Famous Residents: William "Count" Basie, Dorothea Lange, Paul Robeson, Frank Sinatra

NEW MEXICO

Land of Enchantment

Capital: Santa Fe

Admission to Union: Jan. 6, 1912

Total Area: 121,593 sq. mi.

Rank in Size: 5

Flower: Yucca

Tree: Piñon

Bird: Roadrunner

Famous Residents: Billy the Kid, Kit Carson, Bill Mauldin, Georgia O'Keeffe

NEW YORK

Empire State

Capital: Albany

Admission to Union: July 26, 1788

Total Area: 49,108 sq. mi.

Rank in Size: 30

Flower: Rose

Tree: Sugar maple

Bird: Bluebird

Famous Residents: Lucille Ball, Maria Callas, George Gershwin, J. Robert Oppenheimer Jr., Jonas Salk

NORTH CAROLINA

Tarheel State, Old North State

Capital: Raleigh

Admission to Union: Nov. 21, 1789

Total Area: 52,669 sq. mi.

Rank in Size: 28

Flower: Flowering dogwood

Tree: Pine

Bird: Cardinal

Famous Residents: Roberta Flack, Ava Gardner, Billy Graham, O. Henry, Charles Kuralt, Edward R. Murrow

NORTH DAKOTA

Peace Garden State

Capital: Bismarck

Admission to Union: Nov. 2, 1889

Total Area: 70,702 sq. mi.

Rank in Size: 17

Flower: Wild prairie rose

Tree: American elm

Bird: Western meadowlark

Famous Residents: Louis L'Amour, Peggy Lee, Eric Sevareid

OHIO

Buckeye State

Capital: Columbus

Admission to Union: March 1, 1803

Total Area: 41,330 sq. mi.

Rank in Size: 35

Flower: Scarlet carnation

Tree: Buckeye

Bird: Cardinal

Famous Residents: Neil Armstrong,Thomas Edison, Clark Gable, John Glenn, Annie Oakley, James Thurber

OKLAHOMA

Sooner State

Capital: Oklahoma City

Admission to Union: Nov. 16, 1907

Total Area: 69,919 sq. mi.

Rank in Size: 18

Flower: Mistletoe

Tree: Redbud

Bird: Scissor-tailed flycatcher

Famous Residents: Woody Guthrie, Will Rogers, Maria Tallchief, Jim Thorpe

OREGON

Beaver State

Capital: Salem

Admission to Union: Feb. 14, 1859

Total Area: 97,073 sq. mi.

Rank in Size: 10

Flower: Oregon grape

Tree: Douglas fir

Bird: Western meadowlark

Famous Residents: Beverly Cleary, Ann Curry, Chief Joseph, Linus Pauling, John Reed

PENNSYLVANIA

Keystone State

Capital: Harrisburg

Admission to Union: Dec. 12, 1787

Total Area: 45,308 sq. mi.

Rank in Size: 33

Flower: Mountain laurel

Tree: Hemlock

Bird: Ruffed grouse

Famous Residents: Marian Anderson, Andrew Carnegie, Mary Cassatt, Gene Kelly, Margaret Mead, Jimmy Stewart, Andy Warhol

RHODE ISLAND

Little Rhody, Ocean State

Capital: Providence
Admission to Union: May 29, 1790
Total Area: 1,210 sq. mi.
Rank in Size: 50
Flower: Violet
Tree: Red maple
Bird: Rhode Island red hen
Famous Residents: George M. Cohan, Julia Ward Howe, H. P. Lovecraft, Massasoit

SOUTH CAROLINA

Palmetto State

Capital: Columbia
Admission to Union: May 23, 1788
Total Area: 31,113 sq. mi.
Rank in Size: 40
Flower: Yellow jessamine
Tree: Palmetto
Bird: Carolina wren
Famous Residents: Bernard Baruch, John C. Calhoun, Althea Gibson

SOUTH DAKOTA

Coyote State, Mount Rushmore State

Capital: Pierre
Admission to Union: Nov. 2, 1889
Total Area: 77,116 sq. mi.
Rank in Size: 16
Flower: Pasqueflower
Tree: Black Hills spruce
Bird: Ring-necked pheasant
Famous Residents: Tom Brokaw, Mary Hart, Crazy Horse, Cheryl Ladd, George McGovern, Sitting Bull, Laura Ingalls Wilder

TENNESSEE

Volunteer State

Capital: Nashville
Admission to Union: June 1, 1796
Total Area: 42,144 sq. mi.
Rank in Size: 34
Flower: Iris
Tree: Tulip poplar
Bird: Mockingbird
Famous Residents: Davy Crockett, Sequoya, Bessie Smith

TEXAS

Lone Star State

Capital: Austin
Admission to Union: Dec. 29, 1845
Total Area: 266,807 sq. mi.
Rank in Size: 2
Flower: Bluebonnet
Tree: Pecan
Bird: Mockingbird
Famous Residents: Carol Burnett, Babe Didrikson, Howard Hughes, Mary Martin

UTAH

Beehive State

Capital: Salt Lake City
Admission to Union: Jan. 4, 1896
Total Area: 84,899 sq. mi.
Rank in Size: 11
Flower: Sego lily
Tree: Blue spruce
Bird: Seagull
Famous Residents: Maude Adams, Philo T. Farnsworth, John Held Jr., Brigham Young

VERMONT

Green Mountain State

Capital: Montpelier
Admission to Union: March 4, 1791
Total Area: 9,609 sq. mi.
Rank in Size: 43
Flower: Red clover
Tree: Sugar maple
Bird: Hermit thrush
Famous Residents: John Deere, Patty Sheehan, Thaddeus Stevens, Rudy Vallee

VIRGINIA

Old Dominion

Capital: Richmond
Admission to Union: June 25, 1788
Total Area: 40,767 sq. mi.
Rank in Size: 36
Flower: Flowering dogwood
Tree: Flowering dogwood
Bird: Cardinal
Famous Residents: Ella Fitzgerald, Pocahontas, Walter Reed, Booker T. Washington

WASHINGTON

Evergreen State

Capital: Olympia
Admission to Union: Nov. 11, 1889
Total Area: 68,139 sq. mi.
Rank in Size: 20
Flower: Rhododendron
Tree: Western hemlock
Bird: Willow goldfinch
Famous Residents: Bing Crosby, Bill Gates, Mary McCarthy, James Whittaker

WEST VIRGINIA

Mountain State

Capital: Charleston

Admission to Union: June 20, 1863

Total Area: 24,231 sq. mi.

Rank in Size: 41

Flower: Big rhododendron

Tree: Sugar maple

Bird: Cardinal

Famous Residents: Pearl S. Buck, Thomas J. "Stonewall" Jackson, Charles E. "Chuck" Yeager

WISCONSIN

Badger State

Capital: Madison

Admission to Union: May 29, 1848

Total Area: 56,153 sq. mi.

Rank in Size: 26

Flower: Wood violet

Tree: Sugar maple

Bird: Robin

Famous Residents: Gena Rowlands, Spencer Tracy, Orson Welles, Frank Lloyd Wright

WYOMING

Equality State

Capital: Cheyenne

Admission to Union: July 10, 1890

Total Area: 97,809 sq. mi.

Rank in Size: 9

Flower: Indian paintbrush

Tree: Cottonwood

Bird: Meadowlark

Famous Residents: Jackson Pollock, Nellie Tayloe Ross

Acknowledgments

PHOTO CREDITS

8 The Granger Collection, New York; **9** Joe Kohen/Getty Images; **10-17** The Granger Collection; **18** Jason Todd/Getty Images; **19** The Granger Collection; **20** *top* The Mariner's Museum, Newport News, Va., *bottom* The Granger Collection; **22** The Granger Collection; **23** Dorling Kindersley/Getty Images; **24-25** The Granger Collection; **26** The Print Collector /Alamy; **27** The Granger Collection; **29** Library of Congress; **30** Mansell/Time Life Pictures/Getty Images; **31** The Granger Collection; **32** Library of Congress; **33** *top* The Granger Collection, *bottom* Tony Savino/Corbis; **34** The Granger Collection; **35-36** Bettmann/Corbis; **37** *top* The Granger Collection, *bottom* D. Hurst/Alamy; **38** The Granger Collection; **39-40** Bettmann/Corbis; **42** *top* Library of Congress, *bottom* FPG/Getty Images; **43** *top* Bettmann/Corbis; **43** *bottom* Hulton Archive/Getty Images; **44** Minnesota Historical Society/Corbis; **45** United States Mint image; **46** The Granger Collection; **48** NASA-JSC; **49** Michael Smith/Getty Images; **50** *top* Spencer Platt/Getty Images, *bottom* NASA-ARC; **52** Jake Rajs/Getty Images; **53** SuperStock, Inc.; **54** Stock Montage/Getty Images; **55** The Granger Collection; **55-57** The Granger Collection; **58** The National Archives; **60** *top* Glowimages/Getty Images, *bottom* Library of Congress; **62-63** Library of Congress; **64** Edward Percy Moran/SuperStock, Inc.; **65** The Granger Collection; **66** Lee Foster/Alamy; **67** Dorling Kindersley/Getty Images; **68** Library of Congress; **70** *left* Stockdisc/Getty Images, *top right* Musée Frédéric Auguste Bartholdi, *bottom right* Copyright holder unknown. Collection of Andrew Spano. In Oliver O. Jensen, American Album, 1968, p. 248, U.C. Davis.; **71** Photodisc/Getty Images; **72** Digital Vision/Getty Images; **74** W. Eugene Smith/Time & Life Pictures/Getty Images; **75** Johnny Eggitt/AFP/Getty Images; **76** New York Public Library; **77** The Granger Collection; **78** POPPERFOTO/Alamy; **79** *top* Courtesy Gerald R. Ford Library, *bottom* AP Photo; **80** Library of Congress; **81** *top left* Library of Congress, *top right* Library of Congress, *bottom* Library of Congress; **82** FPG/Getty Images; **83-85** Library of Congress; **86** The Granger Collection; **87** Library of Congress; **88** Pictorial Press Ltd/Alamy; **89** The Granger Collection; **91** The White House/Getty Images; **92** *top* Hulton Archive/Getty Images, *bottom* Grey Villet/Time Life Pictures/Getty Images; **93** *top* The Granger Collection, *bottom* Library of Congress; **94** Mansell/Time Life Pictures/Getty Images; **95** *left* Mathew Brady/Courtesy Picture History, *right* Howell/Courtesy Picture History; **96** Blank Archives/Getty Images; **97** *left* Hulton Archive/Getty Images, *right* Library of Congress; **98** U.S. Senate Collection; **99** The Granger Collection; **100** Gil Eisner; **101** Francis Miller/Time Life Pictures/Getty Images; **102** *top* Bettmann/Corbis, *bottom* Francis Miller/Time Life Pictures/Getty Images; **103** The Granger Collection; **104** *top* Paul Buck/AFP/Getty Images, *bottom* Tim Boyles/Getty Images; **105** Tim Sloan/AFP/Getty Images; **106** Robert King/Newsmakers/Getty Images; **107** Chris Hondros/Getty Images; **108** *top* U.S. Senate Collection, *bottom* Photodisc/Getty Images; **109** *top left* U.S. Senate Collection, *top right* Stefanie Keenan/Getty Images, *bottom right* Library of Congress; **110** *left* The Granger Collection , *right* Library of Congress; **111** Polaris Images; **112** Stefanie Keenan/Getty Images; **113** Bettmann/Corbis; **114** *top* Keystone/Getty Images, *bottom* Hulton Archive/ Getty Images; **115** *top* Bettmann/Corbis, *bottom* Hulton Archive/Getty Images; **116** *top* Hulton Archive/Getty Images, *bottom* Library of Congress; **117** Photodisc/Getty Images; **118** *top* The Granger Collection, *bottom* The National Archives; **119** *top* Keystone/Hulton Archive/Getty Images, *bottom* United States Mint image; **120** Hulton Archive/Getty Images; **121** Justin Sullivan/Getty Images; **122** U.S. Senate Collection; **124-125** Bettmann/Corbis; **126** Keystone/Getty Images; **127** Bettmann/Corbis; **128-129** Hulton Archive/Getty Images; **130** Brown Brothers; **131** The Granger Collection; **133** Bettmann/Corbis; **134** The Art Archive; **135** Library of Congress; **136** *top* Stock Montage/Getty Images, *bottom* Topham/The Image Works; **138** *top* American Stock/Getty Images, *bottom* FPG/Getty Images; **139** John Chiasson/Getty Images; **140-141** The Granger Collection; **142** *top* Richard Levine/Alamy, *bottom* Jacques Boyer/Roger-Viollet/The Image Works; **143** Ralph Crane/Time Life Pictures/Getty Images; **144-145** The Granger Collection; **146** J.R. Eyerman/Time & Life Pictures/Getty Images; **147** Brown Brothers; **149** *top* Michael Rougier/Time Life Pictures/Getty Images, *bottom* The Granger Collection; **150** Courtesy Avon Products Inc.; **151** Diners Club; **153** Sam Jones/Time & Life Pictures/Getty Images; **154** *top* Bettmann/Corbis, *bottom* The Granger Collection; **155** Natalia Bratslavsky/Alamy; **156** *top* Robert Harding Picture Library Ltd/Alamy, *bottom* Alfred Eisenstaedt/Time & Life Pictures/Getty Images; **157** *top left* The Kobal Collection, *top right* AP Photo, *bottom left* The Granger Collection; **158** American Stock/Getty Images; **159** James Nielsen/Getty Images; **160** Collection of The New York Historical Society #1952.80; **161** Gil Eisner; **162** Library of Congress; **163-164** The Granger Collection; **167-168** Library of Congress; **170** David Hume Kennerly/Getty Images; **172** St. Louis Mercantile Library Association; **173** Bettmann/Corbis; **175** The Granger Collection; **176** The Granger Collection; **177** Victor Lazzaro; **178** *top* Library of Congress, *bottom* The National Archives; **179** *left* The Granger Collection , *right* Hulton Archive/Getty Images; **182** *top* Bettmann/Corbis, *bottom* Library of Congress; **185** Bettmann/Corbis; **186** The Granger Collection; **187** *left* Hulton Archive/Getty Images, *right* Bettmann/Corbis; **188** AP Photo; **189** *top* Dave Einsel/Getty Images, *bottom left* Reuters/Richard Carson /Landov, *bottom right* Reuters/Richard Carson /Landov; **190** Library of Congress; **191** Bettmann/Corbis; **192** Library of Congress; **193** Hulton Archive/Getty Images; **194** *top* North Wind Picture Archives / Alamy, *bottom* Culver Pictures; **195** Bettmann/Corbis; **197** Culver Pictures; **198** Kelly-Mooney Photography/Corbis; **199** Library of Congress; **200** The Granger Collection; **203** Bettmann/Corbis; **205** SF PALM/StageImage/The Image Works; **207** The Granger Collection; **208** Amoret Tanner/Alamy; **209** *left* Library of Congress, *right* Blue Lantern Studio/Corbis; **210** Library of Congress; **211** *top* Andy Nelson/The Christian Science Monitor via Getty Images, *bottom* Library of Congress; **212-213** Library of Congress; **215** The Granger Collection; **216-218** Library of Congress; **219** *top left* The Granger Collection, *bottom right* Comstock Images; **220** Wildlife Conservation Society; **221-222** Bettmann/Corbis; **224** *top* Corbis, *bottom* The Granger Collection; **225** Photo courtesy of Tishman Speyer and Rockefeller Center Archives; **226** Library of Congress; **227** Bettmann/Corbis; **228** Library of Congress; **229** *top* Bettmann/Corbis, *bottom* Library of Congress; **230** *top* Hulton-Deutsch Collection/Corbis, *bottom* Doug Landreth/Corbis; **232** *top* The Granger Collection, *bottom* Library of Congress; **233** *top right* Bettmann/Corbis, *bottom left* The Granger Collection; **235** *top* Rykoff Collection/Corbis, *bottom* The Granger Collection; **236** *left* Bettmann/ Corbis, *right* The Granger Collection; **237** *left* Courtesy of Alan and Jeanne Abel, *right* Courtesy of Original Appalachian Artworks Inc.; **238** Mansell/ Time & Life Pictures/Getty Images; **239** NASA-HQ-GRIN; **241** Library of Congress; **242** The Granger Collection; **243** Library of Congress; **244-247** The Granger Collection; **248** *top* Bettmann/Corbis, *bottom* The Granger Collection; **251** Corbis; **252** *top* Corbis, *bottom* The Brooklyn Museum/ Corbis; **254** The Granger Collection; **255** Library of Congress; **258** The Granger Collection; **259** Nebraska State Historical Society Photograph Collection; **260** The Granger Collection; **261** Library of Congress; **263-264** The Granger Collection; **265** North Wind Picture Archives; **266** Library of Congress; **268** Nebraska State Historical Society Photograph Collection; **269** Bettmann/Corbis; **270-271** The Granger Collection; **272** Corbis; **274** *left* Leonard de Selva/Corbis, *right* Bettmann/Corbis; **275** Academy of Natural Sciences of Philadelphia/ Corbis; **276-278** The Granger Collection; **279** The Art Archive/Culver Pictures; **281** *top* Library of Congress, *bottom* Corbis; **282** *top* Mary Evans Picture Library/Alamy, *bottom left* Nordicphotos/Alamy, *bottom right* Bettmann/ Corbis; **283-284** NASA-JSC; **285** *top* NASA-JSC, *bottom* Bob Daemmrich/ Corbis; **286** *top* NASA-ARC, *bottom* NASA-JSC; **287** NASA-HQ-GRIN; **288** Topical Press Agency/Getty Images; **289** AP Photo; **290** Hulton Archive/Getty Images; **291** Library of Congress; **292-293** U.S. Patent Office; **295** The Granger Collection; **297** MPI/Getty Images; **298** Margaret Bourke-White/Getty Images; **299** The Granger Collection; **300** Mary Evans Picture Library/Alamy; **301-302** Library of Congress; **304** *top* Frederic Lewis/Getty Images, *bottom* Library of Congress; **305** Blank Archives/Getty Images; **306** The Art Archive/ Domenica del Corriere/Dagli Orti; **307** Mary Evans Picture Library/Alamy; **308** The Granger Collection; **309** *top* Ted Thai/Time Life Pictures/Getty Images, *bottom* Al Fenn/Time Life Pictures/Getty Images; **310** NOAA; **312** Mansell/Time Life Pictures/Getty Images; **313** Bettmann/ Corbis; **315** Mansell/Time Life Pictures/Getty Images; **316** Bettmann/Corbis; **317** San Diego Aerospace Museum; **318** Mary Evans Picture Library/The Image Works; **319** Fred Lyon/Time Life Pictures/Getty Images; **320-321** U.S. Patent Office; **322** New York Public Library; **323** Corbis; **324** ©2007 Crayola. Silly Putty®, The Real Solid Liquid®, used with permission; **325** National Museum of American History, Behring Center/Smithsonian Institute; **326** *top* Clarence Sinclair Bull/Margaret Chute/Getty Images, *bottom* Roger Viollet Collection/ Getty Images; **327** Hulton Archive/Getty Images;

328-329 U.S. Patent Office; **330** The Granger Collection; **331** Michel Gangne/AFP/Getty Images; **332-333** The Granger Collection; **334** Geoffrey Clements/Corbis; **335** North Wind Picture Archives/Alamy; **337** Bettmann/ Corbis; **338** John Trumbull/ Wikipedia Commons; **339** Frances M. Roberts/ Alamy; **341-343** The Granger Collection; **345** *top* The Granger Collection, *bottom* Library of Congress; **346-347** Library of Congress; **348** The Granger Collection; **349** Library of Congress; **350** The Granger Collection; **352** *right* U.S. Senate Collection, *left* Library of Congress; **353** Library of Congress; **354** *top* The Granger Collection, *bottom* North Wind Picture Archives/Alamy; **355-358** Library of Congress; **359** *top right* Mort Kunstler, *bottom left* Library of Congress; **360-361** Library of Congress; **362** Corbis; **363** *top* The Granger Collection , *bottom* The Art Archive/Culver Pictures; **364** Marvin Koner/Corbis; **365** Library of Congress; **366** Oscar White/Corbis; **368** *top left* The National Archives, *bottom right* Wikipedia Commons; **370** Bettmann/Corbis; **371** Hormel Foods Corporation; **372** US Army/Getty Images; **373** AP Photo; **375-377** The Granger Collection; **378** Reuters/Corbis; **379** Stephen Jaffe/ AFP/Getty Images; **380** Brooks Kraft/ Corbis; **382** *top* The Granger Collection , *bottom left* U.S. Senate Collection, *bottom center* U.S. Senate Collection; **382-387** Library of Congress; **388** *top left* Pictorial Press Ltd/ Alamy, *top center* Department of Defense photo, *top right* Library of Congress, *bottom left* LBJ Library photo by Yoichi R. Okamoto, *bottom center* Courtesy Gerald R. Ford Library, *bottom right* Department of Defense photo; **389** *top left* Department of Defense photo, *top center* Department of Defense photo, *top right* White House photo by Eric Draper

SPECIAL APPRECIATION

The staff of this revised and updated edition of *Strange Stories, Amazing Facts of America's Past* would like to acknowledge everyone who worked on the previous edition of this book, including:

Project Editor: Jim Dwyer. **Art Editor:** Kenneth Chaya. **Associate Editor and Research Editor:** David Palmer. **Associate Editors:** Noreen B. Church, W. Clotilde Lanig, Diana Marsh, Paula Pines. **Art Associate:** Nancy Mace. **Research Associates:** Barbara Guarino, Diane Zito. **Library Research:** Nettie Seaberry. **Editorial Assistant:** Vita Gardner. **Editorial Intern:** Melanie WIlliams. **Contributors**. **General Consultant:** Frank B. Latham. **Business Consultant:** The Winthrop Group, Inc. **Military Consultant:** Colonel John R. Elting, U.S. Army, Ret. **Editorial Research:** Mary Hart, Madeleine Walker. **Writers:** Tom Callahan, Davis Caras, Rita Christopher, Ormonde de Kay, Josh Eppinger, Marjorie Flory, Signe Hammer, Jeanne Molli, Don O'Neill, Heindieter von Schoener-marck, David Sicilia, Robert Thurston, Terry Wells, Jeff Yablonka. **Art Research:** Mary Leverty, Lisa Barlow, Sybille Millard. **Illustrators:** Michael K. Conway, Peter de Sève, Gil Eisner, Gerry Gersten, Steve Gray, Gregg Hinlicky, Victor Lazzaro, Rick McCollum, Bill Shortridge, Ed Vebell, Richard Williams. **Copy Editor:** Eva Galan Salmieri. **Indexer:** Sydney Wolfe Cohen.

The editors wish to express special appreciation to the following individuals for their generous assistance with the research for this book:

Carol L. Bagley and Jo Ann Ruckman, Idaho State University. Philip Vander-bilt Brady, Vanderbilt Family Historian. Barnaby Bullard, Loudonville, NY. Theodore Chase, Dover, Mass. Sue Collins, Stillwater Public Library, Stillwater, MN. Hollis N. Cook, Tombstone, AZ. J. Cooper, University of Wisconsin, De-partment of History. David J. Frent, Political Americana Historian. Albert E. Grollin, NY. Helen Harrison, Guest Curator, Queens Museum. Lester J. Harri-son, Brooklyn Masonic Temple. Kenneth Jessen, Loveland, CO. Donald E. Loker, Niagara Falls Public Library, Niagara Falls, NY. Oscar Mastin, Patent and Trademark Office, U.S. Department of Commerce. Dan Morgan, Cincin-nati, for information on Private O'Leary. Douglas C. Moul, Civil War Times Illustrated. Dr. Charles E. Nolan, Archdiocese of New Orleans. Colleen Phillips, Cincinnati, OH. Marcia C. Stein, March of Dimes. Jane Sumpter, Vir-ginia State Library. Bernard Titowsky, Austin Book Shop. Alan D. Weiner, Richmond, VA, for the story on D-Day tanks.

Alabama Department of Archives and History, Reference Division. Alabama Historical Association. Alaska Department of Natural Resources. Alexander Graham Bell National Historic Park. American Bowling Congress. American History Illustrated. Appomattox Court House National Historical Park. Arizona Historical Society. Arkansas Historical Association. AT&T Company Historical Archives. Avon Products, Inc. Baseball Hall of Fame. Basketball Hall of Fame. Baylor University, The Texas Collection. Beersheba Springs Historical Society, Beersheba Springs, Tenn. Berkeley Plantation. Berkshire Athenaeum. Bishop Museum. Booker T. Washington National Monument. Borden, Inc. *The Boston Globe*. Brooklyn Historic Railway Association. Cali-fornia Historical Society. California State Archives. The Chapel of Four Chaplains. Chesebrough-Pond's, Inc. Chicago Historical Society. The Church of Jesus Christ of Latter-day Saints, Historical Department. Cincinnati Histori-cal Society. City of New York, Police Department, Youth Services Division. Civil War Times Illustrated. Colorado Division of Archives and Public Records. Col-orado Historical Society. Comstock Historic House. Connecticut Historical Society. Connecticut State Library. Cornell University, New York Historical Resources Center. Delaware Bureau of Archives and Records Management. Department of the Navy, Naval Historical Center. Department of the Treasury, U.S. Mint. The Dirksen Congressional Center. Dover Public Library, Dover, DE. Dr Pepper Company. Dwight D. Eisenhower Library. *Early American Life*. Essex Institute. F & F Laboratories, Inc. Federal Bureau of Investigation. Fitchburg Public Library, Fitchburg, MA. The Florida State Museum. Fort Boonesboro State Park. Fort Clatsop National Memorial. Franklin D. Roosevelt Library. Frederick Law Olmsted National Historic Site. Fredericksburg National Military Park. The Garibaldi and Meucci Memorial Museum. Georgia Department of Archives and History. Gerald R. Ford Library. Governor Hogg Shrine State Historical Park. Henry Ford Museum and Greenfield Village. Her-bert Hoover National Historic Site. The Hideout Inc. The Historical Society of Delaware. The Historical Society of Pennsylvania. Historical Society of West-ern Pennsylvania. Hubbell Trading Post National Historic Site. Idaho State Historical Society. Illinois Historic Preservation Agency, Galena State Historic Sites. January 12th, 1888 Blizzard Club. Jedediah Smith Society. Jimmy Carter Library. John Brown Historical Association, Inc. John Muir National Historic Site. John Wesley Powell Memorial Museum. Jones Memorial Library, Lynchburg, Va. Judah L. Magnes Memorial Museum, Western Jewish History Center. Kansas State Historical Society. Kentucky Historical Society. La Crosse Chamber of Commerce, La Crosse, KS. Lindbergh Historic Site. Longfellow National Historic Site. Louisiana State Museum. MacArthur Memorial. Maine Historical Society. Manhattan College, College Relations Office. Marshall Gold Discovery State Park. Martin Van Buren National Historic Site. Massachusetts Historical Society. Max Factor & Co. Melrose Plantation. Mississippi Depart-ment of Archives and History. Missouri Historical Society. Montana Historical Society. Montgomery Ward & Co., Inc. Monticello. Morton Thiokol, Inc. Mount Holyoke College. Museum of New Mexico. Natchez Trace Parkway. National Soft Drink Association. Nebraska State Historical Society. Nevada Historical Society. North Carolina Department of Cultural Resources, Division of Archives and History. The Northeastern Nevada Museum. Oklahoma Histori-cal Society. Omaha Public Library. Orange County Historical Society, Va. Oregon State University, Kerr Library. Phillips Petroleum Company. Plimoth Plantation, Inc. Polish Historical Commission of the Central Council of Polish Organizations of Pittsburgh. The Procter & Gamble Co.Pro Football Hall of Fame. Queensboro Public Library, Long Island Division. R. E. Olds Trans-portation Museum. Republican National Committee. Robert E. Lee Memorial Association, Inc., Stratford Hall Plantation. Rosenberg Library. Rough Riders Memorial and City Museum. Rutherford B. Hayes Presidential Center. Rut-ledge Hill Press. Salem Public Library, Salem, MA. The Sam Rayburn Library. San Luis Obispo County Historical Society, CA. Scholl, Inc. Sears, Roebuck and Co. Shelby County Historical Society, TX. Shell Oil Company. Smithsonian Institution, National Air and Space Museum. South Carolina Department of Archives and History. Southern Jewish Historical Society. St. Francis de Sales Church, Cincinnati. State Historical Society of Missouri. State Historical Soci-ety of North Dakota. State Library of Massachusetts. Stephentown Historical Society, NY. Supreme Court Historical Society. Swiss Mennonite Cultural & Historical Association. Tennessee Historical Society. Texas Historical Commis-sion. Texas State Library. Thomas Jefferson Memorial Foundation, Inc. Tubac Presidio State Historic Park. Union Pacific Railroad. U.S. Chess Federation. U.S. Postal Service, History Department. U.S. Senate Historical Office. Uni-versity of Akron, Bierce Library. Utah Division of State History. Uvalde, TX, City Manager's Office. Virginia Department of Conservation and Historic Re-sources, Division of Historic Landmarks. Virginia Historical Society. The Washington State Historical Society. Weaverville Joss House Association. Western Postal History Museum. The White House, Office of Correspondence. Will Rogers Memorial. Wyoming State Archives, Museums & Historical Depart-ment. Yankee Publications, Inc. Yonkers Public Library, Yonkers, NY. YWCA of the City of New York. Zion Evangelical Lutheran Church, Manheim, PA.

The editors gratefully acknowledge their debt to the groundbreaking historical publications of *American Heritage*, which served as an inspiration and occa-sional model in the preparation of this book.

Selected sidebars from Chapter Five were excerpted from The Trenton Pickle Ordinance, by Dick Hyman. Copyright © 1976 by Dick Hyman. All rights reserved. Reprinted by permission of the Stephen Greene Press, a wholly owned subsidiary of Viking Penguin Inc.

Index

Italic page numbers refer to captions.

Georgia, 10, 59, 183, 237, 240, 391
England vs. Spain in, 341–42
governors of, 102, *102*
9/11 fraud in, 51
off-the-wall laws in, 174
German immigrants, 69, 262
Germany, 333, 364–67, 371, 372, 374
germ warfare, 13
Geronimo, 342
Gettysburg, Battle of, 352
Gettysburg Address, 27, 118
Ghost Dance, 344–45, *345*
Giannini, Amadeo Peter, 145
Gibbs, Josiah, 16
GI Bill of Rights, 226
Giddings, Tex., hanging in, 180
Gifford, Walter S., 44, *44*
Gilded Age, The (Twain), 216
Glass, Hugh, 124
G-men, 43, 173
goat sex gland transplants, 113
Goetze, Martin, 329
Goffe, William, 160
gold, 96, 125, 127–28, 137, 145, 185,
261, 268, 272
in California, 24, 133, 261, 348
explorers' searches for, 241, 242
scheme to corner market for, 136–37
Golden Hind, 243–44
goldfish, for Reagan, 49, 91
gold standard, 86, 127
Goldstein, Joseph L., 295
Goldwyn, Sam (Sam Goldfish), 157
Goodnight, Charlie, 270–71, *270*
Gordon, John, 359
Gore Jr., Albert, 51, 104–7
Gorman, Margaret, 229
Gossamer Albatross (plane), 281
Gould, Jay, 135, 147
Black Friday and, 136–37, *136*
Grand Canyon, 265
Grand Ohio Company, 123
Granola, 141
Grant, Cary (Archibald Leach), *323*
Grant, Ulysses S., 81, *84*, 112, 137,
212, 352, 385
Civil War and, 32, 355, 356
in election of 1872, 30, 94
Grasse, François Joseph Paul,
Comte de, 338
grasshoppers, 267–68, *268*
Gravelot, Jean François (The Great
Blondin), 22, *22*
Graves, Abner, 36
Gray, Elisha, 301, 302
Gray, Harold, 226

Great Aerodome, 314–15, *315*, 316
Great Britain, 220, 250, 310
in American Revolution, 10, 14, 15,
55, 76, 161, 247, 310, 332–38,
334, 338
amnesty offer of, 55
germ warfare used by, 13, 342
regicide in, 160
in San Juan Island, 351
in War of 1812, 63, 65, 339, 344
in World War I, 364, 365
Great Depression, 42, 136–39,
224–27, 232, 327
bonus march in, 43, 224–26, *224*
dust storms in, 226–27, *226*
populist politicians in, 113
Rockefeller Center Christmas tree
in, 42, 225
Great Lakes, 202, 250
Great Northern Railway, 280
Great Pacific War, The (Bywater),
368–69
Great Salt Lake, 261
Great Seal, 15, 67
Greeley, Horace, 30, 94
Green, Hetty, 39, 147, *147*
Green, Ned, 147
Green, Sylvia, 147
Green, Talbot, 261
Greenhow, Rose O'Neal, 27, 355, *355*
Green Mountain Boys, 332–33
Griffin, Charles John, 351
Griffin, Clifford, 272
Griffin, Heneage, 272
Grinder, Priscilla, 249
Grinder, Robert, 249
Grinder's Stand, 18, 249
Guadalupe Hidalgo, Treaty of (1848),
347–48, *347*
Guiteau, Charles, 90
Gulf War, 50, *230*, 378, *378*
gum, chewing, 145
Gwinn, W. Charles, 374

H

hair products, 149
Hall, Charles, 30, 276
Halley, Edmund, *37*
Halley's comet, 36–37, *37*
Hamill, Al, 132–33
Hamill, Curt, 132–33
Hamill, Jim, 132–33
Hamilton, Alexander, 12, 59, 250,
336, 338
duel and death of, 18, 164–66

election of 1800 and, 98, 165
Reynolds affair and, 16, 165
Hamilton, Elizabeth, 165
Hancock, John, 54, *55*, 332, *334*
Hancock, Winfield, 105
hangings, 51, 161, 163, 171, 269, 307,
357
of Longley, 180
Murder Castle and, 35, 177
of Surratt, 178–79
Hanson, John, 15, 76
Harding, Mrs. Warren, 114, 115
Harding, Warren, 76, 97, *114*, 387
scandals of, 114–15
Harper's New Monthly Magazine, 210
Harrison, Benjamin, *84*, 86, 97, 313,
386
in election of 1888, 72, 105
White House renovation and, 63, 76
Harrison, William H., *84*, *343*, 344,
383
death of, 95
Harry Hill's, 128
Hart, Richard Joseph (Two-Gun
Hart; Jim Capone), 183
Harvard, John, 193
Harvard-Boston Aviation Meet, 281
Harvard University, 218
Indian College of, 193
Harvey, Thomas, 298
Hastings Cutoff, 175
Hastings Tournament, 220
Haver, Phyllis, 325
Hawaii, 369, 391
Hawley, Joseph R., 28, 29
Hawthorne, Maria, 21
Hawthorne, Nathaniel, 13, 21, 205
Hayes, Lucy, 31, 81
Hayes, Rutherford B., 72, 211, 215,
259, 385
alcohol-free White House and, 31,
81
firsts of, 76
Hearst, William Randolph, 360
Heath, Lillian, 181
Heim, Jacques, 233
Heinman, Henry, 36–37
Heinz, Henry J., 156
Heinz 57, 156
Heller, Richard, 188
Helms, Thomas, 48
Helper, Hinton Rowan, 206
Henderson Island, 264
Henry, Buck (G. Clifford Prout Jr.),
236–37
Henry, Patrick, 59

Monopoly, 36, 127
Monroe, James, 63, 99, 164, 383
Montana, 30, 39, 183, 393
Montez, Pedro, 15–16
Montgomery, Ala., 26
Montgomery Ward, 140–41
Monticello, *117*
moon:
  unicorns on, 14–15
  visit to, 48, 235
Moore, Richard, 28, 259
Moran, Percy, *64*
Morgan, J. P., 39, 130, 187, 318
  railroads and, 144
  on taxes, 138
  Treasury bailed out by, 34, 127–28
Morgan, J. P., Jr., 42
Morgan, Junius Spencer, 42
Mormons, 146, 254–55
Morris, Esther, 29, 73
Morris, Gouverneur, 202
Morrison, Wade B., 156–57
Morrison's Old Corner Drug Store, 157
Morse, Wayne, 116
Morton, Thomas, 11, 246–47
Morton, William, 24, 296–97
Mother's Day, 34–35, *35*
mountain men, 124, 175
Mount Vernon, 77, 85, 250
movies, 146, 325–26, 363, *363*
Mudgett, Herman W. (Henry H. Holmes), 35, 177, *177*
Mueller, Edward, 45
murder, 35, 175–79, 180–81, 269, 276
  cannibalism and, 176, *176*
  getting away with, 44–45
  of Sitting Bull, 345
Murder Castle, 35, 177, *177*
Murrow, Edward R., 101, 309
Mutual Film Corporation, 363
Myers, Apheus, 329
Mystic, Conn., 28–29

N

Napoleon I, Emperor of France, 112, 166, 310
Narváez, Pánfilo de, 242
NASA, 283, 285
NASDAQ, 153
Nash, Jay Robert, 187
Nast, Thomas, 209
Natchez, 257, 258
Nation, Carry, 219
National Colonization Council, 267

National Intelligencer, 339
Native Americans, 131, 202, 242, 245, 256–60, 271, 335, 340–45
  blacks and, 249
  in England, 11, 122–23, 340
  germ warfare used against, 13, 342
  Ghost Dance and, 344–45, *345*
  Harvard's Indian college and, 193
  in Jamestown, 122, 340
  in King Philip's War, 340–41, *341*
  Manhattan sold by, 11, 194
  Morton's relations with, 246, 247
  Prohibition and, 183
  at Thanksgiving, *192*, 193
  tribal nation plan for, 343–44, *343*
  see also specific people and groups
Nauvoo, Ill., Mormons in, 255
Navy, U.S., 311, *365*, 372–74, *373*
  Carter in, 79, *79*
  "Mission Accomplished" banner and, 379–80
Neal, Ralph, 375
Nebraska, 255, 260, 349, 393
  human sacrifice in, 256–57
Neelly, James, 249
Netscape, 153
Nevada, 257, 347, 393
  borax in, 143
  divorce in, 174
Newcomb, Simon, 314
New Hampshire, 59, 80–81, 183, 393
  Mystery Hill in, 240
New Harmony, Ind. (Harmonie), 21, 251–52, *251*
New Haven, Conn., 16, 131, 160, 334–35
New Haven Railroad, 34
New Jersey, 55, 58, 161, 394
  cross-dressing governor of, 160
  female suffrage in, 73
  passport to, 9, 10
New Mexico, 100, 227, 252, 346, 347, 394
  near nuking of, 47, 376
  Pueblo in, 195–96
  Reavis's claim to, 184
New Orleans, La., 140, 166, 205, 250, 346
  Battle of (1814-15), *167*
Newsboys' Lodging House, 125
newspapers:
  advice columns in, 236
  election mistakes made by, 44, *74*, 103
  prison, 29
  see also specific newspapers

New Year's celebrations, *8*, 49
New York (state), 59, 201, 394
  blacks in, 58, 197, *197*, 220–21, *220*
  canals in, 202–3, *203*, 250
  Declaration of Independence and, 54, 55
  electrocution in, 307
  9/11 fraud in, 51
New York, N.Y., 16, 42, 61, 125, 223, 225, 297
  British in, 15, 338
  Bronx Zoo in, 220–21, *220*
  Civil War and, 23, 357
  Crystal Palace Exposition in, 313, 314
  equine flu in, 213
  Kelly's stunts in, 227, *227*
  Kidd in, 162
  orphans and street children in, 269
  police in, 169
  restaurants in, 151
  St. John the Divine in, 234
  skyscrapers in, 48, 230, 314
  slave uprising rumors in, 197, *197*
  Times Square in, *8*, 49
  Tories in, 161
  Twin Towers tragedy in, 50–51, *50*
  U.S. centennial in, 212
New York & Harlem Railroad, 135
New York and Queens Railroad, 39, *39*
New York Central Railroad, 135
New York *Evening Mail*, 61–62
New York Herald Tribune, 46
New York Journal, 360
New York Medical Society, 324
New York Sun, 14–15, 103, 134, 308
New York Times, 88, 110, 237, 281
New York Tribune, 94, 314
New York World, 360, 363, 364
Niagara Falls, *18*, 22, *22*
Niagara River, 18, *18*
Nicaragua, 27, 348, *348*
Nickerson, H. G., 73
Nicola, Lewis, 77
Nimitz, Chester, 369
Niña (ship), 240, 241
9th Army, 371
19th Amendment, 41
Nixon, Richard M., 76, 97, 101–2, 105, 388
  Edsel used by, 236
Noailles, Vicomte Louis-Marie, 11
Noble, William H., 144
Noonan, Fred, 46
North, Frank, 260